macOS Apprentice

by Sarah Reichelt

macOS Apprentice

By Sarah Reichelt

Notice of Rights

Notice of Liability

Trademarks

ISBN: 978-1-950325-94-8

Table of Contents

Book License

Before You Begin

This section tells you a few things you need to know before you get started, such as what you'll need for hardware and software, where to find the project files for this book, and more.

What You Need

To follow along with this book, you'll need the following:

- A **Mac computer with an Intel or ARM processor**. Any Mac that you've bought in the last few years will do, even a Mac mini or MacBook Air. It must be running macOS Tahoe (macOS 26) or later.
- **Xcode 26 or later**. Xcode is the main development environment for building macOS Apps. It includes the Swift compiler, the debugger and other development tools you'll need. You can download the latest version of Xcode for free from the Mac App Store.

Book Source Code & Forums

Where to Download the Materials for This Book

The materials for this book can be cloned or downloaded from the GitHub book materials repository:

- https://github.com/kodecocodes/maca-materials/tree/editions/3.0

Forums

We've also set up an official forum for the book at https://forums.kodeco.com/c/books/macos-apprentice. This is a great place to ask questions about the book or to submit any errors you may find.

For David, who handles everything life throws at him with dignity and courage.

— *Sarah Reichelt*

About the Authors

Sarah Reichelt is the author of this book. She got hooked onto trying to make computers do what she told them a very long time ago, and has never stopped loving it. She is a keen evangelist for developing native Mac apps. When not at her computer, Sarah loves coffee, puzzles, reading and cooking - the day hasn't started until the first cup of coffee is drunk and the crossword is done!

About the Editors

Audrey Tam is a tech editor of this book. As a retired computer science academic, she's a technology generalist with expertise in translating new knowledge into learning materials. Audrey attends many concerts at Tempo Rubato and does most of her writing and zooming at Rubato Upstairs. She also enjoys long train journeys, knitting, and trekking in the Aussie wilderness.

Ehab Amer is a tech editor of this book. He is a very enthusiastic Principal iOS engineer with a very diverse experience, from building games to enterprise applications and POCs, specially when exploring new technologies. In the spare time (or time that can be spared) Ehab enjoys watching a few (more like a lot of) TV series if nothing to watch, video games are just as awesome to say the least :] When trying to move away from a screen Ehab enjoys going through challenging escape-room experience with his amazing wife and awesome friends, & attempt to break the escape records.

Richard Critz did double duty as editor and final pass editor for this book. He has been doing software professionally for over 40 years, working on products as diverse as CNC machinery, network infrastructure, and operating systems. He discovered the joys of working with iOS beginning with iOS 6. Yes, he dates back to punch cards and paper tape. He's a dinosaur; just ask his kids.

Introduction

Writing software is fun!

Using a computer is great but nothing beats the satisfaction of writing your own code. It doesn't have to be a super-complex app — maybe you'd like to write a script for processing some text or a utility that automates part of your workflow. Perhaps you have an idea for a game you'd like to create. But how do you get started?

If you're an Apple user, you begin by learning the Swift language. There are a lot of resources for this and they nearly all assume that you want to write apps for an iPhone. But the main tool for writing Swift is Xcode and it runs on your Mac, so why not write apps that run on the same device?

The Mac is more powerful, more flexible and less restricted than any other Apple device, so learn to code by writing for it. It's a terrific feeling when code that you wrote is running on your own computer.

How to Read This Book

This book is split into four sections.

The first section is designed to get you started using Xcode and programming in Swift. If you're already comfortable with these tools, you may skip right to one of the other sections.

The chapters in sections two and three are designed to take you from start to finish building a particular kind of app. While the book is fun from the first page to the last, if one section especially piques your interest, you're free to dive right in there.

The final section ties together all you've learned in the rest of the book and puts the finishing touches on both sample apps.

Section I: Getting Started

This section shows you how to install Xcode and teaches you the basics of programming in Swift. Along the way, you'll learn several different ways to execute Swift code.

Section II: Building With SwiftUI

In this section, you'll use Apple's newest user interface technology — SwiftUI — to develop a word-guessing game called Snowman. You'll learn about data flow in SwiftUI, managing multiple windows, using charts and adding macOS-specific features such as toolbars and menus.

Section III: Building With AppKit

From the very beginning of macOS X, AppKit has been the workhorse behind the user interface of all apps and there are still a number of tasks where it is the superior choice. In this section, you'll explore such an area while building an app to browse movie data from IMDb, the online movie database.

Section IV: Combining SwiftUI & AppKit

Apple has made it simple to include pieces of both user interface frameworks in a single app. In this section, you'll do just that in order to add some finishing touches to both of the apps from the previous sections.

Section I: Getting Started

Begin your journey by learning how to install Xcode and the basics of programming in Swift. Along the way, you'll learn several different ways to execute Swift code.

Chapter 1: Introducing Xcode

By Audrey Tam

You're eager to dive in and create your first macOS app. If you've never used Xcode before, take some time to work through this chapter. You want to be sure your tools are working and learn how to use them efficiently.

Getting Started

To develop macOS apps, you need a Mac with Xcode installed. If you have an account on GitHub or similar, you can connect to that from Xcode.

macOS

This book requires **macOS Tahoe (v26.0)** or later. To install Xcode, your user account must have **administrator** status.

Xcode

To install Xcode, you need **12 GB** free space on your Mac's drive.

➤ Open the **App Store** app, then search for and **GET Xcode**. This is a large download — 2-3 GB — so it takes a while. Fix yourself a snack while you wait.

➤ When the installation finishes, **OPEN** it from the App Store page:

Open Xcode after installing it from the App Store.

> **Note**: You probably have your favorite way to open a Mac application, and it'll work with Xcode, too. Double-click it in **Applications**. Or search for it in **Spotlight**. Or double-click a project's **.xcodeproj** file.

The *first* time you open Xcode after App Store installation, you'll see this window:

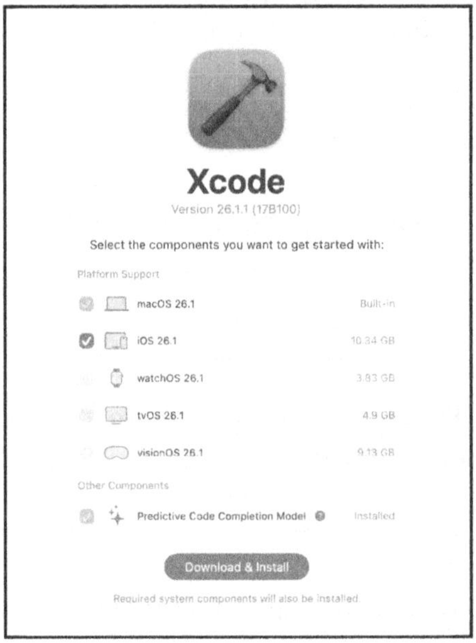

Select the platforms you want to get started with:

➤ macOS is built into the download. Click **Install** and enter your **Mac login password** in the window that appears. This doesn't take long, so don't go away.

➤ When this installation process finishes, you'll see this **Welcome** window:

Welcome to Xcode window

> **Note**: You can manually open this window from the Xcode menu **Window → Welcome to Xcode** or press **Shift-Command-1**. And, there is an Xcode menu item to perform each of the actions listed in this window.

Creating a New Xcode Project

You'll create a new Xcode project just for this chapter.

➤ Click **Create New Project...**. Or, if you want to do this without the Welcome window, press **Shift-Command-N** or select **File → New → Project...** from the menu.

A large set of choices appears (don't worry about the "Downloading iOS 26" message):

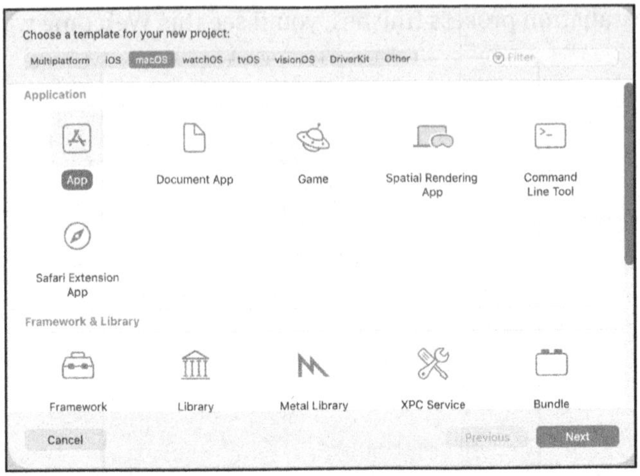

Choose a template for your new project.

➤ Select **macOS** → **App** and click **Next**. Now, you get to name your project:

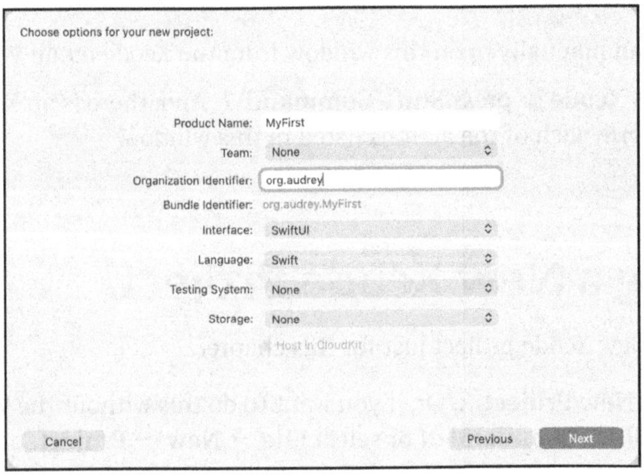

Choose options for your new project.

- For **Product Name**, type **MyFirst**.
- Be sure to leave **Team** as **None** for now.
- For **Organization Identifier**, type the *reverse-DNS* of your domain name. If you don't have a domain name, just type something that follows this pattern, like **org.audrey**. The grayed-out **Bundle Identifier** changes to **your-org-id.MyFirst**.

When you submit your app to the App Store, this bundle identifier uniquely identifies your app.

- For **Interface**, select **SwiftUI**.
- For **Language**, select **Swift**.
- For **Testing System** and **Storage**, select **None**.

➤ Click **Next**. Here's where you decide where to save your new project.

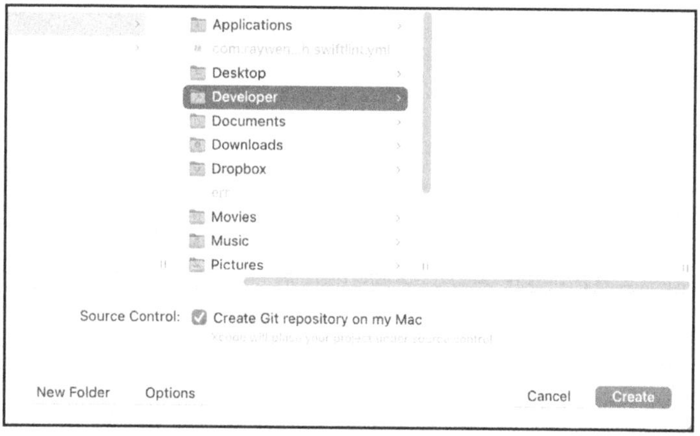

Decide where to save your project.

> **Note**: When a project is open, you can find its location by selecting **File → Show in Finder** from the Xcode menu. If you forget where you saved a project, try looking in the Xcode menu **File → Open Recent**.

➤ If you're saving this project to a location that is **not** currently under source control, click the **Source Control** checkbox to create a local Git repository. Later in this chapter, you'll learn how to connect this to a remote repository.

➤ Click **Create**. Your new project appears, displaying **ContentView.swift** in the editor pane.

In the preview canvas, the app is pretty small. In **Selectable** mode, four zoom buttons appear in the lower right corner of the canvas: Zoom Out, Zoom to 100%, Zoom to Fit and Zoom In.

➤ Click **Selectable**, then click **Zoom to Fit** to get a better look at the app.

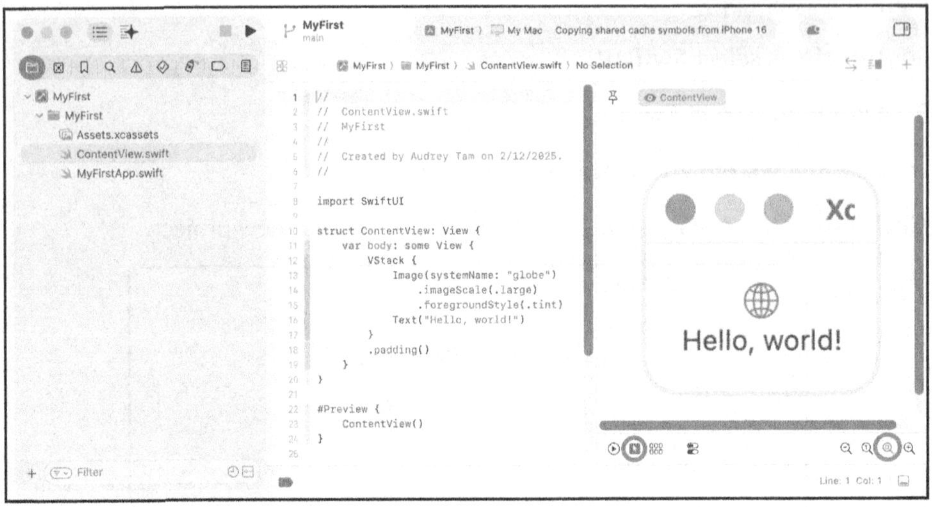

In preview canvas Selectable mode, Zoom to Fit.

➤ Click **Zoom to 100%** to go back.

Looks like there's a lot going on! Don't worry, most macOS developers know enough about Xcode to do their job, but almost no one knows how to use *all* of it. Plus, Apple changes and adds to it every year. The best (and only) way to learn it is to jump in and start using it.

Ready, set, jump!

A Quick Tour of Xcode

You'll spend most of your time working in a **.swift** file:

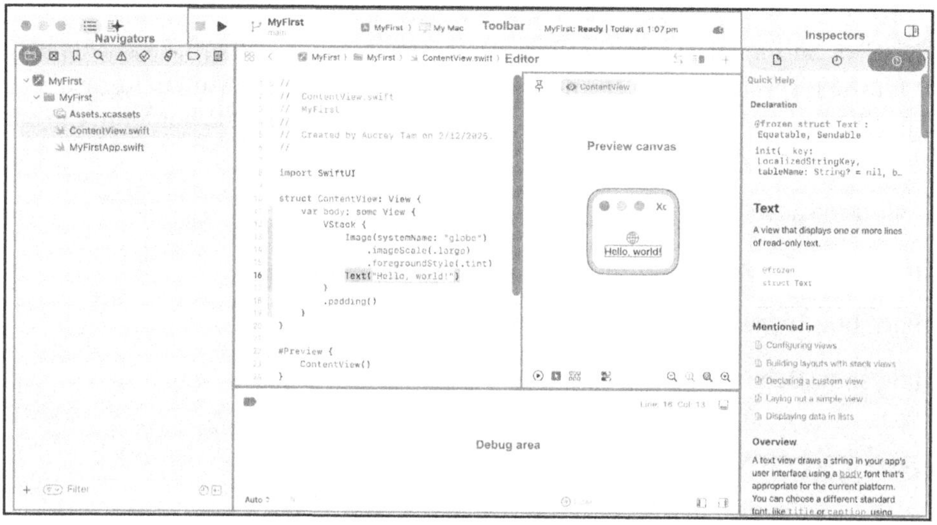

Xcode window panes

> **Note**: If you don't see the file extension `.swift` in the **Project** navigator, press **Command-,** to open **Settings...** then, in the **General** tab, set **File Extensions** to **Show All**:

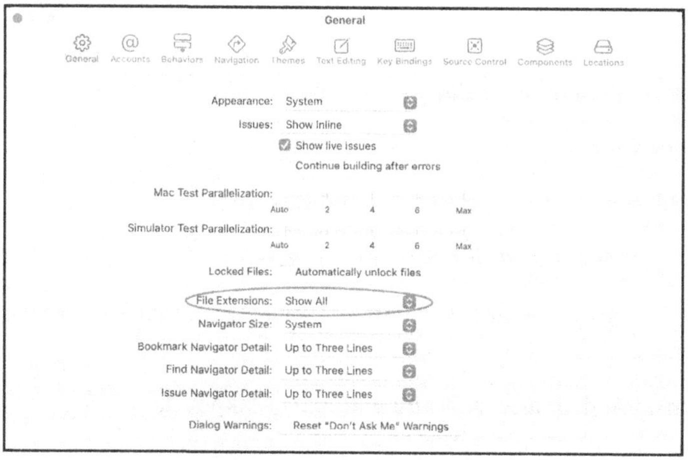

Show all file extensions.

The Xcode window has three main panes: **Navigators**, **Editor** and **Inspectors**. When the app is running, the **Debug Area** opens below the **Editor**. When you're viewing a SwiftUI View file in the **Editor**, you can view the preview canvas side-by-side with the code.

The toolbar button just above the Navigators pane hides or shows it. The same is true for the Inspectors pane. The debug area has a hide/show button in its own toolbar. You can also hide any of these three panes by dragging its border to the edge of the Xcode window.

And all three have keyboard shortcuts:

- Hide/show Navigator: **Command-0**
- Hide/show Inspectors: **Option-Command-0**
- Hide/show Debug Area: **Shift-Command-Y**

Navigators

The **Navigators** pane has nine tabs. When the navigators pane is hidden, you can open it directly in one of its tabs by pressing **Command-1** to **Command-9**:

Navigators bar

1. **Project**: Add, delete or group files. Open a file in the editor.
2. **Source Control**: View Git repository working copies, branches, commits, tags, remotes and stashed changes.
3. **Bookmark**: Hierarchical or flat view of code landmarks and tasks.
4. **Find**: Search tool.
5. **Issue**: Build-time and runtime errors and warnings.
6. **Test**: Create, manage and run unit and UI tests.
7. **Debug**: Information about CPU, memory, disk and network usage while your app is running.
8. **Breakpoints**: Add, delete, edit and manage breakpoints.
9. **Report**: View or export reports and logs generated when you build and run the project.

The **Filter** field at the bottom is different for each tab. For example, the **Project Filter** lets you show only the files you recently worked on. This is handy for projects with a lot of files in a deeply nested hierarchy.

Editor

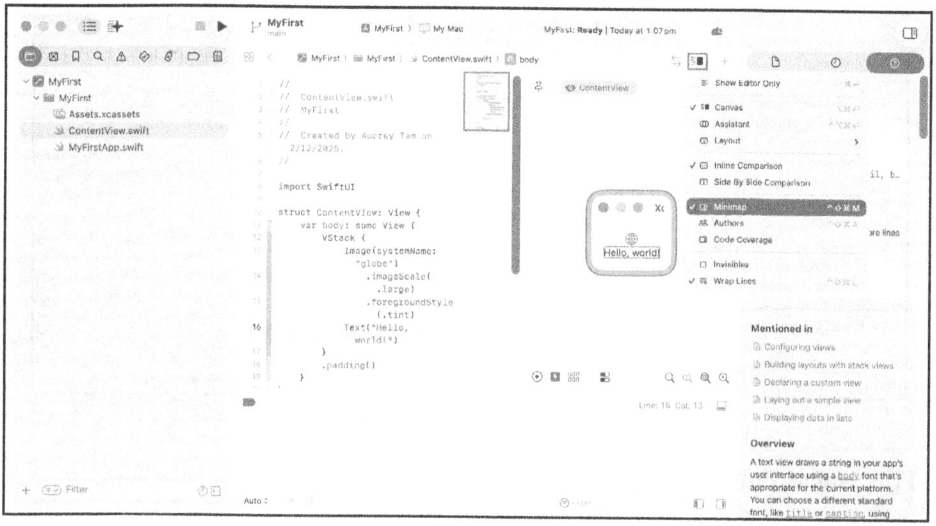

Editor with Minimap

When you're working in a code file, the **Editor** shows the code and a **Minimap**. The minimap is useful for long code files with many properties and methods. You can hover the cursor over the minimap to locate a specific property, then click to go directly to it. You don't need it for the apps in this book, so you may want to hide it via the **Adjust Editor Options** button in the upper right corner of the editor.

When you're working in a SwiftUI view file, **Option-Command-Return** shows or hides the preview **canvas.**

The editor has browser features like tabs and the ability to go back/forward. Keyboard shortcuts for tabs are the same as for web browsers: **Command-T** to open a new tab, **Shift-Command-[or -]** to move to the previous or next tab, **Command-W** to close the tab and **Option-click** a tab's close button to close all the *other* tabs. The back/forward button shows a list of previous/next files, but the keyboard shortcuts are **Control-Command-right** or **-left arrow**.

Inspectors

The **Inspectors** pane has four tabs. When this pane is hidden, you can open it directly in one of its tabs by pressing **Option-Command-1** to **Option-Command-4**:

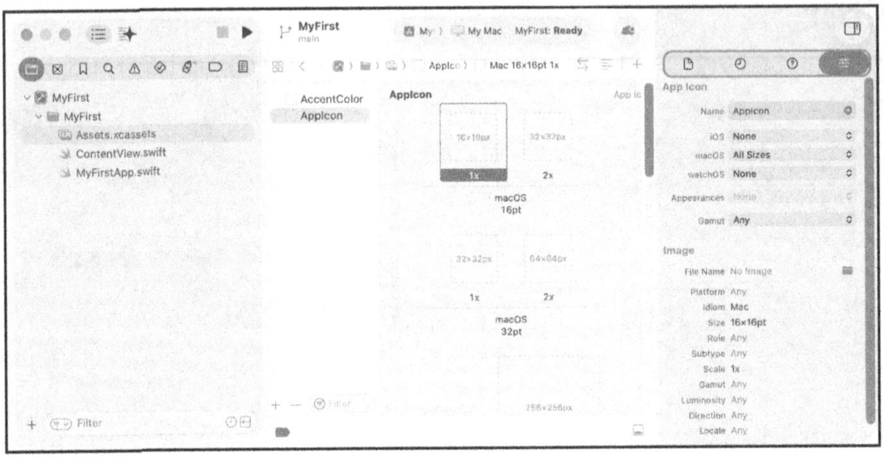

Inspector bar

1. **File**: Name, Full Path, Target Membership.
2. **History**: Source Control and Swift Assist logs.
3. **Quick Help**: Short form of Developer Documentation if you select a symbol in the editor.
4. **Attributes**: Properties of the asset you select in Assets.xcassets.

Tabs 1-3 appear when you select a file or folder in the Project navigator. The Attributes inspector appears only when you select **Assets.xcassets**.

This quick tour just brushes the surface of what you can do in Xcode. Next, you'll use a few of its tools while you explore your new project.

Navigation Settings

In this book, you'll use keyboard shortcuts to examine and structure your code. Unlike the fixed keyboard shortcuts for opening navigators or inspectors, you can specify settings for which shortcut does what. To avoid confusion while working through this book, you'll adjust your settings to match the instructions you'll see.

➤ Press **Command-,** to open **Settings**. In the **Navigation** tab, set:

- **Click on Code With Option** to **Shows Quick Help**
- **Click on Code With Command** to **Jumps to Definition**

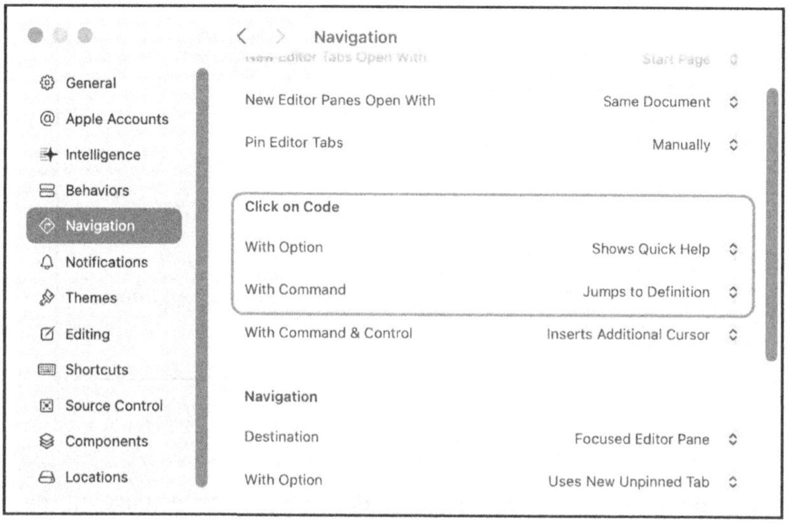

Adjust Navigation Settings.

ContentView.swift

The heart of your new project is in **ContentView.swift**, where your new project opened. This is where you'll lay out the initial view of your app.

➤ If **ContentView.swift** isn't in the editor, select it in the Project navigator.

The first several lines are comments that identify the file and you, the creator.

import

The first line of code is an `import` statement:

```
import SwiftUI
```

This works just like most programming languages. It allows your code to access everything in the built-in SwiftUI module. See what happens if it's missing.

➤ Click the `import` statement line, then press **Command-/**.

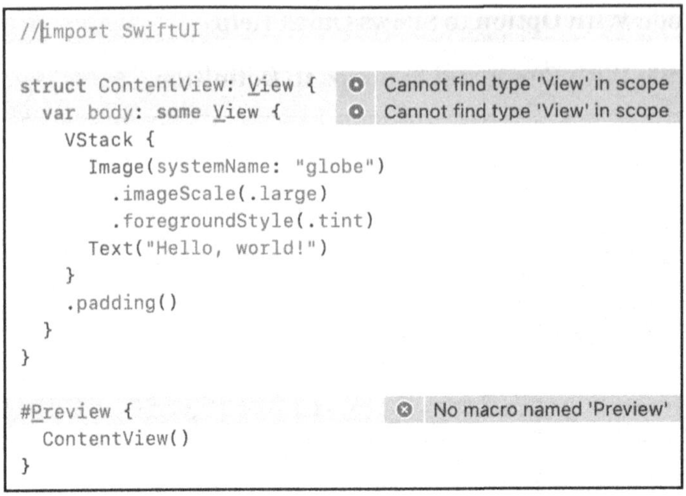

What happens if import SwiftUI is missing

> **Note**: All code on our site uses 2-space indentation to save space on the page. Xcode defaults to 4-space indentation. You can change this in **Xcode Settings → Editing → Indentation**.

You commented out the `import` statement, so compiler errors appear, complaining about `View` and `Preview`.

➤ Press **Command-Z** to undo.

Below the `import` statement is a `struct` definition. A *structure* is a named data type that encapsulates properties and methods.

struct ContentView

The name of the first structure matches the name of the file. Nothing bad happens if they're different, but most developers follow and expect this convention.

```
struct ContentView: View {
  var body: some View {
    VStack {
      Image(systemName: "globe")
        .imageScale(.large)
        .foregroundStyle(.tint)
      Text("Hello, world!")
```

```
      }
      .padding()
    }
  }
```

Looking at `ContentView: View`, you might think `ContentView` *inherits* from `View`, but Swift structures don't have inheritance. `View` is a *protocol*, and `ContentView` *conforms* to this protocol.

The required component of the `View` protocol is the computed property `body`, which returns a `View`. In this case, it returns a `VStack` (vertical stack) that displays a globe image and the usual "Hello, world!" text.

> **Swift Tip**: A computed property returns the computed value. If there's only a single code statement, you don't need to explicitly use the `return` keyword.

The `VStack` view has a `padding` modifier — an instance method of `View` — that adds space around the stack. You can see it in this screenshot:

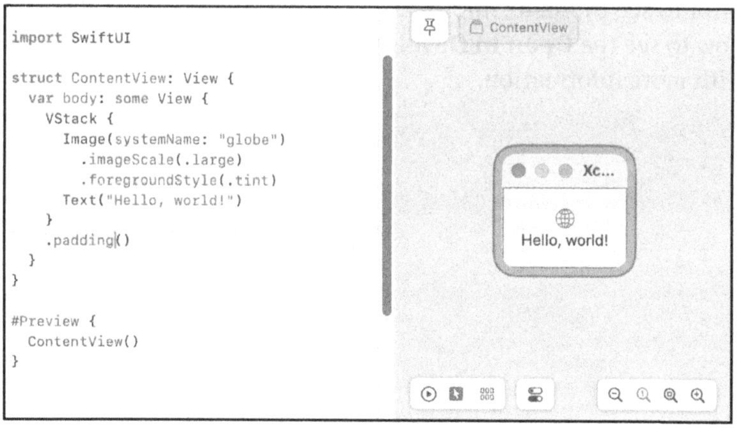

VStack padding

`Image(systemName: "globe")` and its modifiers display a globe symbol. You'll learn about the `Image` view in Chapter 5, "Beginning SwiftUI".

`Text("Hello, world!")` displays the string "Hello, world!".

➤ Click the **Selectable** button below the preview canvas, then click the `Text` view in the canvas and select the **Quick Help inspector**.

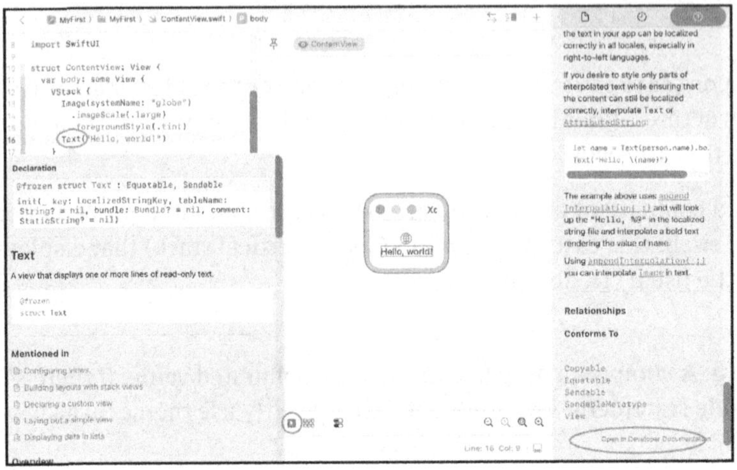

Text Quick Help and Developer Documentation

If you don't want to use screen real estate for this inspector, **Option-click** `Text` in the code editor to see the same information in a pop-up window. Scroll down in either window to see the **Open in Developer Documentation** button, which opens a window with more information.

➤ Now, press **Shift-Command-L** to show the **Library**, then select the **Modifiers** tab and scroll down to the **Text** modifiers. Scan the list to see what's there:

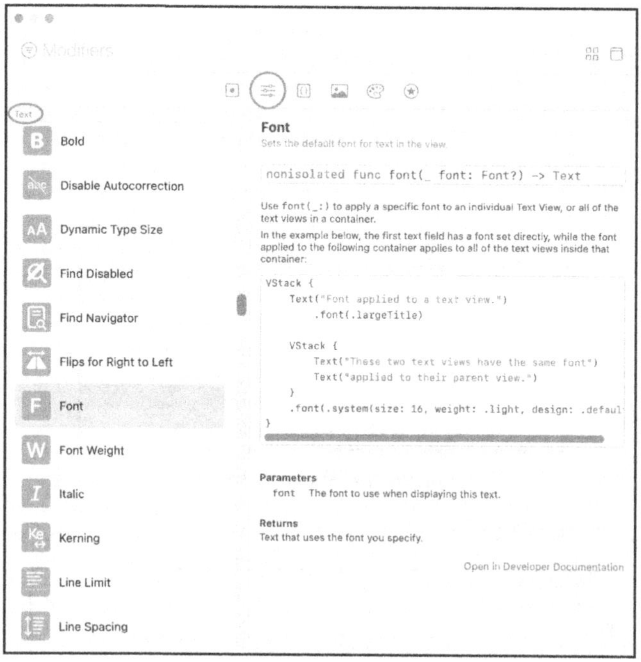

Text Modifiers

> **Note**: The Library window closes when you click anywhere outside it. Press **Option-Command-L** to open it if you want it to remain open.

#Preview

Below `ContentView` is a `Preview` macro.

```
#Preview {
  ContentView()
}
```

You can expand this macro:

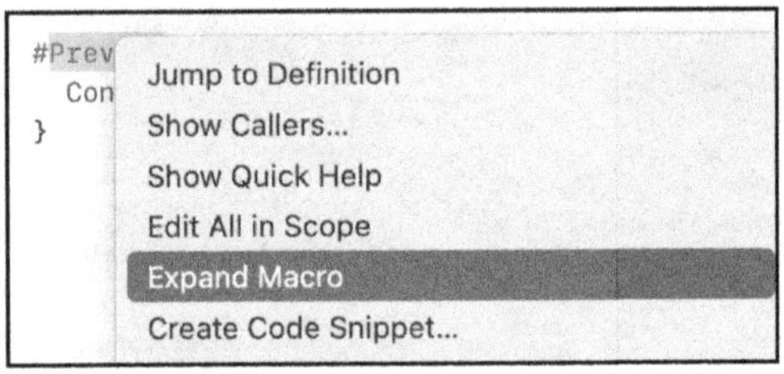

Expand the Preview macro.

This is what the macro contains:

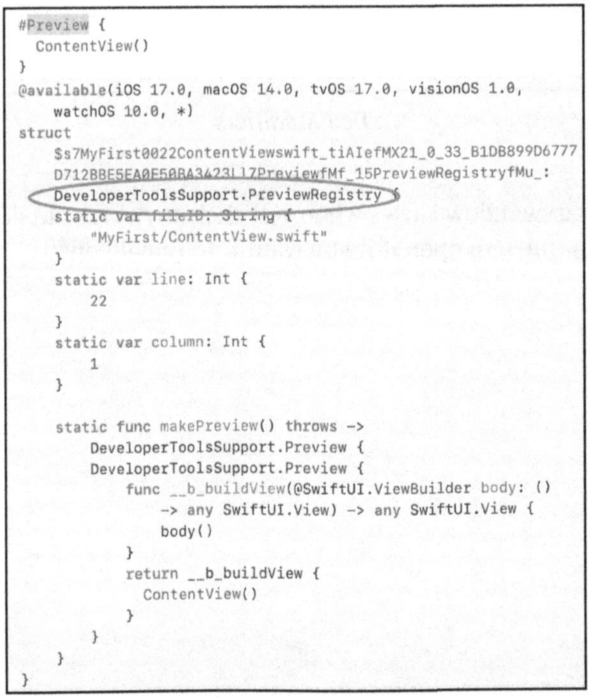

```
#Preview {
  ContentView()
}
@available(iOS 17.0, macOS 14.0, tvOS 17.0, visionOS 1.0,
    watchOS 10.0, *)
struct
    $s7MyFirst0022ContentViewswift_tiAIefMX21_0_33_B1DB899D6777
    D712BBE5EA0E50BA3423LL7PreviewfMf_15PreviewRegistryfMu_:
    DeveloperToolsSupport.PreviewRegistry {
    static var fileID: String {
        "MyFirst/ContentView.swift"
    }
    static var line: Int {
        22
    }
    static var column: Int {
        1
    }

    static func makePreview() throws ->
        DeveloperToolsSupport.Preview {
        DeveloperToolsSupport.Preview {
            func __b_buildView(@SwiftUI.ViewBuilder body: ()
                -> any SwiftUI.View) -> any SwiftUI.View {
                body()
            }
            return __b_buildView {
              ContentView()
            }
        }
    }
}
```

Expanded Preview macro

The `PreviewRegistry` structure is what appears in the canvas on the right of the code editor. See what happens if it's missing.

➤ Press **Command-Z** to hide the macro expansion, then select the three lines of `#Preview` and press **Command-/**.

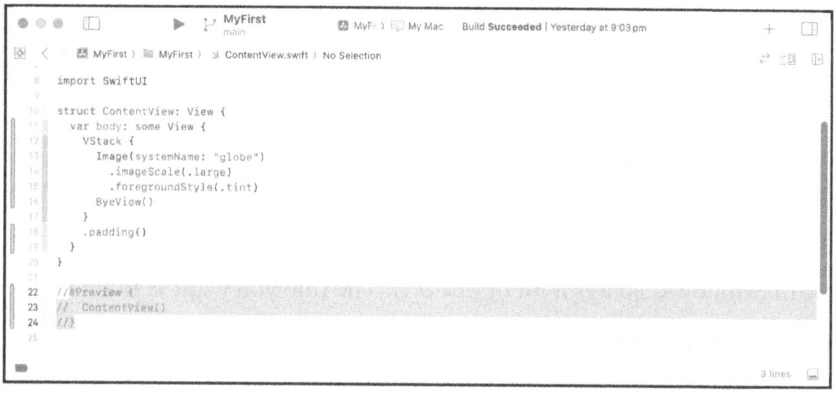

No #Preview so there's nothing in the canvas.

Without `#Preview`, there's nothing in the canvas.

➤ Press **Command-Z** to undo or, if the three lines are still selected, press **Command-/** to uncomment them.

You'll sometimes want to give more space to the code editor, so your code doesn't have to wrap.

➤ Press **Option-Command-Return** to hide the canvas. Press the same keyboard shortcut to show the canvas.

For most apps, **ContentView.swift** is just the starting point. Often, `ContentView` only defines the app's organization, orchestrating several subviews. And usually, you'll define these subviews in separate files.

Creating a New SwiftUI View File

Everything you see in a SwiftUI app is a `View`. Apple encourages you to create as many subviews as you need in order to avoid redundancy and organize your code to keep it manageable. The compiler takes care of creating efficient machine code, so your app's performance won't suffer.

➤ In the Project navigator, select **ContentView.swift** and press **Command-N**. Alternatively, right-click **ContentView.swift** then select **New File from Template...** from the menu.

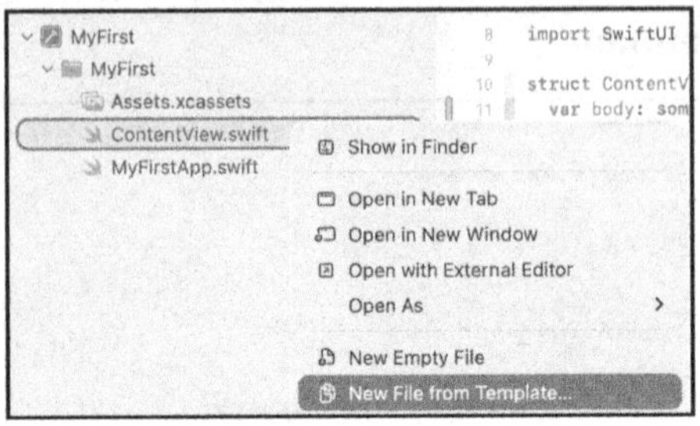

Select New File... from right-click menu.

The new file window displays a lot of options! The one you want is **macOS** → **User Interface** → **SwiftUI View**. In Chapter 6, "Getting Data Into Your App", you'll get to create a **Swift File**.

Choose macOS → User Interface → SwiftUI View.

Naming a New SwiftUI View

➤ Select **SwiftUI View** then click **Next**. The next window lets you specify a file name. By default, the name of the new view will be the same as the file name. You'll define the `ByeView` in this file, so replace **SwiftUIView** with **ByeView**.

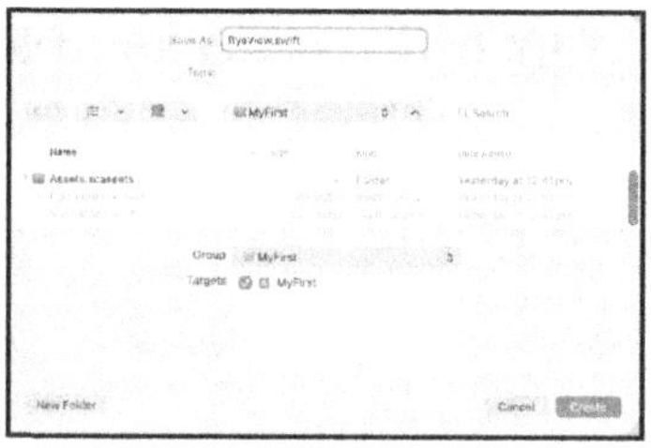

SwiftUI view file name matches the new SwiftUI View.

> **Swift Tip**: Swift convention is to name types (like `struct`) with **UpperCamelCase** and properties and methods with **lowerCamelCase**.

This window also lets you specify where in the project to create your new file. The default location is usually correct — in this project, in this group (folder) and in this target.

➤ Click **Create** to finish creating your new file.

The template code for a SwiftUI view is simpler than the `ContentView` of a new project.

```
import SwiftUI

struct ByeView: View {
  var body: some View {
    Text("Hello, World!")
  }
}

#Preview {
  ByeView()
}
```

The view's body contains only `Text("Hello, World!")` — no `Image`, so you don't need a `VStack`, and no `padding`. Another subtle difference: The "Hello, World!" string is a *token*. It's just a placeholder. Clicking anywhere in it highlights the token so you can type in a new value.

Using Your New SwiftUI View

➤ Click the "Hello, World!" token and change it so the line looks like this:

```
Text("Bye bye, World!")
```

➤ Next, open **ContentView.swift**. In the code editor, delete the `Text` view, then type **bye**. Xcode suggests some auto-completions:

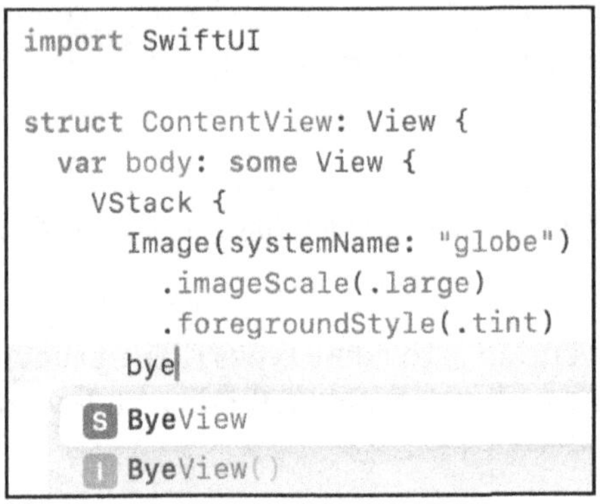

Xcode suggests auto-completions.

Notice you don't have to type the correct capitalization of `ByeView`.

> **Xcode Tip**: Descriptive names for your types, properties and methods is good programming practice, and auto-completion is one way Xcode helps you do the right thing. You can also turn on spell-checking from the Xcode menu: **Edit → Format → Spelling and Grammar → Check Spelling While Typing**.

➤ Select **ByeView()** from the list, so the line looks like this:

```
ByeView()
```

You're calling the initializer of `ByeView` to create an instance of the view.

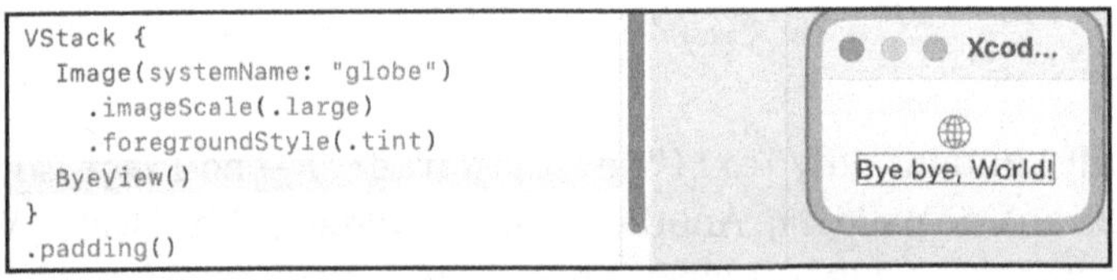

Replace Text view with ByeView.

Your new ByeView has replaced the original Text view. You'll create many new SwiftUI view files and Swift files to develop the apps in this book.

What Else is in Your Project?

The Project navigator lists two other files.

- **Assets.xcassets**: Store your app's images and colors here. AppIcon is a special image set for all the different sizes and resolutions of your app's icon.
- **MyFirstApp.swift**: This file contains the code for your app's entry point. This is what actually launches your app.

```
@main
struct MyFirstApp: App {
  var body: some Scene {
    WindowGroup {
      ContentView()
    }
  }
}
```

The @main attribute marks MyFirstApp as the app's entry point. You might be accustomed to writing a main() method to actually launch an app. The App protocol takes care of this. The App protocol requires only a computed property named body that returns a Scene. And a Scene is a container for the root view of a view hierarchy.

For a macOS app, the default setup is a WindowGroup scene containing ContentView() as its root view. A common customization is to set different root views, depending on whether the user has logged in. In a macOS or iPadOS app, WindowGroup can manage multiple windows.

> **Note**: Don't rename or delete these files. Xcode stores their path names in the project's build settings and will flag errors if it can't find them.

You'll learn how to use these files in the rest of this book.

Xcode Settings

Xcode has a huge number of settings you can adjust to be more productive.

Themes

You'll be spending a lot of time working in the code editor, so you want it to look good and also help you distinguish the different components of your code. Xcode provides several pre-configured font and color themes for you to choose from or modify.

➤ Press **Command-,** to open **Settings**, then select the **Themes** tab:

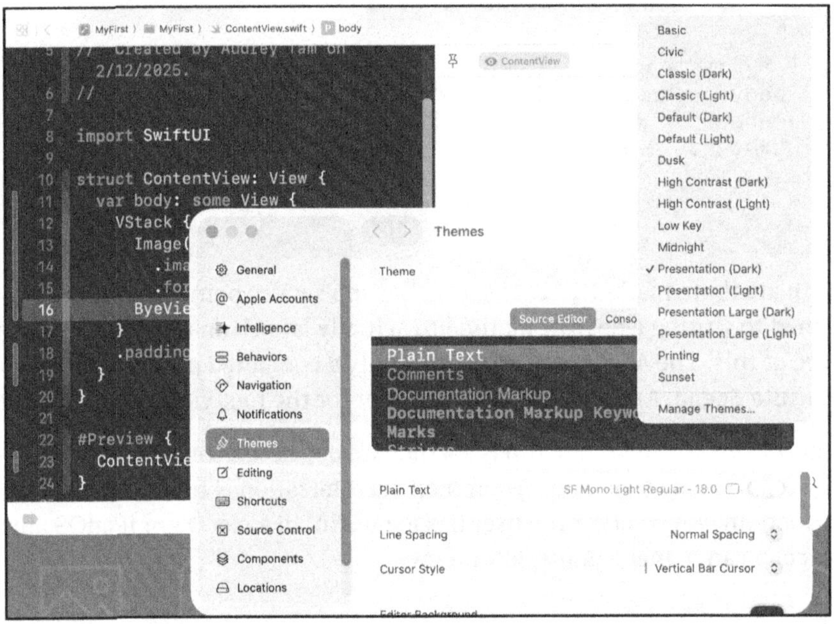

Settings: Font and color themes

Go ahead and explore these. You can customize them or create your own. I'll wait here. ;]

Matching Delimiters

SwiftUI code uses *a lot* of nested closures. It's really easy to mismatch your braces and parentheses. Xcode helps you find any mismatches and tries to prevent these errors from happening.

➤ In **Settings**, select **Editing** → **Completion**:

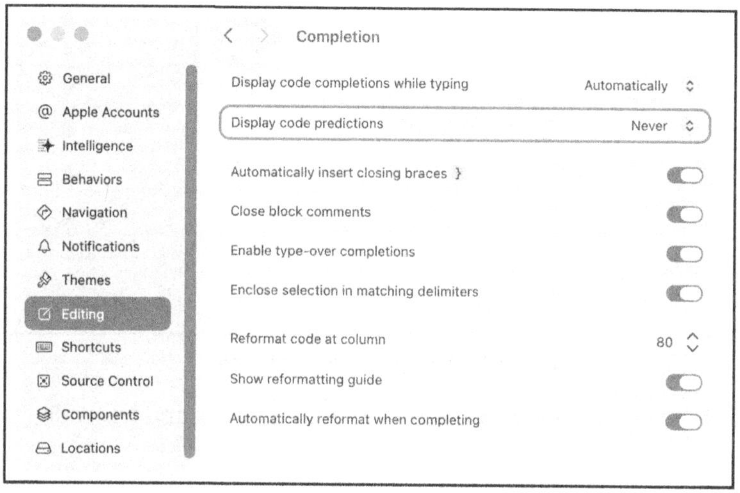

Settings → Editing → Completion

➤ Change **Display code predictions** to **Never**. At this stage of your learning, predictive coding is more confusing than helpful.

The other **Completion** items are super helpful. Although you can copy and paste code from this book, you should try to type the code as much as possible to learn how these aids work.

Here's a big hint that something's wrong or you're typing in the wrong place: You're expecting Xcode to suggest completions while you type, but nothing useful appears. When this happens, it's usually because you're outside the closure you need to be in.

➤ Now select the **Editing** → **Display** tab. Check **Code folding ribbon** and, if you like to see them, **Line numbers**:

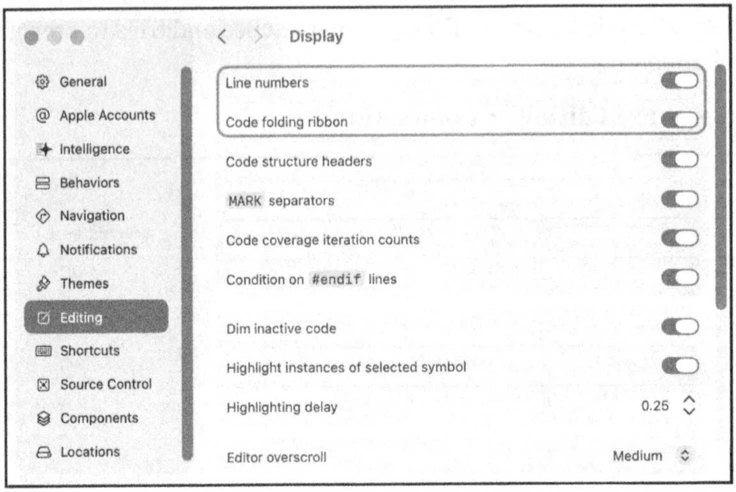

Settings → Editing → Display

So what's a *code folding ribbon*? Between the line numbers and the code, you see darker gray vertical bars.

➤ Hover your cursor over one — anywhere between `VStack {` and `padding()`.

It highlights the start and end braces of that closure:

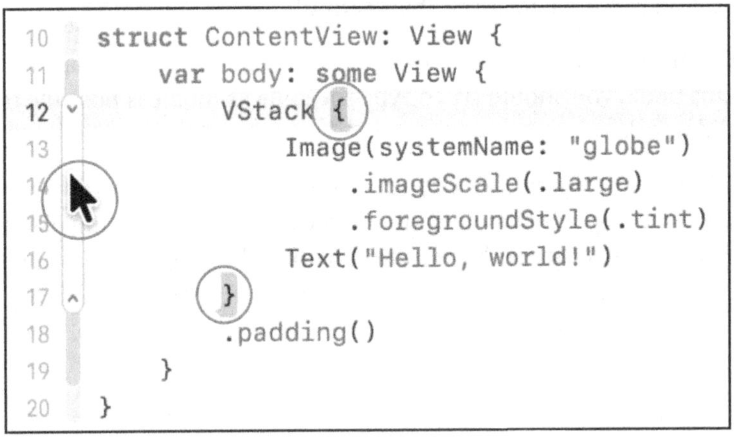

Code folding ribbon: Hover to show matching braces.

Other ways to see matching delimiters:

- **Option-hover** over **{**, **(**, **[** or a closing delimiter: Xcode highlights the start and end delimiters.
- **Double-click** a delimiter: Xcode selects the delimiters and their contents.

➤ Now click the bar (ribbon) to collapse (fold) those lines of code:

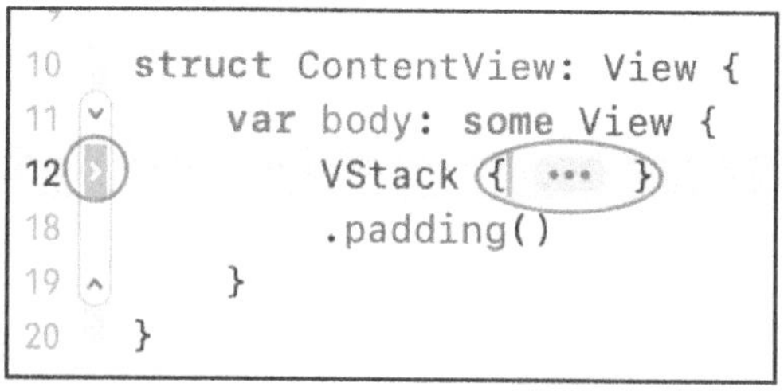

Code folding ribbon: Click to fold code.

This can be incredibly useful when you're trying to find your way around some complex, deeply-nested code.

➤ Click the ribbon to unfold the code.

Adding Accounts

You can access some Xcode features by adding login information for your Apple ID and source control accounts.

➤ In **Settings**, select **Apple Accounts**, then click **Add Apple Account...** and add your Apple ID. If you have a separate paid Apple Developer account, add that too.

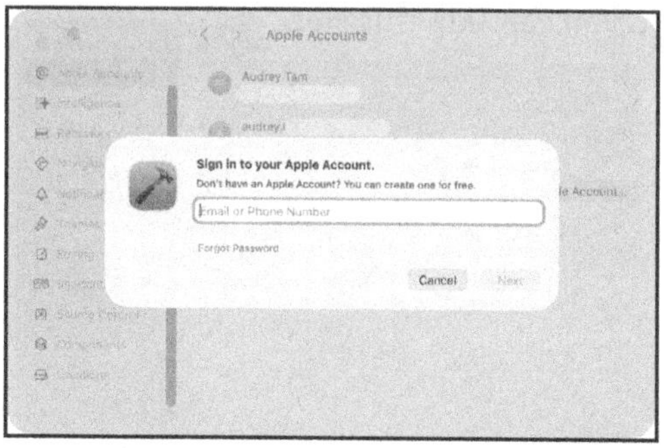

Settings → Accounts

To add capabilities like push notifications or Apple Pay to your app, you need to set **Team** to a Developer Program account. You'd do this in the **Signing & Capabilities** tab of the target.

➤ In **Settings → Source Control**, add your account at Bitbucket, GitHub or GitLab if you want to push your project's local git repository to a remote repository.

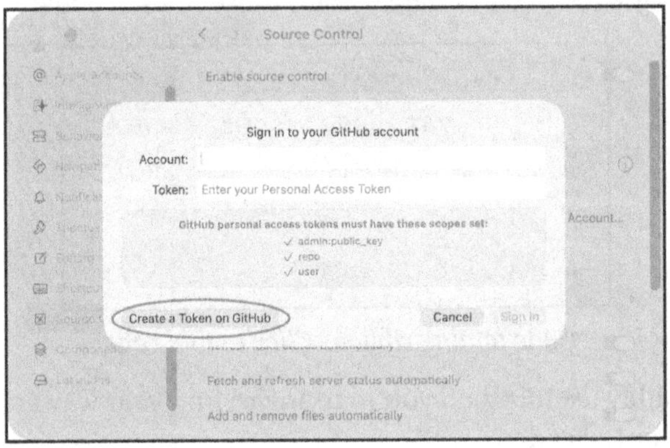

Add a source control account.

Bitbucket Server, GitHub and GitLab accounts require a *personal access token*. If the button to open GitHub's token-creation page doesn't work, open this URL (https://github.com/settings/tokens).

➤ To set up a remote repository, open the Xcode **Integrate** menu and select **New Git Repository...**:

> If you remembered to check **Create Git repository on my Mac** when you created your project, you can skip this step.

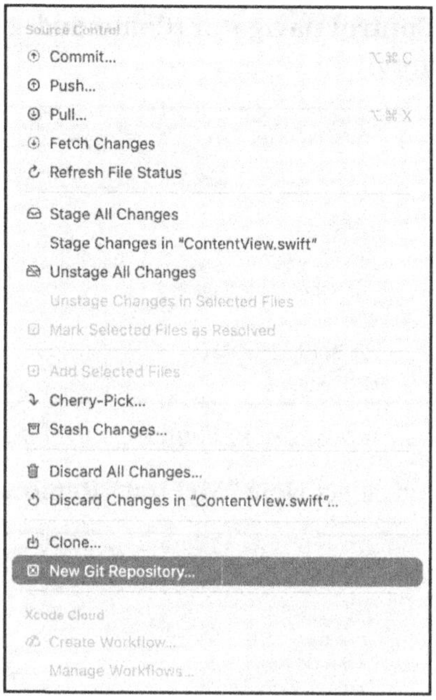

New Git Repositories...

➤ Click **Create**:

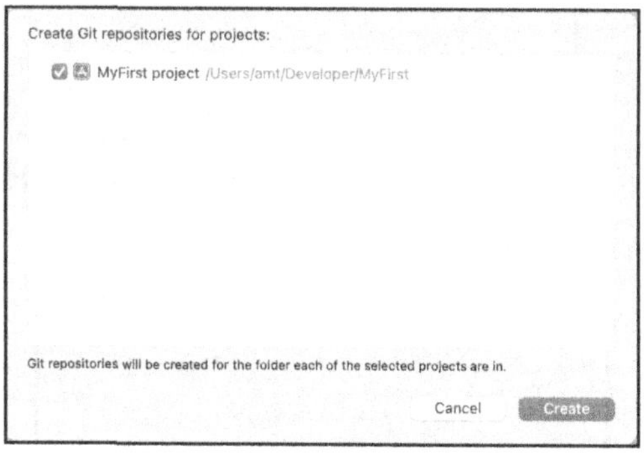

Create Git repository.

➤ Now, open the **Source Control navigator** (**Command-2**), click the **Repositories** tab and expand the repository:

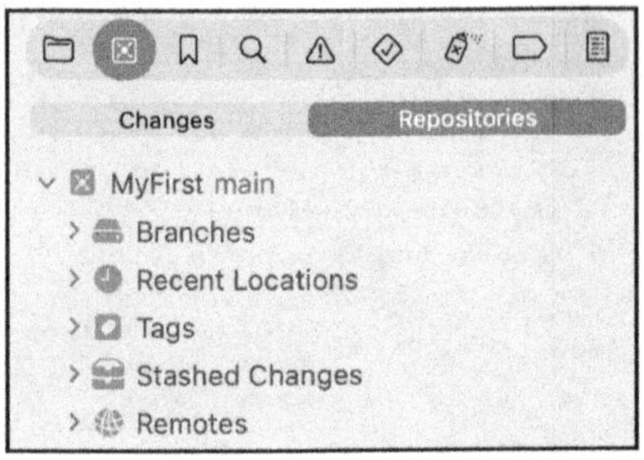

Expand Git repository in Source Control navigator.

➤ **Right-click Remotes** and select **New "MyFirst" Remote...**:

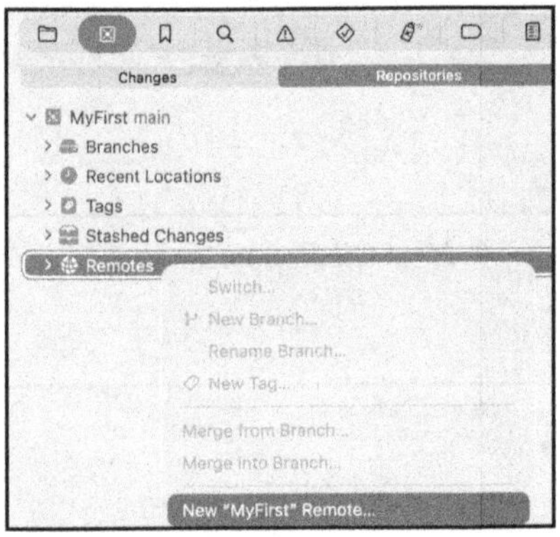

Control-click Remote, select New 'MyFirst' Remote...

➤ Select your options, then click **Create**:

Create-remote options

And here it is:

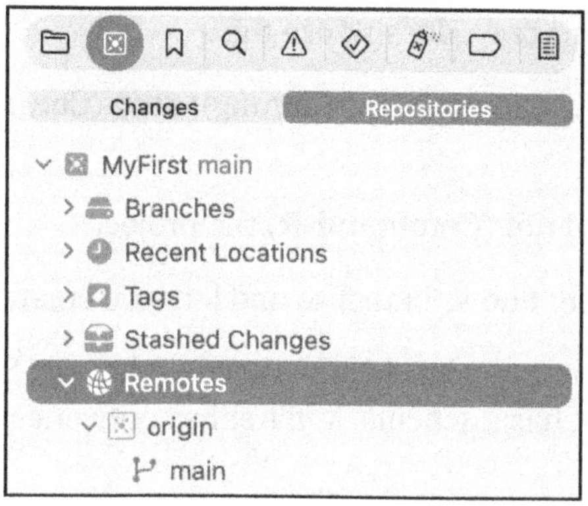

New remote repository created.

Running Your project

So far, you've relied on the preview canvas to see what your app looks like. You can use Live Preview to interact with your app. But some features don't work in Live Preview, so then you need to build and run your app on your Mac.

The Xcode Toolbar

First, a quick tour of the toolbar:

Xcode window toolbar

> **Xcode Tip**: Press **Option-Command-T** to show or hide the toolbar. If this keyboard shortcut conflicts with another app, select the command from the Xcode **View** menu.

So far, you've only used the buttons at either end of the toolbar, to show or hide the navigator or inspector panes.

Working from left to right after the navigation pane button:

- **Coding Assistant**: This book doesn't use this.
- **Stop** button (enabled when project is running): Stop (**Command-.**) the running project.
- **Run** button: Build and run (**Command-R**) the project.
- **Source control** button: Shows branches and lets you create a pull request.
- **Scheme** menu: This button's label is the name of the app. Select, edit or manage *schemes*. Each product has a scheme. MyFirst has only one product, so it has only one scheme.
- **Run destination** menu: This menu defaults to your Mac.
- **Activity** view: A wide gray field that shows the project name, status messages and warning or error indicators.
- **Xcode Cloud** button: This book doesn't use this.

Now that you know where the controls are, it's time to use some of them.

Build and Run

➤ Check the run destination is your Mac, then click the run button or press **Command-R**.

After a short wait, your app appears!

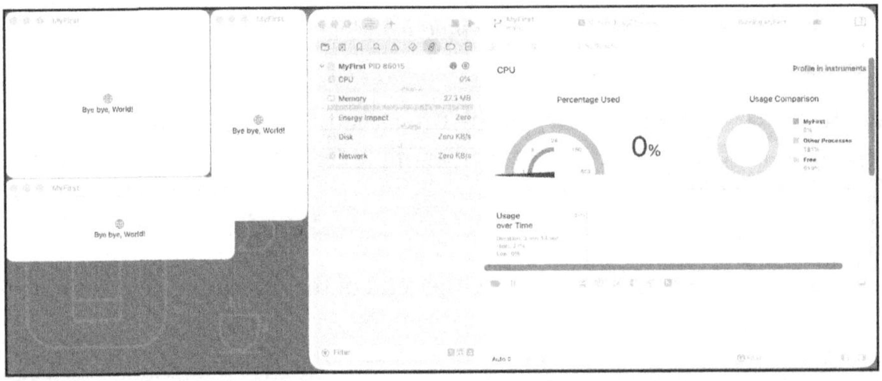

Running app windows, Debug navigator, debug area

There's not much happening in this app, but the debug toolbar appears below the editor window. For this screenshot, I showed the debug area, selected the **Debug** tab in the Project navigator pane, then selected the **CPU** item.

The app itself is just different sized windows showing the globe symbol and "Bye bye, World!" text. The windows are much bigger than the text needs, but they're like any Mac app's windows. You can drag a corner or edge to resize a window, make it full screen or minimize it. You can close a window and open a new one. In fact, you can open lots of new windows.

➤ Open the **MyFirst Window** menu:

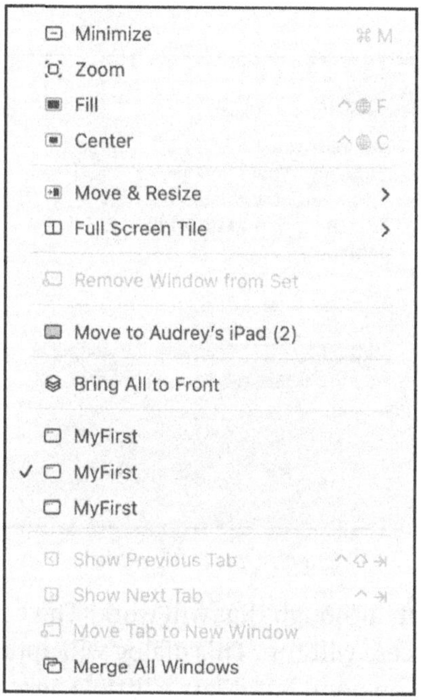

Resize or open new windows and merge them.

All the usual window and tab tools are already there and available to you.

The only control on this window is a static `Text` view, so there's nothing to edit, but the **Edit** menu is there and ready for action, as are all the other standard menus that people expect to see in a Mac app.

Not Stopping

Here's a trick that will make your Xcode life a little easier.

➤ **Don't click** the stop button. Yes, it's enabled. But trust me, you'll like this. :]

➤ In **ByeView.swift**, replace "Bye bye" with "Hello again":

```
Text("Hello again, World!")
```

➤ Click the run button or press **Command-R**.

Up pops this message:

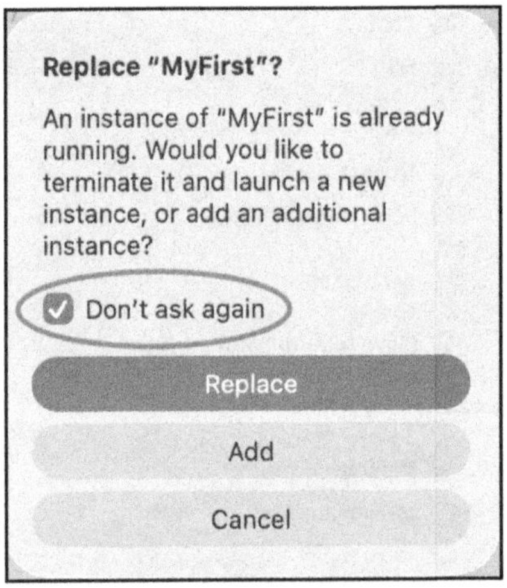

Check Don't ask again.

➤ **Don't click Replace yet**, although that will work: The currently running process will stop, and the new process will run. This dialog will appear every time you forget to stop the app. It's just a moment, but it jars a little. Every time. And it's easy to get rid of.

➤ Check **Don't ask again**, *then* click **Replace** or **Add**.

The app loads with your new change. But that's not what I want to show you.

➤ In **ByeView.swift**, replace "Hello again" with "Hey hey":

```
Text("Hey hey, World!")
```

➤ Once more: Click the run button or press **Command-R**.

No annoying message, no "doh!" moment, ever again! You're welcome. ;]

> **Note**: Depending on which button you clicked, Xcode will either replace your app or add a new one. If you chose **Add**, you can now use the app switcher to move between the different versions. You can reset "Don't Ask Me" warnings in **Settings → General → Dialog Warnings**.

In the rest of this book, you'll create much more interesting apps.

Key Points

- The Xcode window has Navigators, Editor and Inspectors panes, a Toolbar and a Debug Area, plus a lot of Settings.
- You can specify navigation keyboard shortcuts in Settings, to match the instructions in this book.
- The template project defines an `App` that launches with `ContentView`, displaying a globe symbol and "Hello, world!".
- You can view Quick Help documentation in an inspector or with a keyboard shortcut. Or, you can open the Developer Documentation window.
- When you create a new SwiftUI view file, give it the same name as the `View` you'll create in it.
- Xcode's auto-completion, delimiter-matching, code-folding and spell-checking help you avoid errors.
- You can choose one of Xcode's font and color themes, modify one or create your own.

Chapter 2: Beginning Swift

By Sarah Reichelt

In the first chapter, you installed Xcode and configured it. Then, you learned how to create a Mac app from the standard template.

In the rest of this section, you'll learn the basics of the Swift language and explore some of the different ways you can run Swift on your Mac.

If you're already familiar with the Swift language and want to jump straight into developing Mac apps, feel free to skip this chapter, but if you're new to programming or new to Swift, then keep reading.

What is Swift?

Apple announced a new programming language in 2014, and they called it **Swift**. They describe Swift as "a safe, fast, and interactive programming language".

Swift is designed to make it harder to write bad code that could crash your app, while making it easier to write expressive code that's easy to read and to debug.

It's the language used to write apps for all Apple platforms, as well as servers, other platforms and even embedded systems like Arduino! But enough talk — time to code.

Running Swift in the Terminal

When you installed Xcode in the previous chapter, you also installed a suite of tools called the **Xcode Command Line Tools**. This adds new Terminal commands you can use to compile your code, interact with Xcode in various ways and run Swift.

Open Terminal by going to **Applications → Utilities → Terminal.app** or by pressing **Command-Space** to open Spotlight and searching for **Terminal**. The default Terminal window opens as a small window in the top left of your screen. The width is fine, but expand the window so that it's as tall as your screen. This makes it much easier to see the sequence of commands that you're about to run.

In **Terminal**, type `swift` and press **Return**:

```
sarah@sarah-imac ~ % swift

Welcome to Swift!

Subcommands:

  swift build      Build Swift packages
  swift package    Create and work on packages
  swift run        Run a program from a package
  swift test       Run package tests
  swift repl       Experiment with Swift code interactively

  Use `swift --version` for Swift version information.

  Use `swift --help` for descriptions of available options and flags.

  Use `swift help <subcommand>` for more information about a subcommand.
```

Swift in the Terminal.

You're looking at a list of the subcommands that you can run from the `swift` command line tool. Most of these are to do with packages, which are beyond the scope of this book. The one you're interested in is `repl` so that you can "experiment with Swift code interactively".

Type `swift repl` and press **Return** to start the **Swift REPL**. So what is a REPL? It stands for **Read-Evaluate-Print-Loop**. You type in Swift code, the Swift REPL reads it, evaluates the result, prints that result and loops back to its command prompt ready for another command.

> **Note**: In earlier versions of the Xcode Command Line Tools, running `swift` without any extra arguments automatically started the Swift REPL, but since Swift 5.7, you need to select this manually.

To get out of the REPL and back to your usual Terminal, enter `:exit` or press **Control-D**. Pressing **Command-K** at any time clears the Terminal screen.

If you exited the REPL, press **Up-Arrow** to return to the previous command and run `swift repl` again.

Swift Types

Swift is a strictly-typed language, but what does that mean? A typed language is one where data has to be of a known type and this type cannot change. Swift infers the data type depending on what you give it and the Swift REPL makes it easy to see the assigned type.

In the REPL, type `1` and press **Return**:

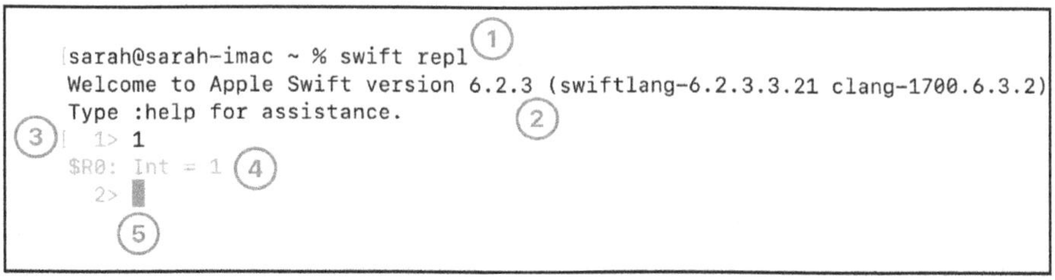

First look at the Swift REPL.

You only entered one character, but there's a lot of information on this screen:

1. The first line shows your standard Terminal prompt — in my case, it's showing my user name and computer name — followed by the command you entered to start the REPL.
2. You get to see what version of Swift you're running. Don't worry if it's not exactly the same as mine.
3. The REPL has its own prompt which numbers the lines as you enter them. You typed `1` on line 1.
4. This is where the REPL printed the result. First, you see **$R0** which is an internal label that the REPL assigns to your result. Then you see **Int = 1**. This tells you that Swift has evaluated what you entered and found it to be an integer with the value of 1. Swift uses `Int` to indicate an integer, which is a whole number with no decimal point.
5. Finally, the REPL loops back and gives you another prompt.

Now that you know how to read what the REPL tells you, enter these lines, pressing **Return** after each one:

```
4.87
"Swift"
true
```

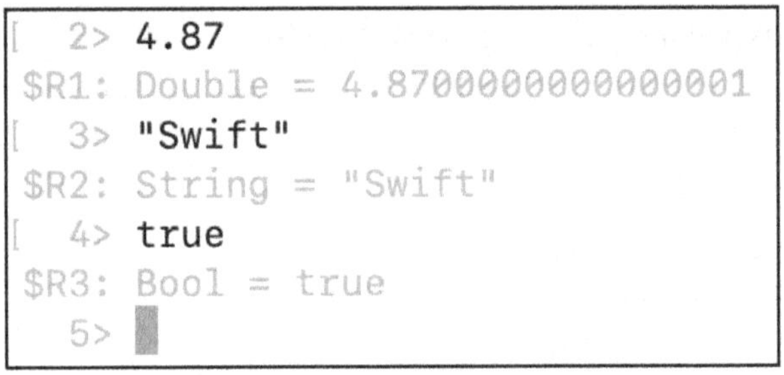

Swift types

Checking the results of these lines, by line number:

2. `Double` is short for **double precision floating point** and means a number with decimals. As you can see from the printed result, computers aren't very good at floating point numbers and often get them a bit wrong, although rarely enough to make any significant difference.

3. `String` describes any text and, in Swift, you surround text with double-quotes.

4. `Bool` (short for `Boolean`) is a value that can only be either `true` or `false`.

These four entries demonstrate the basic or primitive types used by Swift. Later, you'll see how to combine these into more complex types for your own data needs.

Operating on Data

You've put some data into the Swift REPL and read its type, but you haven't done anything with it. You'll use operators to perform operations on your data. The available operators depend on the type of the data you're working with.

Numbers

Numeric operators include the standard mathematical operators with the most usual being addition (+), subtraction (-), multiplication (*) and division (/).

Evaluate these commands one at a time in the Swift REPL:

```
67 + 3
1.45 - 2
9 * 4
7 / 3
```

Which gives these results:

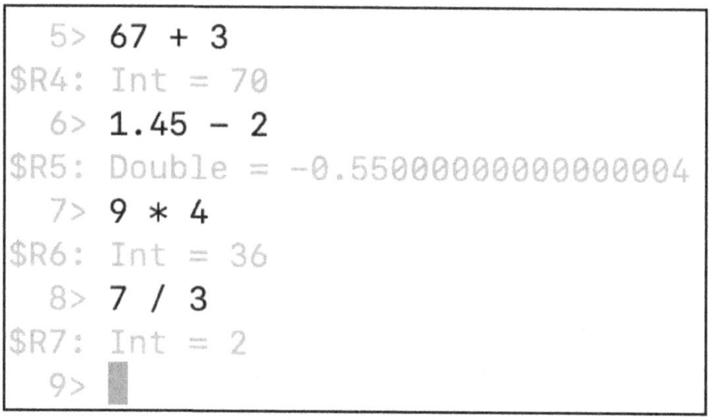

Numerical operators

Looking at these by line number:

5. Adding 2 `Int` values returns another `Int`.
6. The first value here is a `Double`. You can only subtract a `Double` from another `Double`, so Swift has assigned a type of `Double` to the 2. The result is a `Double` and again shows the problems a computer can have with decimals.
7. Again, this operator started with two `Int` values and gives another `Int`.
8. This one may have surprised you with what appears to be the wrong answer. Shouldn't 7 divided by 3 equal 2.3333333? Not in this case, because you started with two `Int` values and so Swift performed an integer operation and returned an integer value. To get the correct answer, enter `7.0 / 3`. To our human eyes, 7.0 is exactly the same as 7, but to Swift, one is a `Double` and one is an `Int`.

> **Note**: The spaces either side of the operator make the expression easier to read. Omitting both spaces — 9*4 — will work, but if you put a space on one side, make sure there's a space on the other side. 9 *4 or 9* 4 won't work. If you use inconsistent spacing, Swift shows a very unhelpful error message: **error: consecutive statements on a line must be separated by ';'**, so if you see that, check your spaces.

Order of Operations

When doing multiple calculations on a single line, Swift evaluates operators in a certain order. Type in this operation, but before pressing **Return**, try to work out what result you expect:

```
2 + 5 * 3
```

If you worked from left to right, you may have expected 21 (2 + 5 = 7, 7 * 3 = 21). But the order of operations dictates that multiplication and division happen first and then addition and subtraction. So for this sum, 5 * 3 = 15, 2 + 15 = 17.

If you want to change the order, wrap sections in parentheses. Swift evaluates these sections first and then evaluates the rest of the line. To get 21, you'd need to do this:

```
(2 + 5) * 3
```

While you can rely on the order of operations, you can always use parentheses to make your meaning clear.

Strings

You can operate on `String` data too. The + operator concatenates strings. Run this command:

```
"Hello" + " Swift!"
```

You'll get a single `String` with the two parts run together. There's a space before the **S** in the second string to make sure the words aren't run together. The + operator does not add a space.

Booleans

The only operator that works on `Booleans` is the negative or **not** operator `!`. You can see it in action like this:

```
!true
```

It toggles `true` to `false` and `false` to `true`.

Storing Data

So far, you've used the Swift REPL in a very transitory way. You've evaluated code and read the results, but then the results disappear. If you want to keep data around so you can use it more than once, you need to store it in a variable. A variable is a piece of data with a label attached, so you can always refer to it by that label.

Still in the REPL, enter:

```
var language = "Swift"
```

Declaring a variable.

The REPL reports back that `language` is a `String`, which is correct. It also shows that instead of giving it a temporary `$R` label, it has assigned it to a variable called `language`. Now you can use that variable:

```
"Hello " + language
```

You've printed your `String` variable with a prefix, but you haven't changed the `language` variable, which you can prove by evaluating `language` on its own.

To change a variable, store the result of your operation back into the same variable, like this:

```
language = "Hello " + language
```

This line says to set the contents of the `language` variable to "Hello " followed by whatever was in there before.

Now when you evaluate `language` (you can press **Up-Arrow** to bring back your previous commands), you'll see that it has changed:

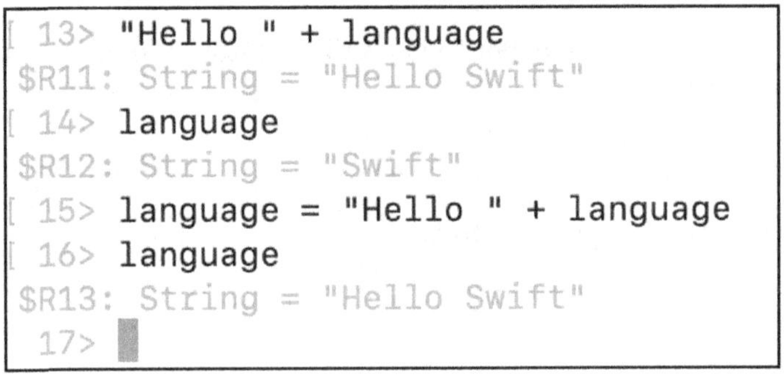

Editing a variable.

You already know that Swift assigns types to data. It does the same to variables, and once assigned, these types can't be changed.

Typing Variables

Run these commands, each of which will give you an error:

```
language = false
language = 42
language = "Swift " + 6.2
```

The first two errors say that you cannot assign a value of a different type to a `String` variable. The last one tells you that a `Double` cannot be converted to the expected argument type `String`. As you saw earlier, + is a valid `String` operator and a valid numeric operator, but it only works if it gets the same type of data on both sides.

Swift uses **Type Inference** to decide what sort of data you're using. You can set the types manually if you want to, but it's better practice to let Swift infer the types for you whenever possible.

To specify the type, follow the variable name with a colon and then the data type, like this:

```
var userName: String = "admin"
var isLoggedIn: Bool = true
var counter: Int = 0
var width: Float = 5.64
```

In these examples, the first three type declarations are redundant since Swift would have allocated those exact types. In the fourth line, the type is different to the default `Double` type for a floating point number, so this is an example of where you do need to specify the type manually.

A `Float` is a single precision floating point number so it's similar to a `Double` but it can't hold numbers as big or as small. It takes up less memory but unless you're writing code for a system where memory usage is critical, it's easier to let Swift make the choices and stick to using `Double`.

Changing Data Types

What if you wanted to produce a `String` that combined text and a number — for example, if you wanted to show the Swift version number?

You use **String Interpolation**. This is a way of inserting the result of any Swift operation into a `String`. You use it by creating a quoted string as usual, and then adding the insertion wrapped in `\(` and `)` like this:

```
var version = 6.2
language = "Swift \(version)"
```

Now when you print out the `language` variable, you'll see that it contains "Swift 6.2".

You can insert almost anything inside a string interpolation, including numbers, other strings, calculations and variables.

So that covers creating strings, but what about converting numbers between the different numeric formats?

Evaluate these three lines and see what happens:

```
var score = 6.8
var bonusPoints = 3
score += bonusPoints
```

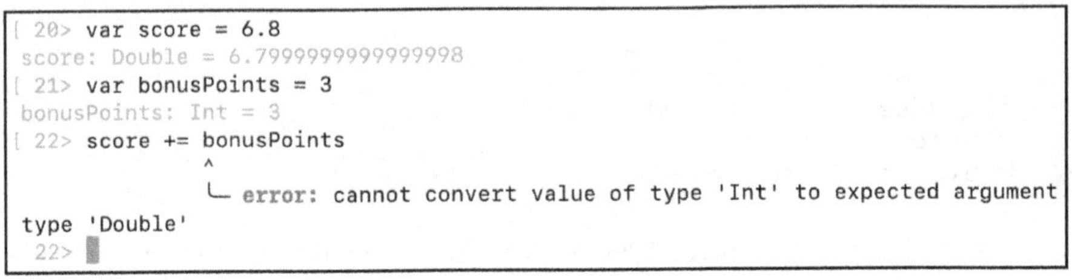

Mixing number types.

Stepping through these lines as numbered in the screenshot:

20. `score` is a `Double` and is almost equal to the number you entered.

21. `bonusPoints` is an `Int`.

22. You're trying to add an `Int` to a `Double`.

The += operator is a shorthand way of saying `score = score + bonusPoints`. You can also use -=, *= and /=. They look strange at first, but once you get used to them, these operators allow you to write code that is neat and efficient.

As before, the last line gives a "cannot convert" error because you've got two different types on either side of the operator. To make this work, you have to change one of these values to the same type as the other. You could use `Int(score)` to convert `score` to an integer. It would lose precision and become 6, but the addition would work.

In this case, a better solution is to convert `bonusPoints` to a `Double` using `Double(bonusPoints)`. This command works:

```
score += Double(bonusPoints)
```

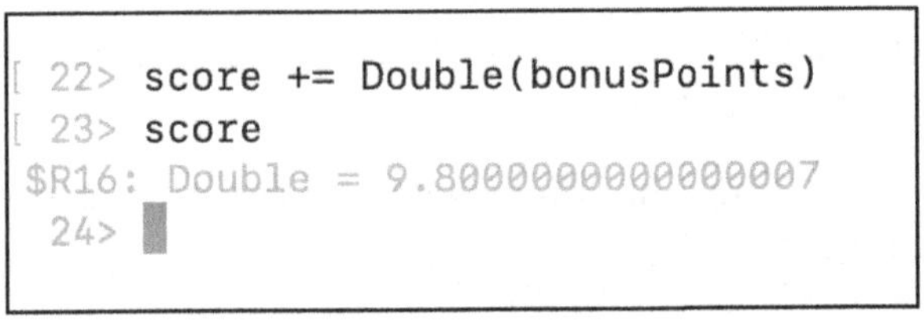

Converting number types.

These `Int()` and `Double()` commands are **initializers**. They're initializing a new instance of their data type starting with the supplied value.

Keeping Data Constant

Variables are very useful for data that may change, but not all data has to have that ability. Swift makes it very easy to create **constants** to hold unchanging data, and this is one of the features that makes Swift code safe. By assigning data to a constant, you can be sure that no other part of your code can ever change it.

Assigning a constant is similar to assigning a variable, but you use the `let` keyword instead of `var`:

```
let userID = "ABCD1234"
```

> **Note**: If you've come from the JavaScript world, this is the opposite of what you expect, but `let` in Swift is the same as `const` in JavaScript, while `var` in Swift is like `let` in JavaScript.

A good rule of thumb when coding in Swift is to start with `let` for every piece of data and only change to `var` if Xcode complains.

Trying to edit a constant gives a series of errors, which helpfully tell you what to do if you actually need to edit the value:

```
 24> let userID = "ABCD1234"
userID: String = "ABCD1234"
 25> userID = "876"
     ^
     └─ note: change 'let' to 'var' to make it mutable
     └─ note: change 'let' to 'var' to make it mutable
     └─ error: cannot assign to value: 'userID' is a 'let' constant
 25>
```

Trying to edit a constant.

Naming Variables

When you're writing code, it's important to make it readable. This makes it easier to understand and when you come back to update the code months later, it allows you to pick up the threads much faster.

Swift encourages code that reads well and a big part of that is choosing good variable names. Compare these two chunks of code:

```
let u = "ABCD1234"
var n = "Jane Doe"
var pw = "super_secret"
var p = 36
```

```
let userID = "ABCD1234"
var userName = "Jane Doe"
var password = "super_secret"
var parkingSpaceNumber = 36
```

Which one would you rather read if you were unfamiliar with the code? Xcode and the Swift REPL have excellent auto-complete options. To see this in action, go back to the Swift REPL, type `l` and press **Tab**:

```
 25> l
Available completions:
        l -- language: String
        l -- lazy
        l -- let
 25> l
```

Auto-complete

Because you previously defined the `language` variable, auto-complete suggests it, along with two key words that also match what you typed.

Type an after the `l` it filled in for you on the next line and this time, pressing **Tab** gives your full variable name. Press **Return** to evaluate it.

So there's no excuse for writing short and unhelpful names as they don't actually save you any time when writing and they'll cost you a lot more time later.

You can use this auto-complete technique for the rest of this chapter to make your life easier as you type in the REPL.

The convention for writing variable and constant names in Swift is **lowerCamelCase**. Names start with a lowercase letter and the subsequent words in the name start with an uppercase letter.

Swift allows for a great deal of variety in variable names including the use of Emoji, but in the interests of clarity, this isn't a great idea. Variable names must start with a letter, but after that, they can contain letters, numbers, underscores and dashes.

Collecting Data

So far, each variable or constant has held a single primitive data point, but you'll often want to gather a collection of data points together under a single variable name.

Arrays

Swift has several ways to do this, and the most commonly used one is an **array**. An array is an ordered collection of items of the same type.

To create an array, you wrap the data in square brackets and separate the individual items by commas:

```
var things = [ "pear", "banana", "grape", "zebra" ]
```

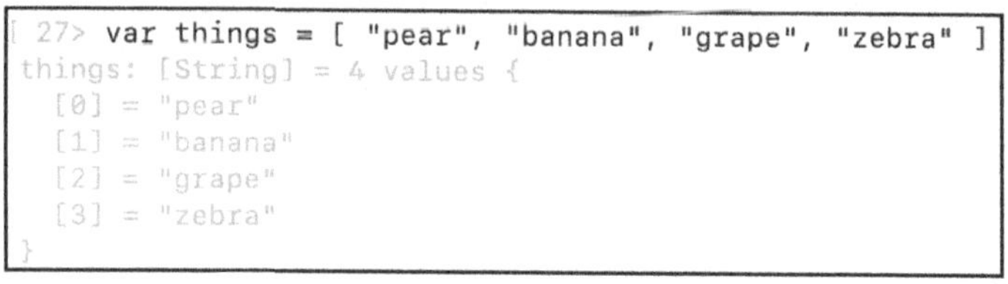

Creating an array.

When you run this line in the REPL, you'll see that `things` has the type `[String]`. The square brackets indicate that it's an array and the `String` says that the elements in the array are all of type `String`. To us, "grape" and "zebra" are very different, but to Swift, they're both strings and that makes them similar enough to have in the same array.

Arrays have operations, too. The + operator combines two arrays:

```
things += [ "aardvark", "artichoke" ]
print(things)
```

`things` now has six elements:

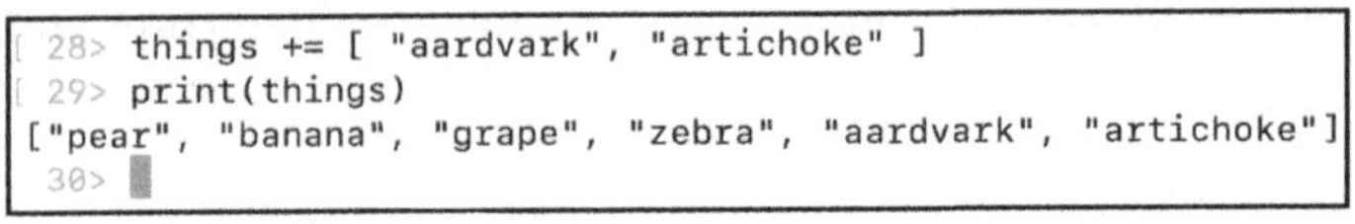

Merging arrays.

> **Note**: In the REPL, you can check the value of a variable by entering its name and pressing **Return**. That gives a lot of information about the variable and its contents. For a more compact display, you can use `print`. You'll find `print` very useful later when it comes to debugging your apps in Xcode.

To access a single item in an array — commonly referred to as an element — you use its position, or **index**, in the array. The `things` array has six elements, but computers like to start counting from zero, so the first element has an index of zero.

Run these commands one at a time, but beware — one of them will crash the REPL:

```
things[0]
things[5]
things[6]
```

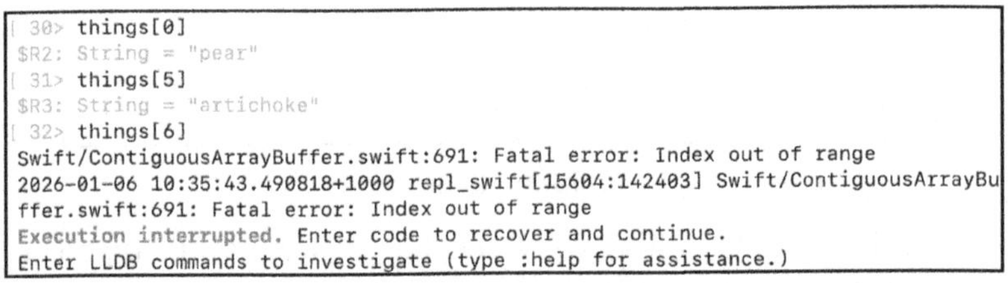

Accessing an array.

The last line gave **Fatal error: Index out of range** which is what happens when you try to read an element that doesn't exist. The key point to remember is that the last element has an index that's equal to the number of elements minus one.

Array Properties and Methods

There are other manipulations that you can perform on arrays, but they don't use operators. Instead, they use methods and properties. Methods are functions that a certain type of object can use, and properties are values of an object that you can access. You'll learn more about these in later chapters, but for now, check these different array properties and methods:

```
var companions: [String] = []
companions.append("Sarah Jane")
companions += ["Amelia", "Rose", "Martha", "Donna"]
print(companions)
companions.count
companions.remove(at: 2)
print(companions)
```

```
  1> var companions: [String] = []
companions: [String] = 0 values
  2> companions.append("Sarah Jane")
  3> companions += ["Amelia", "Rose", "Martha", "Donna"]
  4> print(companions)
["Sarah Jane", "Amelia", "Rose", "Martha", "Donna"]
  5> companions.count
$R0: Int = 5
  6> companions.remove(at: 2)
$R1: String = "Rose"
  7> print(companions)
["Sarah Jane", "Amelia", "Martha", "Donna"]
  8>
```

Array properties and methods.

Going through these different commands:

1. When you create an array with starting data, Swift uses the initial elements to decide the type of the whole array. When starting with an empty array, you must declare the type inside square brackets and then initialize the array as empty with the second set of square brackets after the equals sign.

2. The `append` method adds a new element on to the end of the array. The new element has to match the declared type for the array, in this case a `String`.

3. As you saw already, the + operator merges two arrays, and you can use the += shorthand here too.

4. The `print` command displays the contents of the array.

5. Query the `count` property to see how long the array is.

6. Use `remove(at:)` to delete the element at the specified index. If you use an index that doesn't exist, you'll get another fatal error.

7. Bonus points if you spotted the Doctor Who reference. :]

Arrays are a useful data structure for storing a list of items of the same type and accessing them by index, but what if you wanted to be able to access the elements by name? For that, you need to use a dictionary.

Dictionaries

In a real world dictionary, you look up a key word and get back a definition for that word. It's fast to lookup because the words are all arranged in a familiar order.

In Swift, dictionaries are very similar. Each entry in a dictionary has a **key** and a **value**. The key is like the word that you look up and the value is the definition. Internally, Swift stores the keys very efficiently so it can look them up very fast.

These keys and values can be of any type so long as all the keys are the same type and all the values are the same type. The keys and values don't have to be the same type. Commonly, the keys are strings.

Imagine you're out on a bird-spotting walk carrying your Mac with you. Run these examples one by one in the REPL:

```
var birdsSeen: [String: Int] = [:]
birdsSeen["Robin"] = 3
birdsSeen["Blue Jay"] = 27
print(birdsSeen)
```

```
  8> var birdsSeen: [String: Int] = [:]
birdsSeen: [String : Int] = 0 key/value pairs
  9> birdsSeen["Robin"] = 3
 10> birdsSeen["Blue Jay"] = 27
 11> print(birdsSeen)
["Robin": 3, "Blue Jay": 27]
 12> 
```

Creating a dictionary.

Following this sequence:

1. When creating an empty dictionary you have to set the types for both the keys and the values. Inside the square brackets, the type before the colon is for the key and the type after is for the value. After the equals sign, the square brackets with a colon inside set up an empty dictionary, or as the REPL reports, a dictionary with **0 key/value pairs**.

2. You add an element to an array by setting a particular key for the dictionary to a value of the correct type.

3. Lines 9 and 10 in the image above set integers as the values for two different keys.

4. Printing out the dictionary shows the entered data — yours may appear in a different order.

You retrieve values using their keys:

```
birdsSeen["Blue Jay"]
birdsSeen["Albatross"]
```

```
12> birdsSeen["Blue Jay"]
$R2: Int? = 27
13> birdsSeen["Albatross"]
$R3: Int? = nil
14>
```

Accessing dictionary values.

Interestingly, unlike with an array, you can request an item that doesn't exist without causing a crash. You'll get back `nil` if the dictionary doesn't contain that key.

Looking closely at the result, you'll see that the type is `Int?`. This indicates an optional integer which is a value that might be nothing — `nil` — and might be an integer. You'll learn more about optionals in the next chapter.

Modifying a Dictionary

You've seen how to add values to a dictionary and how to query them, but what about editing existing values? You can overwrite them, using their key:

```
birdsSeen["Blue Jay"] = 2
print(birdsSeen)
```

That's fine if you know the new value, but what if you want to edit the existing value? What happens if you see another robin?

```
birdsSeen["Robin"] += 1
```

```
14> birdsSeen["Blue Jay"] = 2
15> print(birdsSeen)
["Robin": 3, "Blue Jay": 2]
16> birdsSeen["Robin"] += 1
                  ^
                  └─ error: value of optional type 'Int?' must be unwrapped to a val
ue of type 'Int'
                  └─ note: force-unwrap using '!' to abort execution if the optional
 value contains 'nil'
```

Incrementing a value in a dictionary.

This fails because Swift can't be sure that there is a value for the key "Robin". You'll learn all about optionals and unwrapping later, so for now, accept that this can't work.

But there's a convenient way to tell a dictionary to use the value it has, or to use a default value if it doesn't have one already:

```
birdsSeen["Robin", default: 0] += 1
birdsSeen["Penguin", default: 0] += 1
print(birdsSeen)
```

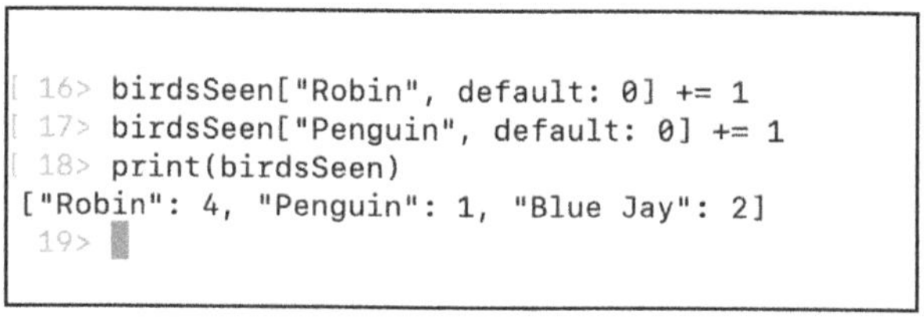

Dictionary default values.

In this example, there was an existing value for "Robin" so Swift was able to increment it by one. There was no value for "Penguin" so Swift incremented the default value of zero.

The number of elements in a dictionary is accessible using the `count` property and you can remove an element by setting its value to `nil`:

```
birdsSeen.count
birdsSeen["Penguin"] = nil
print(birdsSeen)
birdsSeen.count
```

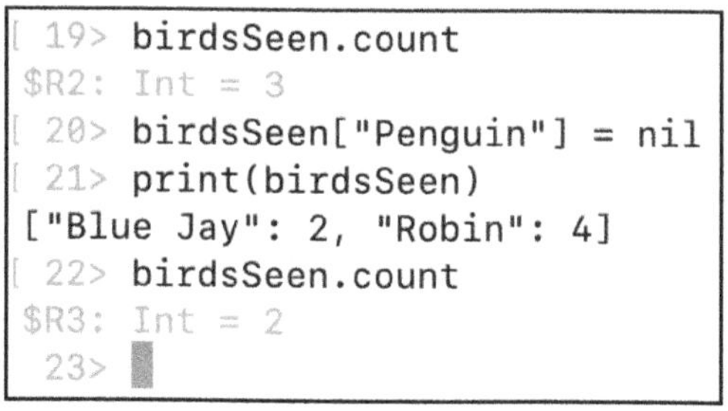

Counting and deleting from a dictionary.

It did seem unlikely that you'd seen a penguin on your walk!

Now that you know about Swift's data types, constants, variables and collections, you're ready to jump back to Xcode in the next chapter.

Key Points

- The Swift REPL allows you to run Swift code in the Terminal. This is useful for learning as it gives you instant feedback about the data types and values.
- Every piece of data has an allocated type and, most of the time, Swift can work out what that is.
- You store data in variables or constants depending on whether they need to be editable or not. In computer terms, variables are **mutable** and constants are **immutable**.
- Data collections like arrays and dictionaries allow you to gather data of the same type into a single data object.

Where to Go From Here?

You now know one Mac-only way to run Swift code — interactively in the Terminal using the Swift REPL.

In the next chapter, you'll expand on your knowledge as you learn a different way to run Swift, this time using Xcode.

For the official Swift information and guides, go to Swift.org.

To read about Swift in more depth, check out our Swift Apprentice: Fundamentals book (https://www.kodeco.com/books/swift-apprentice-fundamentals).

Chapter 3: Using Swift in the Command Line

By Sarah Reichelt

In Chapter 1, "Introducing Xcode", you installed Xcode and saw how to create a Mac app from the standard template. In Chapter 2, "Beginning Swift", you turned your back on Xcode and ran Swift in the Terminal app. You learned about data types, variables, constants and collections.

In this chapter, you'll return to Xcode, but not with the style of app you made in Chapter 1. This time, you'll create a **command line tool**. This is an app without a graphical user interface that runs in Terminal.

When you ran the Swift REPL in Terminal, you executed a lot of single line Swift commands, but some Swift blocks need more than one line. It's easier to edit and follow these in Xcode.

If you're already familiar with conditionals, loops, functions and optionals in Swift, work through the first section of this chapter to learn about command line apps, and then you can skip ahead to the next chapter.

Creating the App

Start Xcode like you did in Chapter 1. If you see the "Welcome to Xcode" window, click **Create New Project...**. If you don't see that window, go to **File → New → Project...**. Either method gets you to the template chooser.

This time, select **macOS → Command Line Tool**:

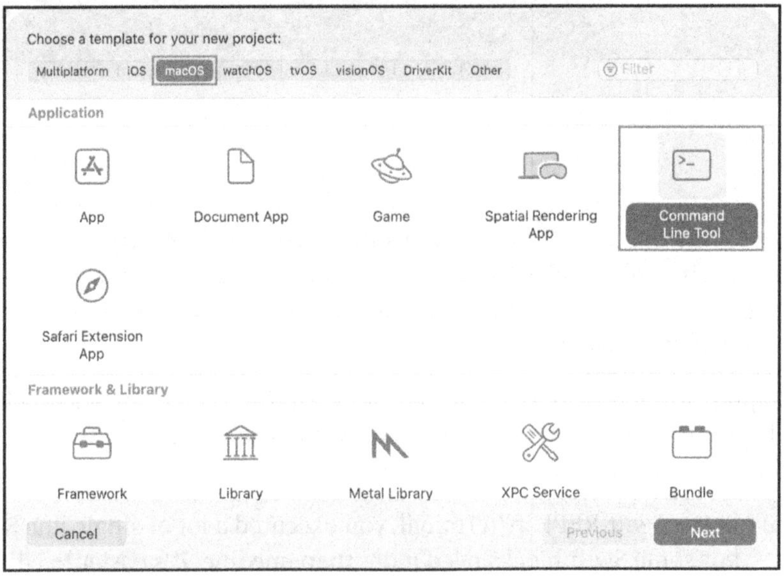

Selecting the Command Line Tool template.

Click **Next** and give your new project the name **swifty**. Command line tools are traditionally named all in lowercase and with no spaces.

Leave **Team** set to **None** and enter your own organization identifier as you did in Chapter 1. Make sure the language is set to **Swift**, or this app won't be very *swifty*. :]

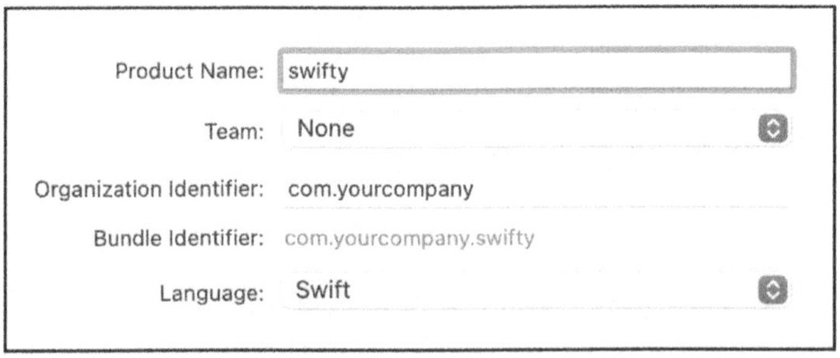

Configuring your app.

Then click **Next** and decide where to save it.

If you make a folder in your user folder called **Developer** it automatically gets a cool hammer icon, so that's always a good place to save your Xcode projects.

Running the App

When the app opens in Xcode, you'll see that it only has one file: **main.swift**. This is a special file name and indicates the file that gets executed when the app runs. Open **main.swift**. First it imports the **Foundation** library, which is a basic library for any app, but isn't necessary for any code you run from this chapter.

Then, as is traditional, it has a single line of code that prints **Hello, World!**. But where does it print this to?

To start, press **Command-R** to build and run the app:

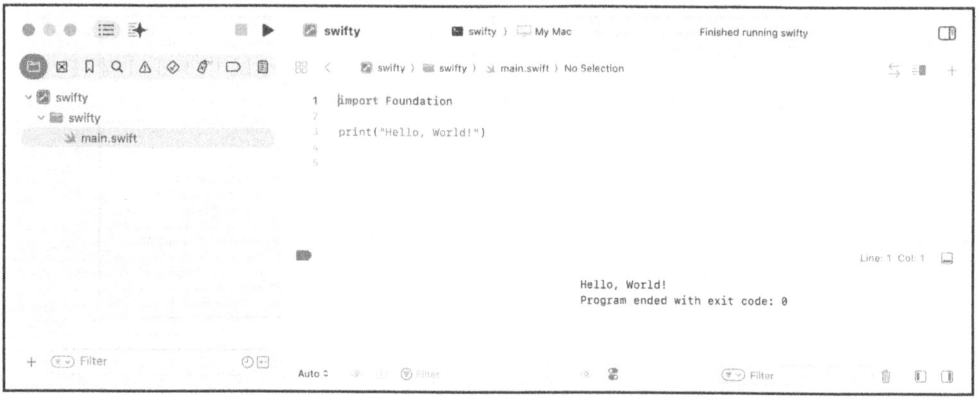

Running the app in Xcode.

What happened? The Xcode status display showed that it was building and now says "Finished running swifty". No app opened and no windows appeared.

Look in the debug console at the bottom of the Xcode window. Use **Shift-Command-Y** to open the console if it's not visible. There's your "Hello, World!", followed by a report that the program ended with an exit code of 0. In command line apps, an exit code of 0 means that the app successfully completed its task and then quit.

If you can't see "Hello, World!", Xcode is only showing the Variables view and not the Console. Click the button at the bottom right of the window with the tooltip that says **Show the Console**.

To make the console display larger from now on, click the second button at the bottom right that shows the **Hide the Variables View** tool tip:

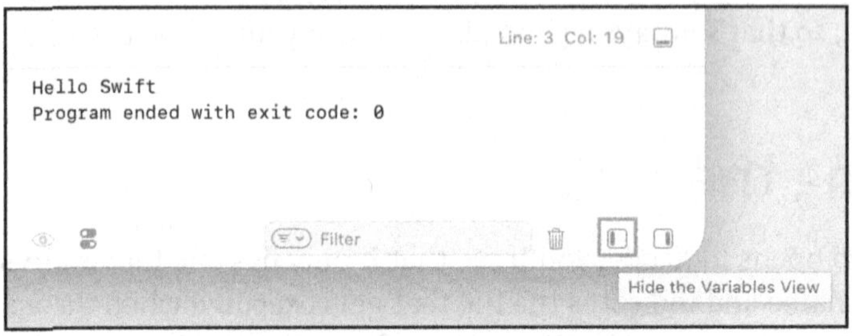

Hide the variables view.

To prove that your app is responsible for this output, change the `print` line to:

```
print("Hello Swift")
```

Press **Command-R** to run again and confirm that the console shows your new text:

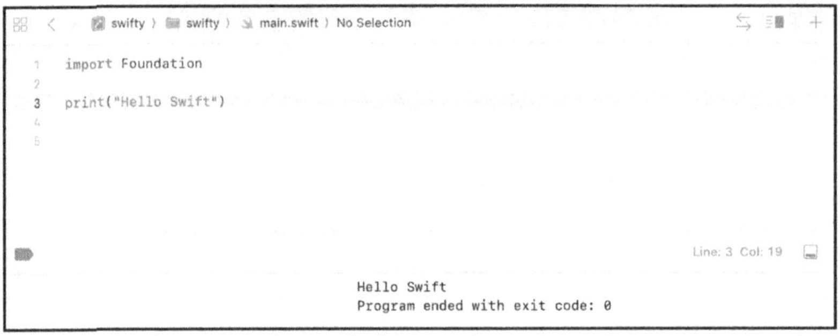

Edited output

Using the Terminal App

Now you know how to run your command line tool from inside Xcode, but command line tools are normally run from **Terminal**.

Open Terminal by going to **Applications** → **Utilities** → **Terminal.app** or by

pressing **Command-Space** and searching for **Terminal**. Press **Command-K** to clear the window so you start with a clean sheet.

Back in Xcode, select **Product → Show Build Folder in Finder**. This opens a Finder window buried deep in your Library folder. Press **Command-3** to get into Columns view and then follow the trail by clicking **Products** and **Debug** until you see the **swifty** executable file:

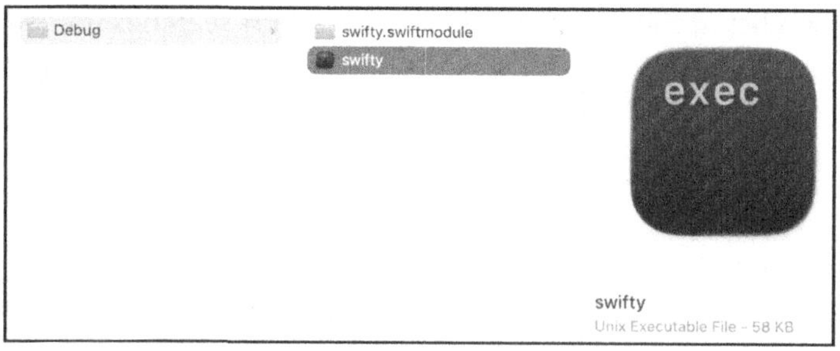

Finding the built executable.

You could run it by double-clicking, but that's not the usual way to run a command line tool. Instead, type `cd` in your Terminal window followed by a space. Then drag the **Debug** folder from your Finder window into the Terminal window.

The `cd` command **c**hanges **d**irectory to whatever you entered and dragging in a folder or file is the same as typing its full path. Press **Return** to switch Terminal into the **Debug** folder.

To run your command, type this:

```
./swifty
```

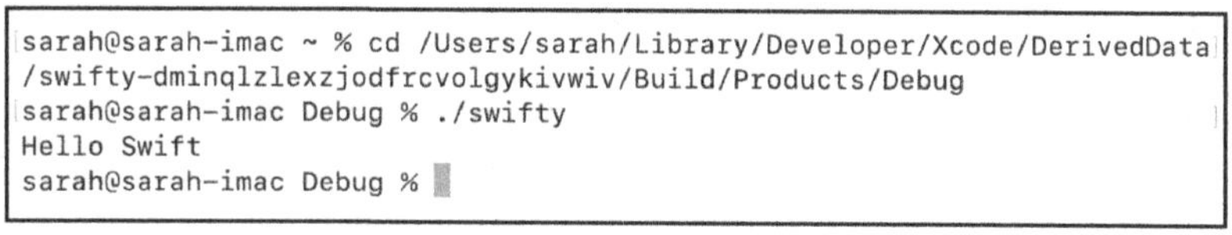

Running the swifty command.

And there's your "Hello Swift" text printed out in Terminal.

Terminal Paths

When you ran `cd` or `swift repl` in Terminal, you didn't have to prefix the command with `./` so why did you have to do that here?

Terminal keeps a list of the directories or folders that it searches for commands. Your app's Debug directory isn't in that list, so you have to tell Terminal exactly where your command is. The `./` prefix is a shorthand way of telling Terminal to look in the current directory.

> **Note**: If you're curious to see where your Terminal searches, type `echo $PATH` in the Terminal window. The output lists all the directories, separated by colons.

Now you know how a command line tool works, it's time to get back to Xcode and learn some more Swift.

Making Decisions

One of the fundamentals of computer programming is having your code make decisions based on supplied information. In Swift, the most common way of doing this is with the `if` statement.

Add this section of code to your **main.swift** file:

```
// 1
if true {
  // 2
  print("This is true")
}
```

This looks simple, but there's a lot of detail here:

1. Start with the `if` keyword and follow it with a condition. The condition must result in either `true` or `false`. After that, type an opening curly brace. When you press **Return**, Xcode automatically gives you a closing brace and puts the cursor in between them.
2. Inside the braces, type the code that runs whenever the condition is true.

Press **Command-R** or click the **Play** button to run this and as you'd expect, "This is true" prints out:

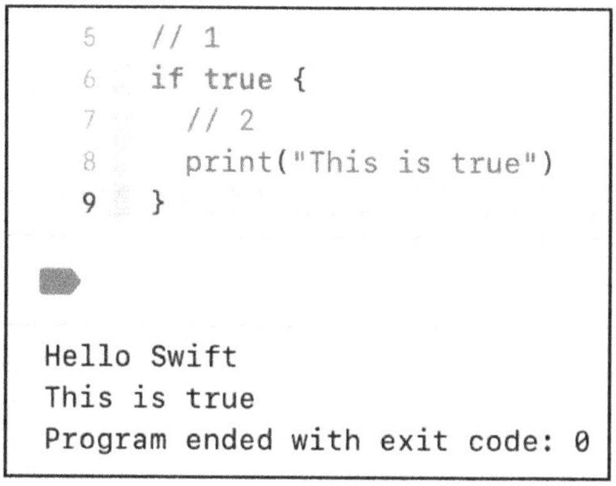

if true

> **Note**: You may be wondering about the lines starting with `//`. What are they and why doesn't the app print them out? Whenever you type `//`, the Swift compiler sees the rest of that line as a **comment** and ignores it. Comments allow you to document your code.

Now you've seen how to construct an `if` block, but this one isn't very useful. To make it do more work, you need to supply a different condition instead of `true`. The condition can be a Boolean variable, or it can be any Swift code that evaluates to either `true` or `false`.

Delete everything you have so far in **main.swift** and type this:

```
// 1
var userIsLoggedIn = true

// 2
if userIsLoggedIn {
  print("Welcome")
}
```

This block is a bit more interesting:

1. You create a Boolean variable. As you learned in the previous chapter, a Boolean variable is one that can only hold one of two values: `true` or `false`.
2. Now you use that variable as the condition for the `if`.

Run the app and see what prints out:

`if` with a Boolean variable

Change the variable to `false` and run again. What do you see this time? Depending on your Xcode settings, the console area may have disappeared. If this happens, click the icon in the bottom right of the edit area or press **Shift-Command-Y** to bring it back. There's nothing to see here because the `if` condition was `false`, so the "Welcome" message never printed.

If ... Else

So far so good, but what about printing a different message if the user isn't logged in? For that, you need to add an `else`.

Replace your `if` block with this:

```
if userIsLoggedIn {
  print("Welcome")
} else {
  print("Please log in")
}
```

You have the `if`, the condition and the curly braces exactly as before, but you've added an `else` followed by another set of curly braces. The code in the first set runs if the condition is `true`, while the second set runs if it's `false`.

Run the app again with `userIsLoggedIn` set to `false`:

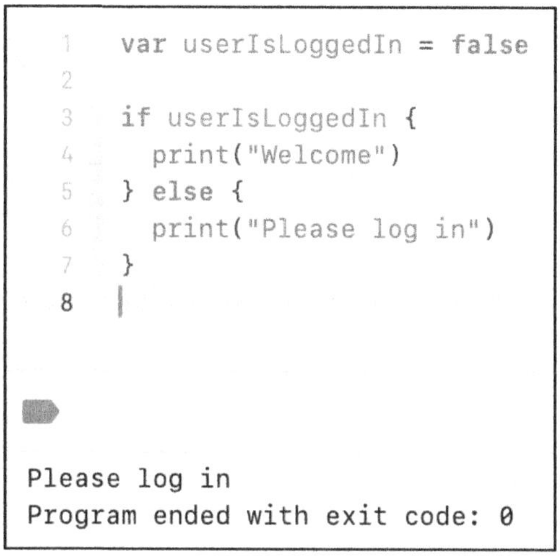

if... else

If you want to make sure the original `if` part still works, change `userIsLoggedIn` back to `true` and test it.

Evaluating Conditions

The condition doesn't have to be a Boolean variable. It can be any code that evaluates to give a Boolean result.

Add this chunk of code to **main.swift**:

```
// 1
var name = "Bob"

// 2
if name.count < 4 {
  // 3
  print("\(name) is a very short name")
} else {
  // 4
  print("Good name.")
}
```

What does this do?

1. Create a `String` variable and give it the value “Bob”.
2. Set up an `if` but this time, the condition is `name.count < 4`.
3. If `name` has fewer than four characters this condition will be `true`, and you use string interpolation to print a message that includes the name.
4. The `else` prints out a message for names with four or more letters.

Run this code to see what happens:

```
var name = "Bob"

if name.count < 4 {
  print("\(name) is a very short name")
} else {
  print("Good name.")
}

```

```
Please log in
Bob is a very short name
Program ended with exit code: 0
```

A short name

Now change “Bob” to a longer name and run the app again:

```
var name = "Veronica"

if name.count < 4 {
  print("\(name) is a very short name")
} else {
  print("Good name.")
}

```

```
Please log in
Good name.
Program ended with exit code: 0
```

A longer name

Comparison Operators

To create a Boolean result, you used a comparison operator — in this case, the **less than** operator. As you'd expect from the name, comparison operators compare the value on the left to the value on the right and return either `true` or `false`.

Here's a list of comparisons you can make:

- > greater than
- < less than
- >= greater than or equal to
- <= less than or equal to
- == equal to
- != not equal to

You're probably wondering why the **equal to** operator has two equals signs. In Swift, as in many languages, there's a different operator for **assign** and for **equality**. A single equals sign assigns the value on the right to the object on the left. The double equals sign checks if the two are the same.

The `!` sign is the **not** operator. You can use it paired with an equals sign, or before any comparison result, to invert it from `true` to `false` or from `false` to `true`.

If ... Else If ... Else

There's an even more expanded way to use `if` to do even more checks. Add this block to your code in **main.swift**:

```
// 1
var score = 70

// 2
if score >= 100 {
  print("You've won")
// 3
} else if score > 80 {
  print("Nearly there...")
// 4
} else {
  print("Keep going")
}
```

Going through these lines:

1. Set up an integer variable called `score`.
2. Check if `score` is greater than or equal to 100. If so, print "You've won".
3. If `score` is less than 100, the code execution falls through to the next `else if` where you test to see if it's more than 80.
4. As neither of the other conditions are `true`, the final `else` prints its report.

Run the app:

```
var score = 70

if score >= 100 {
  print("You've won")
} else if score > 80 {
  print("Nearly there...")
} else {
  print("Keep going")
}
```

```
Please log in
Good name.
Keep going
Program ended with exit code: 0
```

if... else if... else

Enter various values for `score` and confirm that each one does what you expect.

You can keep adding `else if` clauses, but it gets difficult to read and cumbersome to maintain. Once you have more than three possibilities, using `switch` is a better option.

Switching

A **switch** statement is a different method for doing comparisons. You switch **on** a particular value and state what happens at each stage.

Enter this code:

```
// 1
var grade = "B"

// 2
switch grade {
// 3
case "A":
  print("Top of the class!")
case "B":
  print("Excellent work.")
case "C":
  print("Solid effort.")
case "D":
  print("Try harder next time.")
// 4
default:
  print("More effort needed.")
}
```

Stepping through this:

1. Make a string variable called `grade` and set it to “B”.
2. Start a switch statement with the keyword `switch` followed by the variable to test and an opening curly brace.
3. Use `case` statements to check for various values of `grade`. As soon as the switch finds a match, it prints an appropriate message and exits.
4. Every switch must be exhaustive — it must account for all possible input values. Adding `default` at the end catches everything.

Running this gives you:

```
var grade = "B"

switch grade {
case "A":
  print("Top of the class!")
case "B":
  print("Excellent work.")
case "C":
  print("Solid effort.")
case "D":
  print("Try harder next time.")
default:
  print("More effort needed.")
}
```

```
Please log in
Good name.
Keep going
Excellent work.
Program ended with exit code: 0
```

switch

Now you know the basics of how to code decisions in Swift. There's a lot more that `switch` can do, but this is enough to get you going.

Looping

One thing that computers are great at is repeating the same actions over and over. Swift gives us several different ways to loop repetitively.

Open **main.swift** and delete everything. You can always refer back to the code, but the output is getting a bit cluttered.

The most common type of loop is a `for` loop:

```
// 1
for number in 1 ... 5 {
  // 2
  print(number)
}
```

There's a lot of detail in the first line:

1. Start with the `for` keyword followed by the name to use as the index variable — in this case, `number`. You don't have to declare the index variable before this. The `in` keyword comes next and then the starting value for the loop index. The three dots form the **closed range** operator and that tells the loop to repeat, incrementing the loop variable by one each time, until the loop variable equals the number after the operator.

2. Inside curly braces, add the code that executes each time.

Running this code shows you:

```
for number in 1 ... 5 {
  print(number)
}

1
2
3
4
5
Program ended with exit code: 0
```

A for loop with a closed range.

The numbers 1, 2, 3, 4 and 5 printed out and then the loop stopped.

Now edit the `for` line. Change `...` to `..<` and run the app again:

```
for number in 1 ..< 5 {
  print(number)
}

1
2
3
4
Program ended with exit code: 0
```

A for loop with a half-open range.

You changed from using a closed range operator to using a **half-open range** operator. This time, the loop ran as long as the index value was less than 5 and then it stopped.

If you're wondering why this would be any use, remember back in the last chapter where you crashed the REPL by trying to access an extra element of an array? This operator is great for avoiding that crash as you can supply the `count` of the array as the ending value and the loop stops one before that.

> **Note**: You don't have to leave a space before and after these range operators and you'll see a lot of code that doesn't. The spaces make the code easier to read, but you can choose your own style. If you leave a space before, then you must leave a space after.

The `for` loop is the one you'll use most, but `while` loops are also useful.

While Loops

There are two forms of the `while` loop, with an important distinction.

Delete everything in **main.swift** and replace it with this:

```
// 1
var counter = 0

// 2
while counter < 5 {
  // 3
  print("Counter: \(counter)")
  // 4
  counter += 1
// 5
}
```

More verbose than a `for` loop, but stepping through:

1. A `while` loop needs something to test to see if it should stop. In this case, you're using an integer variable.
2. Start with the `while` keyword and then — like for an `if` — add a condition that evaluates to `true` or `false`.

3. As long as the condition is `true`, the code inside the loop executes repeatedly.
4. It's vital to have something inside the loop that changes the condition. If you forget this, you'll be stuck in an **infinite loop** and have to force-quit Xcode.
5. The closing curly brace marks the end of the loop.

Running this code gives you:

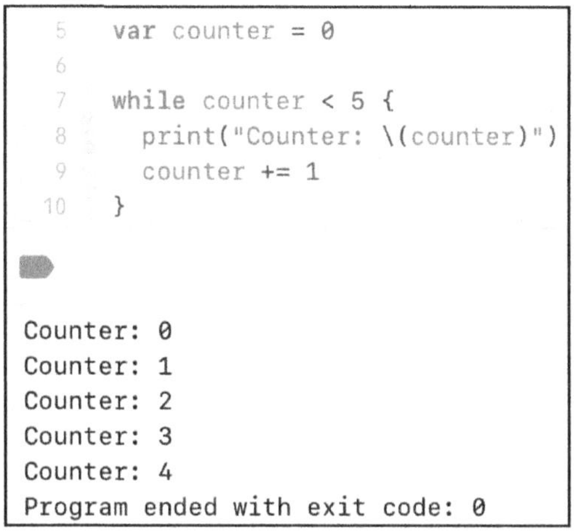

A while loop

Change the starting value for `counter` to 5 and run the code again. There's nothing to see because the `while` loop never ran at all.

Repeat While Loops

That covers the first way to use a `while` loop, but there's a second form called a **repeat ... while** loop.

Replace your **main.swift** code with this:

```
// 1
var counter = 0

// 2
repeat {
  print("Counter: \(counter)")
  // 3
  counter += 1
// 4
} while counter < 5
```

At first glance this looks similar to the `while` loop, but there's one important difference:

1. As before, you create a variable.
2. This time, the loop starts with the `repeat` keyword.
3. The body of the loop executes and increments the counter to avoid an infinite loop.
4. Finally, after the closing curly brace, the `while` evaluates the condition.

Running this code gives you the same as the first `while` gave. But the interesting part happens when you change the starting value of `counter` to 5:

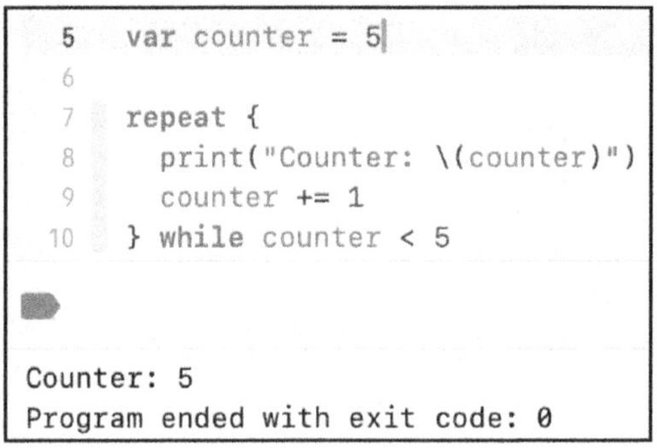

A repeat ... while loop

Despite the fact that the condition never equals `true`, the loop executed once before reaching the `while`. That's the crucial difference between `while` and `repeat ... while`. The `while` loop never executes if the conditional is `false` at the start. The `repeat ... while` loop always runs at least once.

If you want a funny way to remember this, check out this cartoon (https://starecat.com/content/wp-content/uploads/programming-while-vs-do-while-coyote-road-runner.jpg). It's not coded in Swift, but you'll get the idea. :]

Looping Through Arrays

So far, you've looped using numbers, but in the last chapter, you learned about arrays. Swift provides a convenient way to loop through them too.

Clear **main.swift** and enter this array of strings:

```
let toys = ["Andy", "Bo-peep", "Buzz", "Jessie", "Rex"]
```

On the next line, type `for to` and admire the way auto-complete has worked out exactly what you want:

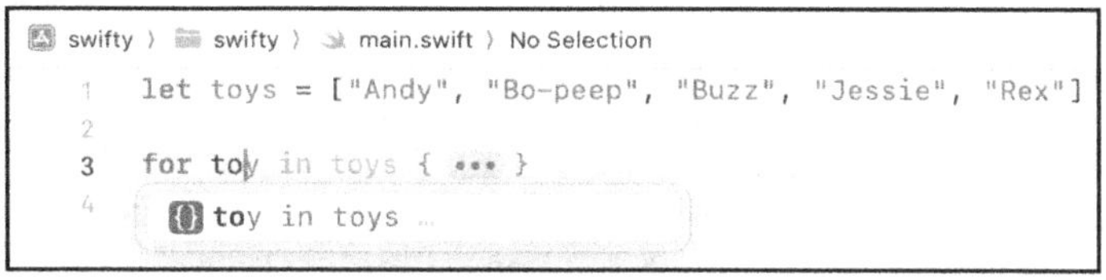

Xcode's auto-complete

Press **Return** to accept the suggestion, and then replace the **body** placeholder with `print(toy)` so you end up with this code:

```
let toys = ["Andy", "Bo-peep", "Buzz", "Jessie", "Rex"]
for toy in toys {
  print(toy)
}
```

Run the app and Swift loops through the elements in the `toys` array. Each time through the loop, `toy` holds the next element:

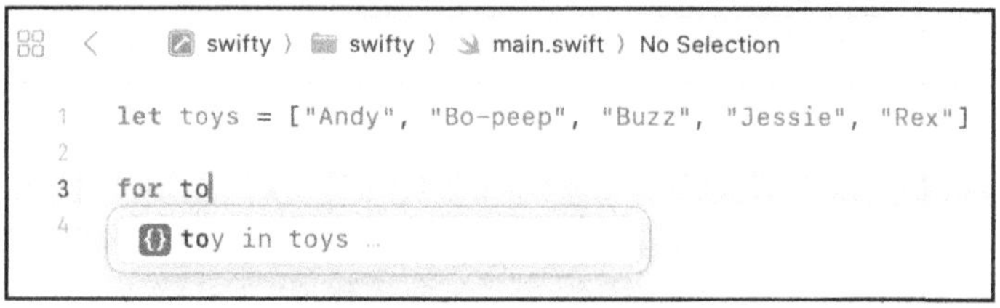

Looping through an array.

You've covered making decisions and looping in various ways. Now, it's time to start having some **fun** with functions. :]

Writing Functions

All the code you've written so far executed immediately. Functions are blocks of code that only run when you call them. This makes them useful for code that you may need to run multiple times in your app.

Clear your code from **main.swift** as usual, and enter this:

```
func showVersion() {
  print("swifty - version 1.0")
}
```

The important stuff is on the first line:

1. Every function starts with the `func` keyword.
2. The next part is the name of the function. Use the same **lowerCamelCase** style that you use for variables, and give your functions descriptive names.
3. The pair of parentheses mark where you can provide data to the function. This function doesn't receive any input, but you still need the parentheses.
4. The curly braces contain the code that executes whenever you call the function.

Don't run the app yet. You've declared a function, but you haven't called it, so it won't run.

Add this line below the function:

```
showVersion()
```

This uses the name of the function without the `func` keyword and it actually makes the function happen. Run the app to see it work:

```
func showVersion() {
  print("swifty - version 1.0")
}

showVersion()
```

```
swifty - version 1.0
Program ended with exit code: 0
```

Running your first function.

You now have a function and it runs, but it'll always do the same thing. Next, you'll send it some information.

Providing Input

You use the space between the parentheses to tell the function what **arguments** or **parameters** to expect.

Replace your code with this version:

```
// 1
```

```
func showVersion(versionNumber: Double) {
  print("swifty - version \(versionNumber)")
}

// 2
showVersion(versionNumber: 1.2)
```

What do these changes do?

1. Inside the parentheses, you assign a name and a type to the incoming argument.
2. When calling the function, you provide a value or a variable with the same label and the same type.

Run the app now to confirm that it uses your provided `versionNumber`:

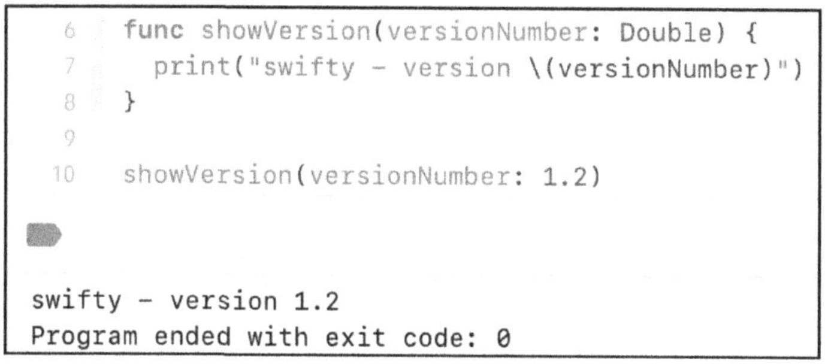

A function with an argument.

Try changing the value you send to the function and checking that the function uses your different value.

Receiving Output

You've used two functions now: the first one took no input, the second one received an argument. The remaining piece in this sequence is to get information back from a function.

Delete your code and add this:

```
// 1
func getVersion() -> Double {
  // 2
  return 1.3
}

// 3
let versionNumber = getVersion()
print("Version \(versionNumber)")
```

There are some interesting things here:

1. You declare the function as before with no arguments, but after the brackets and before the curly brace, you added an arrow — a hyphen followed by a greater-than sign — and then a Swift type. This says that the function returns a `Double`.
2. The `return` keyword precedes the value that the function sends back. Since this function only has one line, you can omit the `return`.
3. When calling the function, you use the result by assigning it to a constant or variable or by using it immediately. In this case, you store it in a constant and then use it in a `print`.

Run the app to see that it works:

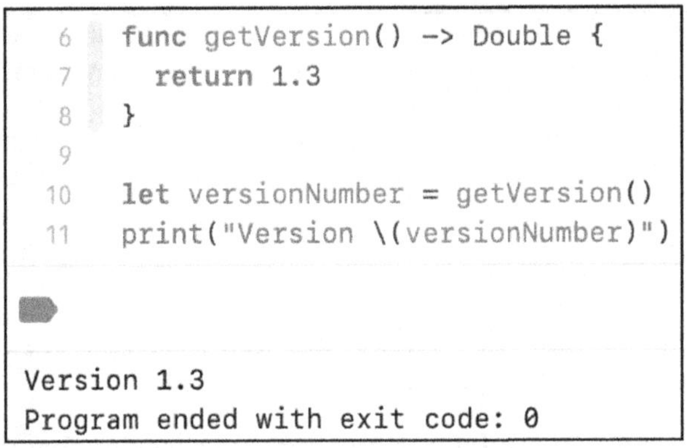

A function that returns a value.

Combining Inputs and Outputs

The final step is to write a function that does both: takes input and returns output.

Clear **main.swift** and add this:

```
// 1
func areaOfCircle(radius: Double) -> Double {
  // 2
  let area = Double.pi * radius * radius
  // 3
  return area
}

// 4
let area = areaOfCircle(radius: 6)
print(area)
```

Things are a bit more complex here:

1. This function declaration sets the name of the function, the name and type of the incoming argument and the type of the return value.
2. Inside the function, the code calculates the area of a circle using the supplied radius. There's a property on `Double` to give a value for `pi`.
3. Since there was more than one line here, the `return` keyword is essential for outputting the calculated value.
4. The caller supplies a radius, stores the result and prints it out.

Run the app now to perform your calculation:

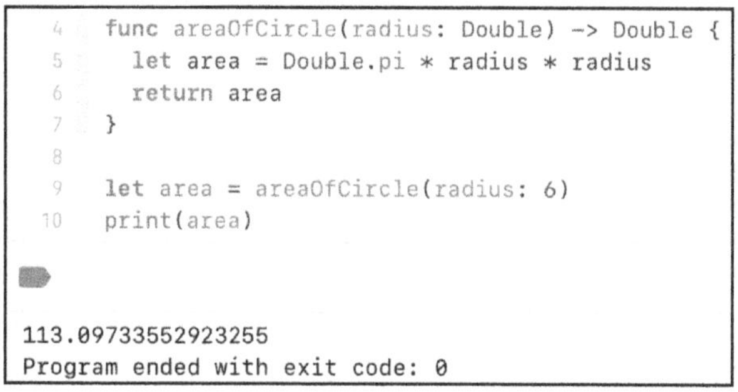

A function with input and output.

Test it by running again with different `radius` values. Does it give the expected results each time?

Optionals

Now to the last topic in this chapter — **optionals**. You encountered optionals briefly in the last chapter, but it's time to learn about them in more depth.

Imagine a box with a big sticker saying `Int?`. You can't see inside the box to tell if there is anything there, but you know that if there's anything inside, it must be an `Int`. This box is an **optional** and to see what's inside, you **unwrap** it.

An example makes this clearer, so empty **main.swift** and insert this:

```
// 1
var mightBeNumber: Int?

// 2
```

```
print(mightBeNumber)

// 3
mightBeNumber = 3

print(mightBeNumber)
```

Ignoring the scary yellow warnings:

1. Set up a variable with the type of `Int?` which means an optional `Integer`.
2. Print out the value. Xcode complains because it can't be sure what type of value you're printing.
3. Assign an integer value to the variable and print again.

Run this to see what you get:

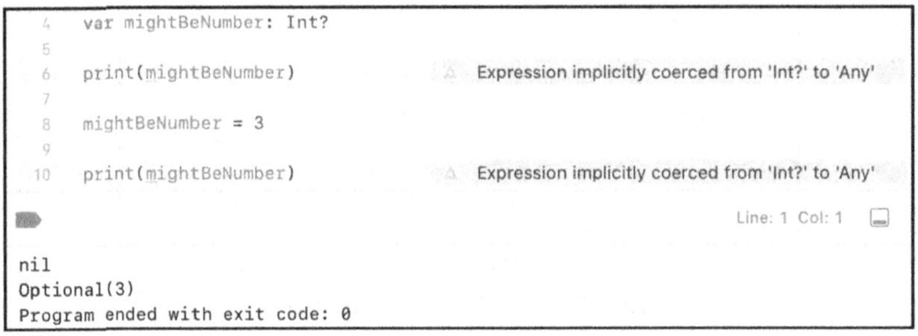

Printing an optional.

The first time, it printed `nil`, which makes sense as there was no value.

The second time, you got **Optional(3)**, which isn't super helpful. How can you use that anywhere else? Don't worry — Swift has this covered with `if let`.

Unwrapping

Replace your code with this new version:

```
// 1
var mightBeNumber: Int? = 3

// 2
if let mightBeNumber {
  // 3
  print(mightBeNumber)
} else {
  // 4
  print("mightBeNumber is nil")
```

```
}
```

All the Xcode warnings have gone, but why?

1. As before, you set up your `Int?` but this time, you initialized it immediately.
2. `if let mightBeNumber` unwraps the optional, and if it has an integer value, uses that to set a temporary constant, also called `mightBeNumber`. The version of `mightBeNumber` inside the curly braces is an `Int`, and not an `Int?`.
3. Now you can use the unwrapped `mightBeNumber` like you would use any non-optional `Int`.
4. If the unwrapping found no value, `if let` falls through to the `else`.

Run your app:

```
var mightBeNumber: Int? = 3

if let mightBeNumber {
  print(mightBeNumber)
} else {
  print("mightBeNumber is nil")
}

3
Program ended with exit code: 0
```

Unwrapping an optional.

This prints **3** as expected. Now remove the `= 3` so that the starting value for `mightBeNumber` is unset. Run the app again and confirm that it prints **mightBeNumber is nil**.

> **Note**: You'll see old code that looks like `if let number = number {}`. Until Xcode 14, this was the only way to use `if let` but as a convention developed of using the same name before and after the equals, the Swift team built a shorter way of writing the same thing.

So when would you ever use an optional? You already saw an example of this when accessing a dictionary. If the key exists in the dictionary, you get an optional value. If it doesn't, you get `nil`. And there are lots of other instances – like network calls – where you can't be sure what you'll get.

Force Unwrapping

Before leaving this topic, there are two more points to cover. The first is **force unwrapping**.

Try this **bad** code:

```
var forcedString: String? = "This really is a string."
print(forcedString!)
```

You set up an optional string and then you printed it with a following `!` symbol. This stopped Xcode giving any warnings because you force unwrapped the variable. You promised Swift there would be a string value in this variable by the time it needed to access it.

In this case it worked, but if you hadn't assigned a value to the variable, your app would have crashed. Xcode will sometimes insert force unwrapping code, but don't do it in your own code.

Guard Let

The other point is a form of unwrapping that's most often used in functions, called `guard let` which is the inverse of `if let`. Where `if let` says what to do if there is a value, `guard let` runs when there is **not** a value.

In a function, it's good practice to exit as soon as possible if there's any problem and `guard let` is good at this.

Here's an example of **not** doing this:

```
func handlingOptionals(name: String?, age: Int?) {
  if let name {
    if let age {
      print("All input data is valid: \(name) & \(age)")
    } else {
      print("age is not an Int")
    }
  } else {
    print("name is not a string")
  }
}
```

This works, but the correct path is deep in nested `if` clauses making the sequence difficult to follow.

Now look at this version which uses `guard let`:

```
func handlingOptionals(name: String?, age: Int?) {
  guard let name else {
    print("name is not a string")
    return
  }

  guard let age else {
    print("age is not an Int")
    return
  }

  print("All input data is valid: \(name) & \(age)")
}
```

This uses `return` to exit the function as soon any unwrapping fails. It produces the same result, but the code looks clean and maintainable.

With both these blocks, if you don't need to check the arguments individually, you can unwrap them both on the same line:

```
func handlingOptionals(name: String?, age: Int?) {
  guard let name, let age else {
    print("One of the arguments is not valid")
    return
  }

  print("All input data is valid: \(name) & \(age)")
}
```

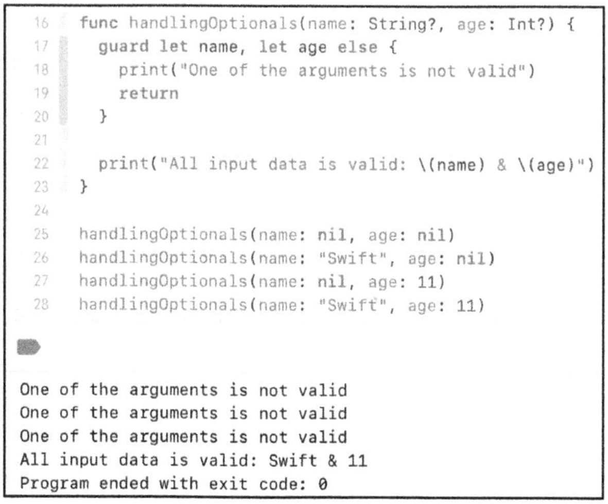

guard let

You can only use `guard` inside a function or loop that you can break out of, because the last command inside a `guard` block must be an exit of some sort.

Key Points

- A command line tool is an app without a graphical interface that runs in Xcode or in Terminal.
- Swift can make decisions using `if` or `switch`. If you have more than three possibilities, use a `switch`.
- Loops use `for` or `while` to step through data.
- Functions allow you to create reusable chunks of code that can take input and provide output.
- Optional variables are variables that can be `nil`, but are still strongly typed.

Where to Go From Here?

In the downloaded materials for this chapter, in **projects → final** there's an Xcode project containing the code used in this chapter.

You've now learned yet another Mac-only way to run Swift code. In the next chapter, you'll use a method that works on both Macs and iPads: Swift playgrounds.

There you'll find out how to create your own data objects by combining what you already know about data types and functions.

For the official Swift information and guides, go to Swift.org.

To read about Swift in more depth, check out our Swift Apprentice: Fundamentals book (https://www.kodeco.com/books/swift-apprentice-fundamentals).

Chapter 4: Running Swift in a Playground

By Sarah Reichelt

In the previous chapters, you used basic Swift types and collections. You learned how to loop, evaluate conditions and write functions. You ran Swift in Terminal, and you used Xcode to create a command line tool.

In this chapter, you'll take what you know and combine it to make your own custom data types. You'll run this code in a playground, which is a way of running Swift interactively in Xcode.

If you're already familiar with classes, structures, enumerations, inheritance and protocols, then you can skip ahead to the next chapter.

Running a Playground

Open **Xcode** and close the “Welcome to Xcode” window, if it appears. Use the menu bar to choose **File → New → Playground...** and select **macOS** and **Blank** from the template chooser. Name your playground **CustomTypes.playground** and save it in your Developer folder or wherever you prefer.

When your playground opens, click the blue **Play** button in the bottom toolbar to run the sample code:

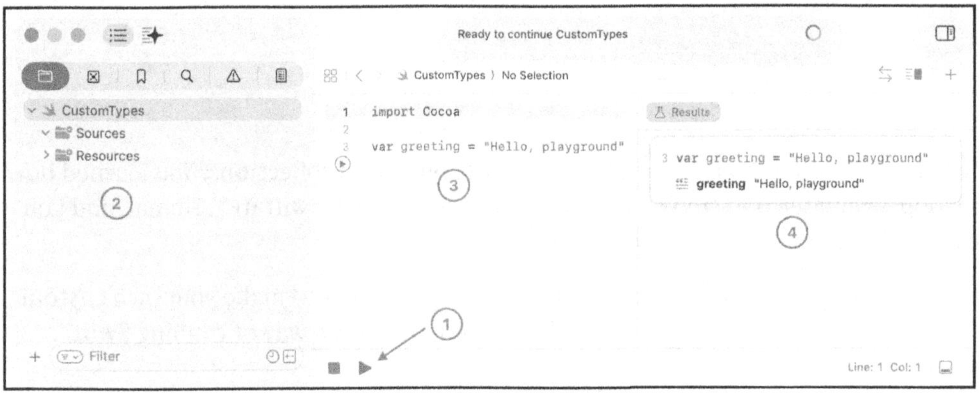

A Swift Playground

There are four things to notice in this window:

1. The **Play** button for running the playground.
2. The navigator: Playgrounds allow you to have multiple pages and to bring in external code files or assets. You’ll see them all listed here. Press **Command-1** if this isn’t visible.
3. The code editor where you’ll type all your Swift.
4. The results panel that shows the result of each line of code.

Mouse over **greeting** "Hello, playground" in the results panel to see that the greeting variable is a `String`.

Long-click on the **Play** button to see its options. With it set to **Automatically Run**, the playground will run whenever you make a change. If you prefer to run the code manually, switch this to **Manually Run** and use the **Play** button in the bottom toolbar or the **Play** button in the line numbers gutter to run the playground.

Classes

So far, every type of data you've used has been one of Swift's built-in types like `String` or `Double`. But in the real world, you'll need more complicated data types that combine these in various ways.

Consider a contacts list that stores names, addresses, phone numbers and email addresses. Or a pizza shop menu that stores pizza types with their bases, sauces and toppings. You can construct these by mixing the types that you already know.

For this section, imagine you're writing an app for a fruit seller who wants to keep track of their stock items.

Clear everything out of your playground and enter this code:

```
// 1
class StockItem {
  // 2
  let name: String
  var numberInStock: Int
}
```

This uses a new keyword:

1. A **class** is a custom type. To create one, you start with the `class` keyword and then set a name. Class names conventionally use **UpperCamelCase**.

2. Inside the class, you declare a constant and a variable. When these are in a class, they're referred to as **properties**. So the `StockItem` class has two properties: one of them is a constant and the other is editable.

Xcode now shows a nasty red error. Click on the red dot to read the full message. The problem is that your new class has no way of setting these properties when it's first used.

To solve this, you'll write an **initializer**. Add a blank line after the properties but before the closing curly brace and insert this code:

```
// 1
init(name: String, numberInStock: Int) {
  // 2
  self.name = name
  self.numberInStock = numberInStock
}
```

This looks almost like a function, but not quite:

1. There's no `func` keyword because `init` is a special method that the class calls automatically whenever you make a new object of that type. The arguments to the `init` function are the starting information sent to fill in the properties. It's common to use the property names for these arguments.
2. In the body of this function, you use the argument values to set the properties. Because the same names appear twice, `self` distinguishes the properties from the arguments.

A class doesn't do anything by itself. It provides a set of instructions for making an **instance** of the class. You'll use this `StockItem` initializer to create instances of the `StockItem` class, each with their own values for the properties.

Creating a Class Instance

To create your first instance of the class, add this outside the class declaration:

```
var bananas = StockItem(name: "banana", numberInStock: 12)
```

When this line has run, mouse over **bananas** in the results panel:

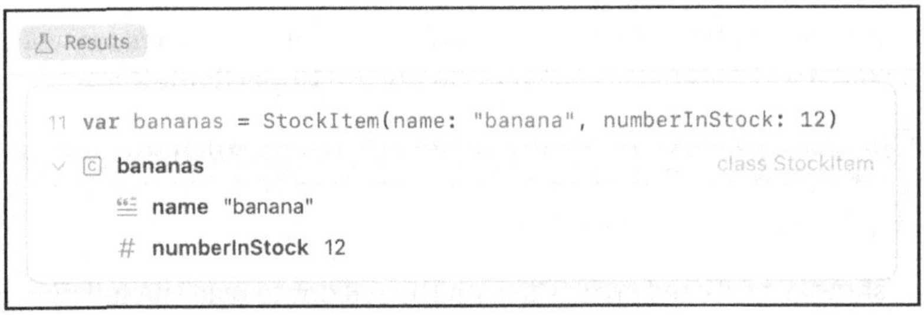

Creating an instance of a class.

This shows that the line of code created a new instance of the `StockItem` class, setting its `name` property to "banana" and its `numberInStock` property to 12.

Now you can work with these properties:

```
// 1
bananas.name
// 2
bananas.numberInStock += 1
// 3
bananas
```

Looking at these lines:

1. You access properties using **dot-notation** that uses the name of the object, a dot and then the name of the property.
2. The `numberInStock` property is a variable that you can edit.
3. This line is here to show the current value of `bananas` in the results panel.

After running, the playground shows this:

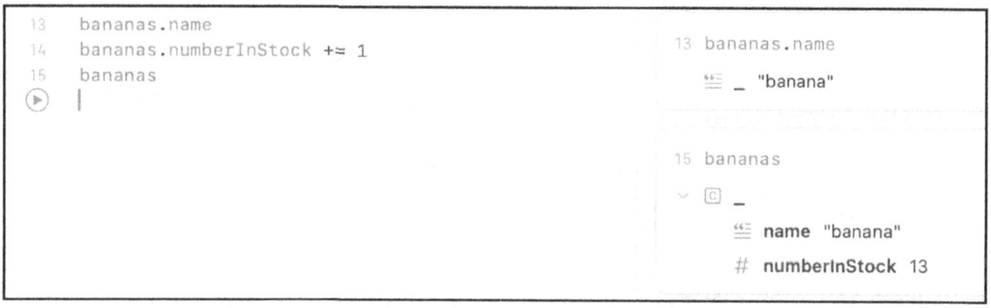

Accessing an instance's properties.

Now you have the ability to create a complex object with more than one property, and you can assign it to a variable.

So far, this looks like a super-dictionary. You have a single variable called `bananas` and it has two properties, which are like the keys of a dictionary. It's more flexible than a dictionary because the properties can have different types and it's easier to access them, but what makes classes better?

The answer is **methods**. Method is the name given to a function that's inside a class. You **call** a method on an instance of the class, and it operates on its own instance properties.

Adding Methods

You already edited the numberInStock property manually, but that doesn't allow for any error checking, so now you'll add methods to do this.

Add a blank line after the end of the init method and type in these new methods:

```
// 1
func buy(number: Int) {
  // 2
  numberInStock += number
}

// 3
func sell(number: Int) {
  // 4
  if number > numberInStock {
    numberInStock = 0
  } else {
    numberInStock -= number
  }
}
```

Here's what you added to the class:

1. You declare a method called buy(number:) that takes an Int argument. A method is a function, so the structure of a method is the same as the structure of a function.

2. You use the argument to increase the numberInStock property.

3. The sell(number:) method starts off the same as buy(number:), but it adds some validation.

4. You can't sell more than you have in stock, so this method checks to make sure numberInStock never goes below zero.

Time to test this by adding these lines at the end of the playground:

```
// 1
bananas.buy(number: 4)

// 2
bananas.sell(number: 2)

// 3
bananas.sell(number: 1000)
```

Each of these sections calls a method:

1. Call `buy(number:)` on your `bananas` instance of `StockItem` to increase the number in stock.
2. Use `sell(number:)` to reduce the stock by a number that you know is less than the current stock.
3. Now, try to sell a large number of bananas and confirm that your validation works.

Running the playground shows these results:

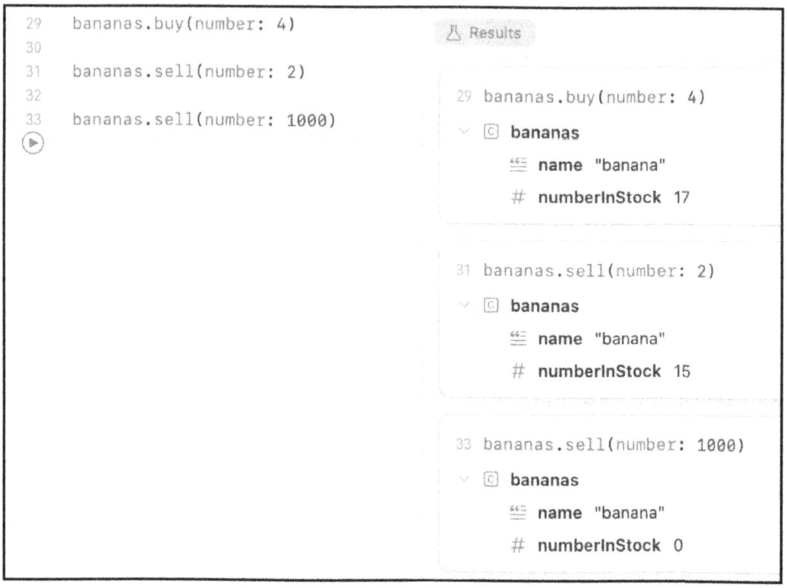

Calling class methods.

Reference Types

It would be a very boring shop that sold nothing but bananas, so create some new instances:

```
let apples = StockItem(name: "apple", numberInStock: 0)
let oranges = StockItem(name: "orange", numberInStock: 24)
```

Now for an interesting twist. These two instances of `StockItem` are both constants, declared using the `let` keyword. Does this mean you can't edit them?

Try it:

```
apples.buy(number: 16)
oranges.sell(number: 3)
```

Running the code, this all works!

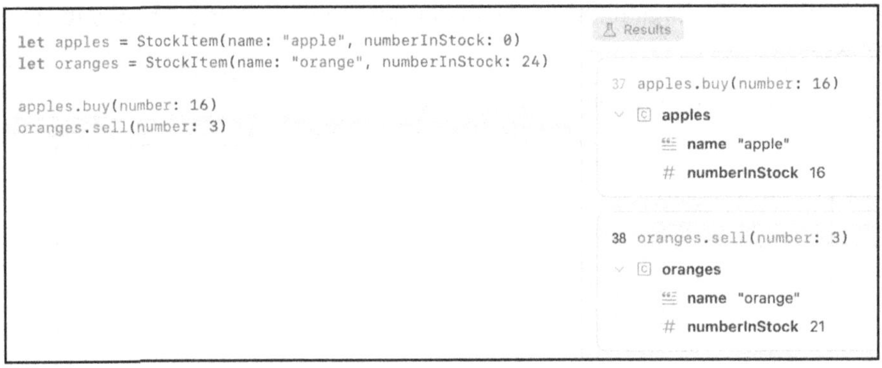

Editing a constant class instance.

Why? Isn't `let` supposed to keep things from changing?

When you made the `apples` instance, the value stored in `apples` was not the data, it was the address of the data in memory. In computer terms, classes are **reference types** and not **value types**.

A `String` is a value type, so when you create a string constant or property using `let`, you can never change it. But `StockItem` is a reference type, so even if it's declared as a constant, you can still edit its variable properties.

You can't edit its constant properties, which you can prove by trying this:

```
apples.name = "Golden Delicious"
```

Running the playground now gives this error:

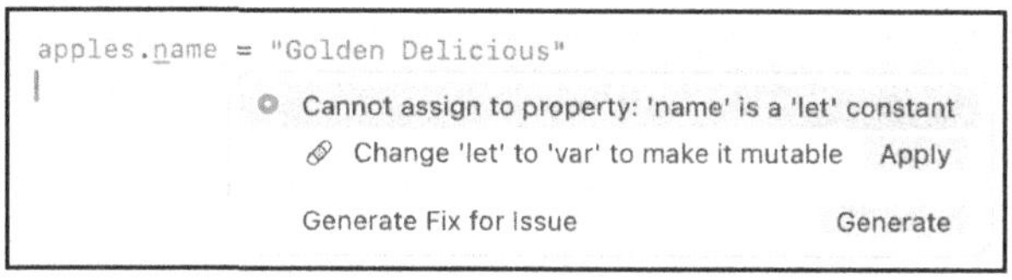

Trying to edit a constant property.

The error message not only tells you what's wrong, but how to fix it. In fact, clicking the **Apply** button will go into your class definition and change `name` from `let` to `var`, but that's not what you want here, so remove the error-causing line.

> **Note**: The **Generate** button will use AI to attempt to solve the problem. This does not always do what you want, so use it with caution and always check the results.

Now you know the basics of defining a class, initializing instances of the class and working with properties and methods, it's time to learn about another way of creating custom types.

Structures

You're going to use another playground page for this, so go to **File → New → Playground Page** or press **Option-Command-N** to add a page.

Xcode adds a new page called "Untitled Page 2". Press **Command-1** to show the navigator if it's not already visible and type **Return** to make the name editable. Set the name of this page to **Structures** and press **Return** again.

Your first page now appears in the navigator as "Untitled Page". Select it and change the name to **Classes**.

Click the **Structures** page in the navigator to get back to it. Your playground now looks like this:

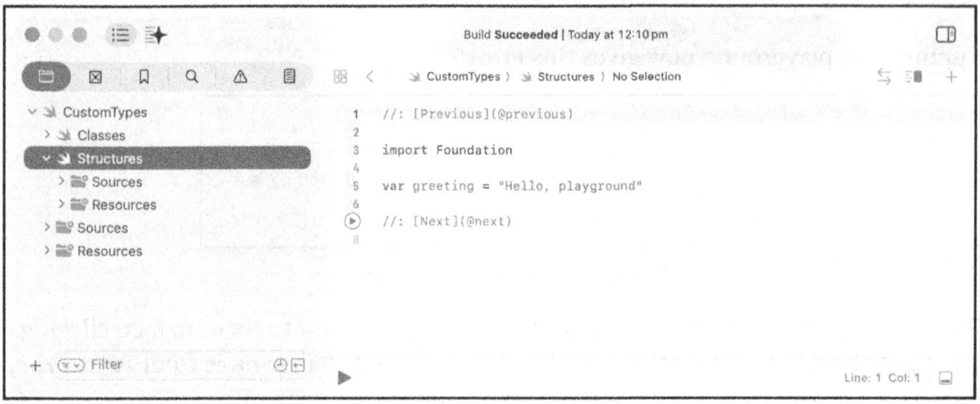

Adding a page to the playground.

The comments at the top and bottom of the code are for navigation. To see this in action, select **Editor → Show Rendered Markup** (all the way down near the bottom of the menu) and use the **Previous** link to jump to the **Classes** page. When you've seen how this works, choose **Editor → Show Raw Markup**. Get back to the **Structures** page and delete all the code in it.

To make it easier to compare classes and structures, you'll create a `StockItem` structure and make it do the same as the class did.

Start by adding this code to your blank **Structures** page:

```
// 1
struct StockItem {
  // 2
  let name: String
  var numberInStock: Int
}
// 3
```

So far, it's very similar to the class:

1. For structures, you start with the `struct` keyword. Again, the name is in **UpperCamelCase**.
2. You define the two properties as before.
3. Xcode isn't showing an error! This is because structures automatically get an initializer, so you don't need to write your own. Hurray! Less code is good code.

To check if it works, add this line to make an instance:

```
var peaches = StockItem(name: "peach", numberInStock: 6)
```

Run the playground (only the current page runs) to see what happens:

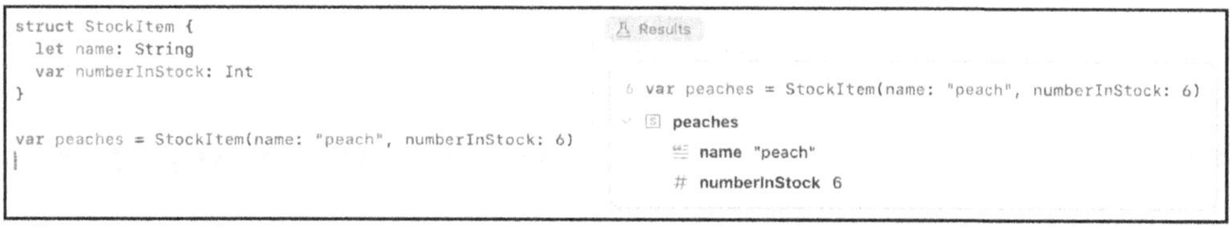

Initializing a structure instance.

So far, structures are looking great — set up the properties and it all just works. But what about methods?

Adding Structure Methods

Add a blank line after the structure's properties and insert these methods:

```
func buy(number: Int) {
  numberInStock += number
}

func sell(number: Int) {
  if number > numberInStock {
    numberInStock = 0
  } else {
    numberInStock -= number
  }
}
```

This is the same as you used in the class, so why is Xcode so upset?

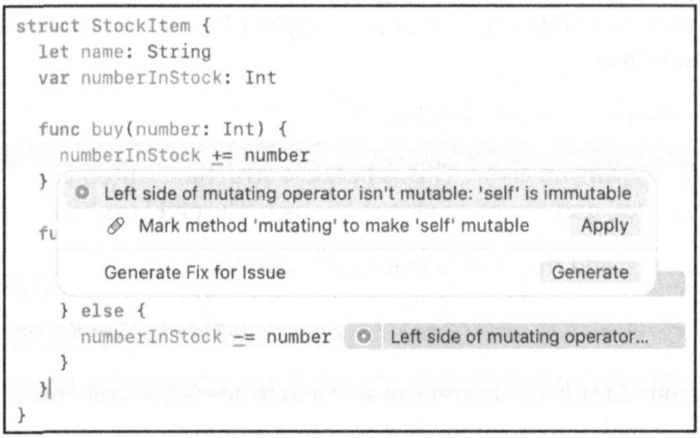

Structure method errors

This looks like a sea of red, but it's only one error repeated. Click the first red dot for more detail and you'll see that **'self' is immutable**. The `numberInStock` property isn't the issue. It really is mutable because you set it up as a `var`. The problem is that the entire structure is immutable — that's what `self` is referring to. This is a feature of structures.

Xcode helpfully offers to solve the problem, so click the **Apply** button on the first and second red dots. This changes the errors to gray while Xcode thinks for a few seconds before removing them.

Now you'll see the `mutating` keyword before `func` in both your methods, indicating that these methods can mutate the structure.

As with deciding between `var` and `let`, always start without `mutating` and only add it if Xcode insists. Like `let`, this is a feature that makes Swift a safer language because you can't change a structure's properties without permission.

With this in place, you can operate on your structure like you did on your class:

```
peaches.name
peaches.numberInStock += 1

peaches.buy(number: 4)

peaches.sell(number: 2)

peaches.sell(number: 1000)
```

Running the playground after adding these lines shows:

Structure operations

Before moving on from structures, there's one more difference you need to be aware of.

Value Types

Try adding this code:

```
let limes = StockItem(name: "lime", numberInStock: 3)
limes.buy(number: 9)
```

With a class, this worked even though the class instance was a constant. But with a structure, it gives an error:

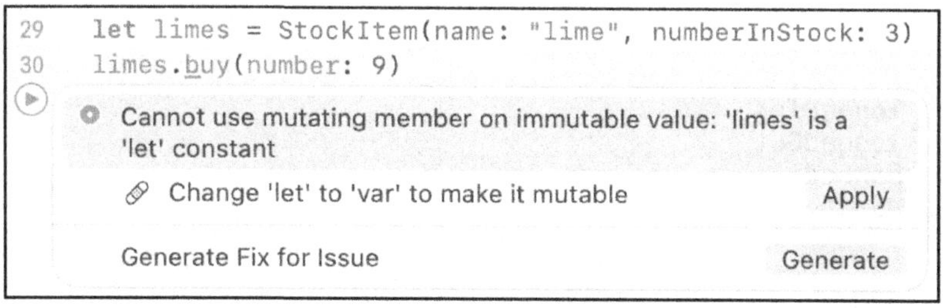

Editing a constant structure instance.

This is actually more logical. When you initialize a structure instance as a constant, it really is a constant and you can't change its properties. You already learned that classes are reference types. Structures are **value types**, so the variable `limes` actually holds the data, not an address in memory. This is another case of Swift making your code safer.

Delete these two lines to clear the error.

Classes and structures are the main two custom types you'll work with, but there's another type that's useful when you have a limited number of options. That type is an enumeration.

Enumerations

An enumeration, or **enum**, is a type where you give it a set of predefined options. Each instance must be one of those options. Imagine you're implementing a login system. What are the possible states for a user?

- Logged in
- Logged out
- Banned
- Logged in as admin

This is a perfect use case for an enumeration because your user has to be in one of these states.

Create a new playground page, set its name to **Enumerations** and clear all its content.

Enter this code to set up your new enumeration:

```
// 1
enum LoginState {
  // 2
  case loggedIn
  case loggedOut
  case banned
  case admin
}
```

How does this work?

1. Start with the `enum` keyword followed by the name in **UpperCamelCase**.
2. For each possibility, add a `case` and a label. The labels use **lowerCamelCase**.

`LoginState` is now a type like `String`, `Int` or `StockItem` and you use it like this:

```
var userStatus = LoginState.loggedOut
```

Now that the type of `userStatus` is set to `LoginState`, you can edit it less verbosely like this:

```
userStatus = .admin
```

Running your playground page shows:

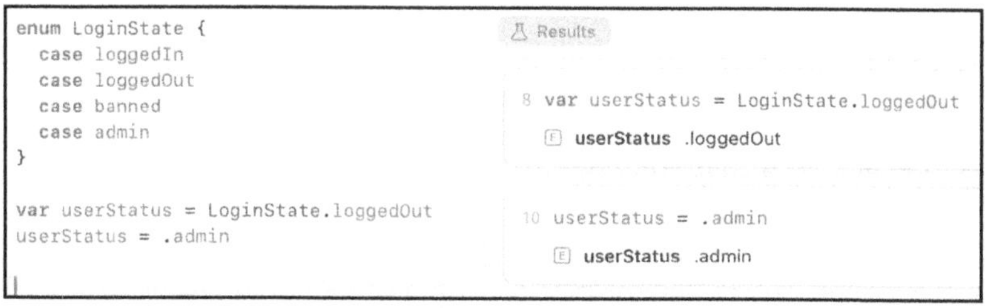

Declaring and using an enumeration.

This is a very convenient way to handle a set of options, but you can also add methods to an enumeration. They can step through the possible options to give a result.

Adding Enumeration Methods

Maybe you'd like to show a message to the user depending on the login status. Add this method before the closing curly brace in `LoginState`:

```
// 1
func displayMessage() -> String {
  // 2
  switch self {

  }
}
```

This looks like it's missing a few parts:

1. You declare the `displayMessage` method. It takes no arguments and returns a `String`.
2. You start a switch statement that switches on `self`, which is the current instance of the enumeration.

Xcode now complains that "Switch must be exhaustive" but since you have a fixed number of options, Xcode can fill in the missing code and save a lot of typing. Click the red dot, scroll down and press the **Apply** button beside "Add missing cases".

> **Note**: If you don't see an error flag, switch to another playground page, then back to **Enumerations**, or close the playground and reopen it.

Xcode adds a case for each of the possibilities with a **code** placeholder for each one. There are warnings because of the placeholders, but you'll fix that now.

Fill in the code blocks so that your switch looks like this:

```
switch self {

case .loggedIn:
  return "Welcome, user"
case .loggedOut:
  return "Log in to access this site."
case .banned:
  return "*** BANNED ***"
case .admin:
 return "Welcome, mighty administrator!"
}
```

It now returns an appropriate message for each state. Xcode isn't always good at formatting, so to tidy things up, delete the blank line after the `switch` line, then press **Command-A** to select all your code and **Control-I** to re-indent it.

A method is one way to provide this message, but another possibility is a computed property. When you have a method that takes no arguments but produces output, consider using one of these instead.

Replace the method declaration with:

```
var displayMessage: String {
```

And now, you've got a computed property, instead of a method, and you can access it with:

```
userStatus.displayMessage
```

These also work in classes and structures.

You have seen three ways to make a custom type in Swift. Now, it's time to go back to classes and learn some more features.

Inheritance

You may have heard of **Object-Oriented Programming** or **OOP**. This is a system of programming that uses classes and subclasses. A subclass is a class that inherits from a parent class.

Open the **Classes** page in your playground and scroll down to the bottom. Your fruit seller has decided to branch out and sell soft drinks, too. In many ways, a soft drink is a `StockItem` like a piece of fruit but it has an extra property: Is the drink fizzy or not?

This make it a perfect case for a subclass. Your `SoftDrinkItem` class can have everything that `StockItem` has, plus more.

Add the subclass like this:

```
// 1
class SoftDrinkItem: StockItem {
  // 2
  var isFizzy: Bool

  // 3
  init(name: String, numberInStock: Int, isFizzy: Bool) {
    // 4
    self.isFizzy = isFizzy
    // 5
    super.init(name: name, numberInStock: numberInStock)
  }
}
```

There's a lot going on here:

1. You declare the new class but, after the class name, type a colon and the name of the parent class.
2. You define the `isFizzy` property, which is unique to this class and not part of the parent.
3. You create an initializer that has both the parent properties and the subclass property as its arguments.
4. You set the subclass property first. You *must* assign all the subclass properties before moving on to the next step.
5. You call `super.init` to initialize the parent with its properties.

Initializing a Subclass Instance

This class has inherited everything from its parent, so you can initialize it and use the parent's methods like this:

```
// 1
let mineralWater = SoftDrinkItem(
  name: "Mineral water",
  numberInStock: 12,
  isFizzy: false)

// 2
mineralWater.sell(number: 3)
```

How does this work?

1. You call the initializer with all three properties. It's perfectly valid to split method calls or declarations over multiple lines, and if you have a lot of properties, this makes your code a lot more readable.
2. You call a parent method on your instance of the subclass.

Run the playground and look at the final result:

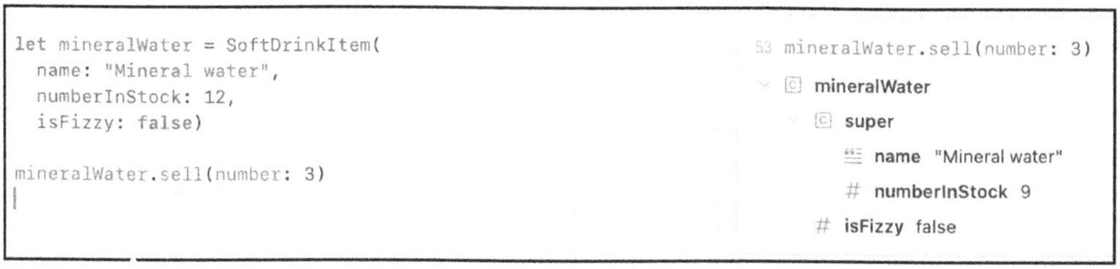

Defining and using a subclass.

Use the disclosure triangle next to **super** in the result panel so you can see the parent class properties separated from the subclass property.

The `SoftDrinkItem` class has no `sell(number:)` of its own so it uses its parent's `sell(number:)`.

Add these two lines to your playground and run:

```
mineralWater is SoftDrinkItem
mineralWater is StockItem
```

They'll both give warnings because they can never be false, but they demonstrate that `mineralWater` is both a `SoftDrinkItem` and a `StockItem`. Select these lines and press **Command**-/ to comment them out and get rid of the warnings.

One benefit of inheritance is that you can have an array containing `StockItem` instances and `SoftDrinkItem` instances without a problem:

Enter this line in your playground:

```
var stocks = [bananas, apples, mineralWater]
```

And then **Option-click** on the variable name `stocks`:

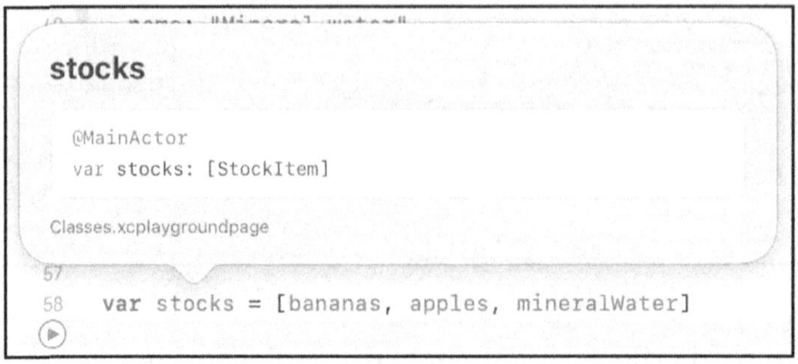

Class array

This confirms that Swift considers it an array with a single type of object in it, but the type is `StockItem`, even though one of the elements is a subclass of `StockItem`.

Overriding Parent Methods

Your fruit seller now tells you that they always buy soft drinks in boxes of 12, so this class needs a custom `buy(number:)` that adds 12 to `numberInStock` for every purchase. `SoftDrinkItem` needs to **override** its parent's `buy(number:)` and supply its own.

Insert this in the `SoftDrinkItem` class definition:

```
// 1
override func buy(number: Int) {
  // 2
  numberInStock += number * 12
}
```

Looking at this method:

1. Since this replaces a parent method, start with the `override` keyword. Xcode will complain and offer to insert it if you forget.
2. Then, insert your custom logic that increments `numberInStock` by 12 for each purchase.

Test your new method like this:

```
mineralWater.numberInStock
mineralWater.buy(number: 2)
mineralWater.numberInStock
```

And run the playground to see the result:

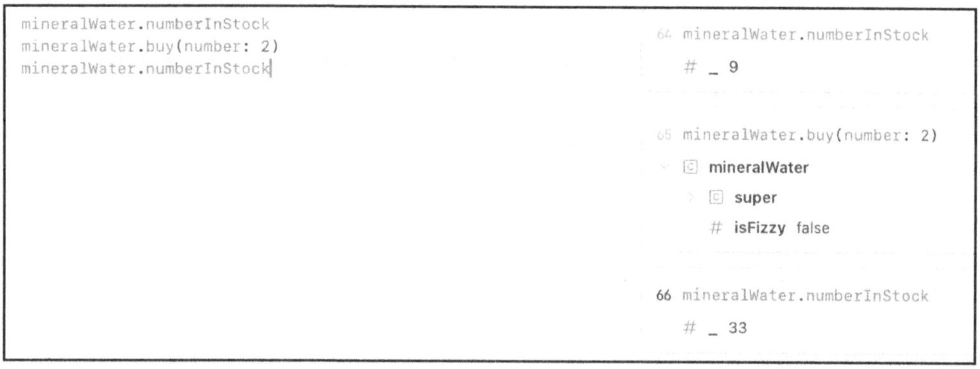

Using an override method.

This covers the key features of inheritance, but it only works for classes. With structures, you'll use a different approach.

Protocols

One alternative to Object-Oriented Programming is **Protocol-Oriented Programming** or **POP**. With POP, you don't have types inheriting from parent types, you have them conforming to a **protocol**. So what is a protocol?

A protocol is a contract — a list of properties and methods that any conforming type must provide.

Implementing the fruit selling app using POP needs a few changes, so create a new playground page and call it **Protocols**.

Clear the page and enter this:

```
// 1
protocol StockItemProtocol {
  // 2
  var name: String { get }
  // 3
  var numberInStock: Int { get set }

  // 4
  mutating func buy(number: Int)
  mutating func sell(number: Int)
}
```

This is different:

1. You declare a protocol by starting with the `protocol` keyword followed by the name in **UpperCamelCase**. It isn't necessary to have **Protocol** as part of the name — that's here to make the example clearer.

2. Any type conforming to this protocol must have a `String` property called `name`. The `get` shows that the type must make it readable, but it doesn't have to be editable.

3. The type also needs an `Int` property called `numberInStock`. The `get` and `set` show that it can be both read and edited.

4. All conforming types must supply two methods called `buy(number:)` and `sell(number:)` that both accept an `Int` argument and return nothing. These methods can mutate the structure's properties.

The methods look very strange since the protocol lists the method declarations but no code, but that's how protocols work. Where class definitions give a blueprint for creating instances, protocols provide a set of rules.

Conforming to a Protocol

Now you'll implement a structure conforming to the protocol.

Type this outside the protocol:

```
struct StockItem: StockItemProtocol {

}
```

You created a structure with a name, and then, you added a colon and the protocol name. This guarantees that `StockItem` will supply all the properties and methods listed in the `StockItemProtocol`.

Right now, it doesn't do any of that, and Xcode is not happy. Click the red dot and then the **Apply** button to get Xcode to fill in what's needed. This supplies the properties and adds method stubs, which are methods with the correct declarations, but using a **code** placeholder.

> **Note**: If you don't see an error flag, switch to another playground page, then back to **Protocols**, or close the playground and reopen it.

Replace the `buy(number:)` code placeholder with:

```
numberInStock += number
```

And the `sell(number:)` placeholder with:

```
numberInStock -= number
```

The `sell(number:)` method doesn't include the validation, but you already know how to do that.

It's a great idea to let Xcode do as much work as possible. You avoid typos, you won't leave anything out and you save yourself time and effort. But as you've already seen, Xcode isn't great at formatting, so get rid of the excess blank lines and press **Command-A** followed by **Control-I** to format your code.

Using your new structure works as before:

```
var mangos = StockItem(name: "mango", numberInStock: 5)

mangos.buy(number: 3)
mangos.sell(number: 1)
mangos.numberInStock
```

So far, this seems a bit pointless. The `StockItem` structure is much the same, and there's an extra protocol that just adds extra code. But what about the soft drinks? That structure can't inherit from `StockItem` but it can conform to `StockItemProtocol`.

Add another structure definition:

```
struct SoftDrinkItem: StockItemProtocol {
  var name: String
  var numberInStock: Int
  var isFizzy: Bool

  mutating func buy(number: Int) {
    numberInStock += number * 12
  }

  mutating func sell(number: Int) {
    numberInStock -= number
  }
}
```

As you can see, this is very similar to `StockItem` but it contains the new `isFizzy` property. A protocol says what must be in a type — it doesn't care if there are extra properties or methods.

Next, create an instance like this:

```
var lemonades = SoftDrinkItem(
  name: "lemonade",
  numberInStock: 24,
  isFizzy: true)
```

Like with the classes and subclasses, you can add different types conforming to the same protocol to an array, if you set up the array correctly.

Try this code:

```
var stocks: [StockItemProtocol] = [mangos, lemonades]
```

The elements in the array are different types, but they conform to the same protocol, so when you declare the array as containing items that conform to that protocol, you can gather them together.

Extending Your Protocol

When you dealt with inheritance, you only had to write a common method once. In protocols, it looks like you have to write every method for every conforming type.

To get around this, you'll use an **extension**. Extensions let you add to existing types or protocols. Often you'll use them as a convenient way of grouping similar methods together, but in protocols they can supply default methods.

Outside the protocol declaration, type this:

```
// 1
extension StockItemProtocol {
  // 2
  mutating func buy(number: Int) {
    numberInStock += number
  }

  mutating func sell(number: Int) {
    numberInStock -= number
  }
}
```

What have you added here?

1. You create an extension using the `extension` keyword followed by the name of the class, structure or protocol that it extends.

2. This extension provides default implementations of `buy(number:)` and `sell(number:)`.

Scroll to where you declared `StockItem` and remove its two methods. It can use the defaults.

In `SoftDrinkItem`, delete `sell(number:)`, but leave `buy(number:)` because it's different from the default.

Now your code is shorter, neater and easier to maintain.

To confirm that this still works and that each type is using the correct `buy(number:)`, add and run these lines:

```
mangos.numberInStock = 0
mangos.buy(number: 2)
mangos.sell(number: 1)

lemonades.numberInStock = 0
lemonades.buy(number: 1)
lemonades.sell(number: 1)
```

Which shows you:

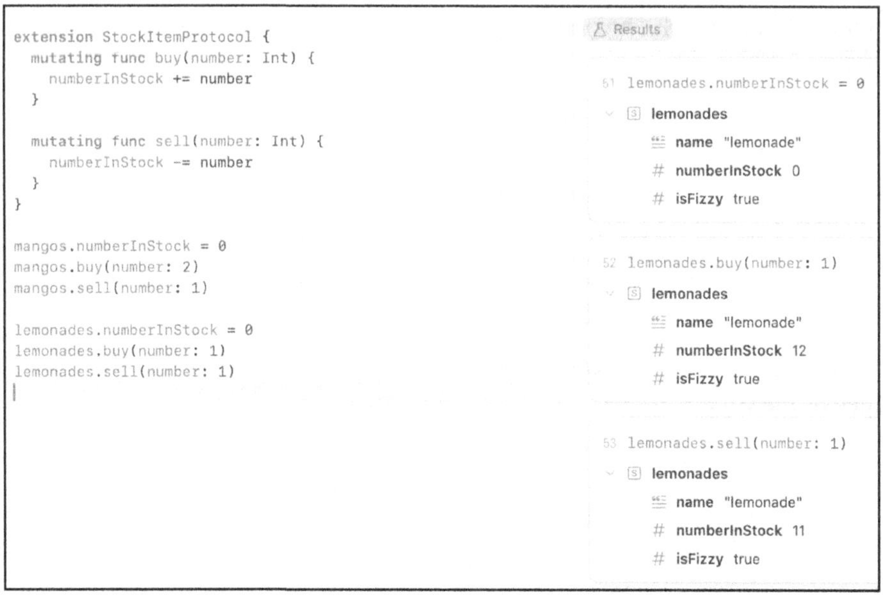

Protocol methods

Protocols work with both structures and classes. Inheritance only works with classes. So, which should you use?

What to Use?

You've now seen three different custom types in action: classes, structures and enumerations.

Enumerations are for when you have a predefined set of possibilities.

Deciding between classes and structures is more complex:

- Classes are **reference types**; structures are **value types.** If you want to pass an object to something else and have the changes flow back to the original, use a class. If you want to pass along isolated instances, use a structure.
- Classes can inherit from another class. Often, especially when working with interface elements, you'll start with existing classes that you want to customize, so you'll have to use a class.
- Both structures and classes can conform to protocols. In fact, a single object can conform to multiple protocols where a subclass can only inherit from one parent class.
- You don't have to pick one only. Any project can have a mixture of classes and structures.

Generally speaking, structures are safer because you know exactly what can change their data. So start with a structure, but if you need to inherit or you need the properties to be more mutable, then switch to a class.

In Section 2 of this book, you'll build an app using SwiftUI. SwiftUI has definite rules about using classes in some cases. A common pattern is to have a main data class that contains an array of data structures.

As you progress to section 3, you'll get into AppKit, which is the Mac's older user interface framework. It uses classes and inheritance extensively.

Key Points

- Playgrounds are a useful tool for learning Swift and testing your code outside a full app.
- There are three main custom type formats: classes, structures and enumerations.
- Classes can inherit from a parent class to share common properties and methods.
- Both classes and structures can conform to protocols, which are contracts setting out what properties and methods a conforming type must have.
- Enumerations allow for predefined sets of options.

Where to Go From Here?

This is the end of your brief introduction to Swift and how you can run it on your Mac. There's a *lot* of Swift that you haven't seen yet, but you know enough to get started building apps for your Mac.

In the next section, you're going to build a full game using Swift and SwiftUI.

For the official Swift information and guides, go to Swift.org.

To read about Swift in more depth, check out our Swift Apprentice: Fundamentals book (https://www.kodeco.com/books/swift-apprentice-fundamentals).

Section II: Building With SwiftUI

In this section, you'll use Apple's newest user interface technology — SwiftUI — to develop a word-guessing game called Snowman. You'll learn about data flow in SwiftUI, managing multiple windows, using charts and adding macOS-specific features such as toolbars and menus.

Chapter 5: Beginning SwiftUI

By Sarah Reichelt

In Section 1, you installed Xcode and used various tools to run Swift code on your Mac. In this section, you'll apply that knowledge to create an entire app for your Mac using Swift and SwiftUI.

Chapter 1 gave a tour of Xcode, explained the basic structure of a Mac app project and showed you how SwiftUI views and previews work together. This chapter builds on that.

The app you're about to create is a word guessing game called Snowman. The computer picks a word and you enter letters to guess the word. Every time you choose an incorrect letter, part of the snowman disappears. If the snowman vanishes completely before you've guessed the word, you lose. :[

Snowman

Setting Up Your App

Start **Xcode** as you've done many times now. Create a new project from the **Welcome** window or by selecting **File → New → Project...**. When you get to the template chooser, select **macOS → App**. Click **Next** and set the details like this:

- **Product Name**: Snowman
- **Team**: If you have a developer team, select it, or leave this set to None.
- **Organization Identifier**: Enter your reverse domain name as you did in Chapter 1.
- **Bundle Identifier**: Xcode fills this in based on your previous entries.
- **Interface**: SwiftUI
- **Language**: Swift
- **Testing System**: None
- **Storage**: None

When your settings look like this, click **Next**:

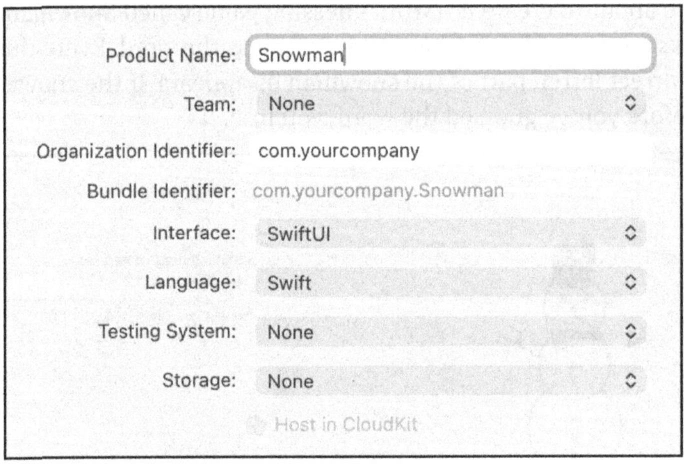

Setting up the new project.

Select where you want to save your project and click **Create**.

The project window appears and you're ready to code.

What is SwiftUI?

When developing apps for the Mac, you have a choice of two layout frameworks. **AppKit** is the older one, and you'll learn about it later. If you've done any iOS programming, it's similar to UIKit. **SwiftUI** is the newer framework, which Apple describes as "a modern way to declare user interfaces for any Apple platform".

SwiftUI is a declarative framework. You don't micro-manage all the details of the user interface. You describe what you want and SwiftUI generates appropriate interface elements for the selected platform.

SwiftUI is also reactive: You connect data to elements in the interface and SwiftUI automatically keeps them in sync. Due to this behavior, the data and the user interface are tightly connected in a SwiftUI app. If you're getting your data from an external source, it works better to design your data structures first and then make the user interface match them. In this app you have total control, so you'll lay out the interface first and then see what data you need to make it work.

Laying Out the User Interface

Looking at the app image at the start of this chapter, there's a sidebar listing the games played and a larger area to display the current game.

This is a common layout for Mac apps, and you'll use a `NavigationSplitView` to create this.

Open **ContentView.swift** and delete everything inside `body`.

Replace it with this:

```
// 1
NavigationSplitView {
  // 2
  Text("Sidebar")
} detail: {
  // 3
  Text("Game view")
}
```

What does this do?

1. A `NavigationSplitView` has several different initializers. This one sets it up to have a sidebar and a detail view, which is exactly what this app requires.
2. The first set of curly braces contains the code to layout the sidebar view. For now, this is a `Text` view.
3. The detail section contains the layout code for the main part of the window. Again, you're using a `Text` placeholder for now.

The preview will update automatically to show your new design. Hide the inspectors pane on the right to give yourself more space, and adjust the width of the preview pane until you see this:

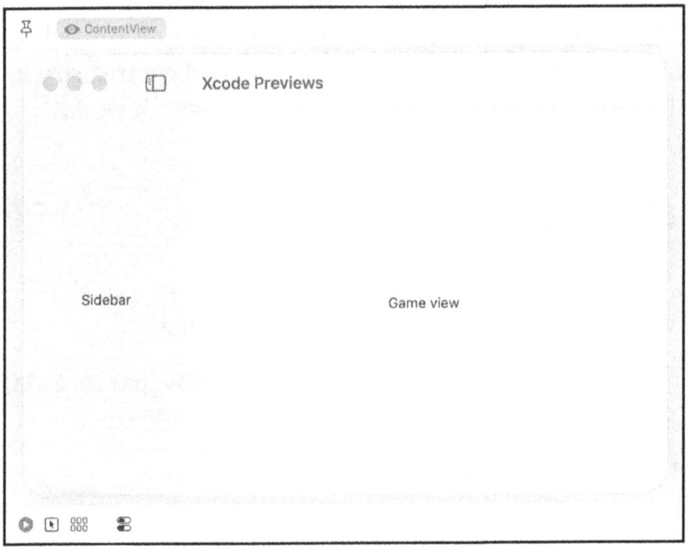

Previewing the split view.

> **Note**: If you don't see the preview, choose **Editor → Canvas** or press **Option-Command-Return**. If the preview pane is open but not active, click the circle arrow beside **Preview paused** or press **Option-Command-P** to start it.

Splitting Up the Subviews

Your views will get more complicated, so it's a good idea to split them out into their own files and structures.

Go to **File → New → File from Template...** or press **Command-N** to open the file template selector. Choose **macOS → User Interface → SwiftUI View** and click **Next**. Set the file name to **SidebarView.swift** and click **Create**.

Repeat this process to make a second SwiftUI view file called **GameView.swift**.

You now have three **View** files and there will be more to come, so to make the Project navigator easier to work with, you'll put them into a separate folder.

In the navigator, select **ContentView.swift**, **GameView.swift** and **SidebarView.swift**. With the three files selected, right-click and choose **New Folder from Selection** from the popup menu. Edit the name of the new folder to **Views** and press **Return** to set it.

Your Project navigator now looks like this:

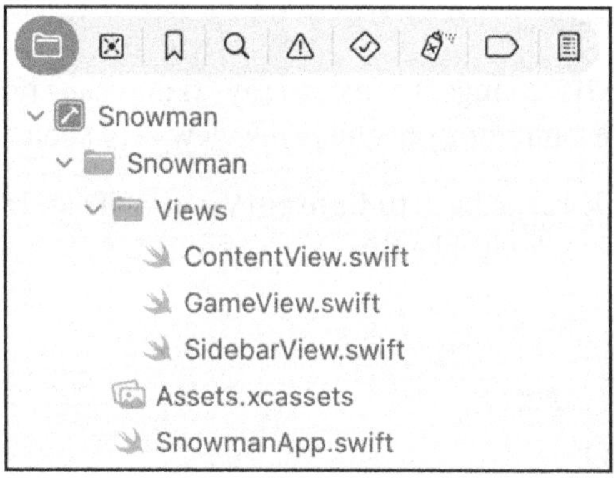

The view files in a folder.

Large projects can accumulate a lot of files, so this sort of organization is really helpful. You can even make sub-folders inside other folders.

You've made two new files, so now it's time to use them.

Open **SidebarView.swift** and look at the default code:

```
// 1
struct SidebarView: View {
  // 2
  var body: some View {
    // 3
    Text("Hello, World!")
  }
}
```

This is a standard SwiftUI view:

1. Every SwiftUI view is a `structure` that conforms to the `View` protocol.
2. The `View` protocol requires a property called `body` that has a type of `some View`. This means that it doesn't matter what sort of a view it is, but it must be something that conforms to `View`.
3. The `body` property returns a single `Text` view containing some starter text. As `body` returns a single object, the `return` keyword in unnecessary.

You're not going to work on the sidebar yet, so edit the default "Hello, World!" to say "Games will be listed here".

Over in **GameView.swift**, change its `Text` to say "Game view here". This is temporary as you'll start building out the game view very soon.

To use your two new views, go back to **ContentView.swift** and replace the two `Text` placeholders so that `body` looks like this:

```
var body: some View {
  // 1
  NavigationSplitView {
    // 2
    SidebarView()
  } detail: {
    // 3
    GameView()
  }
}
```

Going through this:

1. The body property returns a `NavigationSplitView`.
2. The sidebar section of the `NavigationSplitView` displays `SidebarView`.
3. The detail section shows `GameView`.

You've extracted the sidebar and detail views out into their own files and told `ContentView` to display them. The preview shows the placeholder text you added:

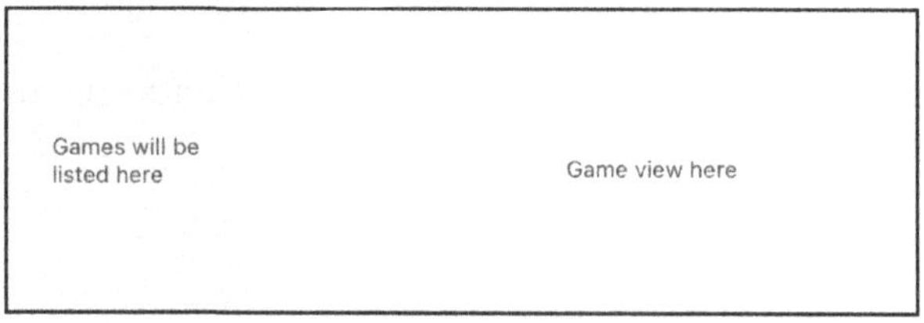

Separated subviews

With this in place, you're ready to design the game view.

Designing the Game View

One of the fundamentals of SwiftUI is that you can build complex views from a set of component views. It looks like the game view has a lot of parts, but if you break it down into components, you can add them one at a time. That way you don't lose yourself in complexity.

Look at this view of the game area with the parts numbered:

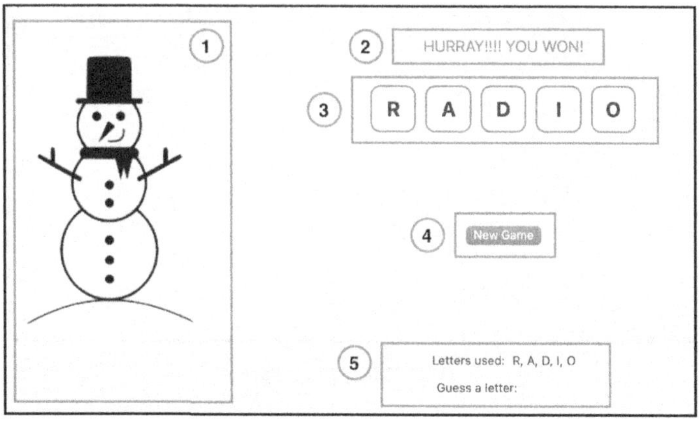

The game view components

Listing these components:

1. The snowman image which changes when you choose an incorrect letter.
2. Some status text.
3. The word displayed as empty boxes for letters the player hasn't guessed yet and blue boxes for correctly guessed letters. After the game is over, this draws a red box around letters the player never guessed.
4. The **New Game** button that appears when a game has ended.
5. The letters the player guessed already and a field for entering further guesses.

The Snowman Images

SwiftUI has an `Image` view that can display a picture, but first, you need the images to show. Open the downloaded materials for this chapter and look in the **assets** folder. There's a folder called **Snowmen** with images for both light and dark mode.

To get them into your project, select **Assets.xcassets** in the Project navigator. It already has entries for **AccentColor** and **AppIcon**. Drag the **Snowmen** folder from the **assets** folder into the sidebar underneath AppIcon:

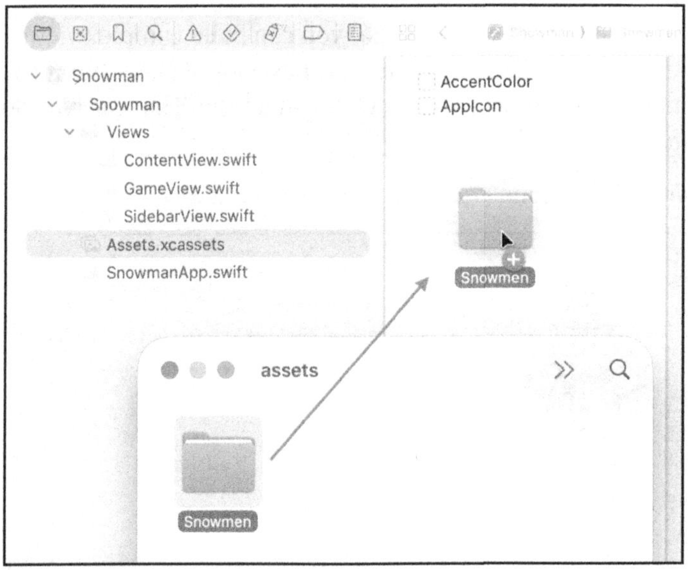

Importing images.

Click the > beside the **Snowmen** folder to expand the folder and see all the imported images:

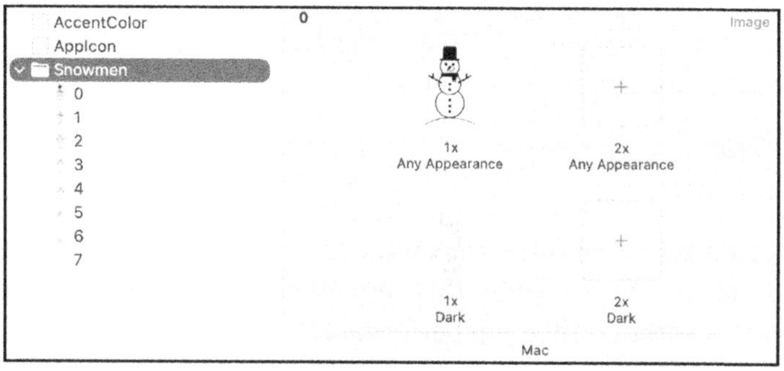

Snowman images

There are eight images named using the numbers 0 to 7. This naming allows you to use the number of incorrect guesses to select the correct image.

Each image has two versions: one "1x Any Appearance" and the other "1x Dark". This accommodates both of the Mac's display modes.

To display an image, open **GameView.swift** and replace the `Text` view with:

```
// 1
Image("0")
  // 2
  .resizable()
  // 3
  .aspectRatio(contentMode: .fit)
  // 4
  .frame(width: 230)
```

What's happening here?

1. `Image` is a view type like `Text`, and it takes the name of an image to use. For now, use "0", which shows the complete snowman.

2. By default, `Image` shows the image at its full size. To control this, you add a modifier to make the `Image` resizable.

3. The aspect ratio of an image is the ratio between its width and its height. If you change this, the image appears distorted. Applying this `aspectRatio` modifier tells the image to use its original ratio. The `contentMode` can be either `.fill` which expands the image to fill the space chopping off extra bits, or `.fit` which makes sure you can see the entire image.

4. Finally, a `frame` modifier sets the width of the image so it doesn't jump around as the window resizes.

But what is a **modifier**? A modifier is a method that takes a view, changes it and returns the edited view. SwiftUI does this very efficiently, so you can add multiple modifiers to a view without affecting performance.

> **Note:** `.fit` and `.fill` are the two cases of the `ContentMode` enumeration. As the `contentMode` argument must receive one of these cases, there's no need to specify the type before the period. You'll see this pattern a lot in SwiftUI. If you're curious about the type of any data, **Option-click** it to show the Quick Help.

The preview shows the complete snowman. Change the number in the `Image` initializer to see different versions. Click the **Variants** button at the bottom of the Preview pane and select **Color Scheme Variants** to see both light and dark modes:

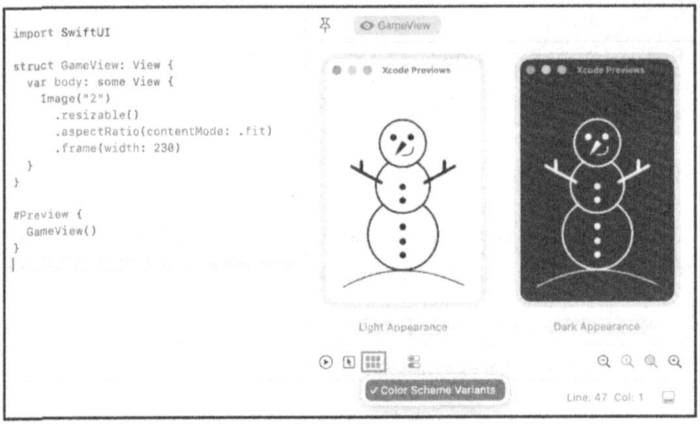

Previewing an image.

Click the **Live** button on the left of the button group to turn off the color variants. This gives more room in the preview for the next part.

That covers the image part of the game view. Now, you'll add the next component.

Stacking

SwiftUI offers various stack views for arranging components in your layout. `HStack` arranges them horizontally, `VStack` arranges them vertically and `ZStack` piles them on top of each other.

Looking back at the design, the image is to the left and everything else is to the right, so this looks like a good place for an `HStack`.

Still in **GameView.swift**, **right-click** `Image` and select **Embed...**. Xcode puts the `Image` and its modifiers inside a pair of curly braces and adds a `Container` placeholder at the start. Change `Container` to `HStack`. Nothing changes yet in the preview. Now, add a blank line after the `.frame` line and then enter this:

```
Text("Enter a letter to guess the word.")
  .font(.title2)
```

This inserts a `Text` view to hold the status text and applies a `font` modifier. There are lots of preset font options you can select. To see what's available, delete `.title2` and type a period — auto-complete now shows you a list of possibilities. Test them out and see how they appear in the preview. Revert to `.title2` when you're done.

You've added one more component, but the next one goes below the status text, so this needs a `VStack`. **Right-click** `Text` and choose **Embed...**. This time, change `Container` to `VStack`.

Again, nothing changes in the preview because there's only one view in the `VStack`, but now you'll add the view that shows the word's letters.

Looping Through Views

To create the letters view, you'll loop through the letters in the word, using `Text` views to show each letter and overlaying this with a rounded rectangle to draw the box.

To start with, you need a test array of letters to work with.

At the top of `GameView`, before `body`, define this property:

```
let word = ["S", "N", "O", "W", "M", "A", "N"]
```

Next, scroll back down to the `VStack` and add a blank line after the `font` modifier before entering this:

```
// 1
HStack {
  // 2
  ForEach(word, id: \.self) { letter in
    // 3
    Text(letter)
      .font(.title)
      .bold()
      .frame(width: 20, height: 20)
      .padding()
      // 4
      .overlay {
        // 5
        RoundedRectangle(cornerRadius: 10)
          .stroke(lineWidth: 2)
          // 6
          .foregroundStyle(Color.accentColor)
          // 7
          .padding(2)
      }
  }
}
```

This is the most complicated view you've used so far, but taking it bit by bit:

1. Since you want the letters arranged horizontally, start with an `HStack`.
2. SwiftUI uses `ForEach` to create views in a loop. The first argument is the array to loop through, and the `id` argument allocates an identifier to each element so that SwiftUI can track it. In this case, you're using each letter as its own identifier. Each time through the loop, the current element has the name `letter`.
3. Next, display the letter in a `Text` view. This has several modifiers to set the font, turn on bold text, specify width and height and add some padding around the letter to space out the border.
4. Any view can have an `overlay` modifier which puts another view on top. In this case, you're adding one of the graphic views. The curly braces for the `overlay` contain the view to lay on top.
5. A `RoundedRectangle` takes an argument to set the corner radius. The `stroke` dictates how thick the line is.

6. Use a `foregroundStyle` modifier to set the color. The `foregroundStyle` modifier expects a `ShapeStyle`. This is a protocol that you can use to add colors or patterns. In SwiftUI, `Color` conforms to `ShapeStyle`, so this is perfectly valid and `Color.accentColor` is a special color that changes depending on the system color scheme and the accent color selected in System Settings.
7. Finally, another `padding` modifier spaces out the letters. This padding specifies an amount of padding instead of using the platform's default.

Now the preview looks like this:

The word view

The last letter is at the edge of the view, so to make it look better, add a `padding` modifier to the `VStack`.

To find the bottom of the VStack, double-click the curly brace on its starting line. This selects all the code inside, including the closing curly brace. Add a new line after that closing brace and type in `.padding()`.

An alternative way to locate the end is to collapse the `VStack` completely using the code folding ribbon, as you saw in Chapter 1, "Introducing Xcode".

Buttons

Now, you'll add the **New Game** button. It goes in the `VStack` underneath the letters view. Collapse the `HStack` that contains the `ForEach` loop and add a blank line after it.

Next, type in this:

```
// 1
Button("New Game") {
  // 2
  print("Starting new game.")
}
```

```
// 3
.keyboardShortcut(.defaultAction)
```

Another new view type:

1. This `Button` view initializer takes the title for the button as its argument.
2. In curly braces after that, add the code to call when the user clicks the button. This prints to the Xcode console for now.
3. A keyboard shortcut allows users to operate without a mouse or trackpad if they want. The `defaultAction` keyboard shortcut means the **Return** key "clicks" the button.

For the first time, press **Command-R** to build and run the game:

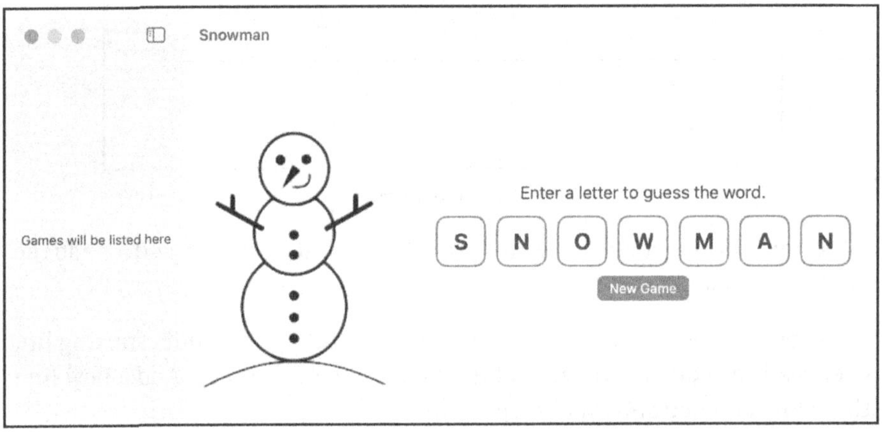

Running the app to see the default button.

There are some interesting features here that you don't see in the preview.

First, you can test that the button works like a default button. Click it and then press **Return**. Check the Xcode console to see "Starting new game." printed twice.

At the top of the window, you see the standard window controls so you can close, minimize or maximize the window. If you close the window, use **File → New Window** or **Command-N** to open another one. You can also drag the corners or edges to resize the window.

Notice that your window has a toolbar with a button for toggling the sidebar — `NavigationSplitView` gives you this automatically. You can resize or hide the sidebar by dragging its divider, but once you've hidden it, this is one way to get it back.

And while you're in the app, check out the menus, which are what you would expect in any standard Mac app.

Now, there's only one more section of the game view to add, so quit the app and get back to Xcode. Press **Option-Command-P** to resume the preview which pauses whenever you run.

> **Note**: If you're using **Stage Manager**, Xcode disappears every time you run the app. This is inconvenient during development, so turn off Stage Manager while you're coding.

Adding the Final Components

The last section is the area that shows the letters guessed and allows you to guess new ones. First, you'll need some test data to hold the guesses.

Open **GameView.swift** and scroll up where you defined `word`. Add this new property on the next line:

```
let guesses = [ "E", "S", "R", "X"]
```

Next, scroll down to where you defined the **New Game** button. Add a blank line after its `keyboardShortcut` modifier and insert:

```
// 1
HStack {
  // 2
  Text("Letters used:")
  // 3
  Text(guesses.joined(separator: ", "))
}
```

This shows the guesses made so far:

1. You want a header before the list of letters, so start with with an `HStack`.
2. The header is a `Text` view with fixed content.
3. The second `Text` view uses an `Array` method to join the `String` elements in the array, separated by comma and space. The `joined` method inserts the `separator` argument between each pair of elements.

The final component is the text field to receive input. This requires some data management, which you'll learn how to do later. For now, add this placeholder after the end of the last `HStack`:

```
// 1
LabeledContent("Guess a letter:") {
  // 2
  Text("Q")
}
```

Here's another new view:

1. `LabeledContent` takes a `String` to use as the label.
2. The view inside the curly braces show what comes after the label — in this case, a `Text` placeholder.

With all this in place, your `GameView` preview looks like this:

GameView preview

Spacing

When you look back at the original design, you'll see that you have all the parts, but SwiftUI has clustered them into the center.

Some SwiftUI views are greedy and take up as much space as they can. Others only take as much space as they need.

With the preview active, change to **Selectable** mode by clicking the second button in the group at the bottom left. Then click the different views in your layout code. Xcode draws a box around the active element in the preview, so you can see the space it occupies. The `VStack` is the one that needs to spread out.

You have two tools for this. First, you can set a `spacing` for any `VStack` or `HStack`.

Change the `VStack {` line to this:

```
VStack(spacing: 30) {
```

The preview updates to show your components with more space between them.

This is definite progress, but it spaces the five parts evenly and that's not what you want. You want a gap at the top, the top two components, another gap, the button and then the remaining two components together at the bottom.

This is where you'll use `Spacer` views. A `Spacer` takes up as much room as it can to push the neighboring elements apart. It works in an `HStack` or a `VStack`.

First, insert a `Spacer` as the top view in the `VStack`, like this:

```
VStack(spacing: 30) {
  Spacer()    // NEW

  Text("Enter a letter to guess the word.")
```

Next, find your `Button` and add two `Spacer` views, so that the code looks like this:

```
Spacer()    // NEW

Button("New Game") {
  print("Starting new game.")
}
.keyboardShortcut(.defaultAction)

Spacer()    // NEW
```

This looks a lot closer, but there's one more thing... The bottom two views should be closer together. To make this happen, you'll embed them in another `VStack` inside the first one. This doesn't change the direction of layout, but does change the spacing between the parts.

Select the two parts: `HStack` and `LabeledContent`. With those views selected, type an opening curly brace. This wraps them in a pair of braces, indents them and places the cursor before the opening brace. Type `VStack` and a space to finish the job.

Now check the preview:

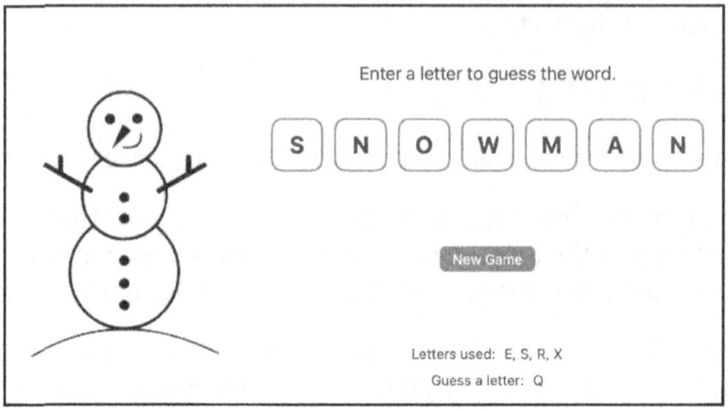

Fixing the spacing.

Doesn't that look good? With stack views, padding and spacers, you've constructed a great looking view from standard components.

Framing the Window

Time for another run, so press **Command-R** to build and run the app:

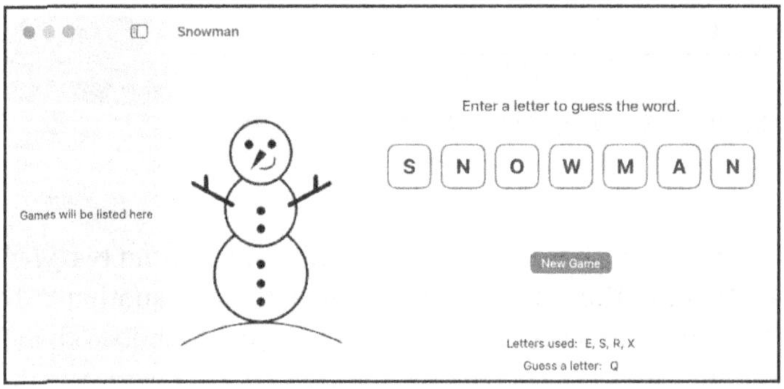

Running the app.

It looks like the preview when it starts up, but what happens when you resize the window?

The views inside `ContentView` are restricting the window from getting too small, but it doesn't look so good when the window is very large. When you're building a Mac app, you have to make it flexible. Some people will run your app on a huge external display and some in a corner of a small monitor. You have to arrange it so that it works no matter what.

The problem with the large window is that the snowman comes towards the center, but you want it to stick to the left.

Looks like a job for another `Spacer`. :]

Insert a `Spacer` between the `Image` and the start of the first `VStack`, like this:

```
Image("2")
  .resizable()
  .aspectRatio(contentMode: .fit)
  .frame(width: 230)

Spacer()     // NEW

VStack(spacing: 30.0) {
```

That pushes the snowman to the left, but it pushes the rest of the layout to the right.

Fix this by adding yet another `Spacer` after the outer `VStack`'s `padding` modifier:

```
}     // end of VStack
.padding()

Spacer()     // NEW
```

Run the app again and check out large and small windows:

Large window

Great work! You've laid out the interface, made sure it works with various window sizes and used a lot of different SwiftUI view types.

Tidying Your Code

You've finished the layout work for your `GameView`, but **GameView.swift** has become long and complicated. Now is a good time to separate out some of this code into subviews.

The first candidate is the `HStack` that displays the letters in their boxes.

Start by selecting **GameView.swift** in the Project navigator and then press **Command-N** to bring up the new file template dialog. Having **GameView.swift** selected means that the new file appears in the **Views** folder. Choose **macOS → SwiftUI View**, click **Next** and name your file **LettersView.swift**.

Go back to **GameView.swift** and find the `HStack` with the `ForEach` inside.

Before the `HStack`, add:

```
LettersView()
```

This tell `GameView` to use your new `LettersView` here.

Select the entire `HStack` block and press **Command-X** to cut it. Over in **LettersView.swift**, delete the `Text` placeholder and press **Command-V** to paste your `HStack` into `body`.

This gives an error because it can't find the `word` property, so cut that property out of `GameView` and paste it into `LettersView`.

Using the same technique, make another new **SwiftUI View** file called **GuessesView.swift**.

In **GameView.swift**, find the second `VStack` and insert this line above it:

```
GuessesView()
```

Cut the `VStack` and paste it to replace the `Text` in **GuessesView.swift**. Move the `guesses` property too, so `GuessesView` looks like:

```
struct GuessesView: View {
  let guesses = ["E", "S", "R", "X"]

  var body: some View {
    VStack {
      HStack {
        Text("Letters used:")
        Text(guesses.joined(separator: ", "))
```

```
        }

        LabeledContent("Guess a letter:") {
          Text("Q")
        }
      }
    }
  }
```

Build and run once more to check that everything looks the same as before. You haven't changed any code, only moved it around, so there are no visible differences. But, you've organized your project in a neater and more maintainable way.

Key Points

- SwiftUI is a framework that allows you to layout your user interface programmatically. You tell SwiftUI what you want and it decides how to do it.
- You build your interface by assembling components and grouping them into stacks.
- Modifiers change the views and you can chain multiple modifiers together.

Where to Go From Here?

Your game view interface is complete. In the next chapter, you'll start making it live with real data instead of placeholders.

For more details on SwiftUI, check out SwiftUI Apprentice (https://www.kodeco.com/books/swiftui-apprentice). It's written for iOS but the fundamentals of SwiftUI are the same on any Apple platform.

Chapter 6: Getting Data Into Your App

By Sarah Reichelt

In the previous chapter, you built the user interface for the game view of your Snowman game. The displayed data was hard-coded into the app and users couldn't do anything to change it.

Now, you'll learn how to create data types for use by SwiftUI. You'll see how SwiftUI passes data around the app, and how it keeps the data and the user interface in sync.

You'll also encounter property wrappers, which are a way of giving properties superpowers. SwiftUI uses these extensively.

Designing the Data Model

Start by opening your project from the last chapter, or use the **starter** project from the downloaded materials for this chapter.

Run the app to remind yourself of the layout and what data it needs:

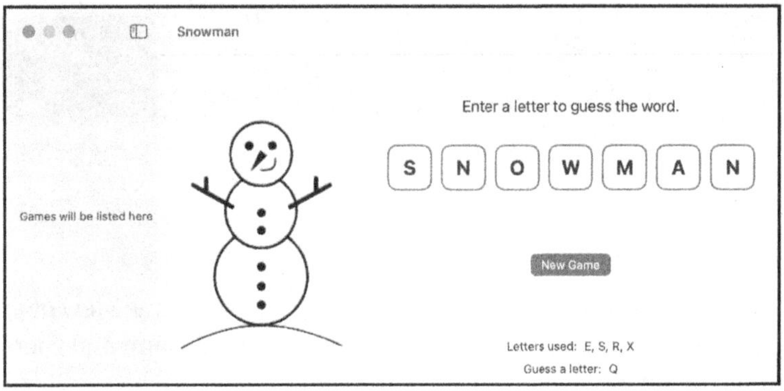

The starter project

Looking at the game view, here's what the app needs to know:

- How many incorrect guesses the player has made.
- What text to show in the status area.
- The secret word.
- The player's guesses.
- Whether the player has won, lost or the game is still in progress.

You'll add all this to a new structure called `Game`.

In the Project navigator, right-click on **SnowmanApp.swift** and choose **New Empty File**. Rename the new **Untitled.swift** file to **Game.swift**.

Start by adding this structure to the new file:

```
// 1
struct Game {
  // 2
  var incorrectGuessCount = 0
  var statusText = "Enter a letter to start the game."
  var word = "SNOWMAN"
  var guesses: [String] = []
}
```

This is similar to code you wrote in Section 1:

1. You define a structure with the keyword `struct` followed by its name.
2. Inside the structure, you declare properties to cover most of the required data. These are all initialized to default starting values.

This doesn't cover the state of the game. Since there are three possible states, this is a great place to use an enumeration.

Adding an Enumeration

Right-click on **Game.swift** to create another empty file and call it **GameStatus.swift**.

Insert this code into the new file:

```
// 1
enum GameStatus {
  // 2
  case won
  case lost
  case inProgress
}
```

To create an enumeration, you:

1. Start with the `enum` keyword and then give it a name.
2. Add each of the possibilities as a `case`.

You may think that having a separate file for these few lines is a bit wasteful, but you'll add to this enumeration later. Also, having each structure, class or enumeration in its own file makes it easier to find them in your project.

You've already arranged your views into a folder in the Project navigator. Now you'll do the same with your models. **Model** is the term for a class or structure that defines a data type.

Select **Game.swift** and **GameStatus.swift** in the navigator. Right-click and choose **New Folder from Selection**. Set the name of the new folder to **Models**.

Now you can go back to **Game.swift** and insert the last property:

```
var gameStatus = GameStatus.inProgress
```

This adds a property with a type of `GameStatus` and sets it to `inProgress` by default.

So far, these properties are static — you don't have any code in place that could change them. But you can still use them in the interface.

Open **GameView.swift** and at the top of `GameView`, right before `body`, add this:

```
@State var game = Game()
```

This looks different! You added a property initialized with an instance of `Game`, but what does `@State` mean?

Property Wrappers

When you see a property definition preceded by a word starting with `@`, you know that this is a **property wrapper**. Property wrappers are ways of enhancing properties to give them extra functionality.

It's possible to write your own property wrappers, but in this book you'll use built-in property wrappers designed to work with SwiftUI.

Remember back when you learned about structures, and you found that their methods can't edit their properties by default? Well here, you have a view structure, but you need to be able to edit its data.

The `@State` property wrapper pulls the property out of the usual structure limitations, stores it in a protected part of memory, so that it persists even when SwiftUI recreates the containing view, and makes it mutable. Pretty cool for a single extra word!

Using the Data Model

Now you have your `game` property, you can start replacing the static elements in your UI with real data.

First, look at the `Image`. It uses a `String` containing the number of incorrect guesses to specify the image name.

Replace the `Image` line with this:

```
Image("\(game.incorrectGuessCount)")
```

This uses string interpolation to convert the integer property into a `String`. Press **Option-Command-P** to restart the preview and, since this uses the value you set in `game`, your snowman gets his hat back.

Click the pin at the top left of the preview. This sticks the preview in place when you open another file in the editor. Open **Game.swift** and test different values of `incorrectGuessCount`.

This is the beauty of SwiftUI — once you connect data to a view, SwiftUI updates the view whenever you change the data.

When you've finished testing, set `incorrectGuessCount` back to `0` and return to **GameView.swift**.

The next property is the one that shows the status text. Scroll down to find `Text("Enter a letter to guess the word.")` and replace it with:

```
Text(game.statusText)
```

You don't need to use string interpolation here because `statusText` is a `String` already.

The preview updates to show the text from `game`:

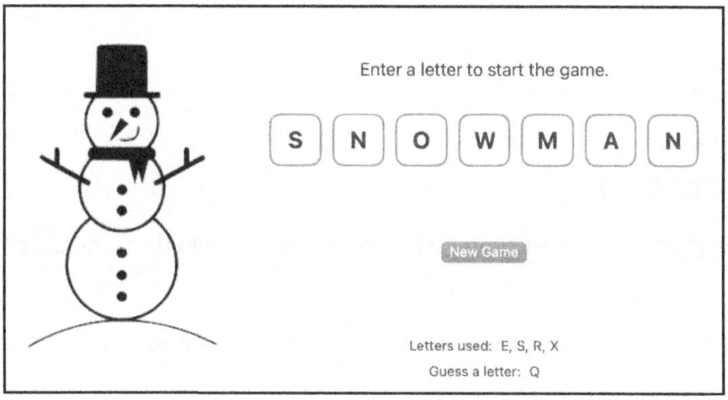

Updated preview

The next property is `word`, and here's where things get a bit more complicated.

Identifying the Letters

You use a `ForEach` loop to display the letters, and this requires that each element in the loop have an identifier. As a temporary measure, you used the letter itself as its identifier.

When you ran the app, you may have noticed warnings in the console about using the same ID multiple times within the collection. This is because the sample word contains **N** twice, so repeats the same ID.

Since it's very common to find repeated letters in a word, you need to solve this. The solution is to make a new `Letter` structure that holds the letter and a unique identifier for each letter. The `Identifiable` protocol requires conforming types to have an `id` property. If you use an `Identifiable` type in a loop, SwiftUI takes the `id` property as its identifier automatically.

And as a bonus, you can use this structure to hold the color for the box around each letter.

Select **GameStatus.swift** to make sure you're in the **Models** folder in the Project navigator. Make a new empty file called **Letter.swift**.

Set the contents of your new file to:

```
// 1
import SwiftUI

// 2
struct Letter: Identifiable {
  // 3
  let id: Int
  // 4
  let char: String
  var color = Color.blue
}
```

What does this give you?

1. One of the properties is of type `Color`, so import `SwiftUI` to be able to use this type.
2. Set up the `Letter` structure and mark it as conforming to the `Identifiable` protocol.
3. Give the structure an `id` property. This is usually a number, a string, or a UUID. In this case, an `Int` is good.
4. Add the other properties to hold the actual character and its color. The `color` property is a variable with a default value.

Now, you need to generate the list of letters for your word.

Open **Game.swift** and add this computed property to the structure:

```
// 1
var letters: [Letter] {
  // 2
  var lettersArray: [Letter] = []
```

```
    // 3
    for (index, char) in word.enumerated() {
      // 4
      let charString = String(char)
      // 5
      if guesses.contains(charString) {
        let letter = Letter(id: index, char: charString)
        lettersArray.append(letter)
      } else if gameStatus == .lost {
        // 6
        let letter = Letter(id: index, char: charString,
  color: .red)
        lettersArray.append(letter)
      } else {
        // 7
        let letter = Letter(id: index, char: "")
        lettersArray.append(letter)
      }
    }
    // 8
    return lettersArray
  }
```

There's a lot to unpack here:

1. This defines a computed property called `letters`, and it's an array of `Letter` instances.
2. Start by creating an empty array.
3. Loop through the characters in `word`, but you want a counter to use as the identifier. `enumerated()` gives two values each time it loops: the position of the element in the array and the value of the element.
4. You're looping over a single `String`, not an array of `Strings`. Each time through, `char` holds the next letter, but its type is `String.Element`. Since `Letter` uses `String`, you must perform the type conversion.
5. If the user has guessed this letter, create an instance of `Letter` with the index and character and add to the the array. Use the default color.
6. If the player lost the game, set the color to show the unguessed letter in a red box. You specify `color` in this initializer because it's not the default blue.
7. If neither of these are true, make an empty blue box.
8. Return the new array.

The line that specifies the color is now showing an error because `Color` is part of SwiftUI. Fix this by adding `import SwiftUI` at the top of this file.

Displaying the Letters

In the previous chapter, you separated `LettersView` into its own file. Open **LettersView.swift** and unpin the `GameView` preview, so that you're seeing the preview for this file only.

Replace the `word` definition at the top with:

```
let letters: [Letter]
```

This tells the view that its property is an array of `Letters`, but it causes some errors. To fix the first one, replace the `ForEach` line with:

```
ForEach(letters) { letter in
```

Notice you no longer need the `id` argument because `letters` is `Identifiable`.

Following the trail of errors, replace the `Text` line with:

```
Text(letter.char)
```

Before, `letter` was a `String`. Now, it's type `Letter`. As a result, you can't use it directly in a `Text` view, but it has a `char` property that you can.

The only error left is in `#Preview`. There's no default value for `letters`, so the preview doesn't know what to display.

Replace `LettersView()` with:

```
LettersView(letters: Game().letters)
```

You're creating a new instance of `Game` and getting its default `letters` property for the preview.

All the errors have disappeared, so why is the preview still not working? There's now an error in `GameView` and any error stops all previews.

Open **GameView.swift** and scroll to the line with the error. Change it to:

```
LettersView(letters: game.letters)
```

This passes `letters` from `game`, through to `LettersView`. There's no need to send the whole `game`, only the part that `LettersView` needs.

Jump back to **LettersView.swift** and now, the preview is working, but since it thinks this is the start of a game, it only shows a row of empty blue boxes.

Pin the `LettersView` preview and open **Game.swift**. Edit `guesses` to hold some of the letters in **SNOWMAN** and save the file:

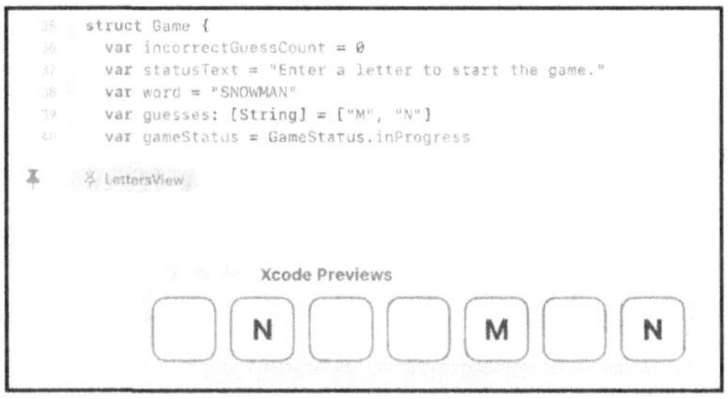

Previewing some letters.

> **Note**: To see the preview below the code like this, select **Editor → Layout → Canvas on Bottom**.

Next, change `gameStatus` to `GameStatus.lost` and save again. The preview updates to show all the letters, but none of them are in red boxes.

Back in **LettersView.swift**, find where you set the `foregroundStyle` for the `RoundedRectangle`. Replace that line with:

```
.foregroundStyle(letter.color)
```

Now, it uses the color set for each `Letter`, and the preview looks correct:

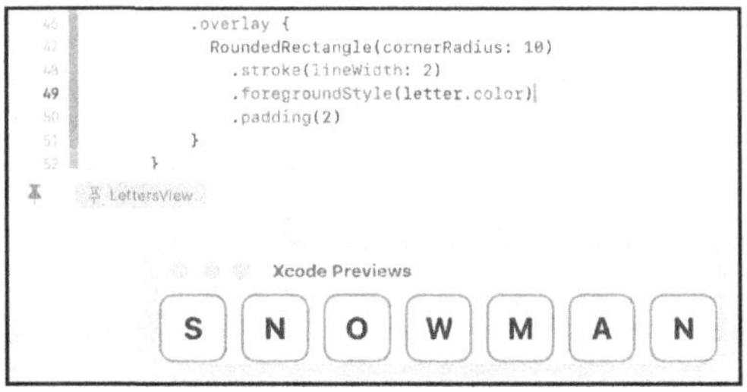

Previewing a lost game.

Pat yourself on the back. That was a complicated bit of code, layout and data flow.

Experiment with other settings until you're sure you know what's happening, and then reset the Game properties to:

```
var guesses: [String] = []
var gameStatus = GameStatus.inProgress
```

Styling the Button

Working down through GameView, the next item is the **New Game** button. It should only appear when the game is over.

An if can show the button conditionally. Don't add this code, but take a look:

```
// 1
if game.gameStatus != .inProgress {
  // 2
  Button("New Game") {
    print("Starting new game.")
  }
  .keyboardShortcut(.defaultAction)
}
```

You haven't used if in layout code before:

1. First, you check if gameStatus is **NOT** inProgress.
2. If this is true, draw the Button.

This works but it's ugly. SwiftUI moves subviews around to fit, so hiding the Button like this means that everything else jumps up or down. A better technique is to display the button but set its opacity to zero, so that it's in position, taking up its usual space, but invisible.

Open **GameView.swift**, find the `Button` code and add this line after the `keyboardShortcut`:

```
.opacity(game.gameStatus == .inProgress ? 0 : 1)
```

This uses an operator called the **ternary operator**. Most operators are binary: They work with two parts like `4 + 19` or `63 / 7`. There are a few unary operators like `!` or `-`. Note that `-` can be binary for subtraction or unary to negate a number.

The ternary operator has three parts: a conditional, an if-true value and and an if-false value. Here's an example:

```
mood = isRaining ? "sad" : "happy"
```

This sets a variable called `mood` to "sad" if `isRaining` is true and "happy" if `isRaining` is false.

The syntax is: `conditional ? if true : if false`

One way to remember is by calling it the **WTF** operator: What ? True : False.

Effectively, this is a one line version of `if...else`, and it's commonly used in SwiftUI when making decisions inside modifiers.

Getting back to the button, if the game is in progress, the button's opacity is set to `0`, so it disappears. If the game is over, the opacity is `1` and the button becomes visible.

There's one more wrinkle to this. The button is there on the screen even though you can't see it. This means that it can still detect the Return key. You have to disable it. Guess what? There's another modifier for that.

Searching for Modifiers

When working in SwiftUI, you'll often think that there must be a modifier for some situation, but you don't know what it's called. Use Xcode's Library to help you find it.

Place the cursor in your code where the new modifier will go: Open a new line under the `opacity` line and make sure the preview is open — press **Option-Command-Return** if it isn't.

Next, choose **View → Show Library** from the menubar, or press **Shift-Command-L** to open the Library:

The tabs allow you to search for views, modifiers, code snippets, images, colors or symbols. Click the one with the sliders icon to choose modifiers and then start typing **disable**.

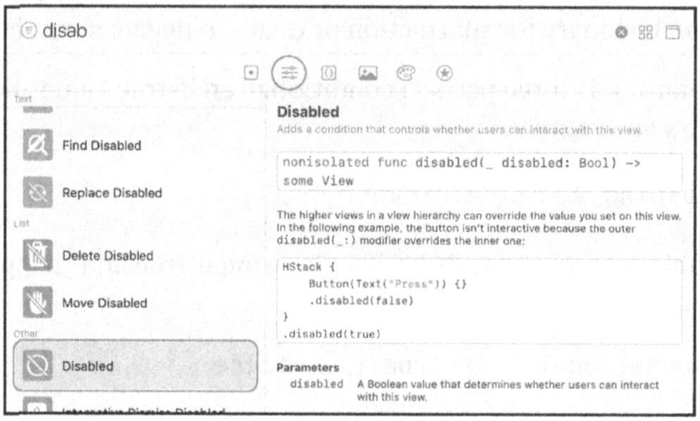

Using the Xcode library.

The one you want is **Other → Disabled**: Read its help, and then drag or double-click it to insert it into your code:

```
.disabled(true)
```

It appears with the placeholder Boolean value `true`. Replace this conditional so the line reads:

```
.disabled(game.gameStatus == .inProgress)
```

If the game is in progress, `disabled` is true, and the keyboard shortcut won't work.

> **Note**: Sometimes, you'll run a SwiftUI app and nothing appears. The app hangs before it draws any windows but there's no error message or crash report. If this happens to you, make sure you haven't forgotten the period before a modifier. Xcode doesn't flag this as an error, but your app won't work.

The Guesses View

The remaining section of the UI to connect is `GuessesView`. The first part you'll add is the text entry field where players enter their guesses.

Open **GuessesView.swift** and add this property at the top of the structure:

```
@State var nextGuess = ""
```

Since `GuessesView` is a structure, use the `@State` property wrapper to make this property mutable and persistent.

Next, find `Text("Q")` and replace it with:

```
TextField("", text: $nextGuess)
```

This uses another SwiftUI view called `TextField`, which is an editable text entry field. The first argument is a placeholder that appears in gray inside the field when it's empty. You don't want one for this app, so set it to an empty string.

The second argument is the interesting one: You've used the new property but why does it have a dollar sign before it?

The dollar sign indicates that this is a **Binding**. So far, your data has all flowed one way. You change `incorrectGuessCount` and the snowman image changes, but the image never edits `incorrectGuessCount`. With `TextField`, the data has to go both ways: Typing into the field changes `nextGuess` and changing `nextGuess` shows new text in the field.

In SwiftUI, this is a Binding, and you pass a property as a binding by adding a $ prefix.

Unpin the `LettersView` preview and refresh `GuessesView`. The field is too wide considering it's only going to take one letter at a time.

Add these modifiers to `TextField`:

```
// 1
.frame(width: 50)
// 2
.textFieldStyle(.roundedBorder)
// 3
.disabled(game.gameStatus != .inProgress)
```

Here's what these three lines do:

1. The `frame` modifier sets the text field to a fixed width.
2. The `textFieldStyle` modifier chooses a style for the field. A lot of SwiftUI views have a `...Style` modifier with preset options and this can save you a lot of time and effort.
3. You don't want players typing in letters if the game is over, so disable it as needed.

The last modifier gives an error because `GuessesView` doesn't have a `game` property yet, but you're about to fix that.

Sending the Game Data

This view needs data from the game, but it also has to edit the game when the player makes a guess.

You learned about bindings for the text field, and now you'll use bindings to send the game data to `GuessesView`.

In **GuessesView.swift**, add this property at the top of the structure:

```
@Binding var game: Game
```

This says that the view receives data in the form of a binding that it can use and edit.

As you'd expect, this gives a missing argument error in the preview, so in the `#Preview`, replace `GuessesView()` with:

```
@Previewable @State var game = Game()
GuessesView(game: $game)
```

Setting a binding argument for a preview takes an extra step as you first create a `Game` and then mark it as `@Previewable` so that the preview can show it as a dynamic property.

Now there's an error in `GameView`, so open **GameView.swift** and scroll to the line with the error.

Replace that line with:

```
GuessesView(game: $game)
```

This passes `game` into `GuessesView` as a binding so that `GuessesView` can edit it as well as display it.

With that in place, jump back to **GuessesView.swift** to add the last piece of game data.

Replace the line displaying the guesses with:

```
Text(game.guesses.joined(separator: ", "))
```

This uses the same `joined` syntax but it's getting the letters from `game` instead of from its static property. Now, you can delete the `guesses` property at the top.

Click the **Play** button or press **Command-R** to run the app:

Running with live data.

Great work. You've switched your UI from using static data to using data from a `Game` model.

Playing the Game

It all looks good, so now it's time to start playing the game. The first step is to process what the player types in the text field.

Open **Game.swift** and add this method:

```
// 1
mutating func processGuess(letter: String) {
  // 2
  guard
    // 3
    let newGuess = letter.first?.uppercased(),
    // 4
    newGuess >= "A" && newGuess <= "Z",
```

```
    // 5
    !guesses.contains(newGuess)
  else {
    return
  }

  // 6
  if !word.contains(newGuess) && incorrectGuessCount < 7 {
    incorrectGuessCount += 1
  }
  guesses.append(newGuess)

  // 7
  // checkForGameOver()
}
```

Taking this bit by bit:

1. Create a method called `processGuess(letter:)` that takes a `String` argument. It can change the structure's properties, so make it `mutating`.
2. Use `guard` to check three different things:
3. Does the string passed to the function have a first letter? If so, convert it to uppercase. This uses **optional chaining**. `first` looks for the string's first character and returns an optional. You can't uppercase `nil`, but the `?` only chains on the `uppercased` method if `first` works. Now, either `newGuess` is a non-optional string or `guard` immediately returns.
4. Is `newGuess` a letter between **A** and **Z**? If not, the guard fails and returns.
5. Has the player already guessed this letter? You don't want to process the same letter twice.
6. If you made it to here, you have a valid letter. If it's not in the word, increment `incorrectGuessCount` up to its maximum. Either way, append the new letter to `guesses`.
7. In a minute, you'll write a method to check if the game is over.

Now to use this method, open **GuessesView.swift**.

Add this modifier to `TextField`:

```
// 1
.onChange(of: nextGuess) { _, newValue in
  // 2
  game.processGuess(letter: newValue)
  // 3
```

```
    nextGuess = ""
  }
```

This is a more complicated modifier:

1. An onChange modifier tracks changes to a property, in this case nextGuess. The code in curly braces executes whenever nextGuess changes, and newValue contains the changed data. This modifier's action receives two arguments — the original value and the new value. You're only interested in the new one, so use an underscore as a placeholder for the old value.

2. Call game's processGuess(letter:) sending the newly typed letter.

3. Set nextGuess back to an empty string to clear the text field.

The game won't ever end, but you can run it now and type some guesses:

Entering guesses

The correct letters appear in the blue boxes, the snowman starts disappearing and the guesses appear at the bottom. It's working!

Ending the Game

The last step is to work out whether the player has won or lost the game.

Open **Game.swift** and add this method:

```
// 1
mutating func checkForGameOver() {
  // 2
  let unmatchedLetters = word.filter { letter in
    !guesses.contains(String(letter))
```

```
    }

    // 3
    if unmatchedLetters.isEmpty {
      gameStatus = .won
      statusText = "HURRAY!!!! YOU WON!"
    } else if incorrectGuessCount == 7 {
      // 4
      gameStatus = .lost
      statusText = "You lost. Better luck next time."
    } else {
      // 5
      statusText = "Enter another letter to guess the word."
    }
  }
```

There are some new features here:

1. Declare a mutating method that has no arguments.
2. Use `filter` to create an array of the letters in `word` that the player has *not* guessed. `filter` loops through the letters, returning the ones that match the condition in the curly braces. Each time through the loop, `letter` holds the next character in the word, passing it in to the conditional.
3. If there are no unmatched letters, the player has won. Set the status and change the status text.
4. If the player has made too many incorrect guesses, the game is lost. Set the status and text to match.
5. If the game is still in progress, change the starting status text.

Uncomment the call to `checkForGameOver` in `processGuess(letter:)` and run the game:

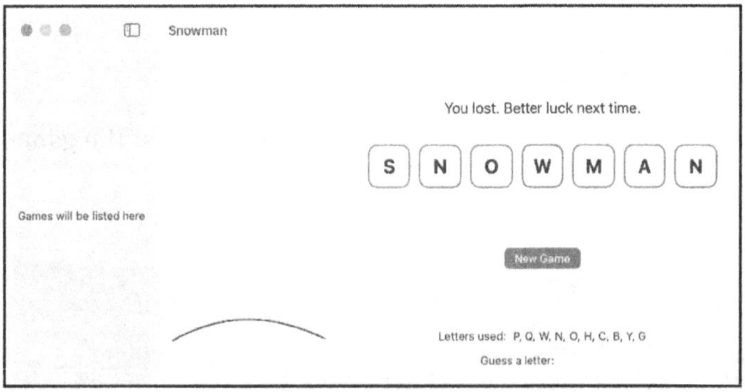

Losing a game.

Knowing that the word is always **SNOWMAN**, test out a winning game. The **New Game** button appears at the correct time, but doesn't do anything yet. To play again, close the window and press **Command-N** to open a new one. This time, try losing the game.

The game works well, but it's a bit boring because there's only one word. And the **New Game** button doesn't work.

Starting a New Game

You'll start with choosing a random word. In the **assets** folder downloaded for this chapter, there's a file called **words.txt** that lists over 30,000 words. Drag this file from assets into the **Models** group in the Project navigator.

Make sure the options look like this, and then click **Finish**:

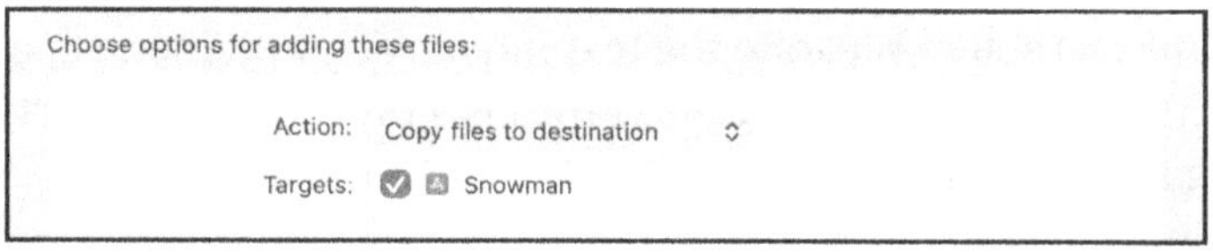

Adding the words file.

A macOS app is actually a folder, which you can prove by **right-clicking** any app and selecting **Show Package Contents**. This file addition tells Xcode to put your **words.txt** file into your application's folder — or **bundle** — whenever it builds.

To use your new file, open **Game.swift** and add this method:

```
// 1
func getRandomWord() -> String {
  // 2
  guard
    // 3
    let url = Bundle.main.url(forResource: "words",
withExtension: "txt"),
    // 4
    let wordsList = try? String(contentsOf: url,
encoding: .utf8)
  else {
    // 5
    return "SNOWMAN"
  }

  // 6
  let words = wordsList.components(separatedBy: .newlines)
```

```
    // 7
    let word = words.randomElement() ?? "SNOWMAN"

    // 8
    print(word)
    return word.uppercased()
  }
```

Another interesting method:

1. This method returns a `String` — the random word.
2. Again, use `guard` to make multiple checks.
3. First, see if **words.txt** exists inside the app bundle.
4. Next, try to read the file into a `String`.
5. If either of these fail, return the default word.
6. Use a `String` method to separate the text into an array of lines. `separatedBy` can take a `String` or a `CharacterSet`. `newlines` is a predefined `CharacterSet` containing all the possible new line characters. This is useful because you don't have to know what operating system created the file and what sort of line feeds it uses.
7. See if you can get a random word out of the array and use the default word if not. This uses the **nil coalescing** operator, which allows you to assign a default value to something that would normally return an optional. If the part before the `??` is `nil`, it uses the part after the `??`.
8. Print the word to help during debugging. Then, convert it to uppercase and return it.

This gets a word from the file, but `Game` isn't using it yet.

To fix this, add an `init` to `Game`:

```
  init() {
    word = getRandomWord()
  }
```

Every time a new game starts, this calls `getRandomWord()`.

Now, you'll make the **New Game** button work. Open **GameView.swift** and replace the `print` in the button's action with:

```
game = Game()
```

And that's it! Your game works, you can start new games, and you get a random word each time.

Run the app and test it.

Winning a game

You can see the random word in the Xcode console, so make sure you test winning and losing. Does the UI do everything you expect? Fantastic work!

Tweaking the App

Playing the game, there are a few improvements to make.

It's inconvenient that when you start a new game, the text field isn't active, so you have to click in it or press Tab. If your first thought was to use another modifier, you're really starting to think like a SwiftUI programmer. :]

There's a `focused` modifier that uses another property wrapper. Open **GuessesView.swift** and insert this property at the top of the structure:

```
@FocusState var entryFieldHasFocus: Bool
```

This is a property with a wrapper that you link to a field. It updates when the field gets or loses focus, and can be set to change the focus.

To apply it, add this modifier to `TextField`:

```
.focused($entryFieldHasFocus)
```

This binds the new property to the focus state of the field. Setting it to `true` places the cursor in the text field. You can use another `onChange` modifier to track `gameStatus` for when to set it.

Time for YAM (yet another modifier) for `TextField`:

```
.onChange(of: game.gameStatus) {
  entryFieldHasFocus = true
}
```

This tracks changes to `gameStatus`. It doesn't care what the status changes to, but it sets the focus on every change. This time, you don't care what the new value is, only that it changed, so you're using a version of the modifier with no arguments.

Run the app, play a game and then click **New Game** or press **Return**. The cursor is in the text field ready for your input:

Setting focus

The other main issue is with the length of the words. Too few letters, and it's almost impossible to guess; too many, and the window isn't wide enough. Also, if the window is narrow, a longer word resizes it.

Start by making the window wider by default. In **ContentView.swift**, add this `frame` modifier to the `NavigationSplitView`:

```
.frame(minWidth: 1100)
```

You saw earlier how to set a frame with a fixed width for the image. This is similar but sets the smallest allowed width for the window.

Now to set some letter count limits. Open **Game.swift** and find `getRandomWord()`:

Locate this line:

```
let words = wordsList.components(separatedBy: .newlines)
```

And replace it with:

```
// 1
let words = wordsList
  .components(separatedBy: .newlines)
  // 2
  .filter { word in
    // 3
    word.count >= 4 && word.count <= 10
  }
```

What does this do?

1. The first chunk is the same as before, but spread over two lines.
2. Next, you use `filter` to loop over the words. Each time through the loop, the `word` variable contains the next word.
3. Only return a word from the loop if it has between four and ten letters.

Run the app again and check that you don't get any words outside these limits:

Tweaked GameView

And if you get a ten letter word, it still fits across the window. With these changes, your app has become a lot more usable.

Key Points

- SwiftUI uses property wrappers to assign behaviors to properties of its views.
- `@State` allows a structure to have persistent, mutable properties.
- `@Binding` sends data to a view and allows that view to send any changes back.
- You can include data files in your Swift apps and read them from the app bundle.

Where to Go From Here?

Your game now works perfectly, but the sidebar is still showing the placeholder text. In the next chapter, you'll create a new model to hold app-wide properties, including an array of games for listing in and selecting from the sidebar.

Chapter 7: Data Flow in SwiftUI

By Sarah Reichelt

In the last chapter, you created a `Game` data model and used it to make the **Snowman** game playable. You imported a data file for generating random words, and you connected the data to all the components of the game view.

In this chapter, you'll extend your data to include the entire app. This uses a new data object that holds a list of games as well as other data your app needs.

You'll learn how do set up data classes and their properties and how to pass this data around to the views.

This involves several more property wrappers, so hover your finger over the @ key and get ready.

Creating an App Model

Start Xcode and open your project from the previous chapter, or use the **starter** project from the downloaded materials for this chapter. Press **Command-R** to run the app to remind yourself of where you ended:

The starter app

The game view is complete, the game is playable and the `Game` model is functional. The sidebar still only displays placeholder text, so that's what you'll add next.

You'll create a new model class to hold a list of games and the data needed to swap between them.

Select the **Models** folder in the Project navigator and press **Command-N** to make a new file. Choose **macOS → Source → Swift File** and name it **AppState.swift**.

Your previous models have been structures or enumerations, but this one has to be a class. When you learned about classes and structures, you found that classes are reference types and structures are value types. SwiftUI has definite rules about places where you must use reference types, and you're about to encounter one.

Replace the contents of the new file with:

```
// 1
import SwiftUI

// 2
@Observable
class AppState {

}
```

What does this do?

1. Start by importing the SwiftUI library. You don't need it yet, but you will. Importing SwiftUI automatically imports Foundation, which is why you can replace the default import.
2. This model is a class called `AppState` and it conforms to `Observable`.

Observable

So what is the `Observable` protocol? A class that conforms to `Observable` is a class that publishes changes to its properties. This is commonly used in SwiftUI to indicate that data has changed and to trigger an update of the views.

Insert this code into the class:

```
// 1
var games: [Game]
// 2
var gameIndex: Int
// 3
var selectedID: Int?

// 4
init() {
  // 5
  let newGame = Game()
  games = [newGame]

  // 6
  gameIndex = 0
  selectedID = 1
}
```

This sets up the new class:

1. Create a property called `games` that holds an array of `Game` objects.
2. Another property holds the index of the current game in the `games` array.
3. The final property is the ID of the game selected in the sidebar. Since it's possible to have no game selected, this is an optional.
4. Use `init()` to assign the starting values for each of the properties.
5. Create a new `Game` and set it as the contents of the `games` array.
6. Set the two index properties.

Identifying the Game

When you defined the `Letter` structure, you made it `Identifiable` so SwiftUI could loop through it using `ForEach` with a way of distinguishing each letter.

Your sidebar has to loop through each entry in the `games` array, so now you'll make `Game` conform to `Identifiable`.

Open **Game.swift** and add the following property:

```
let id: Int
```

This adds the `id` property required by the `Identifiable` protocol.

Next, change the definition line to:

```
struct Game: Identifiable {
```

`init()` shows two errors, but it's really only one. You can't finish initializing a structure before defining all the properties.

To fix this, replace `init()` with:

```
// 1
init(id: Int) {
  // 2
  self.id = id
  // 2
  word = getRandomWord()
}
```

What changes has this made?

1. `init()` now has a single integer argument, called `id`.
2. Set the value of the structure's `id` to the supplied argument.
3. Then, assign the random word as before.

As you can imagine, your app now has some problems because you've already initialized `Game` objects without passing in an argument.

Press **Command-B** to build and then open the Issue navigator to show any errors:

Build errors

Click each error in turn and replace `Game()` with:

```
Game(id: 1)
```

You may not see multiple errors at first — in fact, there are five. Xcode sometimes can't get far enough through the build process to catch everything. Keep pressing **Command-B** and adding the `id` argument until the app builds successfully.

For the previews, a static `id` of 1 is fine. In `AppState`, the first game should have an `id` of 1. You're about to change how `GameView` gets its data, so it can use 1 temporarily.

Adding a State Property

You defined an `Observable` class, but you haven't used it yet. This class defines app-wide settings, so you'll add it to the app itself.

Open **SnowmanApp.swift**. In a SwiftUI app, this file defines the starting point. It's a SwiftUI structure with a `body`, but this `body` returns a `Scene` instead of a `View`. This `Scene` is a `WindowGroup`, which defines a window that you can open multiple times. The content of `WindowGroup` is the view that fills each window.

When you wrote a command line app in Section 1, **main.swift** was the entry point for the app. In the same way here, `@main` marks this file as the starting point for your SwiftUI app.

Now you know a bit about how SwiftUI defines its app and windows, add this property to SnowmanApp, before body:

```
@State var appState = AppState()
```

This creates an instance of AppState and marks it with the @State property wrapper. When you're initializing an Observable class, you use @State to indicate that this structure **owns** the observable object.

Environment Objects

Now that your app has its appState, you can pass it around to the other views. There are two ways to do this, and you'll learn both. The first one uses @Environment.

In **SnowmanApp.swift**, add this modifier to ContentView:

```
.environment(appState)
```

Now ContentView, and all of its subviews, can access appState. To start using it, open **GameView.swift**.

Replace the @State var game line with:

```
// 1
@Environment(AppState.self) var appState

// 2
var game: Game {
  appState.games[appState.gameIndex]
}
```

This has changed a few things:

1. GameView accesses the appState object from the environment by specifying its type with AppState.self. You only explicitly passed it to ContentView, but the environment is available to any subview. An @Environment property receives notifications of any changes to its object.
2. Getting the current game is a bit wordy, so this computed property makes it easier. And as a bonus, it uses the same property name you had before so almost everything works.

Scrolling down the page, there's an error with the binding argument for `GuessesView`. Here's where things get tricky, because you can't use an `@Environment` property as a binding. The solution is to add this line immediately after the body line:

```
@Bindable var appStateBindable = appState
```

This creates a `Bindable` copy of `appState` that you can now pass to `GuessesView` by replacing the error line with this:

```
GuessesView(game: $appStateBindable.games[appState.gameIndex])
```

This uses the long form access, the same as the computed property, but this is necessary for a binding.

Now the **New Game** button gives an error. You haven't written a new game method for `AppState` yet, so **comment out this line**.

And finally, for the preview to work, it requires an `environment` modifier, so add this to `GameView()` in `#Preview`:

```
.environment(AppState())
```

This creates a new `AppState` instance and inserts it into the environment for the preview.

Build and run the game to make sure it works:

Running the game with the Environment object.

The **New Game** button doesn't work yet, but you can play one game. Earlier, you triggered a new game by opening a new window. Try that now by pressing **Command-N** or choosing **File → New Window**. This time, you get the same game back again. This is because you created the `AppState` object at the app level, so its data applies to all windows.

Close the second window before quitting the app.

If you'd created the `@State` property in `ContentView`, each window would have its own data. For an app that needs to show different information in each window, that would be a good plan, but for this app, a single window is sufficient. You'll see later how to stop it creating multiple windows.

Starting a New Game

Next, you need to give `AppState` a way to create a new game.

Open **AppState.swift** and add this method:

```
// 1
func startNewGame() {
  // 2
  let newGame = Game(id: games.count + 1)
  // 3
  games.append(newGame)

  // 4
  selectedID = newGame.id
  gameIndex = games.count - 1
}
```

This code does the following:

1. Adds a method called `startNewGame()` to `AppState`.
2. Creates a new game with an `id` one higher than the number of games. For the second game, there's only one previous entry in `games`, so the new `id` is 2.
3. Appends the new game to the `games` array.
4. Sets the `selectedID` and the `gameIndex`. `GameView` uses `gameIndex` to access the active game.

To use this method, open **GameView.swift** and replace the `Button` action with:

```
appState.startNewGame()
```

This calls the method to create a new game. Because changes to the `AppState` properties are published, `appState` announces the changes to the subviews, and the new game data appears.

Run the app, finish one game and then click **New Game** to test:

New game

You've refactored the data and the game works as it did before, but now you're in a position to show some data in the sidebar.

Populating the Sidebar

Finally, you're ready to start work on the sidebar, so open **SidebarView.swift**. As with `GameView`, you need to give the preview access to an `@Environment` object so it can use its data.

Inside `#Preview`, add this modifier to `SidebarView`:

```
.environment(AppState())
```

Next, replace the entire contents of `SidebarView` with:

```
// 1
@Environment(AppState.self) var appState

// 2
var body: some View {
  // 3
```

```
    List(appState.games) { game in
      // 4
      VStack(alignment: .leading) {
        // 5
        Text("Game \(game.id)")
          .font(.title3)
        Text(game.word)
      }
      // 6
      .padding(.vertical)
    }
  }
```

Stepping through this:

1. As with `GameView`, `SideBarView` gets access to `appState` using `@Environment`.
2. The `body` defines the view.
3. Before, you used `ForEach` to loop through subviews. This time, you're using `List`, which lets you select rows. The argument to `List` is the `games` array and, each time through the loop, `game` holds the current element.
4. Each row in the list displays several pieces of game data, wrapped in a `VStack`. By default, a `VStack` aligns the data centrally, but this `alignment` argument sets it to align to the leading side, which is the left for left-to-right languages.
5. The `VStack` holds two text views: The first one shows the game and its number. The second one shows its word, which makes the game a bit too easy but is good for testing.
6. You've used `padding` before, but padding has several optional arguments. This one tells it to pad the top and bottom, but not the sides.

Run the app now and play a few games. For the first time, you can see data in the sidebar:

Testing the sidebar.

You're making progress, even though the game is no longer challenging. Now, you'll customize the display of each row.

Getting Data for the Sidebar

Right now, the sidebar shows the game header and the word, but you only want the word to appear if the game is over.

Open **Game.swift** and add this computed property:

```
// 1
var sidebarWord: String {
  // 2
  if gameStatus == .inProgress {
    return "???"
  }
  // 3
  return word
}
```

What does this give you?

1. Game now has a computed String property called sidebarWord.
2. If the game is still in progress, return "???".
3. Because the property has already returned "???" if appropriate, there's no need to add an else here. If the code reaches this point, the game must be over, so it can return word.

To use this in the sidebar, go back to **SidebarView.swift** and replace Text(game.word) with:

```
Text(game.sidebarWord)
```

Run the game again to find it a bit more of a challenge:

Hiding the current word in the sidebar.

The next thing to add is an indication of whether the player won or lost the previous games. Since this information is logically part of GameStatus, you'll add it to that enumeration.

Computing Properties

Open **GameStatus.swift** and start by adding this import at the top:

```
import SwiftUI
```

Next, insert this in the enumeration:

```
// 1
var displayStatus: Text {
  // 2
```

```
    switch self {
    case .inProgress:
      // 3
      return Text("In progress…")
    case .lost:
      // 4
      let img = Image(systemName: "person.fill.turn.down")
      return Text("You lost \(img)")
    case .won:
      // 5
      let img = Image(systemName: "heart.circle")
      return Text("You won! \(img)")
    }
  }
```

Here's another computed property, but what does it do?

1. `displayStatus` returns a `Text` view. That's why you imported SwiftUI for this file.
2. Use `switch` to step through all the possible options for `GameStatus`.
3. If the status is `inProgress`, return a plain `Text` view with appropriate content.
4. If the player has lost the game, return a `Text` view containing an `Image` view. The `Image` view contains a symbol.
5. A winning game uses a different image and text.

These symbols come from **SF Symbols**, a library of scalable images provided by Apple for use in our apps. Download the SF Symbols (https://developer.apple.com/sf-symbols/) app from Apple, or search the Xcode library by pressing **Shift-Command-L** and selecting the **Symbols** tab:

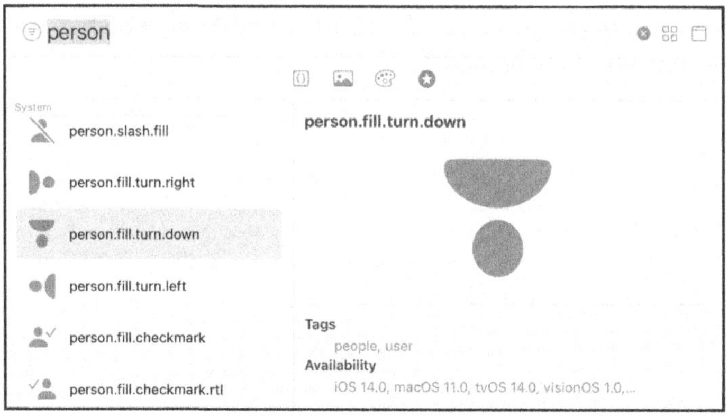

Searching the symbols library.

You can use any named symbol in an `Image` by supplying its name as the `systemName` argument.

Back in **SidebarView.swift**, add this below the other two `Text` views:

```
game.gameStatus.displayStatus
```

Remember, this is already a `Text` view, so you don't need to wrap it in a view.

One final tweak would be to color-code the sidebar entries.

Adding Color

Again, `GameStatus` is the place to do this, so open **GameStatus.swift** and add this:

```
var statusTextColor: Color {
  switch self {
  case .inProgress:
    return .primary
  case .won:
    return .green
  case .lost:
    return .orange
  }
}
```

Another computed property:

1. The property returns a SwiftUI `Color`.
2. Like the previous computed property, step through the possibilities for `GameStatus`.
3. If the game is still in progress, return the `primary` color, which is the default text color for the current display mode.

4. If the player has won, use `Color.green`. This computed property has to return a `Color`, so there's no need to include the `Color` prefix. The shorter version is sufficient.

5. If the player has lost the game, use an orange color. The named SwiftUI colors vary slightly to suit dark and light modes.

To apply this new property, open **SidebarView.swift**.

Add this modifier after the `padding` modifier:

```
.foregroundStyle(game.gameStatus.statusTextColor)
```

This applies the foreground color to every element inside the `VStack`, as you'll see when you run and play the app:

Coloring the sidebar

While you're setting colors, it would look good if the status text used these colors too, so open **GameView.swift**. Find the `Text(game.statusText)` line and give it the same foreground modifier:

```
.foregroundStyle(game.gameStatus.statusTextColor)
```

Whenever you change colors, it's important to confirm that they look good in dark and light modes.

Run the app, then go back to Xcode and click **Environment Overrides** in the button bar under your code. Turn on **Appearance**, and you can swap your app between the two modes without changing the rest of your system:

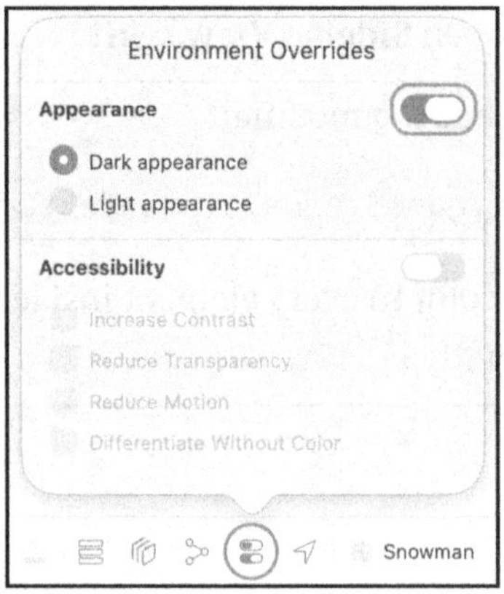

Environment Overrides

The sidebar displays the games and gives useful information, but you can't click a game to reload it.

Making the Sidebar Live

A `List` can have a `selection` parameter. This is an optional value that changes when the user selects or deselects a list item. You already created the optional `selectedID` property in `AppState` for this purpose.

To apply this to the sidebar list, open **SidebarView.swift** and replace the `List` line with:

```
// 1
@Bindable var appStateBindable = appState

// 2
List(appState.games, selection: $appStateBindable.selectedID)
{ game in
```

Here's what these lines do:

1. As you did in `GameView`, create a `Bindable` copy of `appState`.

2. The new part of the `List` initializer is the `selection` argument, which binds the list selection to `selectedID`. This is a two-way binding, so if you set `selectedID`, you select an element in the list and, if you select an element, you set `selectedID`. This property is `nil` if you have no game selected.

Now the sidebar has an active list, so your app can respond to selections and display the chosen game. You've used `onChange` to track changes to properties in SwiftUI views, but `AppState` isn't a view and can't use that modifier. Instead, it uses `didSet`.

Open **AppState.swift** and start by adding this method:

```
func selectGame(id: Int?) {
  // 1
  guard let id else {
    return
  }

  // 2
  let gameLocation = games.firstIndex { game in
    game.id == id
  }
  if let gameLocation {
    gameIndex = gameLocation
  }
}
```

What does this method do?

1. Check to see if the supplied optional `id` is an `Int` and return if it's `nil`.
2. Use an array method to locate the first game in the `games` array with that `id`.
3. If this located a game, use that location to set `gameIndex`. `AppState` publishes the changes to update any views that subscribed to it.

Next, you'll call this method whenever `selectedID` changes. Still in **AppState.swift**, replace the property declaration for `selectedID` with:

```
// 1
var selectedID: Int? {
  // 2
  didSet {
    // 3
    selectGame(id: selectedID)
  }
}
```

What are these changes?

1. Declare the property as before. It's an optional integer, and the class publishes its changes.

2. Add a **property observer** to detect when this changes. In SwiftUI views, you've used `onChange` for this, but that's specifically for view properties. Any Swift property can have a `didSet` property observer.

3. Call the new method with the changed value.

Build and run the app again now. Play a few games so they appear in the sidebar, then click the sidebar entries:

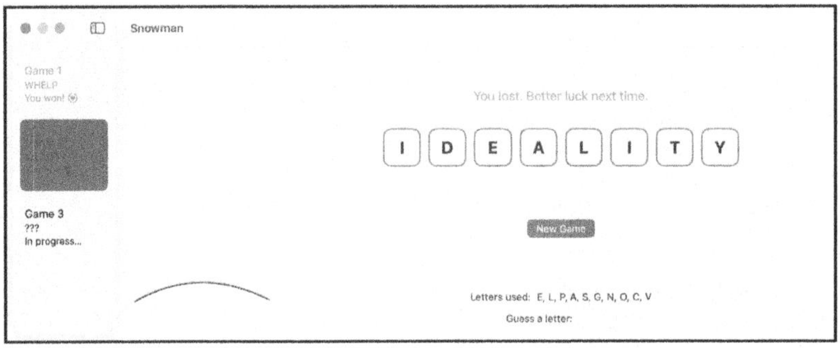

Selecting games from the sidebar.

The only problem here is that the selection background color makes the text hard to read for completed games. These colors used to work but Liquid Glass is messing with us here. To fix this, you'll mix some white in with the game colors.

Open **GameStatus.swift** and replace the `statusTextColor` property with:

```
var statusTextColor: Color {
  switch self {
  case .inProgress:
    return .primary
  case .won:
    return .green.mix(with: .white, by: 0.1)      // CHANGED
  case .lost:
    return .orange.mix(with: .white, by: 0.1)     // CHANGED
  }
}
```

For both the changed colors, you're using the `Color` method `mix(with:by:)` method to blend a small amount of white into the color. This lets you adjust any of the named colors slightly to suit your app, without having to create colors using RGB values. Here, you've lightened it enough to make it readable against the selection background.

Run the app again to check that these colors are readable. Don't forget to test in both dark and light modes:

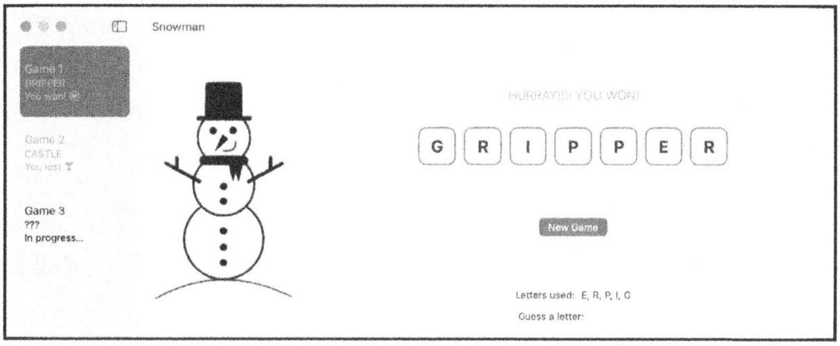

New status colors.

Now the interface for your game is complete, but it's time for some more advanced Swift.

Using Array Methods

You've seen several uses of array methods like `filter` and `firstIndex`. They loop through arrays, but the way they operate can be confusing.

There's no need to add any code from this section into your project, but it's all in a playground in the **assets** folder for this chapter. Run the code and check the results.

Imagine you start with a list of names, and you want a new array of the ones with five letters. This code does the job:

```
// 1
let names = [ "Alice", "Ben", "Celine", "Danny", "Edith" ]

// 2
var fiveLetterNames: [String] = []
// 3
for name in names {
  // 4
  if name.count == 5 {
    fiveLetterNames.append(name)
  }
}
```

What does it do?

1. Start with the list of names.
2. Create a variable to hold the matches.
3. Then, loop through the array, assigning each element to the variable `name` as it loops.
4. Test the element, appending it to the variable array if it matches.

What's wrong with this? It works! Yes, but it gives you a variable instead of a constant, which isn't as safe or memory-efficient.

What about this?

```
// 1
let filteredNames = names.filter { name in
  // 2
  name.count == 5
}
```

You're getting the same result with half the code, but how?

1. Create a constant to hold the matching names. `filter` loops like `for` and again, uses `name` for each element in turn.
2. There's an implicit `return` here that sends back a Boolean. If `true`, `name` becomes part of `filteredNames` and if `false`, it's ignored.

This is neater, but how does it work?

These array methods like `filter` and `firstIndex` take a function as their argument. That's one of the neat things about Swift — functions can be used as arguments. For `filter`, the argument function takes an element of the array and returns a Boolean.

You can use `filter` like this:

```
// 1
func countEqualsFive(string: String) -> Bool {
  string.count == 5
}
// 2
let filteredNames2 = names.filter(countEqualsFive)
```

This separates out the validation function:

1. Write a function that takes a `String` and returns a `Bool`, which is `true` if the string has a count of 5.
2. Use `filter` on the array, but passing this function as the argument.

This does exactly the same thing, but with two separate sections to make it clearer what `filter` does. Writing this yet again:

```
let filteredNames3 = names.filter({ name in
  name.count == 5
})
```

This time, the contents of the function are directly inside the argument parentheses. It uses `in` to pass the internal function its argument. A function embedded inside the arguments like this is a **closure**.

Since this is a common use case, the Swift team devised a cleaner syntax for **trailing closures**. If the closure is the last argument, you can eliminate the parentheses and only use the curly braces. And this gets back to the initial `filter` example, but hopefully you can now see what each of the parts does.

Before leaving this topic, there's one tweak that you'll see used frequently. You don't have to give the closure argument a name, you can use a shorthand version:

```
let filteredNames4 = names.filter {
  $0.count == 5
}
```

This version removes `name in` and uses `$0` to read the first argument. If the function had a second argument, you'd access it using `$1` but, with more than one, it's better to use names for improved readability.

There's a series of methods that operate like this, but if you understand `filter`, you'll understand them all.

Now, return to your project where there's a bug to fix. The text entry field isn't always active when you need it.

Fixing the Focus

To discover the problem, complete one game and start a new one. Next, use the sidebar to get back to your first game and click the **New Game** button. Your sidebar shows two games in progress.

Select one of these, and the text field has focus, but if you select one after another, the focus gets lost. This is because you set focus based on `gameStatus`. When you navigate from a completed game to a game in progress, the status changes. When you select a completed game, it doesn't matter because that disables the field. The problem only occurs when you swap from one active game to another.

When you added the `onChange` modifier, you observed `gameStatus`. But now, every game has a unique `id` which would be a better property to watch.

Open **GuessesView.swift** and look for:

```
.onChange(of: game.gameStatus) {
```

Change that line to:

```
.onChange(of: game.id) {
```

This solves the focus problem even when swapping between incomplete games.

Observing Properties

Earlier in this chapter, you created a `@State` object and used the `environment` modifier to pass it around. But there's another way to use this `@State` object to send data to the subviews.

These changes will cause a lot of errors, but keep going, and the red will disappear. :]

Start in **SnowmanApp.swift** and replace the contents of `WindowGroup` with:

```
ContentView(appState: appState)
```

You've removed the `environment` modifier and added an argument to `ContentView`. Ignoring the error, move to **ContentView.swift**.

Add this new property at the top, before `body`:

```
let appState: AppState
```

This tells `ContentView` that its parent will provide `appState`. Even though `appState` changes all the time, this can be a `let` because the app re-creates `ContentView` for every change.

This makes the error disappear from **SnowManApp.swift** (eventually) but adds a new one to `#Preview` which wants a preview value for `appState`.

Replace `ContentView()` in `#Preview` with:

```
ContentView(appState: AppState())
```

This gives it its own instance of `AppState` for previewing and gets rid of the error, but don't try resuming the preview yet. There's more work to do.

Next is **SidebarView.swift** which has an `appState` property declared using `@Environment`. Change this declaration to:

```
@Bindable var appState: AppState
```

In the `body`, delete the `@Bindable` line and change the `List` line to:

```
List(appState.games, selection: $appState.selectedID) { game in
```

Now that you're not using `@Environment`, you can mark the incoming `appState` as `Bindable` directly and use it for the `List` selection.

And to fix the preview, replace the contents of `#Preview` with:

```
SidebarView(appState: AppState())
```

The last place you used `@Environment` was `GameView.swift`, where you'll do what you did in `SidebarView`.

First, replace the object definition with:

```
@Bindable var appState: AppState
```

Then delete the `@Bindable` from `body` and change the `GuessesView` line to:

```
GuessesView(game: $appState.games[appState.gameIndex])
```

Finally, fix the preview with:

```
GameView(appState: AppState())
```

Press **Command-B** to build and you'll see two remaining errors in the Issue navigator:

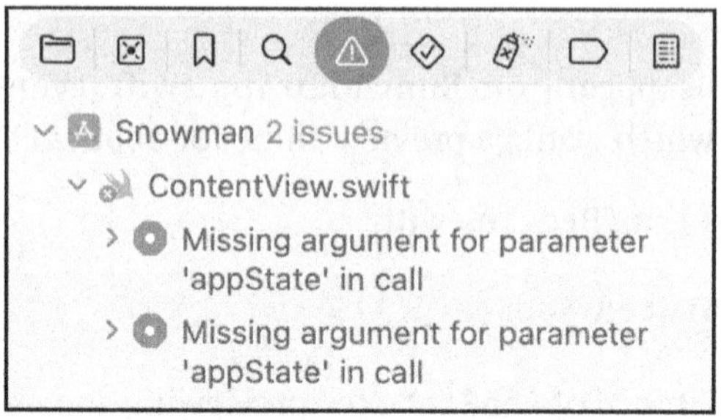

Observed objects build errors

Both of these take you to **ContentView.swift** where you'll add the `appState` arguments. Edit `NavigationSplitView` so it looks like:

```
NavigationSplitView {
  SidebarView(appState: appState)
} detail: {
  GameView(appState: appState)
}
```

Press **Command-B** again to build without errors. So what have these changes done?

In both cases, you started by creating an `@State` property. This is always the same: The view that creates the `Observable` marks it as a `@State`.

The change is in the way you passed the `@State` property down through the views. Originally, you assigned `appState` to `ContentView`'s `environment`. This effectively made it accessible to the entire app. `ContentView` never needed this data directly, but its subviews did. Once it was in the environment of the view hierarchy, they could access it using `@Environment`.

Now, you're using arguments to send the data object to the views directly. One big difference is that there has to be a continuous data trail. You can't skip views that don't need the data. In this case, `ContentView` doesn't need it (yet), but you have to pass it to `ContentView` so that `ContentView` can pass it to `SidebarView` and `GameView`.

Which option is better? This is a big question. Programmers learn that using global variables is a bad idea as it's too easy for unexpected side-effects to occur. `@Environment` feels like a global, so that worries some people. Apple says there are no real performance differences between the two, so it comes down to a matter of personal style.

If you have lots of subviews, some of which need data and some don't, then `@Environment` is easier to maintain. If every view needs the data, then passing the properties directly keeps the data flow more obvious. And as you've seen, working with binding properties is easier without `@Environment`.

You may be wondering about `LettersView` and `GuessesView`, which didn't change during this refactoring. They never had full access to `AppState`. Their parent views passed them the limited data they needed. This is always a good idea. Don't give a subview more data than it needs and it's easier to maintain and more reusable.

You've finished the data flow for your app. This is a big topic, so you should be proud of yourself.

Key Points

- `@Observable` is a protocol for classes that publishes changes to their properties.
- The view that owns the `Observable` declares it using `@State`.
- Subviews can access this object using `@Environment`, `let`, `var` or `@Bindable`.
- Lists can display a selectable array of SwiftUI views.
- Understanding data flow is crucial to working in SwiftUI.

Where to Go From Here?

You've learned a common SwiftUI pattern with a structure for individual data elements and a class to collect them together and pass them round the app.

In the next chapter, you'll learn about more about windows, which are an important part of a Mac app. You'll add a settings window for some user customizations and a secondary window to show a new view.

Chapter 8: Showing Other Windows

By Sarah Reichelt

In the previous two chapters, you set up the data flow for your app. This was a big task and one that can be confusing, so if you feel lost, don't worry about it. Keep going and revisit these chapters at the end of this section if you need to.

Now, you'll move on to dealing with multiple windows. So far, everything has happened in the main window of the app, although you can open it more than once. But Mac apps frequently have more than one type of window, and that's what you'll look into next.

First, you'll create a Settings window to allow users to configure the app.

After that, you'll create an entirely new window with a different SwiftUI view. And you'll see how to pass data around between different windows.

Creating a Settings View

Launch Xcode and open the project you ended with after the last chapter. If you prefer, you can use the **starter** project from the downloads for this chapter, but it contains nothing new.

Press **Command-R** to run the app and open the **Snowman** menu:

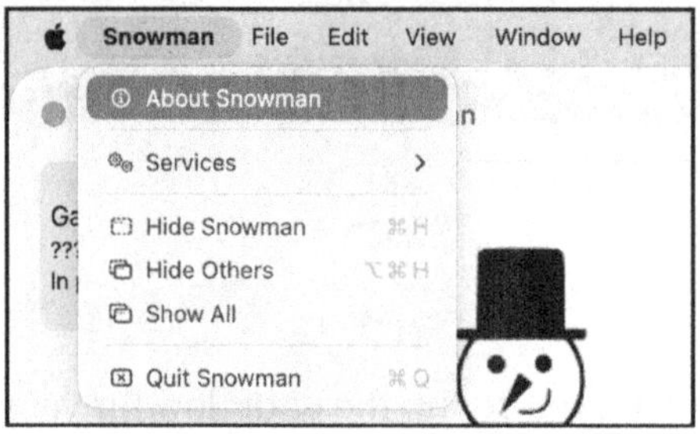

Snowman menu

There are the expected menu items, but no **Settings...** option. Go to to Xcode and open the **Xcode** menu. There's a **Settings...** menu item under the first divider. So how can you add that to Snowman?

Open **SnowmanApp.swift**. The `body` contains a single scene that defines the main window.

Add this after the end of `WindowGroup`:

```
// 1
Settings {
  // 2
  Text("Settings View")
    .frame(width: 250, height: 100)
}
```

What's this?

1. `Settings` is a new scene type that makes SwiftUI add a **Settings...** menu item and link it to the enclosed view.
2. For now, this is a placeholder view for the Settings window to show. It has a default frame so the window is large enough to see when it opens.

Run the app and look at the **Snowman** menu again:

Snowman menu with Settings.

Now it has a **Settings...** option, and it has allocated the default keyboard shortcut: **Command-,**.

Select this option or press **Command-,** to see your new window with the placeholder text:

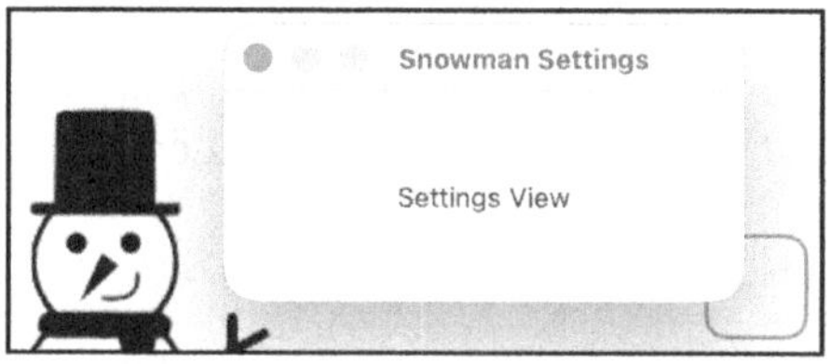

Settings window with placeholder.

Note: Until macOS Ventura, these were Preferences windows and the system options were System Preferences. Ventura brought macOS more into line with iOS, which has always used the term Settings.

A feature of the Settings scene is that it never opens its window more than once. Press **Command-,** with the Settings window already open, and it brings it to the front without duplicating it.

Configuring @AppStorage

You've created a Settings window, and it's linked to the correct menu item — now to add some content.

When you imported the words list and added a method to find a random word, you hard-coded some word length limits. It would be better to let the user change these, so you'll add an upper and lower limit to the Settings view.

Start by making a new view. Select the **Views** folder in the Project navigator so the next file will appear inside it.

Choose **File → New → File from Template...** or press **Command-N** to make a new file. Select the **macOS → User Interface → SwiftUI View** template and click **Next**. Name the file **SettingsView.swift** and click **Create**.

The first thing to add is the data. At the top of `SettingsView`, before `body`, insert these lines:

```
@AppStorage("minWordLength") var minWordLength = 4
@AppStorage("maxWordLength") var maxWordLength = 10.0
```

Another property wrapper!

1. The `@AppStorage` property wrapper is responsible for saving and retrieving user settings and does a lot of work. Any time one of these properties changes, the property wrapper saves it, and any time the app uses one of these, it reads the saved data, so any changes carry over between app launches.
2. The name in brackets after the property wrapper name is an identifier that the user configuration storage system uses.
3. After that, you have a standard variable property declaration, with a name and a default value. It's a good idea to use the same name for the property and its storage label to avoid confusion.
4. The app uses the default values if the user hasn't set anything yet. `maxWordLength` is a `Double` — you'll see why when you use it.

That's a lot of work for a couple of lines! Now to use them.

Adding a Stepper

Still in **SettingsView.swift**, replace the `Text` view with:

```
// 1
Form {
  // 2
  Stepper(
    // 3
    value: $minWordLength,
    // 4
    in: 3 ... Int(maxWordLength)
  ) {
    // 5
    Text("Minimum word length: \(minWordLength)")
  }

  // more items here
}
```

Stepping through this code:

1. A `Form` is another way of grouping SwiftUI views. You've used `HStack` and `VStack` before. This is a more specialized group type designed for settings and similar data entry interfaces.
2. A `Stepper` is an interface element for incrementing and decrementing numbers.
3. Its `value` is bound to the `minWordLength` property. The `$` shows that this works both ways, so changing the property adjusts the stepper and changing the stepper edits the property.
4. The `in` argument is a `range` to limit its upper and lower limits. The lower end is set to 3, and the upper end uses `maxWordLength` because it doesn't make any sense to allow a minimum word length that's longer than the maximum length. Since this is a `Double`, you convert it to an `Int` first.
5. Inside the curly braces, you have the `label` argument. This displays a header and the current value.

This provides the UI for the first setting, but if you run the app now, it won't appear. Open **SnowmanApp.swift** and, in the `Settings` scene, replace the `Text` placeholder with:

```
SettingsView()
```

This tells the `Settings` scene to use your new `SettingsView` as the content for the **Settings** window. Leave the `frame` modifier there for now, and run the app.

Open **Settings** and test your stepper:

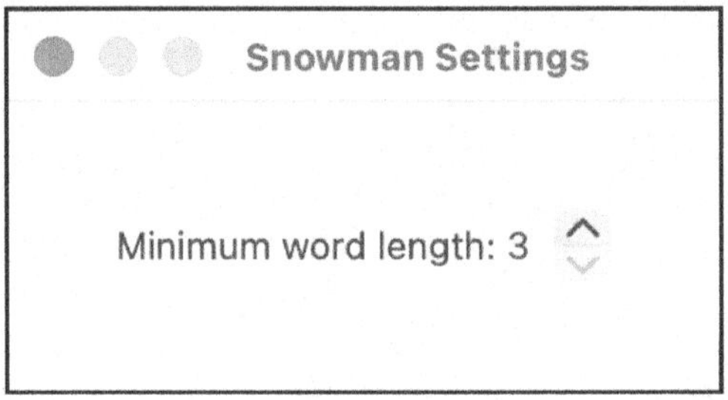

Stepper in Settings window.

Click the arrows to go up and down between 3 and 10. Choose something different to the default 4. Quit the app, then run it again and open Settings. The property wrapper restores your selection.

Adjusting the Settings Window

This app has very few settings, but many apps have a lot more — look in Xcode's Settings for an example. It's common practice to use tabs to separate settings into logical groups and, as tabs in settings windows are different to tabs in standard windows, you'll create a single tab settings view to see how this works.

In Xcode, open **SettingsView.swift**, **right-click** `Form` and select **Embed....** This wraps the form in curly braces, indents the code and gives a `Container` placeholder. Replace `Container` with:

```
// 1
TabView
```

> **Note:** If you don't see **Embed...** in the menu, make sure the preview is visible. It doesn't have to be active, but it must be open, so press **Option-Command-Return** to show it if necessary.

Next, **right-click** `Form` and choose **Embed...** again. This time, change `Container` to:

```
// 2
Tab("Settings", systemImage: "snowflake")
```

How does this make tabs?

1. First, you wrap the `Form` view in a `TabView`. A `TabView` can have multiple tabs.
2. Next, inside the `TabView`, add a `Tab` and give it a title and an image. The `Tab` contains the `Form`.

When using the standard tab settings in a Mac window, you only see the title, but you must supply an image when initializing. You can see this tab if you resume the preview. When used in a Settings window, a tab displays both the title and the image. As before, this image comes from SF Symbols.

Run the app now and open **Settings**:

Tab view in Settings.

It seems a bit odd to have a single tab, but this is an important technique to learn.

While you're working on `SettingsView`, add this modifier after the close of `TabView`:

```
.frame(width: 420, height: 160)
```

With most app windows, you'll set a minimum frame and allow users to expand them, but for a window like Settings that has fixed content, you can set the frame exactly.

Previously, you set a frame for `SettingsView()` in **SnowmanApp.swift**. Delete that `frame`. Now that you have a `SettingsView` structure, the frame is better attached to it, so that the preview is accurate.

Back in **SettingsView.swift**, resume the preview to see your new frame:

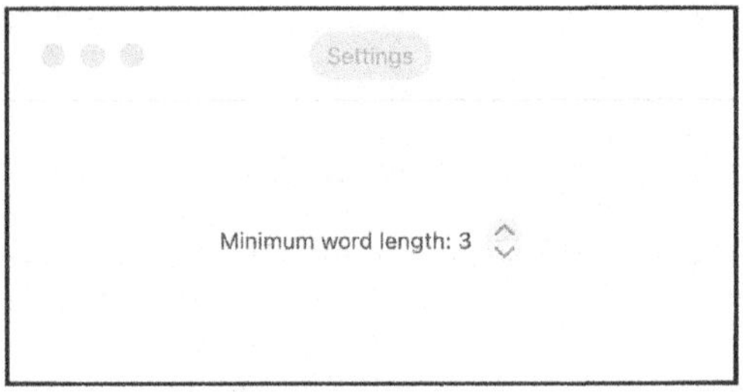

Settings preview

Notice how the preview only shows the standard text tab label. You have to run the app to see the special Settings tab label.

Limiting the Maximum Word Length

You've used a `Stepper` to set the minimum word length. Now you'll use a `Slider` to set the maximum. In a production app, you'd keep the user experience (UX) consistent and only use one type, but for a learning app like this one, it's more interesting to see some variety.

Open **SettingsView.swift** and resume the preview if it isn't already running. Add a few blank lines before `// more items here` and position the cursor there.

Open the Xcode library by pressing **Shift-Command-L** or choosing **View → Show Library** from the menus. Select the **Views** tab icon and search for **label**. When you find `LabeledContent`, drag it into the blank space:

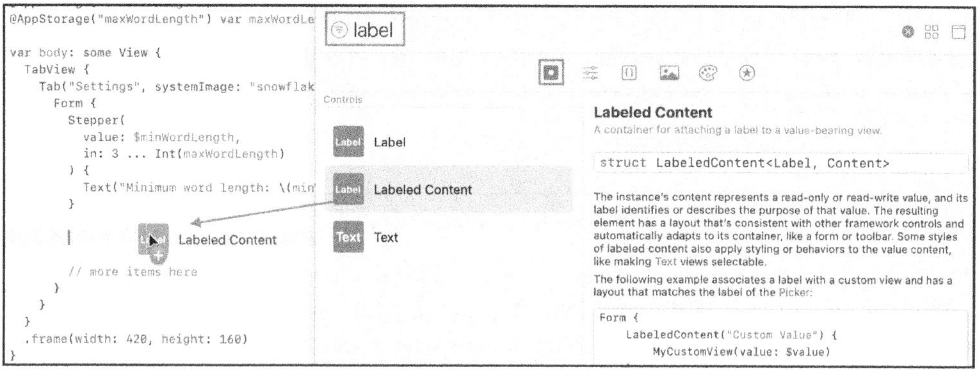

Adding a view from the library.

Replace "Label" with:

```
"Maximum word length: \(Int(maxWordLength))"
```

This gives a label in the same format as you used for the Stepper. You don't want the selected length to show any decimals, so you convert it to an Int for display.

Now, to add the Slider, delete the Content placeholder and type:

```
Slider
```

Xcode now suggests a lot of options. Use the arrow keys to move up and down through the list. The one you want is **Slider(value:in:)**, ignoring its optional italicized arguments:

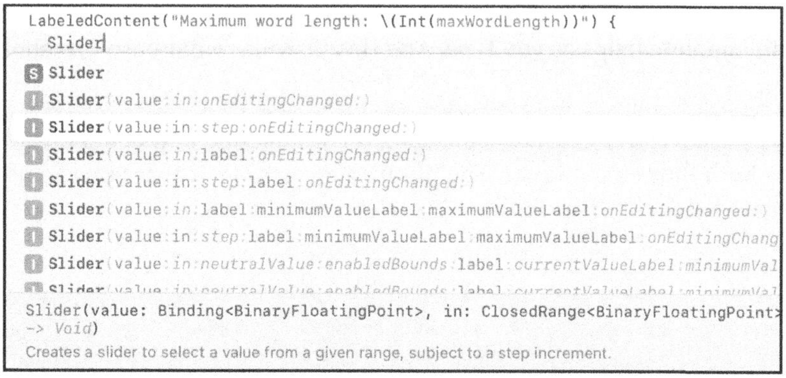

Slider autocomplete options

> **Note:** If the autocomplete menu disappears, press **Esc** to bring it back.

Double-click the relevant line or arrow to it and press **Return** to insert it into LabeledContent. And now you get some strange placeholders and a lot of red:

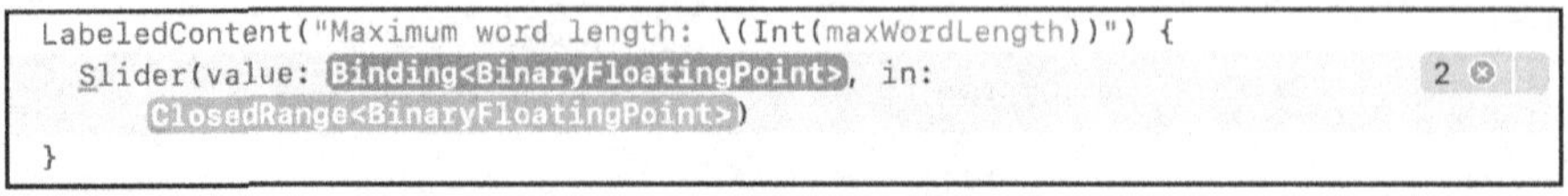

Slider argument errors

Don't panic! Providing valid arguments will make the red vanish. The placeholder for the first argument tells you that it expects a value with a type of Binding<BinaryFloatingPoint>. This means that it wants a binding to a floating point number that can be either a Double or a Float. And that's why you initialized maxWordLength as a Double.

Replace the value placeholder with:

```
$maxWordLength
```

The remaining placeholder has the type ClosedRange<BinaryFloatingPoint>. Remembering back to the earlier chapters, ... is the closed range operator, and it creates a range going from the first number to the last, inclusively.

Add this instead of that placeholder:

```
Double(minWordLength) ... 12
```

The slider can't go lower than the minimum word length, but that's an Int, so you convert in to a Double and fix the upper limit at 12.

Again, autocomplete helps as you type. And this provides what both placeholders specified.

While it may seem clumsy to add code using the library and autocomplete, it's good to practice both those techniques. The library suggests views that you can use, and autocomplete helps fill them in.

Using a Toggle

There's one more setting to add: The word list contains some proper nouns — mostly place names. Your users may not want these to show up.

First, add a new `@AppStorage` property after the others:

```
@AppStorage("useProperNouns") var useProperNouns = false
```

The first two properties are numbers, but this one is a Boolean. You've seen several different input views now, and it's important to choose one that suits the data type. A `Toggle` is an on/off switch and that's perfect for a Boolean property.

Next, replace `// more items here` with:

```
Toggle("Allow proper nouns", isOn: $useProperNouns)
```

Like `Slider`, `Toggle` has several initialization options. This one sets a title and a Boolean binding.

The toggle is a standard Mac checkbox by default. But to keep up with the look of modern versions of macOS, this should be a switch like the ones in the System Settings app.

Add a new line after the `Toggle` line, and type:

```
.toggle
```

Press **Return** to accept the suggestion when autocomplete offers `toggleStyle`.

Now you have a placeholder, looking for a `ToggleStyle`. Select the placeholder and type a **period** to show the possible options:

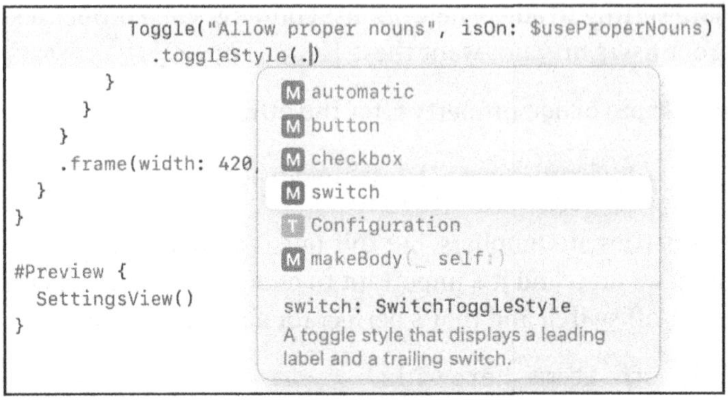

Toggle style options

Choose `switch` and check the preview. Use **Option-Command-P** to resume it if necessary:

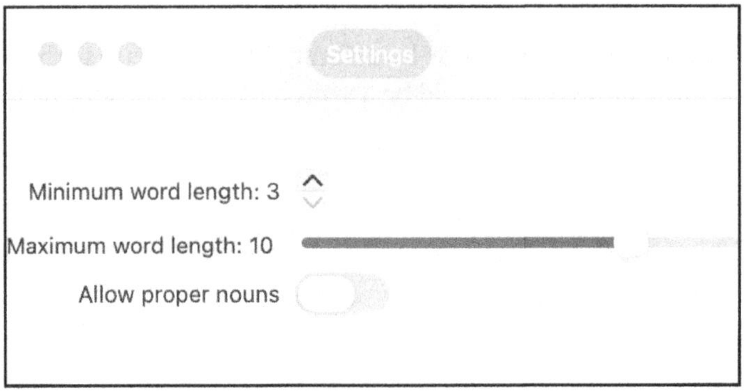

Settings preview

> **Note**: The minimum word length you'll see is the value you set in Settings.

The Toggle is using the switch style but it's huge, like on iOS. For a Mac where you have a precise pointing device, there's no need for a big switch. The System Settings app has small versions of these toggles, so how can you make this one small?

The answer may surprise you. It isn't a Toggle style, it's a Form style.

Add this after the frame modifier:

```
.formStyle(.grouped)
```

If you want more practice using autocomplete, start typing formStyle, select the suggestion and then press **period** to see the options.

The preview has changed, but as it doesn't show the tab properly, run the app and open Settings:

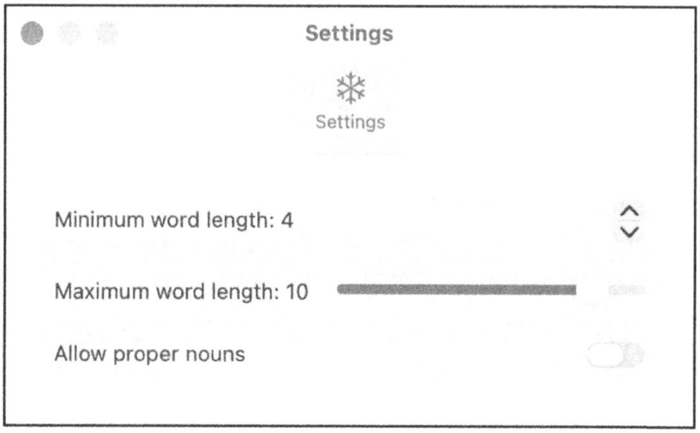

Settings formatted.

Doesn't that look great! Everything is neatly arranged, the toggle switch is small, the labels and controls all line up. Terrific work!

Now to apply these settings in the app.

Applying the Settings

All these user settings change how Game selects a random word, so open **Models → Game.swift**.

Next, add the three @AppStorage properties to the other properties:

```
@AppStorage("minWordLength") var minWordLength = 4
@AppStorage("maxWordLength") var maxWordLength = 10
@AppStorage("useProperNouns") var useProperNouns = false
```

These are the same as in SettingsView except that here, maxWordLength is an Int and not a Double. @AppStorage can extract its value in either format. It had to be a Double for the Slider, but here it works better as an Int.

Scroll down to getRandomWord and insert these lines before the let words = line:

```
let storedMinWordLength = minWordLength
let storedMaxWordLength = maxWordLength
let storedUseProperNouns = useProperNouns
```

The settings are used inside a filter loop, and for performance reasons, you don't want to access @AppStorage every time through the loop. These lines take a snapshot of the current settings for fast and efficient access.

Next, find where you filtered based on word.count with fixed values of 4 and 10.

Replace word.count >= 4 && word.count <= 10 with:

```
word.count >= storedMinWordLength && word.count <=
storedMaxWordLength
```

And that takes care of the word length limits. Whenever you start a new game, this method reads the latest settings for minWordLength and maxWordLength and filters out words that are outside either limit.

Now, you need to implement the setting for proper nouns. These all start with an uppercase letter, so that's what you'll use to remove them if needed.

Add a second filter block after the first:

```
// 1
.filter { word in
  // 2
  if storedUseProperNouns {
    return true
```

```
    }
    // 3
    let firstLetter = word[word.startIndex]
    // 4
    return !firstLetter.isUppercase
  }
```

How does this work?

1. You can chain filter methods to perform a sequence of operations. You already limited the words by length, and now you're filtering the words that remain.
2. If `storedUseProperNouns` is true, return `true` to include all the remaining words.
3. Get the first letter of the word. This isn't a simple process in Swift. Many languages allow you to use `word[0]` to get the first character, but Swift strings are fully Unicode compliant. This means that a single visible symbol isn't always one character long: Accented characters are two different characters superimposed, and some Emoji can include four or five symbols. But a `String` has a `startIndex` property that you can use as the index value to find the first character.
4. Apply a `Character` method to check if the first letter is uppercase. The **not** operator reverses the result and returns it. So if the first letter is uppercase, `isUppercase` is `true` and applying `!` changes it to `false` to exclude that word.

Build and run the app. Play one game with the current settings, but before clicking New Game, open the Settings window and make some changes:

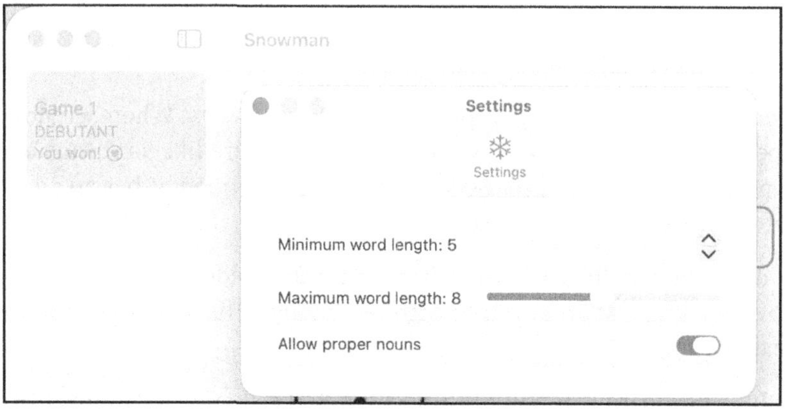

Applying Settings

Notice how changing the stepper or the slider adjusts the limits on the other so you can't choose an impossible combination.

Now click **New Game** and `Game` uses your settings to decide on a new word.

And that's how you create a Settings window, store the user options and apply them to the app.

Opening a Secondary Window

The Settings window is a special case, and SwiftUI provides a preset `Scene` for handling that. But you''ll often want to have more than one window type in an app. You can add more scenes to the `@main` body to do this.

You'll add a secondary window with a tab view. In the next chapter, you'll draw charts in these tabs to display your game statistics, but for now, you'll set up a new window and pass data into it.

Begin by adding the new `Scene`; open **SnowmanApp.swift**.

Add a blank line after the end of `Settings` and insert this:

```
// 1
Window("Statistics", id: "stats") {
  // 2
  Text("Statistics will go here")
}
// 3
.keyboardShortcut("t", modifiers: .command)
```

This adds a new scene, but how?

1. A `Window` is a type of scene that presents a single window. Where `WindowGroup` can open multiple copies of its window, `Window` is more like `Settings` and only ever opens one, bringing it to the front if it's already open. It has an `id` so you can refer to this window to open it programmatically, if required.
2. When developing in SwiftUI, using `Text` as a placeholder view is a convenient way to set up and test an interface without having to have all the structures ready in advance.
3. This adds a keyboard shortcut of **Command-T**. The `keyboardShortcut` modifier changes the supplied letter to uppercase. The default modifier key is **Command**, so you can omit this argument, but leaving it in makes your intentions clearer.

You're probably wondering where this keyboard shortcut appears, so press **Command-R** to run the app and open the **Window** menu:

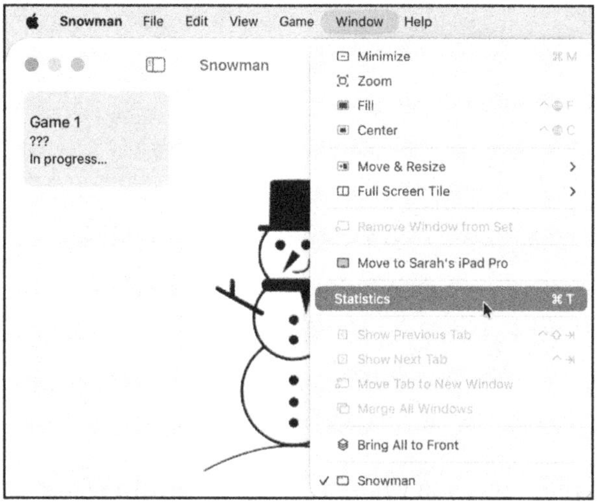

Statistics menu item

Select the menu item or press **Command-T** to see the new window. Command-S would have been more logical for the **Statistics** menu item, but it's always used for **Save** and even though this app doesn't save, it's a bad idea to change a standard shortcut to do something completely different.

You can open a single instance of the Statistics window, but its very boring.

Populating the Statistics Window

Now, you'll replace the placeholder `Text` with a new view for your new window. In the Project navigator, select **Views** and press **Command-N** to make a new file.

Choose **macOS** → **User Interface** → **SwiftUI View** and click **Next**. Set the file name to **StatsView.swift** and click **Create**.

Replace the contents of `body` with:

```
// 1
TabView {
  // 2
  Tab("Games Won & Lost", systemImage: "gamecontroller") {
    // 3
    Text("Games view")
  }

  // 4
  Tab("Length of Words", systemImage: "ruler") {
    Text("Words view")
  }
}
// 5
.padding()
```

More tabs:

1. Like with `SettingsView`, you wrap the contents in a `TabView`.
2. Add a `Tab` with a title and a system image, even though the image will not appear.
3. This `Text` is another placeholder for the contents of the tab until you create a new view to show here.
4. Repeat the process to create a second tab.
5. Add some padding to inset the tab view and its contents from the edges of the window.

Resume the preview to show your tabs with the first tab selected, but don't run the app yet. You need to set the `Window` scene to use this view.

Open **SnowmanApp.swift** and replace `Text("Statistics will go here")` with:

```
StatsView()
```

Build and run the app, open your new window and switch between the tabs:

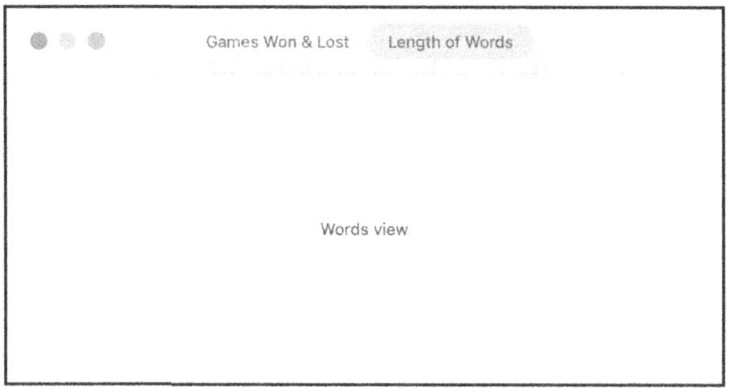

Statistics tabs with placeholders.

The tabs are in place, and now you can add some real content.

Passing Data to the New Window

If this window is to show any game data, it must be able to read `games` from `appState`.

First, open **StatsView.swift** and add this property at the top of the structure:

```
let games: [Game]
```

This tells `StatsView` that its parent view will pass it `games`. Any changes to games are published so this view will be refreshed to receive the updates.

Now that `StatsView` expects this property, the preview has an error. Replace the contents of `#Preview` with:

```
StatsView(games: [])
```

This provides the preview with an empty array of `Game` objects. The preview won't show anything interesting, so you'll run the app and play some games to see the new views in action.

Press **Command-B** to build the app. Now, there's an error in `SnowmanApp`, because it isn't providing the expected data.

Open **SnowmanApp.swift** and click the red dot beside the error:

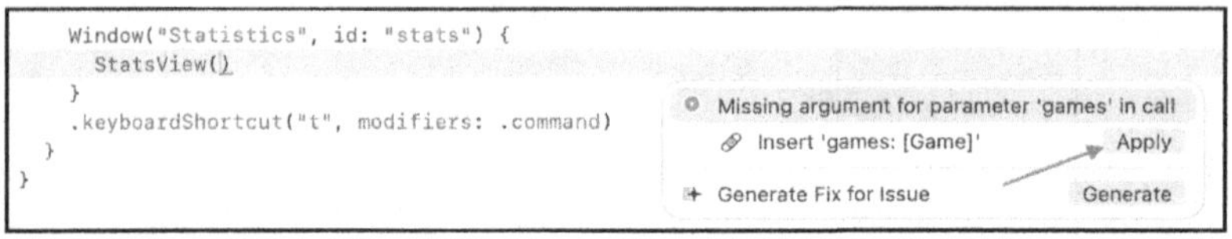

Xcode apply error fix

Click the **Apply** button in the error report, and Xcode adds the missing argument label and a placeholder. Type `appState.games` into the placeholder and you'll end up with this:

```
StatsView(games: appState.games)
```

And now `SnowmanApp` passes its `appState.games` to `StatsView`, which is expecting it.

Next, you'll add some views to use this data.

Adding the Subviews

You'll add two new SwiftUI view files: one for each tab. Select **Views** in the Project navigator and use the technique you used before to create two new **SwiftUI View** files called **GameStats.swift** and **WordStats.swift**.

You now have three views related to the Statistics window. They are already in the **Views** folder, but you can make a sub-folder to keep them together. You've done this using Xcode, but this time you'll use Finder.

Select **GameStats.swift**, right-click and choose **Show in Finder**. In the Finder window that opens, select **GameStats.swift**, **StatsView.swift** and **WordStats.swift**. **Right-click** and choose **New Folder with Selection (3 items)**. Set the name of the new folder to **Statistics**.

Xcode picks up this change and when you switch back, you can see your new folder in the Project navigator:

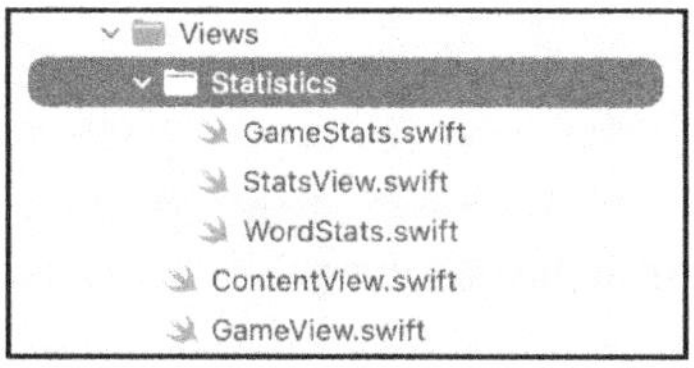

Statistics group

This app won't end up with hundreds of files, but developing organizational skills like this will make your life a lot easier when you start working on large projects.

Both of these new structures need access to `games`, so add this property to both `GameStats` and `WordStats`:

```
let games: [Game]
```

Both also need the argument for the previews, so change their `previews` to:

```
GameStats(games: [])
```

And:

```
WordStats(games: [])
```

These views will end up showing charts, but for now, make them show text so you can see the data changing.

Showing the Game Statistics

Open **GameStats.swift** and add this computed property:

```
// 1
var gameReport: String {
  // 2
  let wonGamesCount = games.count {
    $0.gameStatus == .won
  }
  // 3
  let lostGamesCount = games.count {
    $0.gameStatus == .lost
  }

  // 4
  return """
```

```
        Games won: \(wonGamesCount)
        Games lost: \(lostGamesCount)
        """
  }
```

Stepping through this:

1. The computed property returns a `String`.
2. It uses an array method similar to `filter` to find the number of games that match the condition. In this case, that's the number of games the player has won.
3. Another `count` gets the number of games that the player has lost. Remember there may be one or more games in progress.
4. This is a multi-line string. Enclosing text inside three quotes lets you format a string over multiple lines.

Change the `Text` view to:

```
Text(gameReport)
```

This displays the new property in the `Text` view.

To use `GameStats`, open **StatsView.swift** and replace `Text("Games view")` with:

```
GameStats(games: games)
```

Run the app now, open the Statistics window and play a few games. Remember you're still printing the random word in the Xcode console, so you can always cheat to make sure you get some wins and some losses. ;]

You can see the `GameStats` view updating as you play:

Wins and Losses

In the Settings view, data had to flow both ways, but these views never change the data, they only display it, reacting to any changes. And you're passing only the required data, which is the `games` array.

Showing the Words Statistics

Adding data to `WordStats` is a similar process, so open **WordStats.swift** now. This view will list each completed game, showing how many letters were in each word.

Insert this computed property to supply the `String`:

```
// 1
var wordCountReport: String {
  // 2
  let completedGames = games.filter {
    $0.gameStatus != .inProgress
  }

  // 3
  let gameReports = completedGames.map { game in
    // 4
    let statusText = game.gameStatus == .won ? "won" : "lost"
    // 5
    return "\(game.id): \(game.word.count) letters - \
(statusText)"
  }

  // 6
  return gameReports.joined(separator: "\n")
}
```

This has some familiar code and some new code:

1. Define a computed string property.
2. Use `filter` to get a list of completed games.
3. Next, use `map` to convert `Game` instances to strings. `map` works like `filter`, looping through each element in the array, but where `filter` includes or excludes certain elements, `map` transforms each of them into something else.
4. Apply the ternary operator to get a string showing the game status.
5. Create a report for each game using string interpolation.
6. `gameReports` is an array of `Strings`. Merge this into a single string using the `joined` method.

Like before, change `Text` to:

```
Text(wordCountReport)
```

With this in place, open **StatsView.swift** and replace `Text("Words view")` with:

```
WordStats(games: games)
```

Run the app again. Play a few games and open the Statistics window. Check the data in both tabs, then play a few more games and confirm that the statistics update:

Word length statistics

Now you have a secondary window, opening from the **Window** menu and receiving live game data.

Key Points

- A `Settings` scene adds a **Settings…** menu item and keyboard shortcut that you can link to any SwiftUI view to show as the user settings interface.
- The `@AppStorage` property wrapper saves and restores user settings.
- SwiftUI has a variety of input views, so you can choose the ones that suit your data types.
- You add secondary windows using a `Window` scene, which adds an item to the **Window** menu.

Where to Go From Here?

You've configured two different additional windows. The Settings window is complete, but the Statistics window only shows plain text reports.

In the next chapter, you'll learn about SwiftUI's Charts framework and add two styles of chart to display these two sets of statistics.

Chapter 9: Charting Your Progress

By Sarah Reichelt

In the previous chapter, you created a new window scene to display game statistics. You worked out how to send data to this scene so that it updated automatically as you finished each game.

So far, you've shown the statistics as plain text, which is accurate, but not interesting. It's not even easy to comprehend at a glance.

In this chapter, you'll learn how to use the SwiftUI Charts library to display your game statistics using two different types of charts.

Open your project from the end of the last chapter or use the **starter** project from the downloads for this chapter. Run the app, play a few games and then press **Command-T** to open the Statistics window and see the current display:

Statistics as text.

This window could certainly do with an upgrade. :]

Preparing the Data

To draw a chart, you start with data points. Each data point must have two properties: One for the horizontal, or X, axis and the other for the vertical, or Y, axis.

Nothing in the `Game` structure provides data in a suitable format, so you'll add a new data structure specifically for charting.

Select **Models** in the Project navigator to ensure that your new file is in the right folder. Now, right-click and choose **New File from Template...**. This time, select **macOS → Source → Swift File** and create a file called **ChartPoint.swift**.

Add this to your new file:

```
// 1
struct ChartPoint: Identifiable {
  // 2
  let id = UUID()
  // 3
  let name: String
  let value: Int
}
```

What does this structure do?

1. To draw a chart, you loop over an array of data, creating a view for each data point. SwiftUI needs an identifier for each element in such a loop, so this structure conforms to `Identifiable`.
2. `Identifiable` requires a property called `id`. Here, you set this property to a `UUID`. The `ChartPoint` initializer creates one for every new instance.
3. The remaining two properties define what appears in the chart. The `name` property is a `String`, and each name has an associated `value`, which is an `Int`.

In previous `Identifiable` structures, you've used integer `ids`. `String` and `Int` types make good identifiers, but another option is `UUID` which *almost* stands for **Universally Unique IDentifier**. :] This is a "128-bit value guaranteed to be unique over both space and time". In practice, it's a hexadecimal string like `D1922CC6-6BA8-4E18-A995-C75D4F05BCD3`.

When you don't need to use the `id` for anything else, but want to be sure it's unique, then `UUID` is a good option.

Now that you've set up `ChartPoint`, you can start to use it.

Creating Chart Points

Open **Views/Statistics/GameStats.swift** and look at where you defined `gameReport`. This uses the data in `games` and produces a computed `String` for display. Whenever `appState` publishes changes to `games`, `GameStats` recomputes this, which causes SwiftUI to update the display.

You'll use a similar technique for the charts, but this time, you'll use the data in `games` to compute an array of `ChartPoint` elements.

Add this new property to `GameStats`:

```
// 1
var gameStatsPoints: [ChartPoint] {
  // 2
  let wonGamesCount = games.count {
    $0.gameStatus == .won
  }
  let lostGamesCount = games.count {
    $0.gameStatus == .lost
  }

  // 3
  let chartPoints = [
    ChartPoint(name: "Wins", value: wonGamesCount),
    ChartPoint(name: "Losses", value: lostGamesCount)
  ]

  // 4
  return chartPoints
}
```

Stepping through this code:

1. The new computed property is an array of `ChartPoint` elements.
2. Use the same code you used in `gameReport` to count the won and lost games.
3. Create an array with two elements. The first one has its `name` property initialized to `Wins` and `value` set to the number of games the player has won. The second holds the lost game data.
4. Return this array as the value for the computed property.

And with this in place, you have the data you need to show a chart.

Displaying a Chart

Still in **GameStats.swift**, start at the top by adding this import:

```
import Charts
```

You won't be able to create any charts without including the `Charts` library in your project.

And now, you get to draw your first chart. In `body`, replace `Text(gameReport)` with:

```
// 1
Chart(gameStatsPoints) { point in
  // 2
  BarMark(
    // 3
    x: .value("Count", point.value),
    // 4
    y: .value("Name", point.name))
  // 5
  // bar modifiers here
}
// chart modifiers here
```

There's a lot of new code there:

1. Initialize a `Chart`, passing in the array of data points. This loops through them and each time through, `point` contains the current `ChartPoint`.
2. For each point, initialize a `BarMark`. This is the structure that creates a single bar for a bar chart.
3. Set the `x` property for the `BarMark` to a `PlottableValue`. A `PlottableValue` has a `label` and a `value`. In this case, the `label` is `Count`, and the `value` is the `ChartPoint`'s `value` property.
4. Set the `y` property to another `PlottableValue`, using `Name` for the label and `ChartPoint`'s `name` for its value.
5. You'll add modifiers to style each bar and the chart as a whole later.

Press **Command-R** to build and run the app. Play a few games and open the Statistics window:

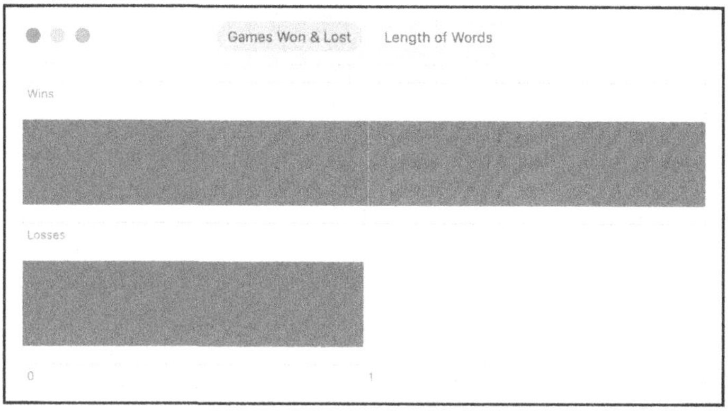

A basic bar chart

And there it is — a bar chart showing how many games you've won and how many you've lost.

> **Note**: When you provided the `gameStatsPoints` array to `Chart`, you used a convenient shortcut. In the long form, you start with a `Chart` and then use a `ForEach` to step through the array. This is such a common use case that the SwiftUI Charts team allows us to combine the two. You'll see the longer version later in the chapter.

Now that you have a basic chart, there are things you can add to make it look even better.

Providing Preview Content

It gets a bit tedious having to run the app and play a few games to see any statistics data. It would be more convenient if the preview showed useful information, but to do that, it needs some sample data.

Open **Game.swift**, scroll to the end, past the final closing brace, and add this:

```
// 1
extension Game {
  // 2
  static var sampleGames: [Game] {
    // 3
    var game1 = Game(id: 1)
    game1.word = "SNOWMAN"
    game1.gameStatus = .lost

    // 4
    var game2 = Game(id: 2)
    game2.word = "FROST"
    game2.gameStatus = .won

    var game3 = Game(id: 3)
    game3.word = "ANTARCTICA"
    game3.gameStatus = .won

    // 5
    return [game1, game2, game3]
  }
}
```

What's happening here?

1. Create an extension to `Game`. This code is part of `Game`, but it's separated for organizational reasons.
2. A `static` property or method is one that belongs to the class or structure, not to an instance of that class or structure. This allows you to use `Game.sampleGames` to query `Game` for an array of games.
3. Initialize a `Game` with an `id` and then set its `word` and `gameStatus` properties.
4. Repeat this to make two more sample games.
5. Assemble them into an array and return it.

To use this property in the `GameStats` preview, return to **GameStats.swift** and change the contents of `#Preview` to:

```
GameStats(games: Game.sampleGames)
```

Resume the preview to see this:

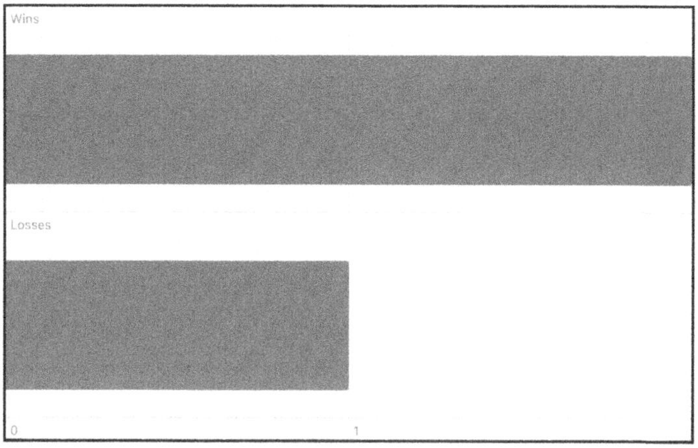

Previewing the bar chart.

And now it's much faster to see the result of any changes you make to the chart.

Styling the Bar Chart

The bars in the chart are blue by default. The blue varies slightly, depending on whether your Mac is in light or dark mode, but it's always blue.

To change this color, stay in **GameStats.swift**, and replace `// bar modifiers here` with:

```
.foregroundStyle(.red)
```

Check the preview now to see two red bars.

Both bars are the same color, whether you set a `foregroundStyle` or not, but having each bar use a different color would be more effective.

Varying the Colors

There are a couple of ways you can do this. For the first, replace the current `foregroundStyle` modifier with:

```
.foregroundStyle(by: .value("Name", point.name))
```

Checking the preview now, you see a blue and a green bar. And as the bars are now visually different, the Charts library has added a legend at the bottom:

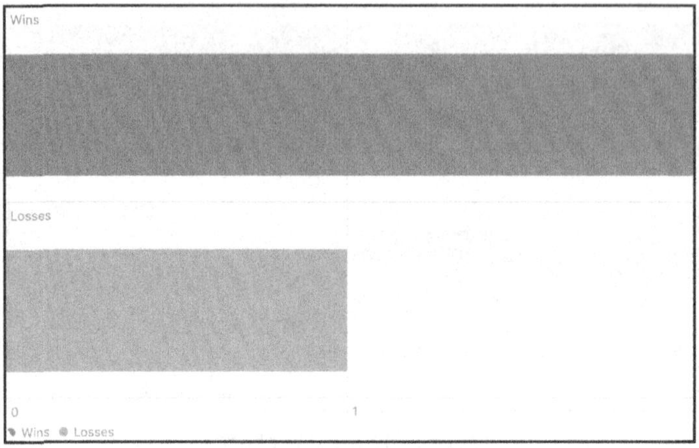

Colored bars and legend

So it worked, but how? By default, a `BarMark` has a `foregroundStyle` of `Color.blue`. This version of the modifier tells the bar to vary its color based on a `PlottableValue`. Here it uses the value of its data point's `name` property, so every time `name` changes, the color also changes. The legend shows the `name` properties for the two `ChartPoint` objects you used to populate the chart.

The Charts library allocates up to seven different colors. If your chart has more than seven bars, the colors start to repeat.

This is a great method if you want the bars different, but don't care what colors they use. But in the main window, you use green text to symbolize a win and orange text for a loss, so it would be more consistent to repeat those colors here.

This requires a modifier for the chart itself. Replace `// chart modifiers here` with:

```
// 1
.chartForegroundStyleScale([
  // 2
  "Wins": Color.green.gradient,
  "Losses": Color.orange.gradient
])
```

What does this do?

1. `chartForegroundStyleScale` is a modifier that takes a set of key-value pairs which is effectively a dictionary.

2. The keys represent the data points. When you set the `y` property for the `BarMark`, you labeled it using the `name` property of the `ChartPoint`, so this is what identifies each bar. The values are the `ShapeStyle` to use for each bar. This time, as well as having colors, they each include a gradient. In SwiftUI, you can add `.gradient` to any color to add a subtle gradient.

And now the preview looks like this:

Defining bar colors.

> **Note**: This `Chart` modifier overrides the individual `BarMark` modifier. Leave the `foregroundStyle` modifier in as a reference and a placeholder, but it no longer does anything.

Adding More Style

There are a few more modifiers that'll make your chart stand out. These all go after the `chartForegroundStyleScale` modifier.

First, you don't want to let the user make the chart too small, so add this:

```
.frame(minWidth: 350, minHeight: 300)
```

You're familiar with `frame` modifiers already. This one lets the `Chart` get as big as the user wants, but stops it getting any smaller than 350 x 300.

After that, the next thing to add is:

```
.padding()
```

The chart was filling all the available space and pushing it right to the edges. Adding some padding makes it look better.

Finally, to make those bars really stand out, add this:

```
.shadow(radius: 5, x: 5, y: 5)
```

This adds a shadow to each bar with a radius of 5. The shadow is offset to the right and down to give a more 3D effect.

Bars with shadows and padding.

Look back to see where you started with this chart. By adding a few modifiers, you've made a great looking chart.

Annotating the Bars

Your chart looks impressive, but there's more you can do. Annotations are a way to add more textual information to the chart.

Still in **GameStats.swift**, add this after `BarMark`'s `foregroundStyle` modifier:

```
// 1
.annotation(
  // 2
  position: .overlay,
  // 3
  alignment: .leading,
  // 4
  spacing: 20
) {
    // 5
    Text("\(point.name): \(point.value)")
      .font(.title2)
  }
```

Taking this line by line:

1. The `annotation` modifier adds a view to each `BarMark`.
2. There are a lot of `position` options. To see them all, delete `overlay` and press **Escape** with the cursor after the period. Then, choose `overlay` again to place the annotation view over the bar.
3. Like `position`, `alignment` has many alternatives. `leading` puts the annotation at the start of the bar.
4. With no spacing, the annotation would start right at the edge of the bar, but the `spacing` argument insets it.
5. The content of the annotation is a `Text` view which uses string interpolation to combine the name and value. The `font` modifier makes this text larger than usual.

With this in place, the legend is now unnecessary, so add this modifier after the shadow:

```
.chartLegend(.hidden)
```

And after all that work, you end with this:

Final bar chart design

Now that you've finished the `GameStats` chart, it's time to move on to `WordStats` and draw a different style of chart.

Preparing Line Chart Data

You know how to create a bar chart, but SwiftUI can create many different types of charts. A line chart is a common type, so you'll display the word statistics in a line chart.

Conveniently, the SwiftUI Charts library works much the same for every type of chart.

Open **WordStats.swift** and add this computed property:

```
// 1
var wordStatsPoints: [ChartPoint] {
  // 2
  let completedGames = games.filter { game in
    game.gameStatus != .inProgress
  }

  // 3
```

```
    let chartPoints = completedGames.map { game in
      // 4
      ChartPoint(
        name: "#\(game.id)",
        value: game.word.count)
    }

    // 5
    return chartPoints
  }
```

This prepares the line chart data points:

1. Create a computed property to return an array of `ChartPoints`.
2. As with the text version, get an array of completed games.
3. Use `map` to convert the completed games into a array of data points.
4. Initialize each `ChartPoint` with the `id` of the game as part of the `name` and the length of the word as its `value`.

The bar chart only ever has two data points, but this chart has a data point for every completed game.

Now you have an array of `ChartPoints`, you can draw the chart. As before, add this at the top of the file:

```
import Charts
```

So you can see some results, scroll down to the `PreviewProvider` and change the contents of `#Preview` to:

```
WordStats(games: Game.sampleGames)
```

And with the data in place, you're ready to draw some lines.

Drawing a Line Chart

In body, replace `Text(wordCountReport)` with:

```
// 1
Chart {
  // 2
  ForEach(wordStatsPoints) { point in
    // 3
```

```
    LineMark(
      // 4
      x: .value("Game ID", point.name),
      // 5
      y: .value("Word Count", point.value))
    // line modifiers here
  }

  // another mark here
}
// chart modifiers here
```

Most of this is familiar:

1. Create a `Chart`. This time, you aren't using the shorthand method of passing data directly to it.
2. Pass the array of `ChartPoints` to a `ForEach` loop. Each time through the loop, `point` contains the data point to draw.
3. For each data point, initialize a `LineMark`.
4. Like a `BarMark`, this needs a `PlottableValue` for `x` which uses the point's `name`.
5. And for `y`, use the point's `value`.

Resume the preview to see this:

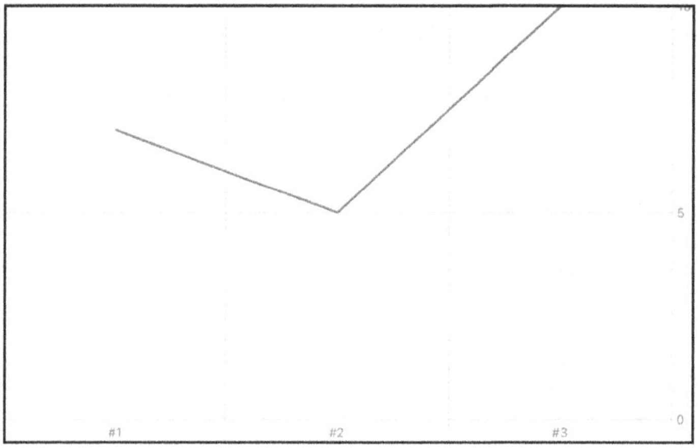

Basic line chart

You have a basic line chart, so now you can style it.

Modifying the Line Chart

The chart goes right to the edge of the view and crops some numbers, so to start, replace `// chart modifiers here` with:

```
.frame(minWidth: 350, minHeight: 300)
.padding()
```

This sets the same minimum height and width as the bar chart which is a good technique because it stops the window changing size as the user switches tabs.

The padding moves the content away from the edges so that all the numbers are now visible.

The Y-axis starts at zero. This is perfect for a lot of charts, but for this one, you know that the minimum number of letters per word is three or higher, so there's a lot of wasted space at the bottom of the chart.

The Charts library adjusts the axes automatically to fit, but you can tell it not to include the zero point for the Y-axis.

Add this new chart modifier to the `frame` and `padding` modifiers:

```
.chartYScale(domain: .automatic(includesZero: false))
```

This is a strange line of code:

1. The `chartYScale` modifier configures the scale of the Y-axis.
2. It can take various arguments, but you're using `domain`.
3. The `domain` argument is a `ScaleDomain`, which is a protocol that sets the span for the axis.
4. The `domain` is always `automatic`, which means that the Charts library works it out for itself based on the data, but you can set various conditions.
5. The `includesZero` argument is `true` by default, but setting it to `false` tells the library that it does not have to show the zero point on the axis if the data doesn't warrant it.

> **Note**: There are a lot of modifiers that are similar for both axes. You'd use `chartXScale` to configure the scale on the X-axis.

Checking the preview now, it already looks better:

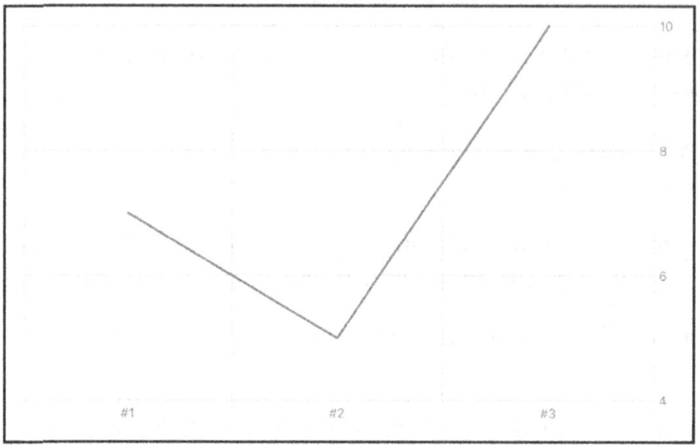

Line chart with padding and axis setting.

You've configured the chart, so it's time to improve the lines.

Configuring the Lines

By default, the line has a thickness of 2. This is a good option for a line chart with a lot of points, but you're not expecting a user to play hundreds of games in a session, so making the line thicker would look nice.

Replace `// line modifiers here` with:

```
.lineStyle(StrokeStyle(lineWidth: 4))
```

Another line that packs in a lot of detail:

1. The `lineStyle` modifier styles each `LineMark`.
2. Its argument is a `StrokeStyle`.
3. The `StrokeStyle` initializer can take a lot of optional parameters, but the only one you're changing here is the line width.
4. Specifying a `lineWidth` of 4 makes each line twice as thick as usual.

So far so good, but in this chart, it's the points between each line that are important, not the lines themselves. You can make them stand out by adding a symbol.

After the `lineStyle` modifier, add:

```
.symbol(.diamond)
```

The `symbol` modifier sets the shape that Charts draws at each point. There are a bunch of basic shape options. Delete `diamond` and press **Escape** with the cursor after the period to see them all. Select `diamond` when you've finished looking.

Look at the preview now and you'll see a small blob at each point. They're too small to distinguish any shape, so you need to make them bigger.

Add another modifier after `symbol`:

```
.symbolSize(200)
```

The `symbolSize` dictates the size of every symbol. This seems like a very large number, but it specifies the *area* of the symbol and not its width or height. An area of 200 means it covers a square roughly 14 high and 14 wide.

And now the preview shows this:

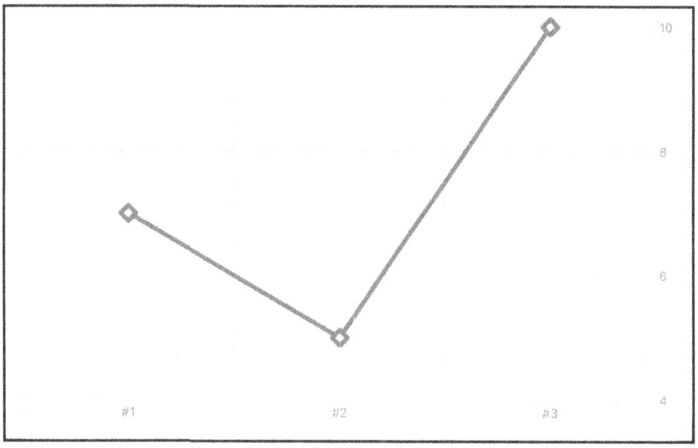

Styling the lines.

This looks good, but is there any way to include win/loss data?

Adding Some Color

It's not possible to vary the symbols or colors of individual points and still get the line chart — you get colored symbols and no lines. But you can use a conditional to adjust the color of the entire chart.

Add this new computed property:

```
// 1
var lineChartColor: Color {
  // 2
  let wonGamesCount = games.filter {
    $0.gameStatus == .won
  }.count
  // 3
  let lostGamesCount = games.filter {
    $0.gameStatus == .lost
  }.count

  // 4
  if wonGamesCount > lostGamesCount {
    return .green
  } else if wonGamesCount < lostGamesCount {
    return .orange
  }

  // 5
  return .blue
}
```

Working through this:

1. The computed property returns a `Color`.
2. Use `count` to count the number of games the player has won.
3. Do the same for the lost games.
4. If the player has won more than they've lost, return `green`, which is the color you've used already to indicate a win.
5. If the player has lost more than they won, use the `orange` failure color.
6. If the program flow makes it to here, the player has won and lost the same number of games, so use a neutral `blue`.

To apply this new property, add another modifier after `symbolSize`:

```
.foregroundStyle(lineChartColor)
```

In the preview, the color changes to green. Open **Game.swift** and check `sampleGames`. Two of these are wins and one is a loss, so the green is correct. Change `game3.gameStatus` to `.lost` and go back to **WordStats.swift**.

When the preview resumes, you'll see:

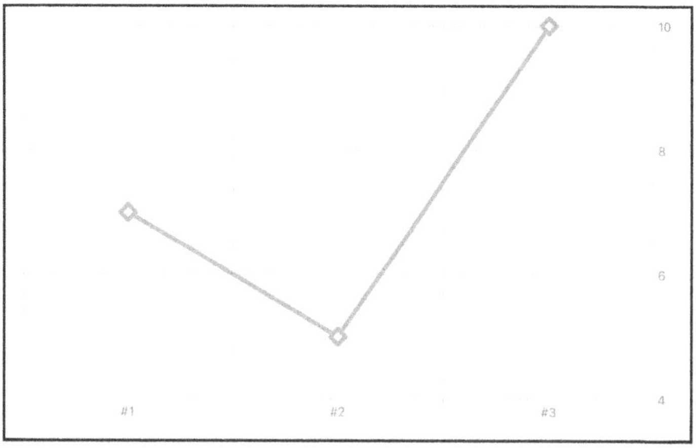

Line colors

Within the limitations of the line chart, you can still use color to provide information to the user. And that's the key to any chart — design to enhance the readability of data, not to confuse or deceive.

Showing More Data

So far, the charts have displayed a single data set, but you can add more than one. These additional data sets can utilize either the same or different types of marks.

In the bar chart, you used the shorthand method of passing data to `Chart`. This is convenient, but restricts you to a single data set. The line chart uses the expanded method with `ForEach` and that lets you to add more data sets.

For this example, you'll add a horizontal line showing the midpoint between the maximum and minimum word lengths.

Replace `// another mark here` with:

```
RuleMark(y: .value("Average", 7.5))
```

A `RuleMark` is a special type of mark that can draw a straight line on the chart. Using this initializer draws a horizontal line at the specified y value.

The words are all between 3 and 12 characters long, so the midpoint is 7.5.

And now, the preview shows:

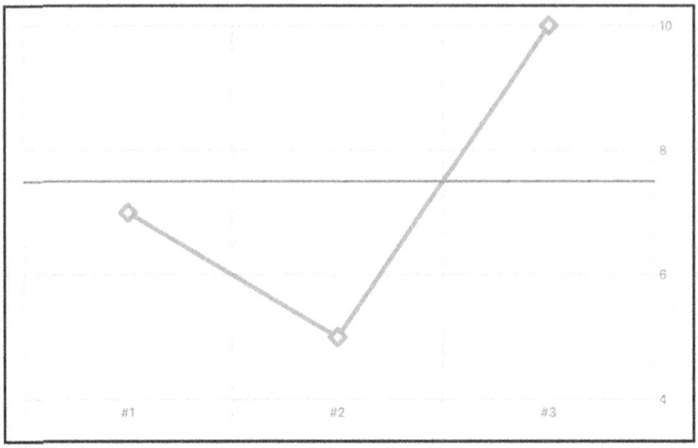

Chart with a RuleMark.

Where you added `RuleMark` is where you could add another `ForEach` loop to insert lines, bars or any of the other mark types.

Accessibility

The SwiftUI Charts team made the Charts library accessible by default. To hear this in action, open **System Settings**. Go to **Accessibility → VoiceOver** and turn on **VoiceOver**:

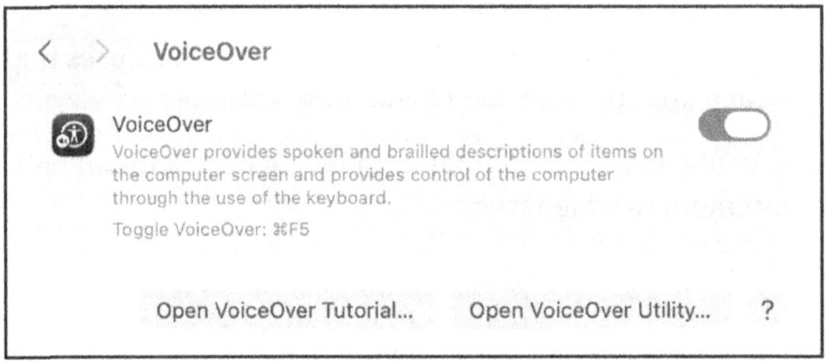

Turn on VoiceOver

You'll see a black box with white text that will describe what's inside its focus box.

To test the default accessibility reports, run the app, play a few games and then go to **Statistics → Length of Words**. Use **Control-Option** with the arrow keys to move the VoiceOver focus box around the window and hear what it says. When over a chart point you'll hear something like "7 #2".

> **Tip**: If the focus box gets stuck on the tab buttons at the top, press **Control-Option-Escape** to change it. The VoiceOver box also provides hints about usage if you give it a second.

This speech gives the coordinates of each point, but you can adjust it to suit the app better.

To improve the VoiceOver content, insert this after the `foregroundStyle` line in **WordStats.swift**:

```
// 1
.accessibilityValue("Game \(point.name)")
// 2
.accessibilityLabel("had \(point.value) letters in the word")
```

This adjusts the speech by:

1. Adding an `accessibilityValue` to each point. Think of this as being the text version of the `x` value.
2. Setting an `accessibilityLabel` to each point that describes the `y` value.

Run the app again and after playing a few games, you'll hear something like "Game number two had six letters in the word", which provides a lot more information.

It's great that charts are accessible by default, but sometimes the defaults need a bit of tweaking to make them more useful.

Turn off **VoiceOver** now and have a go at the challenges.

Challenges

Challenge 1: Flip the bars

The `GameStats` bar chart has horizontal bars. Can you change it so the bars are vertical?

Hint: `x` becomes `y` and `y` becomes `x`.

When you've done that, adjust the position of the annotation to suit the new orientation.

Challenge 2: Use different marks

You've used `BarMark`, `LineMark` and `RuleMark` but there are others. Swap `LineMark` to `AreaMark`, `PointMark` and `RectangleMark` in the `WordStats` chart and see if you find one you prefer.

Try to work these out for yourself, but if you get stuck, look in the **challenge** folder for this chapter.

Key Points

- The SwiftUI Charts library allows you to display data graphically.
- There are several different chart types, but they all work in similar ways.
- Once you've drawn the chart, you can style the chart or the data points.
- Accessibility is built-in, but you can customize it.

Where to Go From Here?

There are some great videos from WWDC 2022 introducing the Charts library and discussing how to use it effectively:

- Hello Swift Charts (https://developer.apple.com/videos/play/wwdc2022/10136/)
- Swift Charts: Raise the bar (https://developer.apple.com/videos/play/wwdc2022/10137/)
- Design an effective chart (https://developer.apple.com/videos/play/wwdc2022/110340/)

In WWDC 2023 and 2024, Swift Charts got even more features:

- Explore pie charts and interactivity in Swift Charts (https://developer.apple.com/videos/play/wwdc2023/10037)
- Swift Charts: Vectorized and function plots (https://developer.apple.com/videos/play/wwdc2024/10155)

After this diversion into charting, which isn't Mac-specific, the next chapter takes you back into the Mac world. You'll handle toolbars and menus and find out how to get your app out of Xcode and into your Applications folder.

Chapter 10: Adding Toolbars & Menus

By Sarah Reichelt

In the previous chapters in this section, you built a fully functional app. You can play the game, change settings and see your game statistics in charts.

Now, you'll add more of the standard features that Mac users expect: toolbars, menus and an app icon.

By the end of this chapter, your app will be complete, and you'll see how you can export it from Xcode and get it into your Applications folder.

Toolbars

Open your app in Xcode or use the project from the **starter** folder in the downloads for this chapter. Run the app and look at the main window. You already have a toolbar:

Initial toolbar

This is because your view uses `NavigationSplitView`. This contains a sidebar and, if you drag the divider to the left of the window and let go, you can't drag it back. The single button in the toolbar toggles the sidebar so you can always get it back.

You have no control over that toolbar item, but you can add your own items. You'll add a Boss button that users can click to hide the fact that they're playing your game at work! ;]

Open **ContentView.swift** and add this after the `frame` modifier:

```
// 1
.toolbar {
  // 2
  ToolbarItem {
    // 3
    Button("Boss", systemImage: "person.fill") {
      // 4
      // action goes here
    }
    // tooltip goes here
  }
}
```

Stepping through this:

1. Add a toolbar to `NavigationSplitView`. Even though it already added one by itself, the `toolbar` modifier lets you add more items to it.
2. Insert a `ToolbarItem` into the toolbar. This is a view type designed for this purpose.
3. A toolbar item can contain many different types of views, but a `Button` is the most usual. Views in a toolbar can show text, icon or both. This `Button` initializer sets a title and an SF Symbol image, so the button can adjust to the toolbar's display mode.
4. You'll add the button's action — what it does when the user clicks it — later.

Run the app again to check out your new toolbar item:

Toolbar item

It doesn't do anything yet, but it's there.

Before making it work, there are a couple of options to set. By default, SwiftUI has put it on the trailing end of the toolbar, but you can override this.

Replace the `ToolbarItem` line with:

```
ToolbarItem(placement: .navigation) {
```

Resume the preview to see the difference:

Toolbar placement

The options you'll use most often are `navigation`, `primaryAction` and `principal`. Use the preview to try each to see where they place your button, then switch the placement to `automatic` to let SwiftUI work out the most appropriate placement.

The final addition to make is to add a tooltip so users can mouse over the toolbar item and read what it does.

Replace `// tooltip goes here` with:

```
.help("Quick, the boss is coming!")
```

This adds a modifier to the `Button` that provides a tooltip and an accessibility hint:

Toolbar button tooltip

Now, it's time to add the action.

Coding the Toolbar Button

The Boss button has to hide the game and display a blank window with an appropriate window title instead.

First, you need a property to store whether to show or hide the game.

Open **AppState.swift** and add this new property:

```
var bossMode = false
```

This is a Boolean that's `false` by default, and `AppState` publishes any changes to it.

Back in **ContentView.swift**, replace `// action goes here` with:

```
appState.bossMode.toggle()
```

This uses a Boolean method that switches `true` to `false` and `false` to `true`.

You have the property, and you have the code to change it. Next, you need to decide what views to show.

Still in **ContentView.swift**, delete all the lines between `body` and `frame`. Those are the selected lines in this screenshot:

```
var body: some View {
  NavigationSplitView {
    SidebarView(appState: appState)
  } detail: {
    GameView(appState: appState)
  }
  .frame(minWidth: 1100)
```

Lines to delete

Fill that gap with:

```
// 1
Group {
  // 2
  if appState.bossMode {
    // 3
    Color.white
      // 4
      .navigationTitle("Work")
  } else {
```

```
    // 5
    NavigationSplitView {
      SidebarView(appState: appState)
    } detail: {
      GameView(appState: appState)
    }
  }
}
```

This looks like a lot:

1. You're deciding between two different view types, but SwiftUI needs to know in advance what type of view `body` returns. One way to work around this is to embed the two options in a `Group` so that `body` always returns a `Group` view.
2. Check if `bossMode` is `true`.
3. If it is, use `Color.white`. In SwiftUI, `Color` is a view and it always expands to fill the available space, so this fills the entire window with white.
4. It would spoil the whole "work" look if the window still had the Snowman title. A `navigationTitle` overrides the default app name title.
5. This chunk is the same as before and ensures that `ContentView` displays the game views if `bossMode` is `false`.

Run the app and toggle the toolbar item:

Boss mode

Animating the Change

Now you and your users are safe if the boss wanders past, but the switch from one mode to the other is rather abrupt.

Add this after the `frame` modifier:

```
.animation(.easeInOut, value: appState.bossMode)
```

The `animation` modifier monitors its `value` and, when it changes, applies the specified animation type. In this case, you're using `easeInOut`, which starts the animation slowly, speeds it up and then slows down near the end.

To see the other options, delete `easeInOut` and press **Escape** to list the autocomplete suggestions. Some variations allow you to specify the duration, but this one needs to stay fast to fool the boss.

Run the app again and toggle to see a smoother change. There's a slight stutter on the `navigationTitle`, but the main view changes more gently.

Now you have a functional toolbar with one automatic item and one that you added yourself.

Menus

Every standard Mac app uses the system menu bar at the top of the screen. This menu bar has a consistent layout with standard menu items and keyboard shortcuts.

You'll often find app controls duplicated in the menus as a way of providing keyboard-based operations and improving discoverability. Menu items display their shortcuts, and the **Help** menu allows you to search the menu items.

You've already added two new menu items by creating new scenes. These both have keyboard shortcuts — one is standard, and the other is your custom shortcut.

Now, you'll add more menu items and a completely new menu.

Including Preset Menu Groups

To start with, you'll tell SwiftUI to include some preset menu groups in your app. Open **SnowmanApp.swift** and add this after the end of `WindowGroup`:

```
// 1
.commands {
  // 2
  SidebarCommands()
  // 3
  ToolbarCommands()
}
```

Stepping through this:

1. The `commands` modifier adds commands to your scene. For macOS apps, this means adding to the system menu. The contents of this modifier are what `commands` adds to the menu bar.

2. The default SwiftUI app includes a basic set of menus and menu items, but not a complete set, since they aren't all needed for every app. There's a collection of pre-built menu groups that provide specific functionality in the standard formats. `SidebarCommands` is one of these, and it adds menu controls for the sidebar.

3. `ToolbarCommands` is a similar pre-configured set that allows users to control the toolbar.

Run the app now and check out the **View** menu:

Expanded View menu

The tabs items and the full screen option were there before, but you now have toolbar and sidebar commands, complete with keyboard shortcuts.

> **Note**: These presets include standard keyboard shortcuts, like **Command-Option-T** for toggling the toolbar, but sometimes developers use these standards for different purposes. This doesn't matter if it's confined to their own app, but can cause confusion if they create global shortcuts that work from anywhere. Trello is an example of this, as it sets **Command-Option-T** as the default global shortcut to toggle the app from anywhere. This means that the toolbar shortcut won't always work in any other app.

The sidebar menu item may seem unnecessary since you already have a toolbar button for that, but it's the only way to control the sidebar if the user hides the toolbar, and it supplies the keyboard shortcut.

Test these new menu items using the menu bar and the keyboard shortcuts. Notice how the text of the menu items changes to suit your choices.

SwiftUI doesn't let you say where you want these items to appear — it places them in the conventional locations with the expected titles, icons and shortcuts.

There are more of these preset groups. Most of them deal with text editing and formatting. To see what's available, search Xcode's **Developer Documentation** for **Menus and commands,** then scroll down to **Getting built-in command groups**. Always use these if possible instead of creating your own menus, as they provide your users with the most consistent and familiar interface.

Customizing the Toolbar

The menu bar has disabled the **Customize Toolbar...** item because you haven't set up the toolbar for customization yet. To make it editable, the toolbar, and each item in it, must have an `id`.

Open **ContentView.swift** and replace the `ToolbarItem(placement: .automatic) {` line with:

```
ToolbarItem(id: "boss_mode_toolbar_item", placement: .automatic)
{
```

This assigns a `String` `id` to the Boss Mode toolbar button.

Next, replace the `toolbar {` line with:

```
.toolbar(id: "content_view_toolbar") {
```

And now, you've set `id` properties for both the toolbar and the item you added.

Run the app and check out the **View** menu again. The menu bar has enabled **Customize Toolbar...** and you can use it to add or remove the **Boss Mode** button and change the **Show** settings. You can't remove the **Toggle Sidebar** button:

Customizing the toolbar.

You can also right-click in the toolbar to set how you want the toolbar items to appear. This works even without toolbar customization.

> **Note**: There is a bug in SwiftUI that crashes the app if you have more than one window open with a customizable toolbar. The `id` for the default sidebar toggle is duplicated, which isn't allowed. This isn't a problem for this app because you're about to restrict it to a single window, but if your app requires multiple windows, then do not make the toolbar customizable.

Adding a Custom Menu Item

The pre-built menu groups are useful and cover a lot of options, but sometimes, your app needs more. In this app, there's an item in the **File** menu to create a new window. Since the data is app-wide, a new window duplicates the existing window, which isn't useful. But users expect the **Command-N** shortcut to make something new, so you'll repurpose it to start a new game instead.

In **SnowmanApp.swift**, add a blank line after `ToolbarCommands()` and insert:

```
// 1
CommandGroup(replacing: .newItem) {
  // 2
  Button("New Game", systemImage: "plus") {
    // 3
    appState.startNewGame()
  }
  // 4
  .keyboardShortcut("n")
}
```

Some of this is new to you:

1. A `CommandGroup` adds its content to an existing menu. You tell a `CommandGroup` where to put its content and it can be `before`, `after` or `replacing` a standard menu item. To see a list of the known menu items, delete `newItem` and press **Escape** with the cursor after the period. In this case, you're replacing **New Window**, so reselect `newItem` when you've read the options.

2. A `CommandGroup` can contain one or more menu items. A menu item can be one of a number of SwiftUI views, but it's most often a `Button`. In this case, you add a `Button` with the title **New Game** and an appropriate SF Symbol to match the new look of macOS menu items, which can show both text and icons.

3. The button action calls `appState`'s `startNewGame()`, which is what the **New Game** button in the game view does.

4. Set a keyboard shortcut of **Command-N**, taking over the previous **New Window** shortcut while keeping the general usage consistent. Remember that the default shortcut modifier key is **Command**, so you don't have to specify this.

Run the app now and open the **File** menu. Select **New Game** or press **Command-N** to see a new game appear in the sidebar:

New Game

You've created a new menu item, positioned it to overwrite an existing menu item that you didn't want and given it the expected keyboard shortcut. That's good user interface design work!

Hiding a Standard Menu Item

In the previous section, you repurposed an existing menu item to suit your app. But what if you want to delete an item instead of replacing it?

Right now, if you select **Snowman Help** from the **Help** menu, you get no help at all:

Snowman Help

Maybe you'll add some help information later, but for now, you'll hide that menu item.

Type a blank line after the end of the new `CommandGroup` and add this:

```
// 1
CommandGroup(replacing: .help) {
  // 2
  EmptyView()
}
```

Looking at this code, it:

1. Adds another `CommandGroup`. This one replaces the help menu item.
2. One of the views you can put into a `CommandGroup` is `EmptyView()`, which shows nothing.

And now, the **Help** menu only contains the menu search:

Truncated Help menu

Deleting the Help menu item may not provide a great user experience, but knowing how to delete an unwanted menu item is useful.

Inserting a Custom Menu

Sometimes, you need to add a completely new menu. You'll add a **Game** menu that has a couple of items to help the user control the game.

To do this, you'll add a new container to the `commands` modifier in **SnowmanApp.swift**.

Add a blank line after the last `CommandGroup` and then insert:

```
// 1
CommandMenu("Game") {
  // 2
  Toggle("Boss Mode", systemImage: "person.fill", isOn:
$appState.bossMode)
    // 3
    .keyboardShortcut("b")
```

```
    // 4
    Button("Different Word", systemImage: "arrow.clockwise") {
      // change word action
    }
    .keyboardShortcut("d")
  }
```

What does this do:

1. A `CommandMenu` inserts a new menu into the main menu bar. The argument is the menu title, and the contents dictate the menu items.
2. A `Toggle` is a great view to use as a menu item if it's linked to a Boolean value. It looks different from the `Toggle` you used in `SettingsView` — in a menu, it gets a checkmark before the title whenever the connected Boolean value is `true`. In this case, it's bound to `appState.bossMode` so selecting this toggles the value. And because its a two-way binding, changing the value using the toolbar button adds or removes the checkmark in the menu item. Again, this includes a title and an SF Symbol.
3. It has a keyboard shortcut because you may need to engage Boss Mode in a hurry! The toolbar item could have a shortcut, but it's not discoverable. The menu item makes it quite clear. And the menu lets you toggle Boss Mode even with the toolbar hidden.
4. Next, add another `Button` with title, system image and shortcut to allow the user to choose a new word. You'll write the code for that soon.

Run the app now to see your new menu:

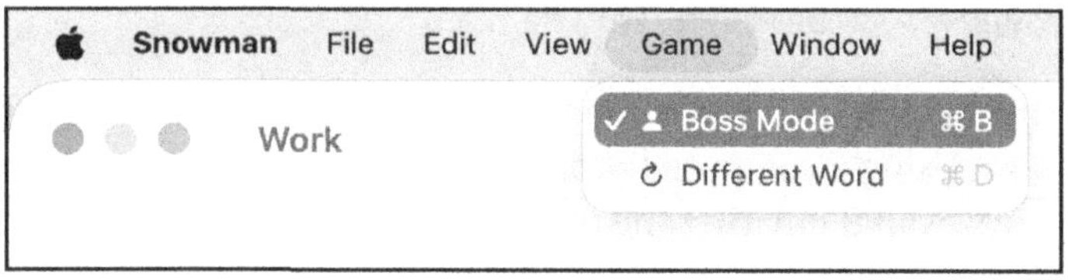

Game menu

The **Different Word** item doesn't do anything yet, but **Boss Mode** works, and its checkmark appears and disappears automatically.

Disabling a Menu Item

Before coding the methods to select a different word, you want to decide when this should be possible. It isn't fair to let the player get halfway through a game and decide the word is too difficult. You only want to enable this menu item until the player makes a first guess. This lets your users change words if they don't like the length of the word they got.

To make this easier to use, you'll create a computed property in `AppState`. Open **AppState.swift** and add:

```
// 1
var gameHasStarted: Bool {
  // 2
  !games[gameIndex].guesses.isEmpty
}
```

This packs a lot in:

1. The computed property is a Boolean — either `true` or `false`.
2. Since it's all on one line, the `return` keyword isn't required. This line gets the current game and checks to see if its `guesses` array is empty. The leading `!` reverses the result, so if `guesses.isEmpty` is `true`, this returns `false` and if `guesses.isEmpty` is `false`, it returns `true`.

To use this, go back to **SnowmanApp.swift** and add this to the **Different Word** button, after `.keyboardShortcut("d")`:

```
.disabled(appState.gameHasStarted)
```

This disables the menu item if the game has started, which is true if the player has made any guesses. Using a computed property for this makes it much more readable at the usage point, even if creating the property was confusing.

Run the app and check the menu item. Then enter a single guess and check it again:

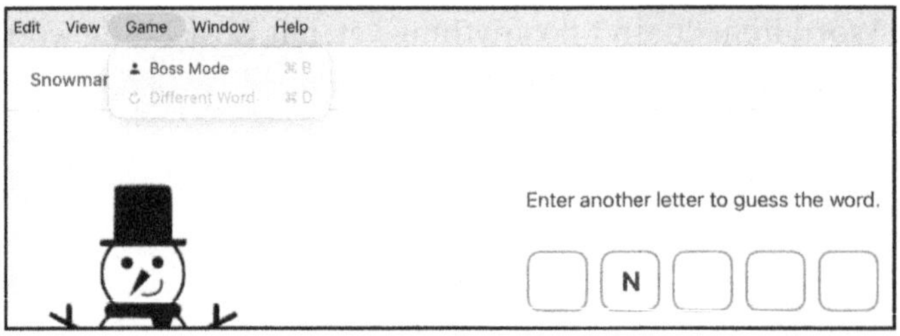

Disabled menu item

Since all completed games must have at least one guess, this only enables the menu item for games that are in progress, but not started.

And with this in place, you're ready to code changing words.

Choosing a Different Word

Implementing changing words requires changes to several files. First, open **Game.swift** and add this method:

```
// 1
mutating func chooseNewWord() {
  // 2
  word = getRandomWord()
}
```

What's happening here?

1. Because this method changes a value in a structure, you must mark it as `mutating`.
2. Then, use `getRandomWord()` to assign a new word to this game.

The next step is to add a method to `AppState` to call this, so open **AppState.swift** and add this:

```
// 1
func getDifferentWord() {
  // 2
  games[gameIndex].chooseNewWord()
}
```

Stepping through this:

1. `AppState` is a class, so editing a property doesn't require the `mutating` keyword.
2. Find the current game in the `games` array and call `chooseNewWord()` on it.

The final step is to hook this up to the menu item. Back in **SnowmanApp.swift**, replace `// change word action` with:

```
appState.getDifferentWord()
```

This calls the AppState method, and that calls the Game method. You could have combined all this into the button action, but that would not have been so clear. This way, the button talks to AppState. AppState knows which is the current Game, and Game has the method for finding a random word so it can change its own word. Each part takes responsibility for its own properties, and any changes are easy to trace.

Run the app and, before making any guesses, select **Game → Different Word** or press **Command-D**. Look in the Xcode console to confirm that the game has chosen a new word:

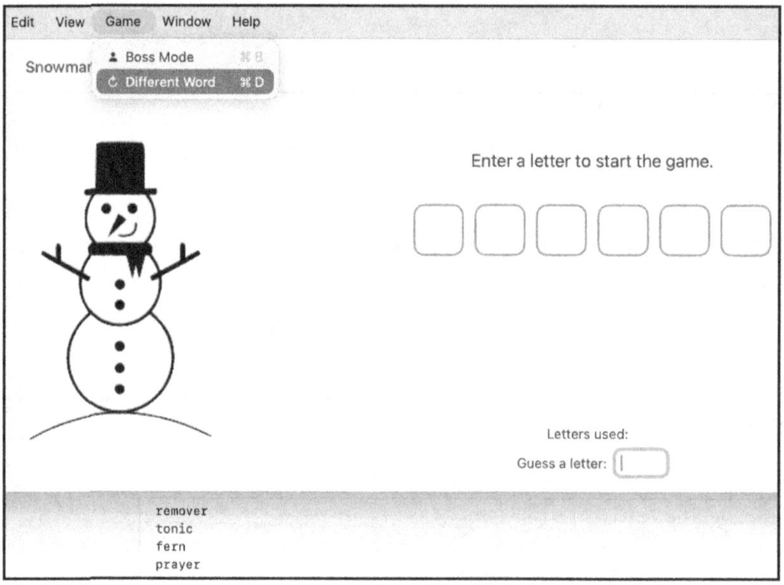

Choosing different words.

You've added preset menu groups, menu items and complete menus. You've used different view types in the menu items, and everything has a keyboard shortcut. Great work! Mac users will appreciate your efforts.

Adding an App Icon

Take a look at the app icon in the Dock. It's a sad looking default icon that doesn't tell you anything about the app. Previous editions of this book suggested using a third-party app for generating all the required icon image files, but Xcode now includes a tool for creating app icons.

Right-click the **Xcode** icon in your Dock and select **Open Developer Tool → Icon Composer**:

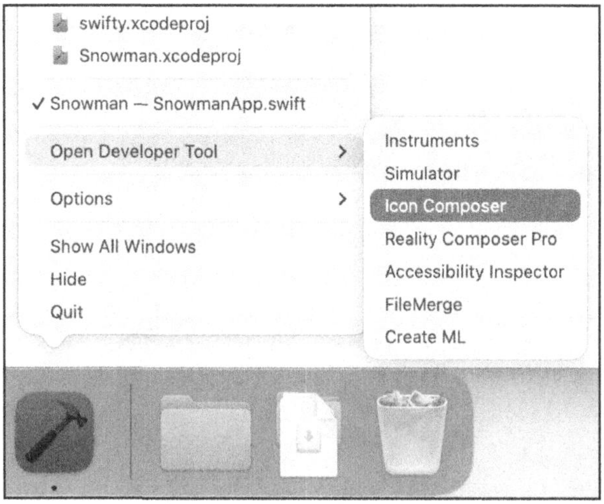

Opening Icon Composer.

Once the app opens, click **New Document** in the file dialog or choose **New** from the **File** menu. If this is the first time you've opened the app, click **Agree** and then it will open a new document. You'll see a window with a default gradient icon in the center and sidebars on the left and right. Since this is for a Mac app, the first thing is to turn off the iOS options. Click the document icon in the top right of the right sidebar to switch to the options. Select **macOS Only** from the **iOS, macOS** popup menu and turn off **watchOS**:

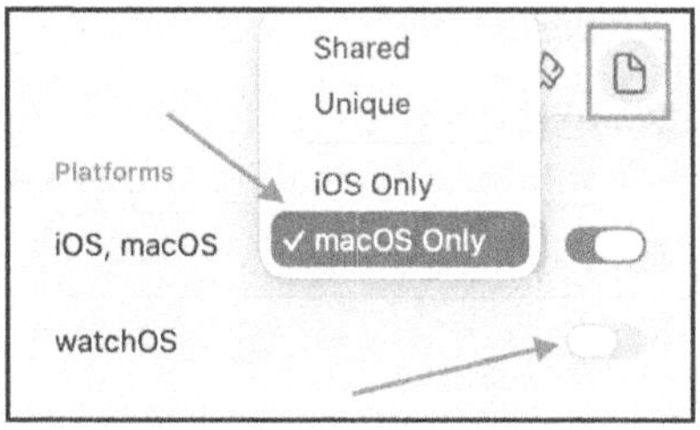

Setting the icon options.

Click the paintbrush icon in the right sidebar to switch to the drawing tools. The first task is to set a gradient for the background. Click the default icon to show the **Fill** section, with two color wells. The top one is set to **Auto**, meaning that when you select a color for the bottom one, the top one adjusts automatically to create an appropriate gradient.

We want the background to look like paper, so click the bottom color well and use the color picker to choose mostly white with a hint of yellow — **FFFFED** in hexadecimal. The top color well changes to match:

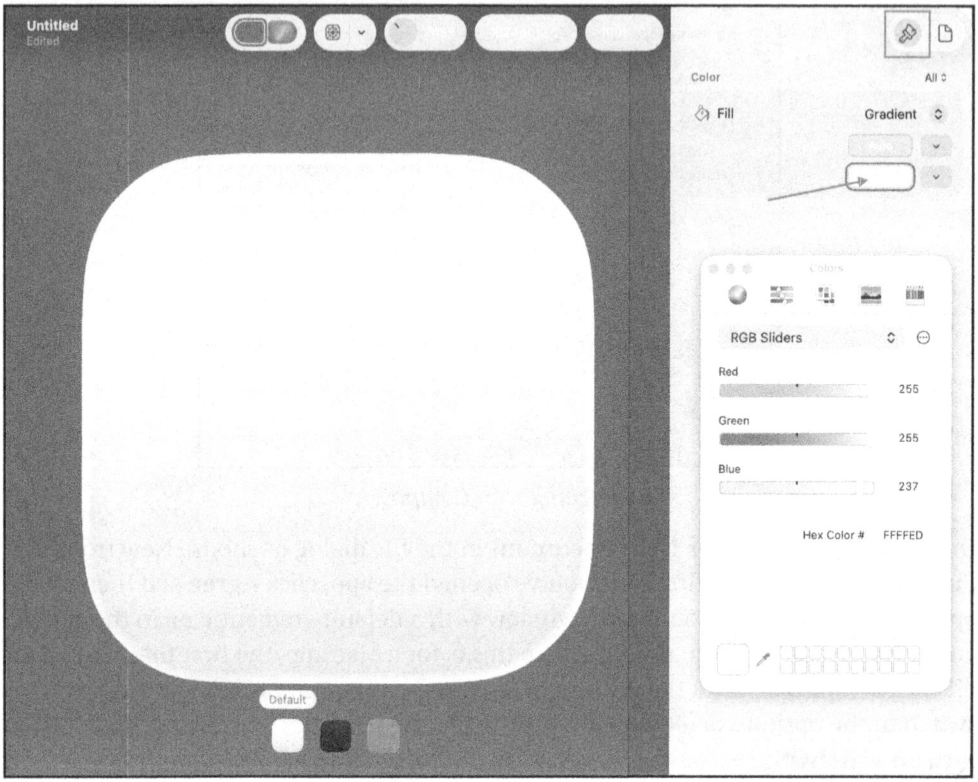

Choosing the icon background.

Next, add one or more images to the foreground. These can be SVG or PNG files. The assets folder for this chapter contains a file called **snowman_head.png** that you can use.

Drag this file on to the icon's background in Icon Composer:

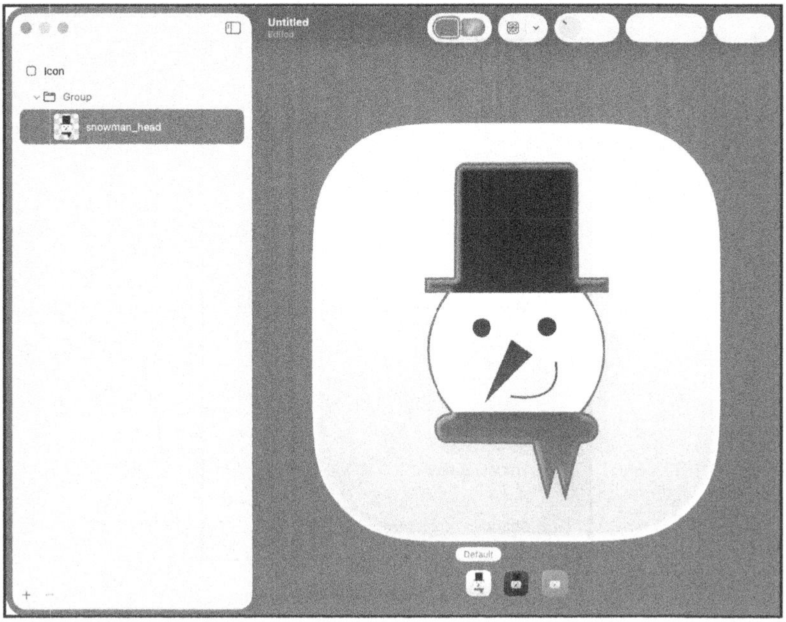

Adding the icon image.

Now it's your turn to have fun experimenting with all the options. In the left sidebar, the image is inside a group. Both the group and the image have options you can adjust. The bottom of the main area has three buttons so you can preview your icon in the various view modes.

Each setting group in the right sidebar has a popup to allow you to select **All** or the current preview mode, so use the mode buttons at the bottom to switch so you can customize settings for each mode.

Turn off **Translucency** for the group in all modes, and in Mono mode, change the group's **Blend Mode** to **Plus Darker**:

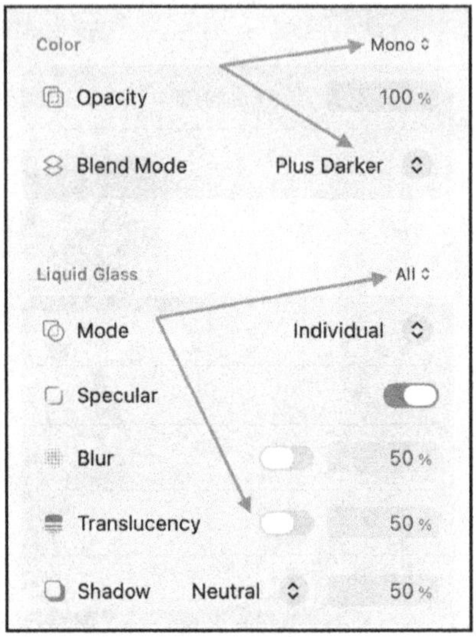

Icon group settings

When you're happy with your icon, choose **File → Save**. In the save dialog, set the file name to **AppIcon.icon** and save it in the same folder as your **SnowmanApp.swift** file.

To see your new icon in operation, choose **Product → Clean Build Folder...** and then run the app. Whenever you change a non-code file, cleaning the build folder makes sure that Xcode implements the changes.

> **Note:** Xcode may show a dialog asking you to confirm that you really want to clean the build folder. If you see this, check **Don't ask again** and click **Clean.**

As well as seeing your icon in the Dock, you can choose **About Snowman** from the **Snowman** menu and see it in the About box:

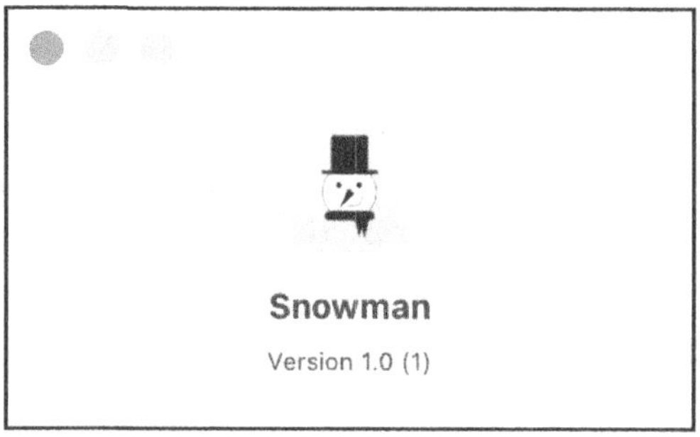

About box with icon

And now you've added the extras that Mac users expect and appreciate in all native Mac apps.

Exporting your Mac app

So far, you've always run your app from Xcode. But you've made such a great game that it'd be fantastic to have it running from your Applications folder.

Quit the app if it's still running and then in Xcode, choose **Product → Archive**. If you get a message about Xcode Cloud, click **Remind Me Later**. Xcode runs the app in **Debug** mode, which adds extra diagnostic tools, uses more memory and is less efficient. Archiving builds the app in **Release** mode.

When it's finished, it opens the **Organizer** window. You can get back to this window at any time by selecting **Window → Organizer**:

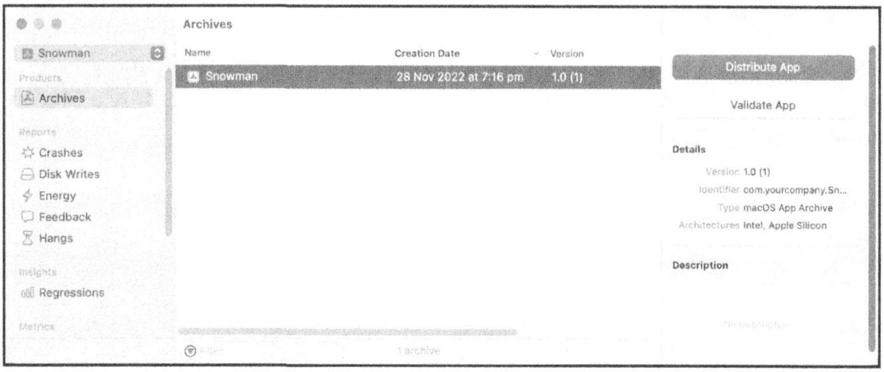

Archived app in Organizer window.

Select the archive and click **Distribute App**. This is the start of the process you'd go through for full app distribution, but that's outside the scope of this book. For all those details, check out macOS Apps Step by Step (https://troz.net/books/macos_apps_step_by_step/).

Select **Custom** and click **Next**. On the next screen, choose **Copy App** and click **Next**, then choose a save location for the export folder and click **Export**. You don't get any feedback from Xcode at this point, but switch to **Finder** and locate the new folder. The export process calls it something like **Snowman 2026-01-23 15-26-04** depending on when you create the export. Inside that folder is your app, and you can drag it into your **Applications** folder and run it.

But you won't be able to see the word in the console anymore, so no more cheating. ;]

macOS happily runs the app on your computer, but complains if you give it to someone else. They'll see a message saying that macOS can't open the app because Apple has not checked it for malicious software. Of course you know there's nothing malicious in your app, so tell your friends that it's OK, but that there's a process to go through before they can run the app for the first time:

1. After the first warning, open **System Settings** and go to **Security & Privacy**.
2. Scroll down to see a message saying "Snowman.app was blocked to protect your Mac".
3. Click **Open Anyway**.
4. You'll see another warning dialog, but this time click **Open Anyway** and enter your password when asked.

This is only for the first time they run the app — after that, they can run it without any further warnings.

So there it is. You've written a real native macOS app using SwiftUI, and you've archived it so you can run it and give it to your friends. You're definitely a Mac app developer now!

Challenge

Your boss may not be convinced by a totally blank white window with no actual work showing. Take a screenshot of a real work window and use that instead. This requires several steps:

1. Get a suitable image and name it **work.png**. There's one in the **assets** folder if you prefer to use that.
2. Import the image file into **Assets.xcassets**.
3. Replace `Color.white` in **ContentView.swift** with an `Image` using the **work** file.
4. Add modifiers to make the image fill the window. Check out **GameView.swift** to see what modifiers you added to the `Image` there. Are some of them appropriate? Maybe with different settings?

Try to work this out for yourself, but if you get stuck, look in the **challenge** folder for this chapter.

Key Points

- Mac users expect standard apps to operate in similar ways. This includes adding toolbars to main windows and using the menu bar.
- SwiftUI has options for including preset menu groups. Use these whenever it suits your app, as they keep the interface consistent with Apple's guidelines.
- Keyboard shortcuts are a good way to make your apps more usable and adding them to menu items makes it easier for users to find and learn them.
- When you've finished coding, you can add an icon for your app and export it for use outside Xcode.

Where to Go From Here?

You've done a terrific job and created a great little app. What could you do with it now?

One idea would be to add a different word list. You could make a version for children or one to teach a different language.

Then there are the graphics. There are many variants of this game with different images as the player guesses. Search for **hangman game variations** to get some ideas, or create your own image sets. **Game.swift** expects the last image to be number 7, so you'll need to edit that if you have a different number.

For more information on the new Icon Composer, check out Create icons with Icon Composer (https://developer.apple.com/videos/play/wwdc2025/361) from WWDC 2025.

In the next section of this book, you'll leave SwiftUI and dive into AppKit which is the other layout framework available for macOS apps.

Section III: Building With AppKit

From the very beginning of macOS X, AppKit has been the workhorse behind the user interface of all apps and there are still a number of tasks where it is the superior choice. In this section, you'll explore such an area while building an app to browse movie data from IMDb, the online movie database.

Chapter 11: Beginning AppKit

By Sarah Reichelt

In the previous two sections, you learned some basic Swift and built a complete app using SwiftUI. Apple provides two different layout frameworks for building macOS apps and in this section, you'll use the other one: AppKit.

This chapter starts the process of building an app to list movies from IMDb (https://www.imdb.com). By the time you're finished, you'll be able to search, sort, filter and edit your movies list.

You'll start from scratch with a new style of app template and build your interface graphically using a storyboard. Then, you'll learn how to get data into an AppKit table.

When you're finished, your app will look like this:

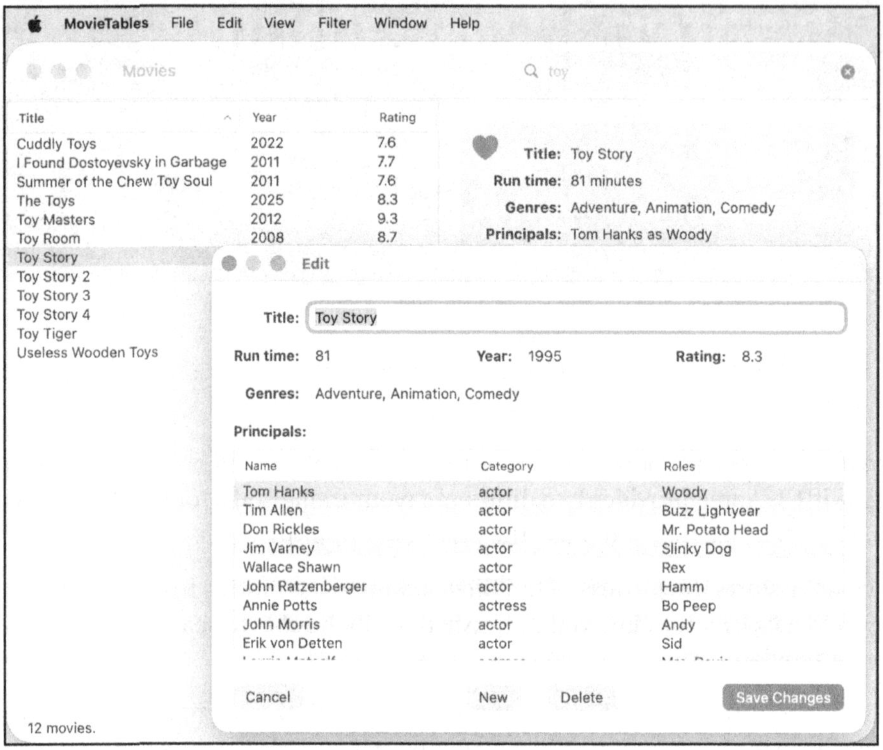

Movie Tables app

I'm sure you're excited to proceed, so start Xcode and get ready to code.

Creating an AppKit App

Once you've started Xcode, create a new project from the **Welcome to Xcode** window, or by selecting **File → New → Project...**. As before, choose **macOS → App** before clicking **Next**.

Set the Product Name to **MovieTables** and leave Team as **None** or select your own developer team. Enter your reverse domain for the organization identifier — you can make one up, it doesn't have to be a real domain.

Now for the different setting: Select **Storyboard** for the interface. Leave language set to **Swift** and when your options look like this, click **Next**:

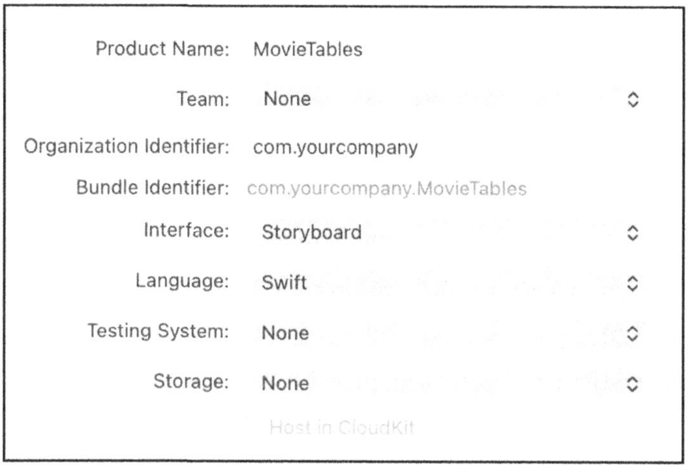

Setting project options.

Decide where to save your project and click **Create**.

> **Note**: It always works best to name your Xcode projects with no spaces and no characters apart from letters and numbers. You can change the app name later, but you'll avoid Xcode issues if you start like this.

Click the **Play** button in the toolbar or press **Command-R** to run the app:

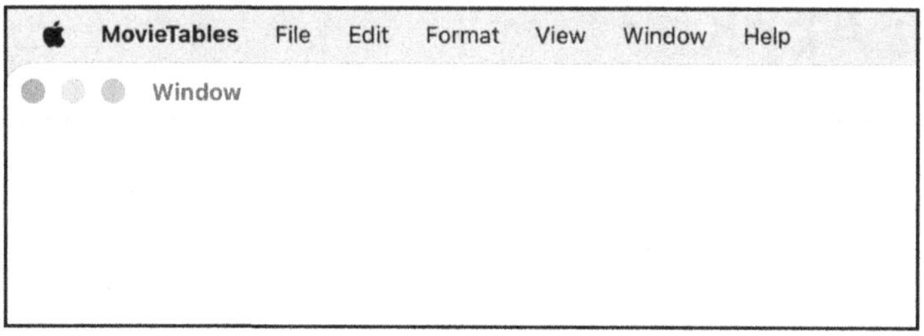

Running the AppKit template

There's a single empty window and if you click the menus, you'll see a *lot* of menu items.

Return to Xcode and look at the starting files:

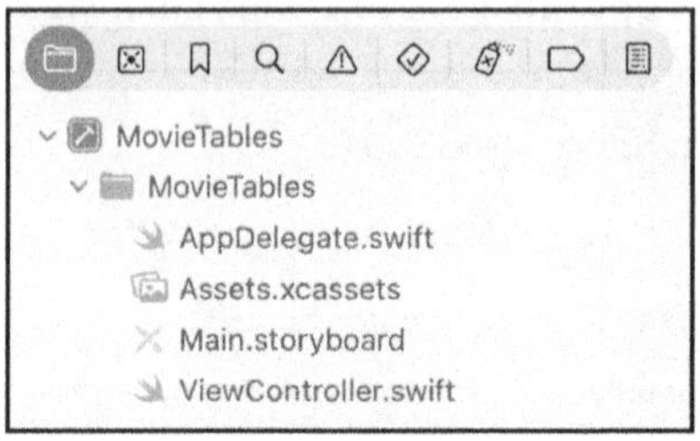

Starting files

Your SwiftUI app had **Assets.xcassets** for images, icons and other graphical assets but the others are new:

- **AppDelegate.swift**: A delegate is an object that receives events from, and provides information about its parent. `AppDelegate` is a subclass of `NSApplicationDelegate` and it handles interactions with the application itself.
- **Main.storyboard**: This is where you'll design the user interface. You'll spend a lot of time in this file as you work through this chapter.
- **ViewController.swift**: In SwiftUI, you create `Views` that the app shows in `Scenes`. In AppKit, you create subclasses of `NSViewController`. Each view controller has a view that contains the interface. The view controller acts as the middleman between the view and the data models. This is the **Model-View-Controller** or **MVC** pattern and is the default pattern for AppKit apps.

What is AppKit?

By this stage, you may be wondering what AppKit is and why you're using it.

AppKit is the original layout framework created for OS X and, later, macOS apps. You'll notice that all the main classes have names that start with `NS`. This stands for NeXTSTEP, which was the company that developed what became OS X. Any time you see a class with the `NS` prefix, you know you're using AppKit.

You created SwiftUI views programmatically, but you'll design your AppKit views visually in a storyboard.

SwiftUI is a great layout framework, but it's still young. This means that most established macOS apps — and jobs — still use AppKit. As part of your journey to becoming a Mac developer, it's important to learn both.

The other reason for using AppKit is that SwiftUI doesn't do everything yet. And some of the things that it does aren't suited to all apps. This app lists thousands of movies. SwiftUI gets very slow and unresponsive with that much data, so this is an example of where AppKit is better than SwiftUI.

Adding Data

In the SwiftUI app, you built the interface first and then constructed the data model to suit. This time, you're getting data from an external source so it works best to look at that first and then build the interface around it.

Open the **assets** folder in the downloaded materials for this chapter and drag **movies.json** into the Project navigator.

Select **Copy files to destination** and check the **MovieTables** target, then click **Finish**.

Select the new file to open it in Xcode. It's a large file — over 54 MB — so Xcode takes a while to open it, but you only need to do this once to examine the structure. The file contains data downloaded from IMDb datasets (https://datasets.imdbws.com).

This is a **JSON** file, which stands for **JavaScript Object Notation**. JSON has become the standard for transferring object data and Swift handles it well, but first you need to discover the data properties.

After collapsing some entries, this is the first movie in the list:

```
[
  {
    "genres": "War",
    "id": "tt0001498",
    "isFav": false,
    "principals": [
      {
        "category": "actor",
        "id": "nm0095809",
        "name": "Sydney Booth",
        "roles": "Lord Nelson"
      },
      { ··· },
      { ··· },
      { ··· },
      { ··· },
      { ··· },
      { ··· },
      { ··· }
    ],
    "rating": 7.9,
    "runTime": 51,
    "title": "The Battle of Trafalgar",
    "year": "1911"
  },
```

Structure of the JSON data

Looking at the top of the file, the opening square bracket indicates an array of objects. The curly braces delimit each object. The data fields and types are:

- genres: `String`
- id: `String`
- isFav: `Boolean`
- principals: `Array`
- rating: `Double`
- runTime: `Int`
- title: `String`
- year: `String`

`principals` is another array of objects but you can ignore it for now.

Armed with this knowledge, you can construct your data model.

Creating the Data Model

Press **Command-N** or use the **File** menu to make a new file. Choose the **macOS → Source → Swift File** template and click **Next**. Name the file **Movie.swift** and click **Create**.

Add this class definition to the new file:

```
// 1
class Movie: Codable {
  // 2
  let id: String
  // 3
  var title: String
  var runTime: Int
  var rating: Double
  var genres: String
  var year: String
  var isFav = false
  // 4
}
```

This defines the main data structure:

1. To work with AppKit tables, you must use a `class`, not a `struct`. The class conforms to `Codable`, which means that it works with JSON data.
2. The `id` property is a constant so it can never change.
3. Later on, you'll let users edit the rest of the movie data, so the other properties are variables.
4. All the properties from the JSON data are there, except for `principals`. That needs its own data object, so omit it for now. The names of the class properties match the names of the JSON properties.

If you remember earlier chapters, a structure doesn't need you to define an initializer, but a class does. However, you don't need to type it out.

Right-click on the word `Movie`, then select **Refactor → Generate Memberwise Initializer**:

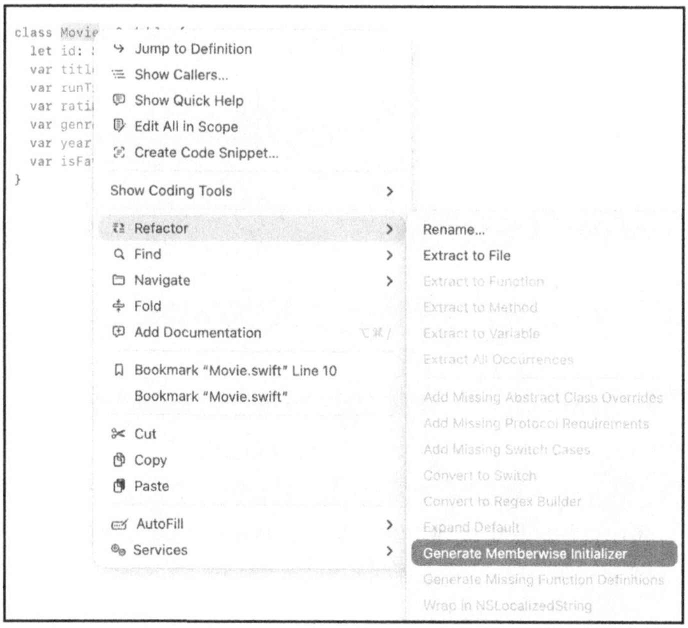

Generate initializer

This adds an `init` method that assigns the arguments to the matching properties.

Note: The `internal` keyword sets an access level for this method so that it's only accessible from within this project. This is the default setting for all methods and properties.

Now that you have the object structure, you can decode the JSON data into this format.

Converting the JSON

Before you can display the data in a table, you need a method that reads **movies.json** and converts the JSON into an array of `Movie` objects.

Still in **Movie.swift**, but outside the class, add this:

```
// 1
extension Movie {
  // 2
  static func readBundleData() -> [Movie] {
    // 3
    guard let fileURL = Bundle.main.url(
      forResource: "movies",
      withExtension: "json")
    else {
      // 4
      return []
    }

    // 5
    do {
      // 6
      let jsonData = try Data(contentsOf: fileURL)
      // 7
      let movies = try JSONDecoder().decode([Movie].self, from:
jsonData)
      // 8
      let sortedMovies = movies.sorted { movieA, movieB in
        movieA.title < movieB.title
      }
      return sortedMovies
    } catch {
      // 9
      print(error)
      return []
    }
  }
}
```

Taking this bit by bit:

1. Create an extension of the `Movie` class. This is part of the class, but separating it like this makes it clearer that this is a class method.
2. Define a `static` method. You call this method on the class itself, not on any particular instance of `Movie`. It returns an array of `Movie` objects.
3. Start by trying to get the `URL`, or file address, of **movies.json** in the application bundle.
4. If this fails, return an empty array.
5. If the file exists, start a `do` block. This allows you to do a series of actions, any of which may fail. As soon as one fails, the program drops down to the `catch` block, ignoring the rest of the `do` block.
6. Try to read `Data` from the file. This operation may fail, so the `try` keyword tells your code to make an attempt and use the `catch` block if there's a problem. The `Data` type is a general type to store any data.
7. If you got `Data` from the file, create a `JSONDecoder` and use its `decode(_:from:)` to convert it. The first argument tells the decoder the data type to return — in this case, an array of `Movie` objects. The `self` property of a type returns the type itself. Again, this can fail, especially if the JSON doesn't match the object structure, so use `try`.
8. Next, sort `movies` using `sorted(by:)`. This takes two `Movie` objects and checks which `title` comes first. Return the sorted array.
9. Finally, if anything went wrong, print the error message and return an empty array. The `catch` has an automatic `error` argument. Printing the error is a good way to detect mismatches between your data structure and the JSON.

Phew! That was intense, but now you can finally start using the data.

Reading the JSON

Open **ViewController.swift** and add this property at the top:

```
var movies: [Movie] = []
```

This sets up the array to hold the movies, starting it off as an empty array.

Next, delete `representedObject`. You won't use it in this app.

Finally, replace the `// Do any additional setup` line with:

```
movies = Movie.readBundleData()
print(movies.count)
```

This calls the `Movie` method you wrote for reading the data file and, as a confirmation, prints the number of elements in `movies`.

Run the app now. There's nothing visually different, but check the Xcode console:

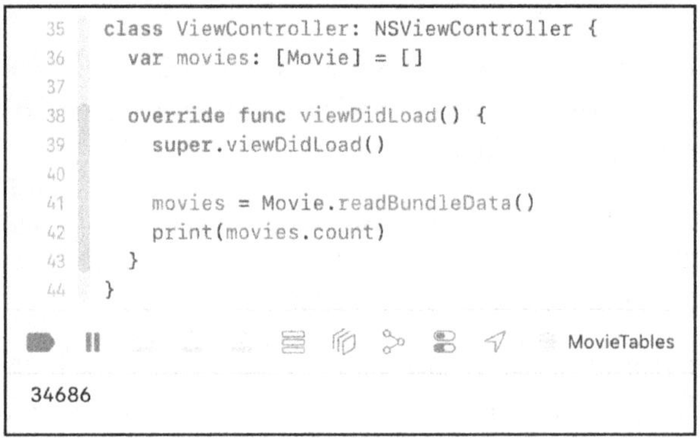

Reading the movies data.

After all that work, you have over 34,000 movie records in your app. Now, it's time to display them.

> **Note**: You may see some warnings in the console, mostly about menus. These are warnings about Apple's code, not yours, so while they should not be appearing, it isn't your problem.

Storyboarding

There's been a lot of coding so far with little visual result, but finally you get to the user interface.

Open **Main.storyboard** and take a look around:

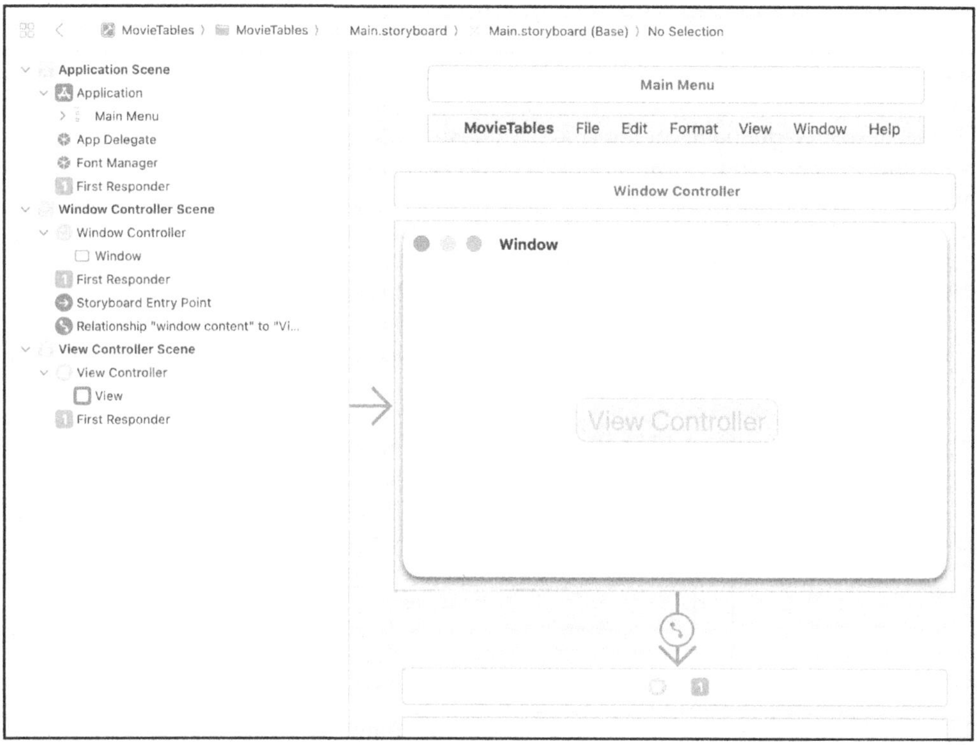

Main.storyboard

Down the left, the outline view shows three scenes. Use the disclosure arrows to expand them so you can see the contents. **Application Scene** holds the menu bar. **Window Controller Scene** has a window and a link to **View Controller Scene**. It holds the view controller, which contains the `view`. The view is where you'll add your interface elements.

In the graphical layout pane, the plain arrow pointing to the `Window` shows that it's the initial window that the app displays when it runs. The window shows the text **View Controller** because that's what it contains. The arrow with the squiggle connects the view controller as the window's content.

Configuring the Window

Start by selecting **Window** by clicking inside the box labeled **Window** or by selecting **Window Controller Scene → Window Controller → Window** in the outline view.

Every window in an AppKit app has a window controller to manage the window, create it from the storyboard, handle its content, display the title and control the size.

Open the Inspectors pane on the right by clicking the sidebar toggle button at the top right or by pressing **Command-Option-5**. The keyboard shortcut opens the Attributes inspector directly, but if you used the toolbar button, click the button with the sliders to open it.

Change **Title** to **Movies** and set **Autosave** to **MoviesWindow**:

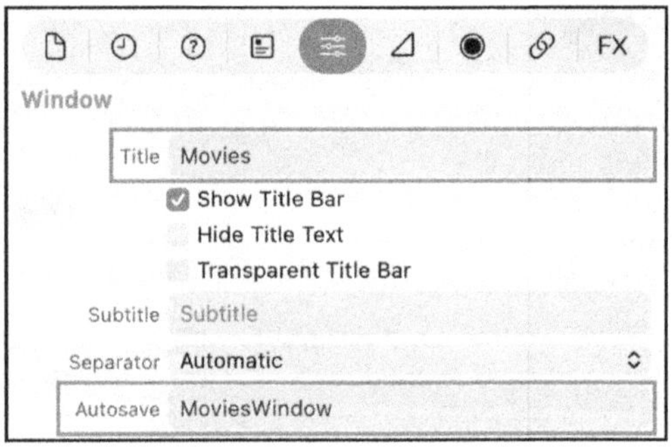

Setting window attributes

The top of the window and the outline view both change to show your new window title. **Autosave** provides a key so the app can save your window size and location for restoring next time you run the app.

The default window is small and this makes laying out the interface more difficult, so now choose the Size inspector — the next tab along.

Set **Width** to **800** and **Height** to **400**. Then check **Minimum Content Size** and enter the same values there:

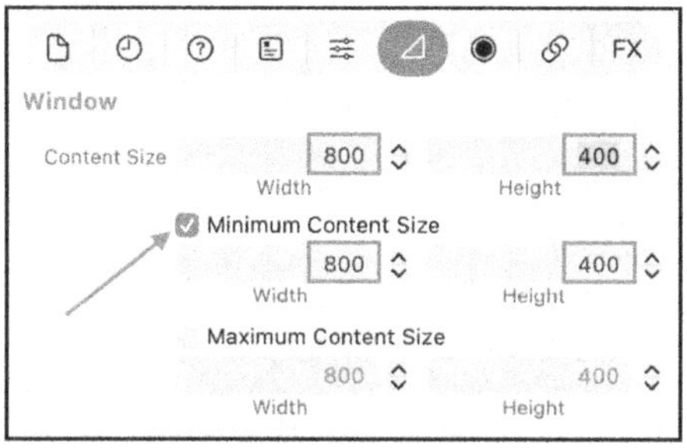

Sizing the window

You don't care how big the window gets, but you don't want it to get too small.

That messed up the display so drag things around so they don't overlap. If the graphics get too big to fit in your window you'll see a floating navigation pane that you can click to move around.

Now that you've configured the window, you can move on to the view controller.

Setting Up the View

Click inside the View Controller box or select **View Controller Scene → View Controller → View** in the outline view. In the Size inspector, set **Width** to **800** and **Height** to **400** to make this view the same size as its containing window.

Drag the elements around to avoid any overlaps. And now you can start to add some interface elements!

Inserting a Table View

Press **Shift-Command-L** or click the + button in the bottom toolbar to open the **Library**. You've used the library before to find SwiftUI views and modifiers. Now it shows AppKit objects instead.

Search for **table** and drag a **TableView** into the `View`:

Inserting a table view.

You only asked for a table view, but the library has inserted a *lot* more. In the outline view, click the disclosure arrow beside **Bordered Scroll View** and then **Option-click** it to expand fully:

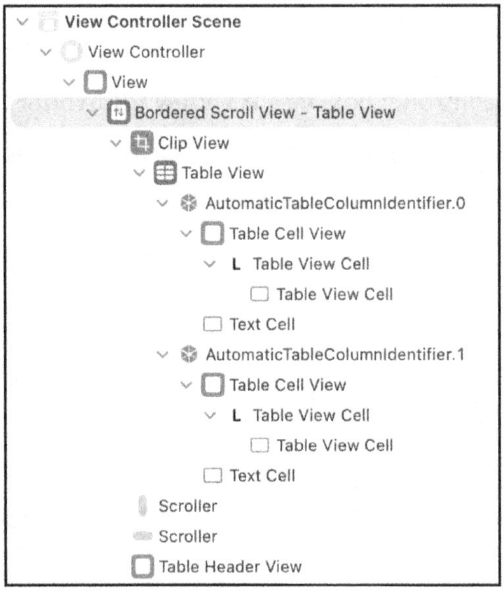

Expanded table outline

There's a **Table View** there, but it's inside a **Clip View** which is inside a **Bordered Scroll View**. This allows your table to scroll and ensures it won't overflow its designated size.

Inside the table view, you have two columns, each with their own sub-components. And finally, you have two scrollers and a header.

Not a bad result for adding a single object from the library! Now, it's time to configure the table.

Positioning the View

In SwiftUI, the layout engine works out the optimum size and location, depending on the view type and its contents. With AppKit, you have to explicitly tell the view where to go and what size to be.

But your users can resize the window and the views need to adjust accordingly. To allow for this, you use **Auto Layout**. With Auto Layout, you provide **constraints** to set spacing between objects and provide size limits.

This can get tricky when you have multiple views as you'll see in later chapters, but now, you only have a single view to constrain.

Click in the outline view to select the **Bordered Scroll View**. Then, click the **Add New Constraints** button in the bottom toolbar.

Enter **1**, **1**, **400** and **30** for the top, left, right and bottom spacing to nearest neighbor. Leave the other options unchecked. When your settings look like this screenshot, click **Add 4 Constraints**:

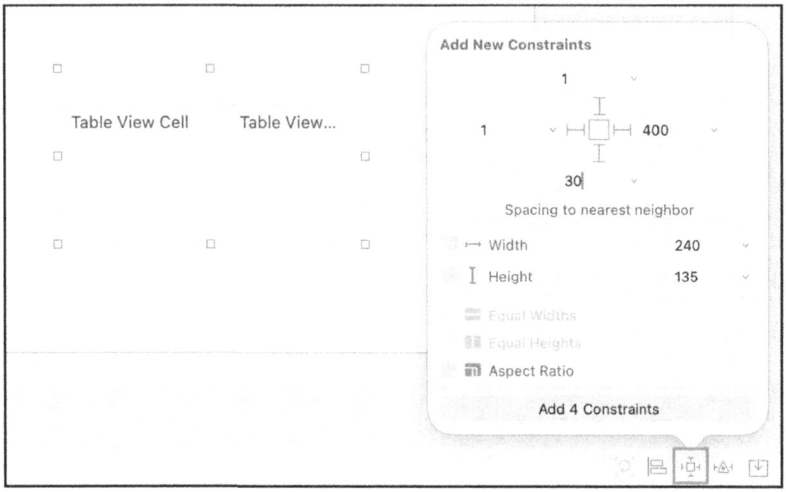

Adding constraints

Since this is the only subview in the view, the spacing is to the edge of the parent view. When you click the button, the table jumps into place. Check back to the image at the start of this chapter. This positions the table as expected, leaving space at the right for the movie details and at the bottom for the count.

> **Note**: You probably expected to use zero for the top and left constraints to place the table at the top-left of the parent view, but there is a layout bug in macOS Tahoe that messes up the scroll if you have spacing at the bottom but not at the top. Any spacing, even a single pixel, fixes this. The left spacing is not required, but makes the display more symmetrical.

Run the app now and resize the window to confirm that the table adjusts as expected and that the window never gets too small:

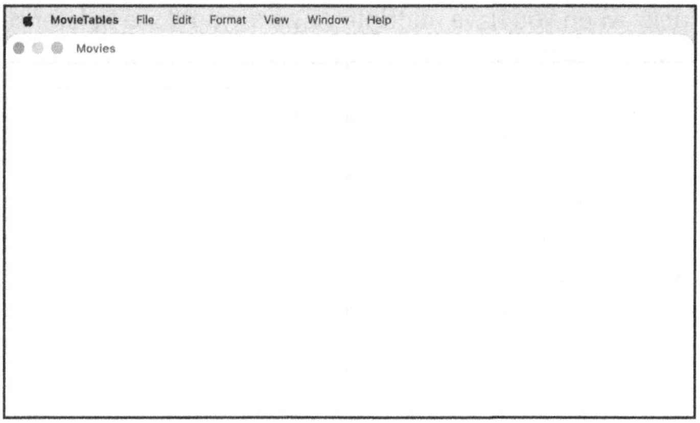

Resizable table

It may feel like nothing's happening yet, but you're making great progress.

Ignore the yellow warning blob beside the View Controller Scene — you'll fix that when you configure the table columns.

Setting Table Columns

The final table has three columns showing the title, year and rating for each movie. The default table comes with two columns, so now you'll fix that.

You need to configure the table itself, but it can be difficult to select it when it's embedded in other objects. Hold down **Shift** and **right-click** in the table view to see a menu of the nested components:

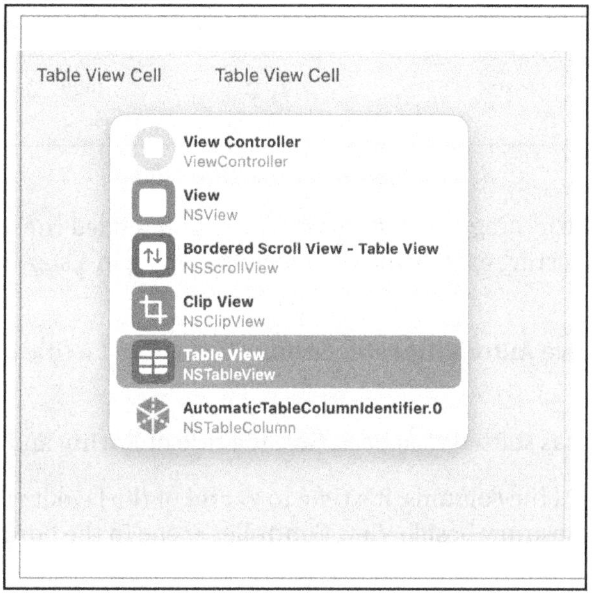

Selection menu.

Select **Table View**, open the Attributes inspector on the right and change **Columns** to **3**:

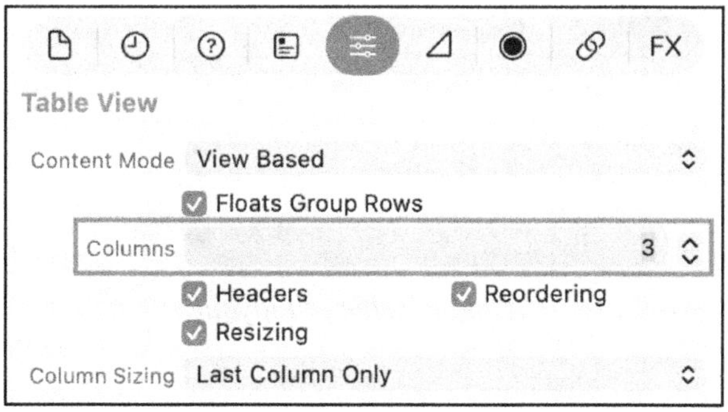

Setting the number of columns.

Visually, nothing has changed because the third column is outside the box, but you can see a new **Table Column** in the outline view.

Select **AutomaticTableColumnIdentifier.0** in the outline view and, in the Attributes inspector, set its Title to **Title**. Click the next inspector icon to get to the Size inspector and set Width to **200**:

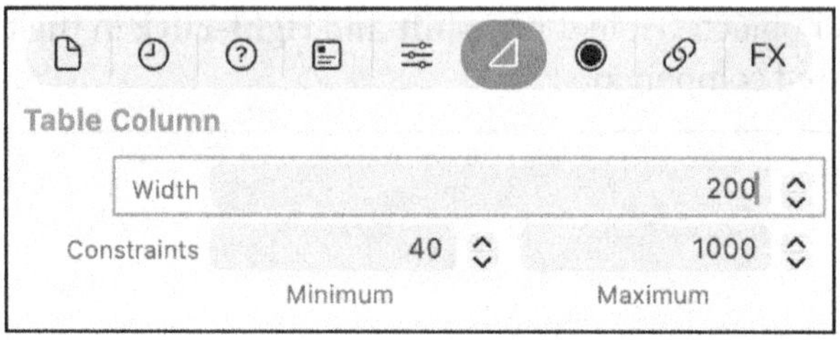

Setting the size for the Title column.

You can set the size by dragging, but this can have unintended consequences due to the difficulty of selecting exactly the right view, so typing in a size is a more reliable method.

In the same way, give **AutomaticTableColumnIdentifier.1** a title of **Year** and a Width of **100**.

The third column has started to appear. Give it a title of **Rating** and a width of **50**.

Now that you see all the columns, it's time to get rid of the layout warnings. Click the yellow blob with the arrow beside View Controller Scene in the outline view. This slides sideways to show a new pane with the three Table View Cells listed as needing constraints.

Click each **Table View Cell** line in turn and, in the Size inspector, change Layout to **Autoresizing Mask**:

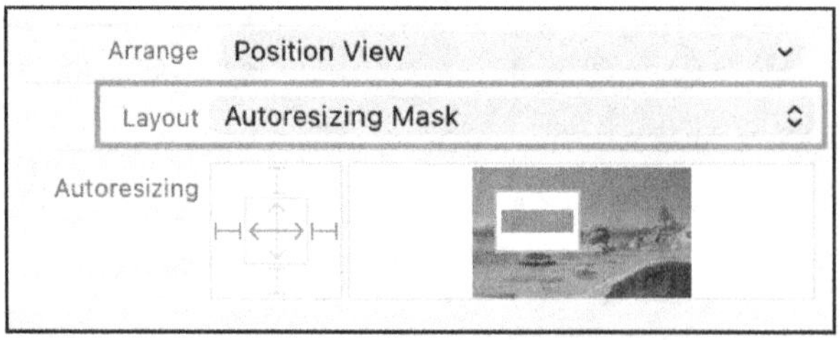

Changing table cell layout.

This tells the individual table cells to use an older layout style and expand to fill the available space. Xcode doesn't detect that you've fixed these errors. The fastest way to get rid of the yellow marker is to save, then quit and restart Xcode.

Preparing the Table for Data

Now that you've set the number of columns and their titles and widths, there are only a few more details to add in the storyboard before you jump back to the code and make the data appear.

First, each column needs an identifier so your code knows which piece of data to provide. Select the **Title** column in the outline view, or **Shift-right-click** in the first column and select it from the menu. Open the Identity inspector from the icon or by pressing **Command-Option-4**.

This column has a preset Identifier of **AutomaticTableColumnIdentifier.0**, which is descriptive but not informative. Change this to **TitleColumn**:

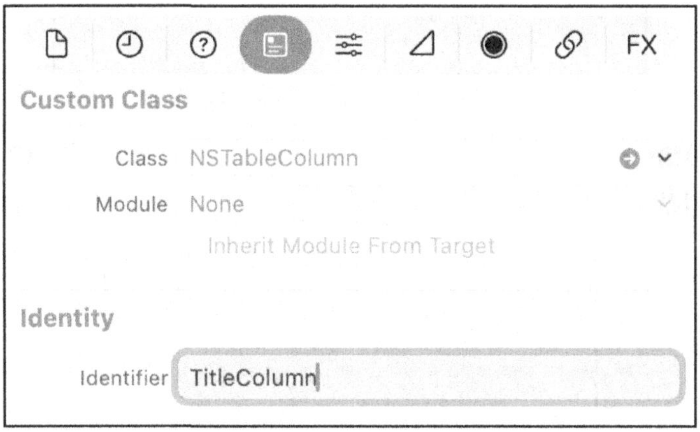

Setting the column identifier.

Next, change the **Year** column's Identifier to **YearColumn** and set the **Rating** column's to **RatingColumn**.

That identifies each column, but you also need to identify the cell inside the column. This allows the code to place the valid data in the correct view.

Shift-right-click in the cell at the top of the **Title** column where it shows **Table View Cell.** Choose **Table Cell View** from the menu:

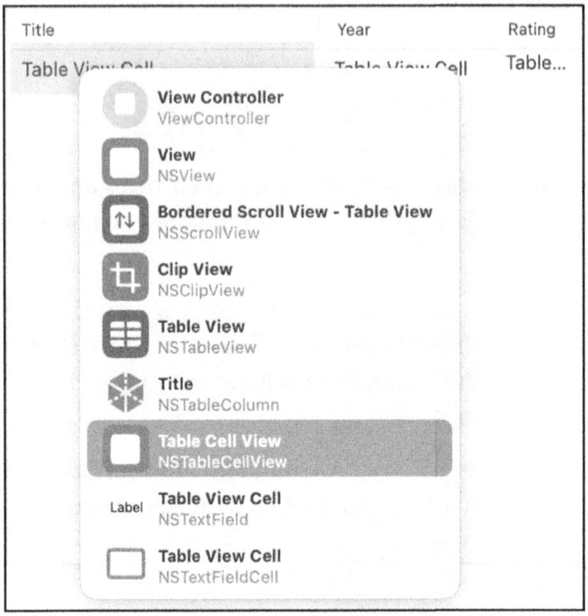

Selecting the table view cell.

In the Identity inspector, you'll know you chose the correct one if the **Class** is **NSTableCellView**. Set the Identifier to **TitleCell**:

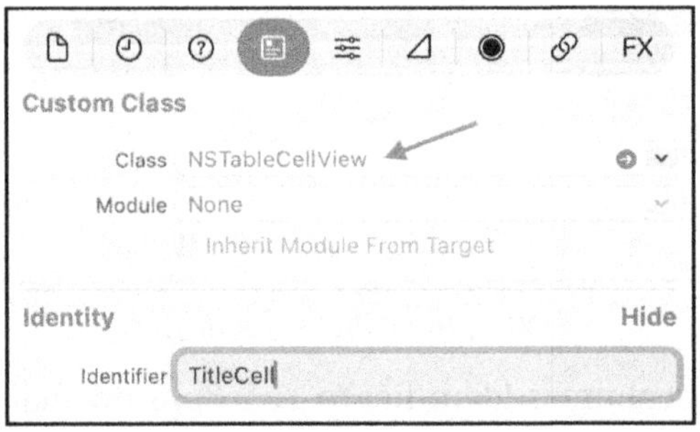

Setting the cell identifier

Do the same with the cells at the top of the other two columns, setting their identifiers to **YearCell** and **RatingCell** respectively.

You're nearly finished in the storyboard, but you still have to link the table to your code.

Select the table view using whatever method you prefer. Open the Connections inspector by clicking the seventh icon in the Inspectors toolbar or by pressing **Command-Option-7**.

In the Outlets section, drag from the circle beside **dataSource** to the **View Controller** in the outline view. Do the same for **delegate**. The Connection inspector now shows these links:

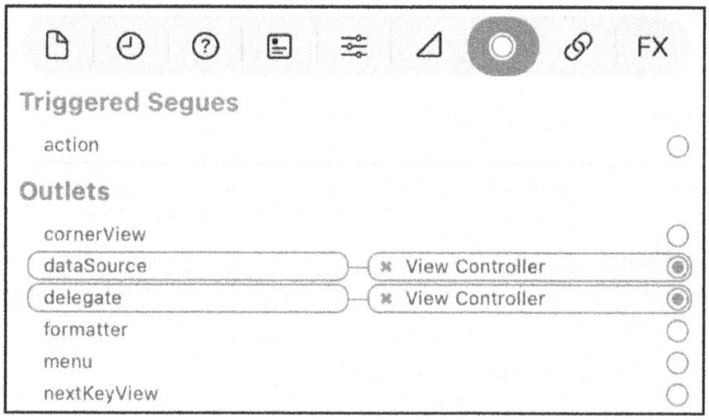

Table view connections

Finally, **Shift-Option-click ViewController.swift** in the Project navigator to open it in a separate editor beside the storyboard. Add some blank lines before the `movies` property declaration.

Control-drag from **Table View** in the storyboard's outline to this blank space and release the mouse button when you see the **Insert Action or Outlet** tooltip:

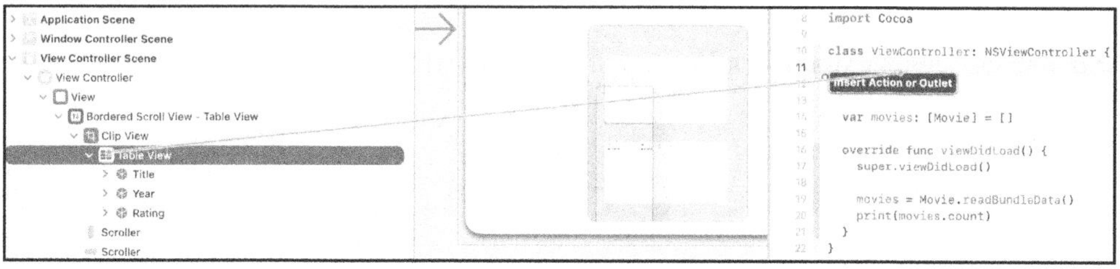

Connecting the table view.

Enter **moviesTableView** as the **Name** and confirm the other settings are as shown here:

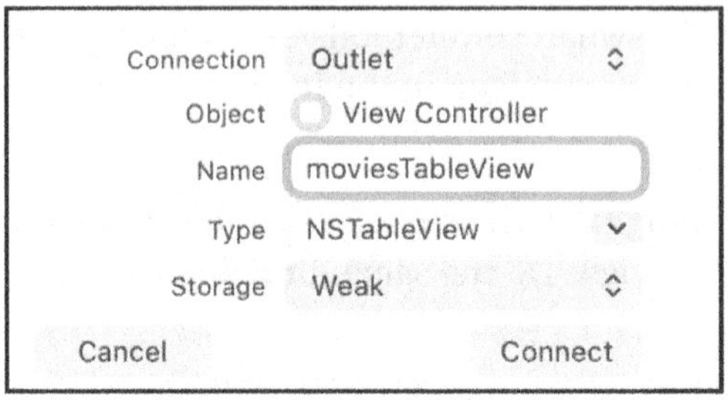

Creating an outlet

Click **Connect** to add this code to `ViewController`:

```
@IBOutlet weak var moviesTableView: NSTableView!
```

There's a lot of detail in this line:

1. `@IBOutlet` marks this as an **Interface Builder** outlet — an object created in the storyboard that your code can now address.
2. A `weak var` defines a property that won't get stuck in memory. When your view controller closes, it frees the memory allocated to this property.
3. The property type is `NSTableView`.
4. This is an optional but the exclamation mark force-unwraps it. Xcode promises to have created the table view from the storyboard by the time you need it. As a general rule, don't use force-unwrapping, but if Xcode puts it in for you, then it's OK.

You may not believe it, but you're very close to showing data now!

Adding a Data Source and Delegate

You're finished with **Main.storyboard** for this chapter, so close its editor.

Right-click **ViewController.swift** in the Project navigator and select **New Empty File**. Set its name to **TableData.swift**.

Insert this into the new file:

```
// 1
import AppKit

// 2
extension ViewController: NSTableViewDelegate,
NSTableViewDataSource {
  // methods go here
}
```

This is where your table gets its data:

1. You're using several AppKit classes here, so import AppKit to start.
2. This is an extension of `ViewController`, so it's still part of the same class but separated out for readability. It states that `ViewController` conforms to the `NSTableViewDelegate` and `NSTableViewDataSource` protocols. In the storyboard, you set `ViewController` as the `dataSource` and `delegate` for the table view, so this is the code side of that.

These two protocols provide data to the table, configure the display and respond to any user interactions.

It sounds like `NSTableViewDataSource` provides the data and `NSTableViewDelegate` detects events, but the distinction isn't as clear as that, so you're using a single extension to supply both.

Next, you'll add the protocol methods to populate the table.

Providing the Methods

In place of `// methods go here`, start typing `number` until you see this autocomplete suggestion:

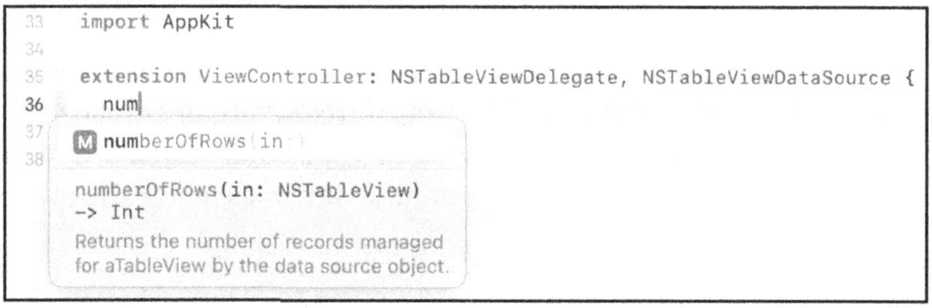

numberOfRows autocomplete

Press **Return** to accept the suggestion, and replace the code placeholder with:

```
movies.count
```

This is a method in `NSTableViewDataSource`. The argument is the table view (useful if your view has more than one table), and it returns the number of elements in `movies`.

The next method returns the view to show in each cell. Add some blank lines below the last method and start typing **viewfor** to get these suggestions:

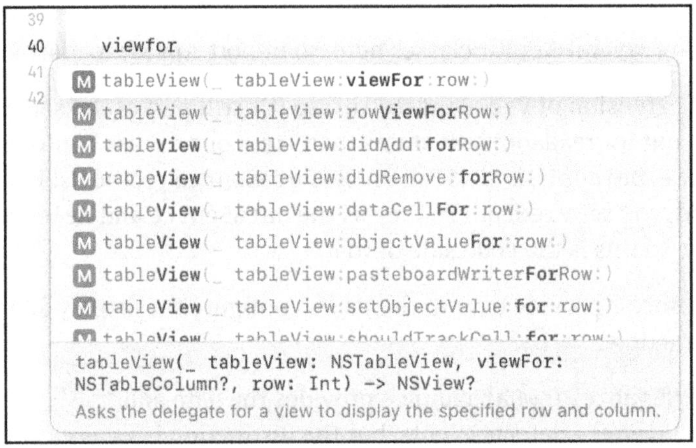

viewForRow autocomplete

Select `tableView(_ tableView:viewFor:row:)`.

This is an `NSTableViewDelegate` method that returns the view to show in the specified column and row, but there are some oddities in the arguments.

Swift has a feature where any function argument can have two labels: The caller uses the first one and the method uses second one. For the second argument, the caller uses `viewFor`, but inside the method, you'll access it with `tableColumn`.

The first argument uses an underscore as the external label. This means that the caller doesn't have to supply a label at all. Using different argument labels is a great way to make your code readable. You can write methods that read like almost like a sentence when called, but still have logical argument names inside the method.

Next, replace the code placeholder with:

```
// 1
guard let columnID = tableColumn?.identifier else {
  return nil
```

```
}

// 2
let movie = movies[row]
var cellID = ""
var cellText = ""

// 3
// get data for each column and cell

// 4
let cellIdentifier = NSUserInterfaceItemIdentifier(cellID)
// 5
if let cell = tableView
  .makeView(withIdentifier: cellIdentifier, owner: nil) as?
NSTableCellView {
  // 6
  cell.textField?.stringValue = cellText
  return cell
}

return nil
```

That's a lot of code!

1. First, check that the column has an identifier. You set these in the storyboard. If there's no identifier, return `nil` and nothing appears in this cell.
2. Get the movie that corresponds to this row number. Define two variables to hold the cell's identifier and text.
3. You'll add code to set these variables in a minute.
4. `cellID` is a `String`. This converts it into an `NSUserInterfaceItemIdentifier`, which is what the next line expects.
5. `makeView(withIdentifier:owner:)` is an `NSTableView` method that returns a view with the correct identifier. The view loads from the storyboard originally, but once a cell view has scrolled out of sight, this method re-uses it, which makes `NSTableView` very efficient even with lots of data. This gets the view, and if it's an `NSTableCellView`, sets `cell`.
6. If you make it to here, `cell` is a non-optional `NSTableCellView`. If it has a `textField`, set its `stringValue` to whatever went into `cellText` and return it.
7. If anything went wrong, return `nil`.

Well done for getting through that. You're nearly there.

Finally, replace `// get data for each column and cell` with:

```
// 1
switch columnID.rawValue {
// 2
case "TitleColumn":
  cellID = "TitleCell"
  cellText = movie.title
// 3
case "YearColumn":
  cellID = "YearCell"
  cellText = movie.year
// 4
case "RatingColumn":
  cellID = "RatingCell"
  cellText = "\(movie.rating)"
// 5
default:
  return nil
}
```

This is where you work out what to put in each cell:

1. `columnID` is another `NSUserInterfaceItemIdentifier`. In the previous chunk, you created one of these from a string. You can do the reverse and read its `rawValue` to get the string back out. Since there are several possibilities, `switch` is a good choice for stepping through the options.

2. If the column identifier is **TitleColumn**, then the matching cell identifier is **TitleCell**. The data to show in the cell is the `title` of the `movie` for this row.

3. The **YearColumn** works the same, since `movie.year` is a string.

4. `movie.rating` is a `Double`, so you use string interpolation to convert it into a `String`.

5. Every `switch` must be exhaustive, so it can handle every possibility. The `default` block deals with any other `columnID` and returns `nil`.

And with this in place, you're ready to see your table in action.

Viewing the Table

Press **Command-R** to run the app:

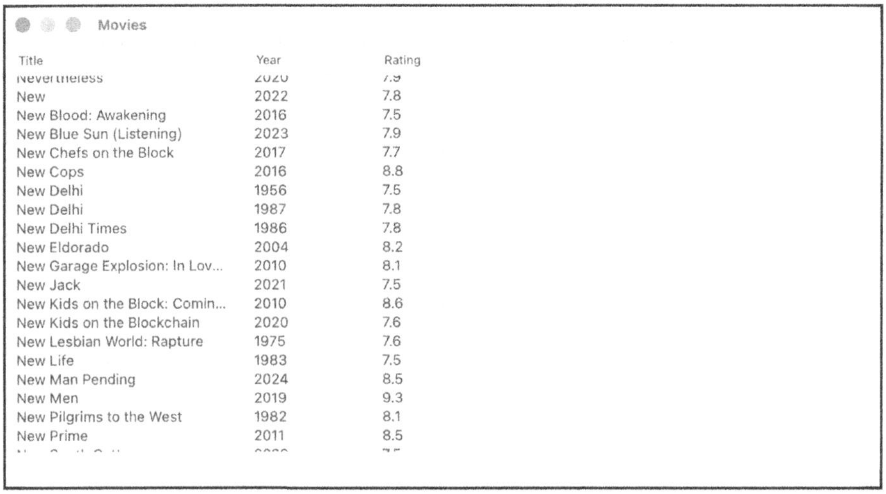

Table view with data

And there it is — your table showing over 34,000 rows!

If everything went well, you'll see all the data with three columns for each row. But there was a lot to set up, so maybe you don't see what you expect.

If this happens to you (and it happens to everybody at some stage), here are the things to check in **Main.storyboard**:

- Confirm that `ViewController` is the `dataSource` and `delegate` for **Movies Table View**.
- Check the **Column Identifiers** for each column.
- Make sure you set the **Cell Identifiers** on the correct subviews. They are for the `NSTableCellViews`.

With those fixed, run the app again to see your data appear. You can scroll up and down the list, resize columns, even move columns. This chapter was a lot of work, but you made it. Congratulations!

Key Points

- AppKit is an alternative layout framework for macOS apps.
- You design the layout visually using a storyboard and use auto layout to position components.
- JSON is a commonly used data format that you can transform into Swift objects.
- AppKit tables are a great way to display large amounts of data.

Where to Go From Here?

In the next chapter, you'll add more functionality to your table. Users will be able to search, sort and see the selected movie's details.

Chapter 12: Building the User Interface

By Sarah Reichelt

In the previous chapter, you loaded in the **movies.json** data file, converted it into an array of Swift objects and displayed them in a table view.

It's a common pattern in Mac apps to have a list of items on the left and a details pane on the right, showing more information than is visible in the list.

In this chapter, you'll add this pattern to **MoviesTable**. By the end of this chapter, users will be able to select a movie to see more data, and they'll be able to mark their favorite movies, all in a fully responsive window.

Selecting a Movie

Open the project you worked on in the last chapter or use the **starter** from the downloaded materials for this chapter. The **starter** folder has a compressed version of the **movies.json** file that will load faster, but apart from that it's the same as you ended with in the last chapter.

Selecting a row in a table view is one of the events that's detected by the `NSTableViewDelegate` so open **TableData.swift** and add these two method stubs:

```
// 1
func showSelectedMovie(_ movie: Movie) {
  print("You selected \(movie.title)")
}

// 2
func clearSelectedMovie() {
  print("Selection cleared")
```

```
}
```

You'll add more code to these methods when you've set up the user interface, but for now, they'll print reports so you know what's happening:

1. The first one gets a `Movie` as the argument and prints its title.
2. The other method detects when the user clears the selection.

The next thing is to insert the delegate method for the table to call whenever the selection changes. Add some blank lines after the last method and type `tvs`. Xcode uses the initials to suggest these autocomplete options:

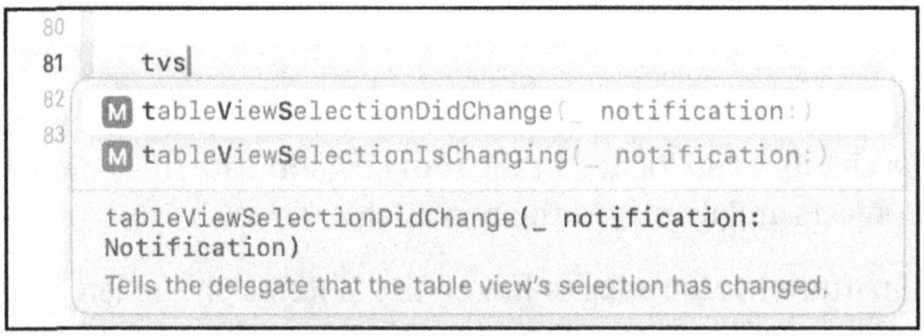

selection autocomplete

Choose `tableViewSelectionDidChange(_ notification:)` and replace the `code` placeholder with:

```
// 1
let row = moviesTableView.selectedRow
// 2
if row < 0 || row >= movies.count {
  // 3
  clearSelectedMovie()
  return
}

// 4
let selectedMovie = movies[row]
showSelectedMovie(selectedMovie)
```

What does this do?

1. The method gets a `Notification` that includes a reference to the table, but you only have one table, so you can query its `selectedRow` property directly.
2. If the user hasn't selected anything, `row` equals `-1`. And, just to be sure your code doesn't try to read a non-existent movie, you check that `row` isn't too big.

3. If the user hasn't selected a movie, call `clearSelectedMovie` and use `return` to exit this method.
4. Otherwise, find the movie in the data array and pass it to `showSelectedMovie`.

Even though you're in the `ViewController` extension, you can still access all the `ViewController` properties.

Run the app now and select a few different movies. Check that the titles appear in the Xcode console. **Command-click** the selected movie to clear the selection and confirm that this prints the correct text:

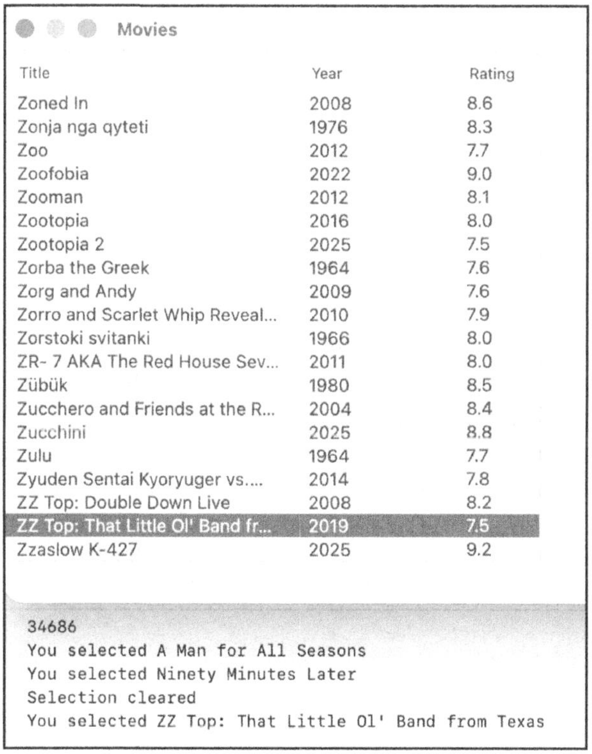

Selecting and deselecting.

Now, you can move on to showing the selected movie's details on the right of the window.

Adding the Details Fields

Open **Main.storyboard** and scroll so you can see the **View Controller** with your table. Press **Shift-Command-L** to open the Library. Search for **box** and drag a `Box` into the empty space. This will draw a nice border around the details display.

With the box still selected, open the Attributes inspector and set **Title Position** to **None**:

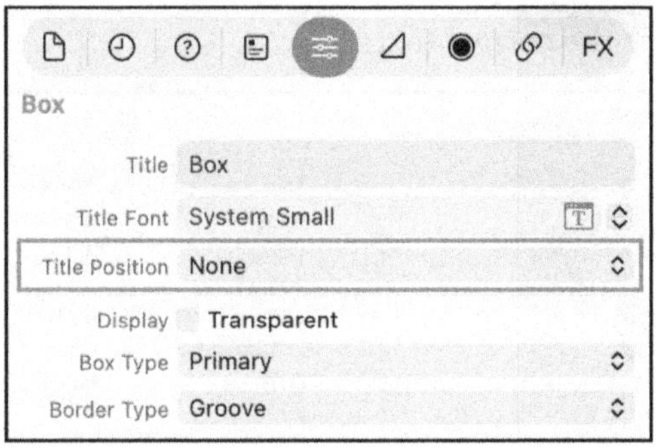

Turning off the box title.

Next, you need to add some Auto Layout constraints. Click the **Add New Constraints** button and enter **20** for the spacing on the left. For the other three, click the little arrow in the box and select **Use Standard Value**. The standard value is 20 when spacing from the sides of the view, but it's less for the spacing to another object. You want them all the same, which is why you set the left spacing manually.

When your settings look like this, click **Add 4 Constraints**:

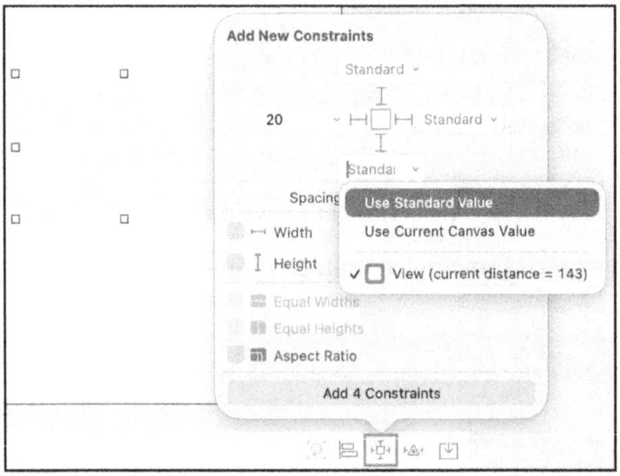

Setting box constraints.

You've now positioned your new box neatly filling the right side of the window. Look at the outline view: **Box** has its own **View**. The detail display elements all go into this subview.

You want to show the movie details in text fields, but you're not going to let the user edit them here. Open the Library again by pressing **Shift-Command-L** and search for `label`. This is perfect for what you need:

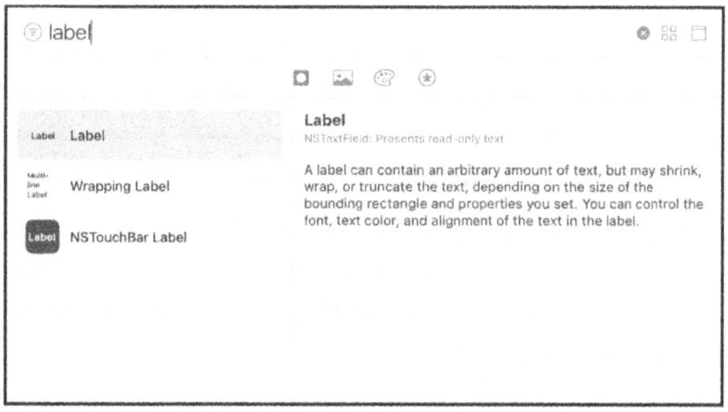

Label in Library

Drag a **Label** from the library into the **Box**. Drag the side handles out until the width is 240, keeping the height at 16:

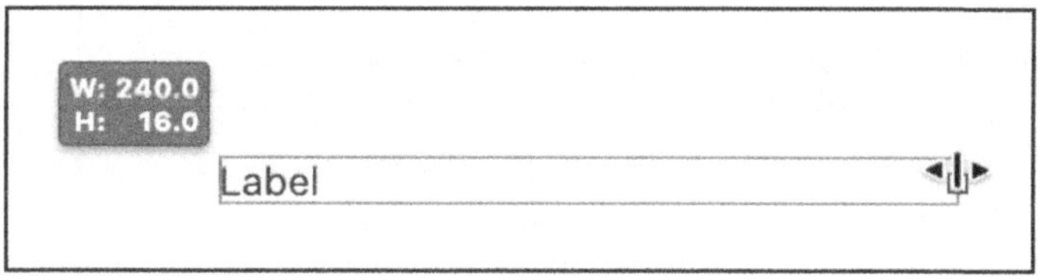

Resizing the label.

Next, drag the label towards the top right corner of the box until you see two blue guides appear. Release the mouse button when the top right of the label is at the intersection of these. Use the vertical guide inset from the edge, like in this screenshot:

Aligning the label.

Now that you've resized this label, you can copy it to create the other data labels at the same size. Select the original and press **Command-D** to duplicate. Then drag the copy down and left until you get the alignment guides at the sides and it *clicks* into the standard spacing from the original at the top:

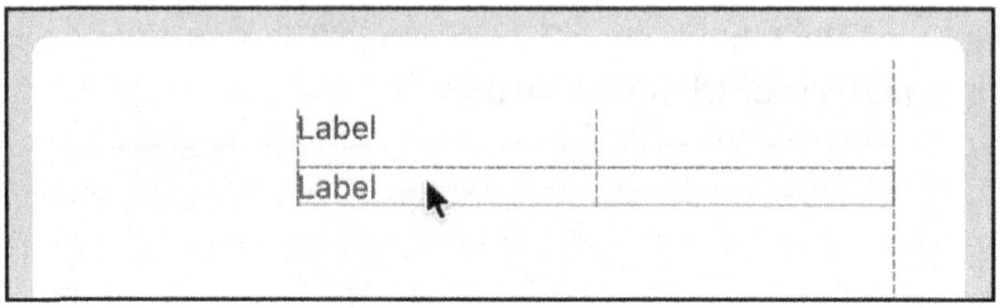

Position the duplicate.

Repeat this process twice more until you have four labels, all lined up.

Next, drag or Shift-click to select all four labels, click **Resolve Auto Layout Issues** and choose **Reset to Suggested Constraints**:

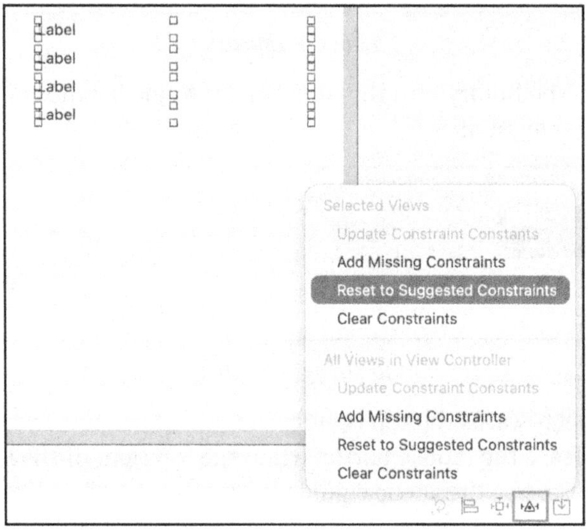

Reset to Suggested Constraints

This tells Auto Layout to add the constraints it thinks are best, given your current positioning. You can see what it's done by selecting any label and opening the Size inspector. This is the top label:

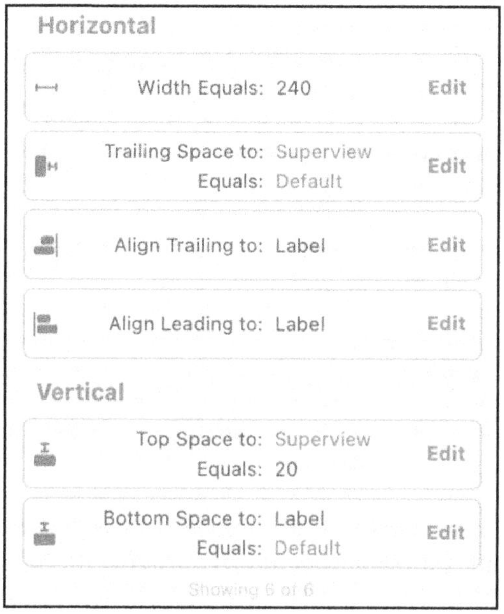

Suggested constraints

Vertically, the label has spacing to the edge of its parent view and to the top of the next label. Horizontally, it has spacing from either edge of the containing superview, and it's aligned with some of the other labels.

> **Note**: You may see a horizontal leading or trailing space constraint instead of the width constraint. If you do, great! If you see the width setting, don't panic — Xcode will ask you to adjust it soon.

Working with Auto Layout

To achieve a responsive design that adapts to user settings, you must use Auto Layout, but it can be tricky. Here are some tips to make it easier to work with:

- If any change makes things look wrong, press **Command-Z** to **undo** immediately. Trying to fix a mistake only leads to more problems.
- Add and position major elements first. Then, you can use them as anchors for less important elements.
- Use the alignment guides to position elements using standard spacing before adding constraints.
- Use **Reset to Suggested Constraints** as a starter, but have your fingers ready on **Command-Z** to undo if it does something unexpected.
- Leave any placeholder text visible while setting up the layout. It's much easier to see what's happening.
- Don't test by resizing the view in the storyboard. Leave your storyboard view set to its minimum size and test responsiveness by resizing the window in the app.
- If everything gets in a complete muddle, use the **Resolve Auto Layout Issues** button to **Clear Constraints** from selected views or from the entire view controller.

Everyone struggles with Auto Layout at some point, but these suggestions will save you some grief.

> To learn more about Auto Layout, check out our book: _Auto Layout by Tutorials (https://www.kodeco.com/books/auto-layout-by-tutorials)_.

Inserting Title Fields

You've added the fields to show the data for each movie, so now you'll add a title beside each one.

These are also read-only text fields, so drag a new label into the box from the Library. Open the Attributes inspector (**Command-Option-5**) and set Title to **Title:** and Alignment to **Right**:

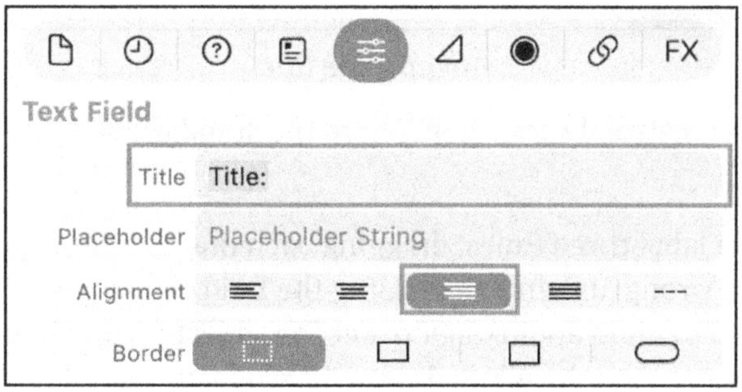

Configuring the Title label.

The Font is set to **System Regular** by default. That's perfect for the data fields, but the title fields will look better if they're a bit different.

Click the icon of a window with a **T** in it, beside where it says **System Regular**. Open the **Font** menu in the popup and select **Headline**, then click **Done**:

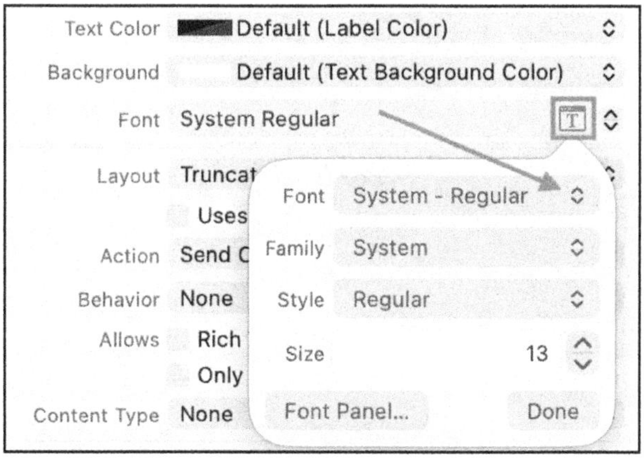

Setting the font.

Next, drag the new title field so that it aligns with the top and left edges of the first data label. You want to get the three horizontal guides as shown:

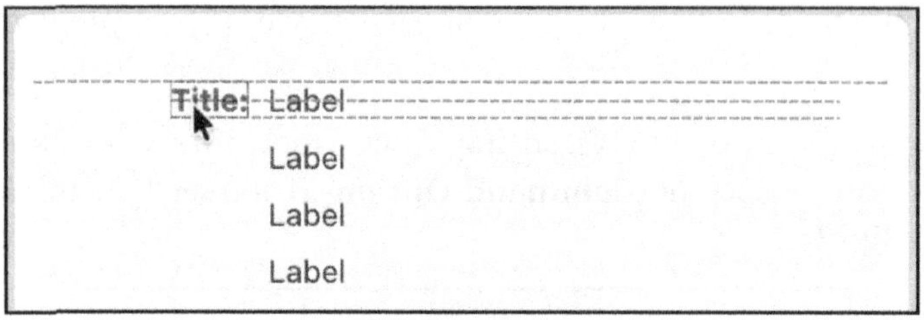

Aligning the title.

Again, you'll detect a virtual *click* when you're the standard distance away from the data label.

Duplicate this title label three times, dragging each one to left of the next data label. If you get the drag wrong and end up resizing the field or dragging the wrong object, press **Command-Z** to undo and try again. Set the titles to **Run time**:, **Genres:**, and **Principals:**. Because you right-aligned these titles, they expand to the left to show the longer strings, which is exactly what you want.

When you've finished, your labels look like this:

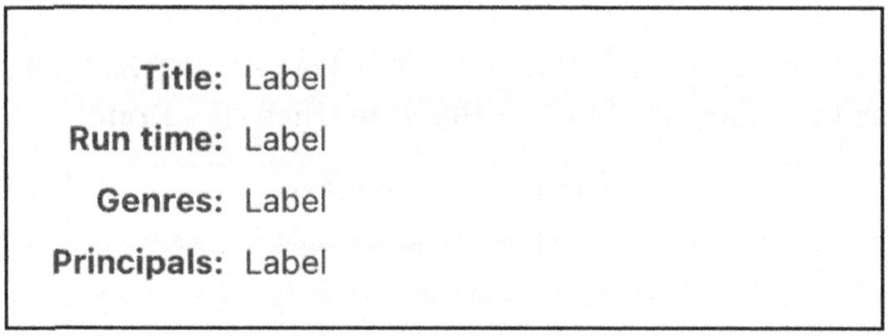

Box labels

Constraining the Titles

You still have to set Auto Layout constraints for the titles, so select all four titles, click **Resolve Auto Layout Issues** and choose **Reset to Suggested Constraints**.

This still leaves a yellow warning symbol beside **View Controller Scene** in the outline view, so click it to see the problems:

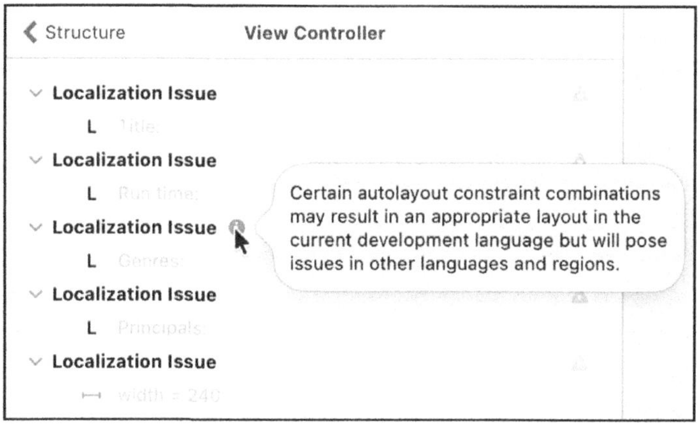

Layout issues

There are four or five warnings for the titles. Mouse over one and click the **i** button to see that the layout works in the current development language but may not work in other languages. The problem is that the header labels have a trailing constraint at the right but no constraint at the left. Ignore the width warning for now, if you see one. For each of the other four issues, click the yellow triangle, select **Use Fixed Leading and Trailing Constraints** and click **Confirm**:

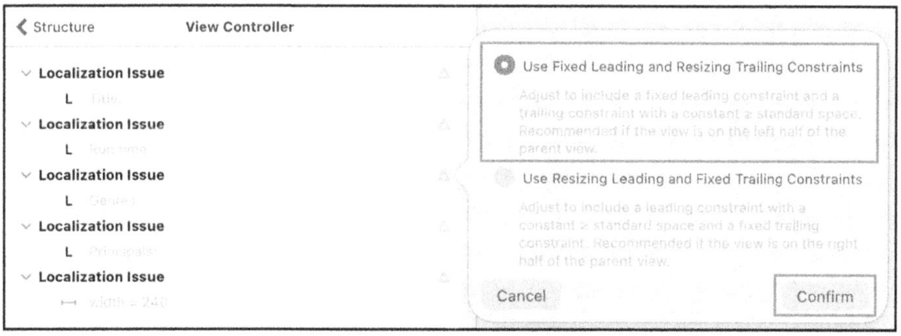

Fixing constraint issues.

This adds the missing leading constraint and changes the spacing between the title and the data label to greater than or equal to the standard. As the dialog says, this is the recommended option for views on the left side of the parent view. This title is to the left of the box that is its parent.

If Auto Layout set a fixed width for one of the data labels, you'll see a fifth warning about **width = 240**. Click its yellow triangle and choose **Set Constraint to >= Current Width**:

Fixing the width constraint.

This allows the label field to expand as much as it needs, but makes sure it can never get too narrow.

Once you've got rid of all the warnings, click **< Structure** to return to the outline view.

As a final check, run the app. Resize the window and confirm that all the labels stay aligned and positioned like this:

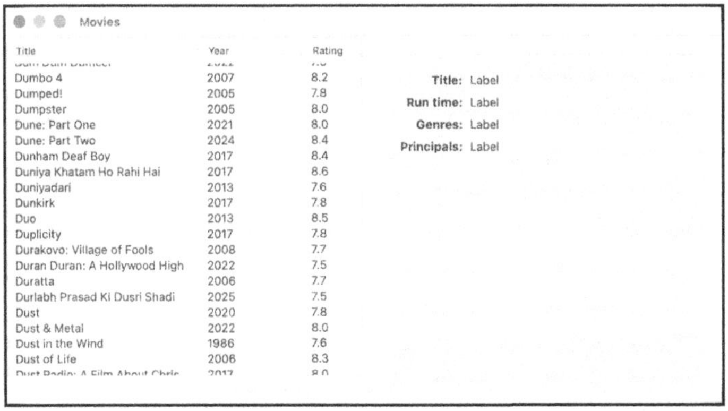

Testing the constraints.

Connecting to the Code

You have the fields set up, but your code needs to have a way to refer to them so it can put the correct data in the correct slot.

Shift-Option-click ViewController.swift in the Project navigator to open it in a secondary editor pane beside the storyboard.

Add some blank lines after `moviesTableView`, then **Control-drag** from the top data label to this space until you see the **Insert Action or Outlet** tooltip:

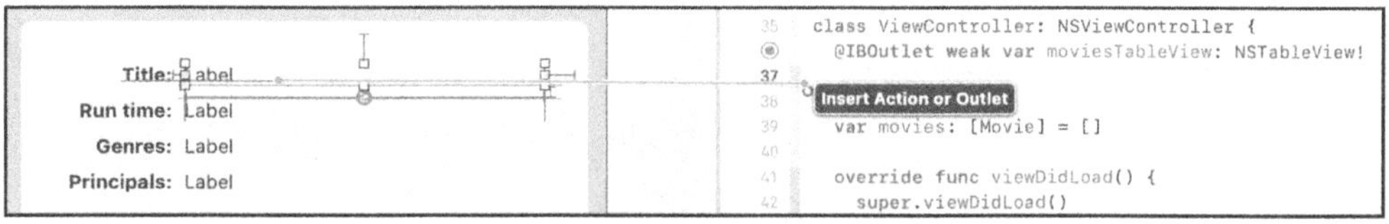

Connecting the label to code.

Set the name to **titleLabel** and click **Connect**:

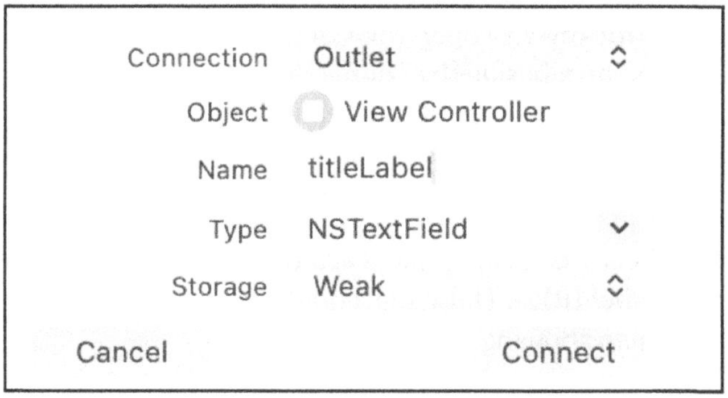

Setting the label name.

Repeat this for the other three data labels, setting their names to **runtimeLabel**, **genresLabel** and **principalsLabel**.

If the drag keeps wanting to connect to an existing outlet instead of making a new one, drag into the beginning of a line, before there's any text.

When you've finished, your code looks like this:

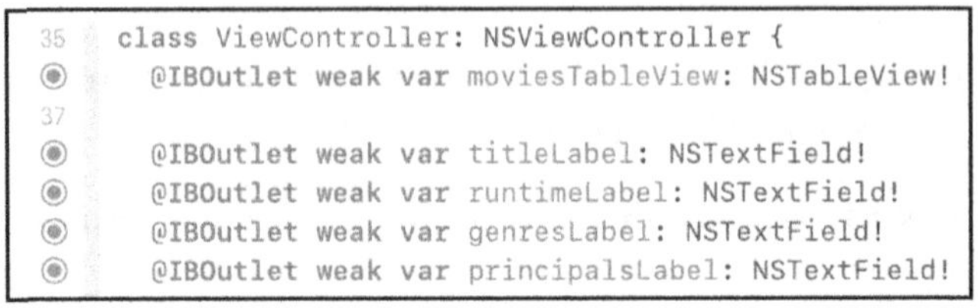

Connected outlets

Mouse over the black blobs in the line numbers gutter — the connected view highlights in the storyboard.

> **Note**: You've created links between the storyboard and the code using exact names. Once you've made those connections, **do not** edit any names in the code or you'll break the link and your app will crash.
>
> If you did edit a name, the easiest fix is to undo your edit. If you prefer to replace the link, go back to the storyboard and select the connected object. Press **Command-Option-7** to open the Connections inspector and find the changed one. Press the **x** beside the connection to delete it, then drag from the circle to connect to the new name. This applies to outlets and to actions, which you'll encounter later in this chapter.

Now that the data labels are set up, select each one and use the Attributes inspector to clear the default **Label** titles. These placeholders are useful during configuration, but you don't want them showing up in the app.

With all the connections in place, you're ready to show some movie information.

Displaying the Selected Movie

Close the secondary editors so you only have one editor pane open and go to **TableData.swift**.

Replace the `print` line in `showSelectedMovie` with:

```
// 1
titleLabel.stringValue = movie.title
// 2
runtimeLabel.stringValue = "\(movie.runTime) minutes"
```

```
// 3
genresLabel.stringValue = movie.genres
```

Stepping through these lines:

1. You supply `movie` as an argument to this method, so you can use it to populate your new fields. `NSTextField` has a `stringValue` property for showing text.
2. `runTime` is an `Int`, so use string interpolation to convert it to a `String`, adding the units.
3. `genres` is already a `String`, so you can use it directly.

Set `clearSelectedMovie` to:

```
titleLabel.stringValue = ""
runtimeLabel.stringValue = ""
genresLabel.stringValue = ""
principalsLabel.stringValue = ""
```

This puts empty strings into the four fields to clear them. You aren't populating `principalsLabel` yet, but you can add the code to clear it.

Run the app and select a movie:

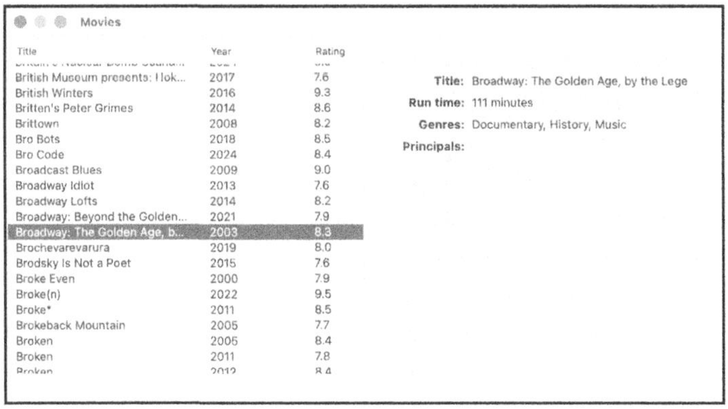

Selecting a movie.

Test **Command-clicking** the selection to clear the display.

Notice what happens if you select a movie with a long title — the table truncates the title, which is what you want, but it would be better if the data views wrapped to show the full text.

Adjusting Auto Layout

Back in **Main.storyboard**, select the first data view. The easiest way is to click **Title Label** in the outline view.

In the Attributes inspector, set **Layout** to **Wraps**. This changes **Line Break** to **Word Wrap**:

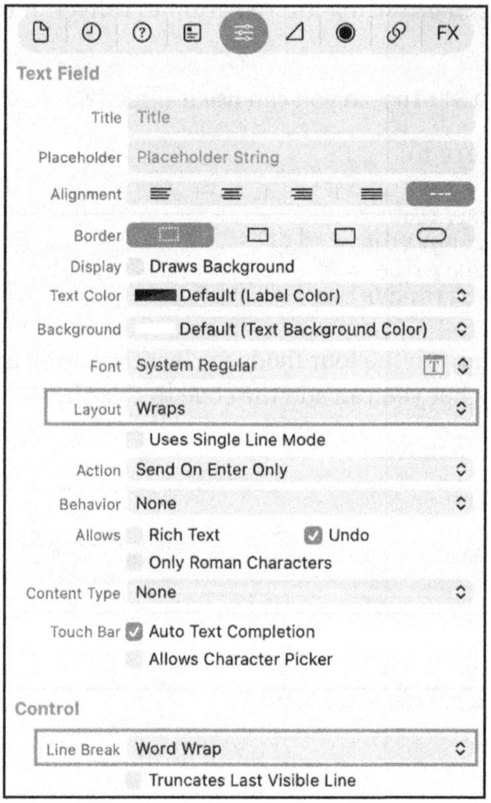

Wrap settings

The **Runtime Label** never has many characters, but apply the same changes to **Genres Label** and **Principals Label**.

Selecting a movie with a long title now shows a different problem: Auto Layout has aligned the title header to the bottom of the title data instead of the top:

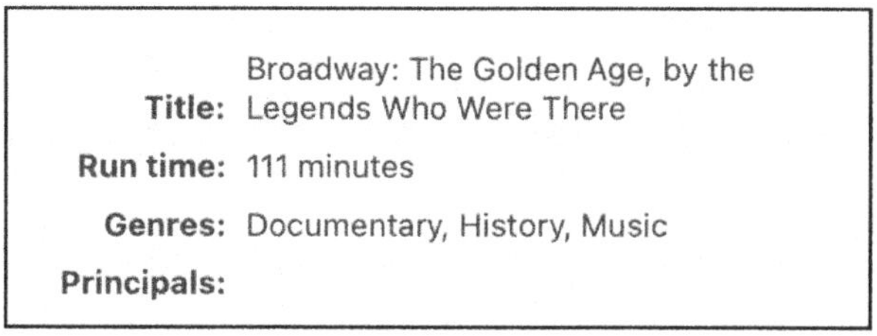

Misaligned text

This is the sort of layout error you get when you let Auto Layout set the constraints, but it's still easier to accept the suggestions and tweak as needed rather than setting them all manually from the start.

To fix this misalignment, select **Title Label** again and open the Size inspector. In the list of **Vertical** constraints, find the one that sets **Last Baseline Space to: Title:**:

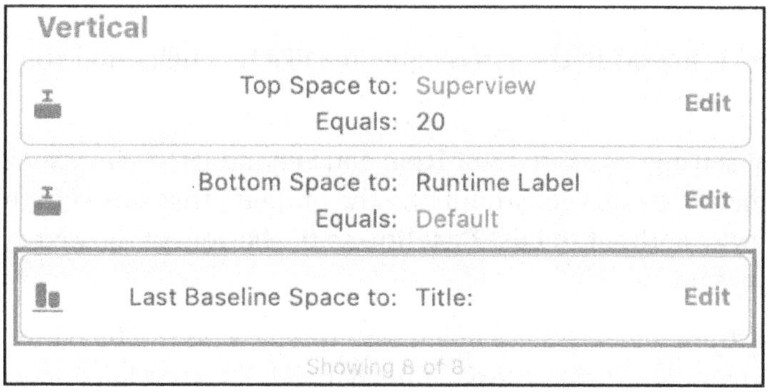

Last Baseline Space

The **Edit** button lets you adjust the constraint distance, but you need to change the constraint completely, so **double-click** in the box to open the Size inspector for the constraint itself:

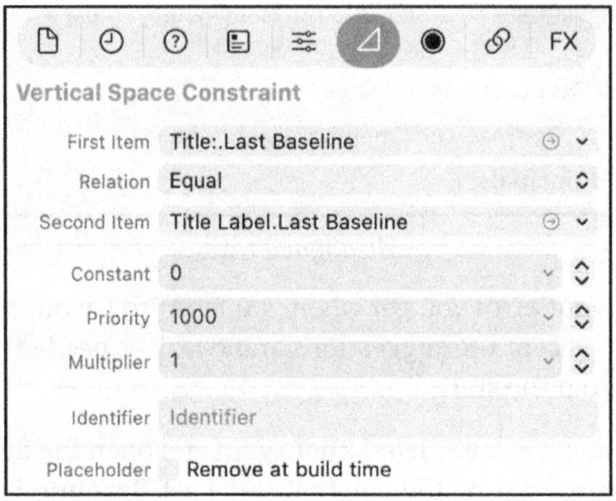

Constraint attributes

Constraints are elements in the storyboard, just like text fields and you can edit them using the inspectors.

The important settings here are **First Item** and **Second Item**. They show the two elements connected by this constraint and the property that's used in the constraint. Right now, they're both set to **Last Baseline** so the bottom of the text on the last line of each lines up.

Click the **First Item** menu to see a menu with three sections. The bottom section selects the element and you can leave it unchanged. The top element is where you set the constraint property. Change it to **Top**:

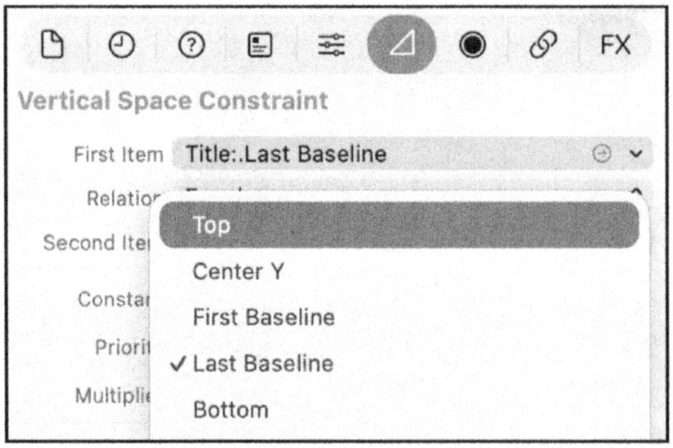

Aligning the tops.

Do the same for **Second Item**, setting its property to **Top** but keeping the element at **Title Label**.

Repeat this process for the other three data labels, double-clicking on the **Last Baseline Space** constraint and changing both items to **Top**. Then run the app again:

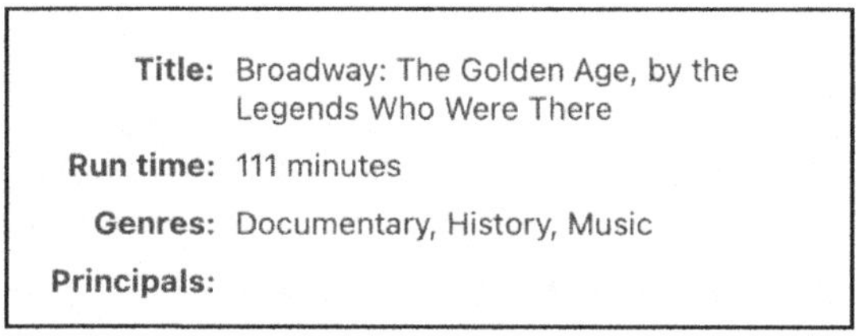

Correct wrapping and alignment.

Now you've sorted this out, you can add in the principals display.

Adding the Principals

The JSON data starts with an array of movies, each with their own properties. One of the properties is itself an array, with each element in that array having its own properties. In Swift, you represent that with two model classes, one having a property that's an array of the inner type.

Add a new **Swift File** to the project and name it **Principal.swift**. This gives you three files related to the models and the data, so now's a good time to put them in their own folder.

Select **Movie.swift**, **Principal.swift** and **movies.json** in the Project navigator. **Right-click** and choose **New Folder from Selection**. Set the name of the folder to **Data & Models**.

Open **Principal.swift** and add this:

```
// 1
class Principal: Codable {
  // 2
  let id: String
  var name: String
  var category: String
  var roles: String

  // 3
  var display: String {
    if roles.isEmpty {
      return "\(name): \(category)"
```

```
      }
      return "\(name) as \(roles)"
    }
  }
```

This defines a new class:

1. `Principal` conforms to `Codable` so you can use it with JSON.
2. Checking back to the image of the JSON data in the previous chapter, you can see that each element in the `principals` array has four properties with these names. They're all strings and `id` is the only one you don't want people to edit.
3. Each principal has `roles` if it represents an actor, or it has a `category` like writer. This computed property returns a valid string to describe either type.

> **Note**: It's possible to change property names when converting between JSON and Swift objects, but it's much easier to keep them the same.

So far, your JSON decoding has ignored the principals. To change this, open **Movie.swift**.

Under the other properties, add:

```
var principals: [Principal]
```

Now the definition of each `Movie` includes an array of `Principal` objects. But this causes an error in the initializer because it isn't setting `principals`.

You didn't type the initializer in the first place, so easy come, easy go. Delete the whole `init` method. You could ask Xcode to generate a new initializer, but there's another technique.

Add some blank lines after `principals` and type `init`. Autocomplete suggests several options. Choose the one with all the properties as arguments:

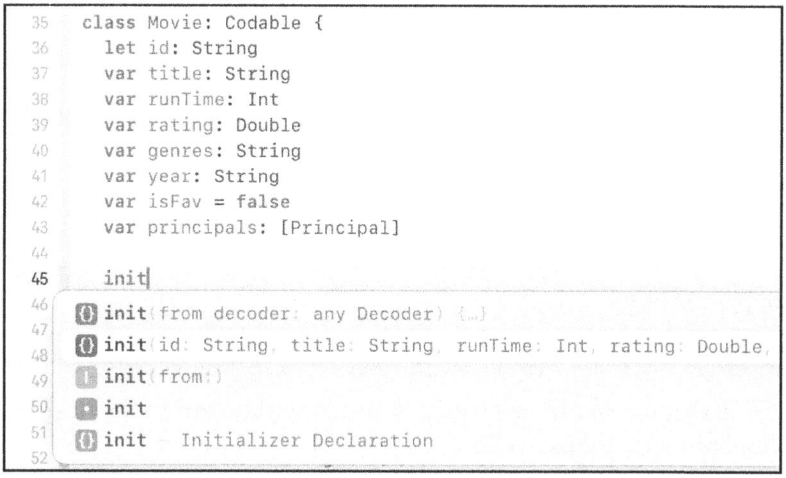

init autocomplete

This fills in a new `init` method that includes `principals`. Unless your initializer does some custom setup, you can always delete it and regenerate it any time you change the properties.

These additions mean that `JSONDecoder` now adds `principals` to `Movie`, but you still need to supply a way to display them.

> **Note**: You may be wondering why you didn't have to provide an explicit initializer for `Principal`. Didn't we say earlier that classes required an initializer? Indeed they do, but `Codable` provides one by default. Technically, you can omit the initializer for `Movie` since it, too, conforms to `Codable`. But, it's also important to understand how to get Xcode to write the code for you when you need it.

Displaying the Principals

Add this computed property to `Movie`:

```
// 1
var principalsDisplay: String {
  // 2
  let principalDisplays = principals.map { $0.display }
  // 3
  return principalDisplays.joined(separator: "\n")
}
```

What's happening here?

1. The computed property returns a `String`.
2. It uses `map` to loop over the elements in `principals`, getting the `display` computed property for each one.
3. Then, it converts the array into a single string, joining them with `\n`, which is what you type to get a line feed in a string.

Now, open **TableData.swift** and add this line to `showSelectedMovie(_:)`:

```
principalsLabel.stringValue = movie.principalsDisplay
```

This inserts the computed property into the final data label.

Run the app and check it out:

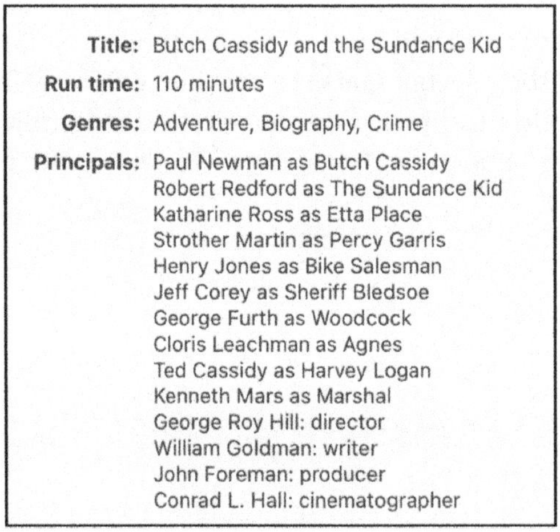

Details display

And there it is. Your selected movie display is fully functional. This section covered a lot of ground, so great work!

Picking Favorites

Nobody likes a teacher who has favorites, but everyone has their favorite movies. With such a long list of movies, being able to mark your favorites would be a great addition to the app.

`Movie` already has a Boolean property called `isFav`. The first step is to add the user interface for displaying and changing this.

Open **Main.storyboard** and scroll so you can see the top of the selected movie box. Press **Shift-Command-L** to open the Library. Search for **image** and drag an **Image Button** into the top left of the box. This is an `NSButton` that's pre-configured to have an image and no title.

To set the position for the new button, click **Add New Constraints** in the bottom toolbar. Enter **8** for the top and left spacings. then check **Width** and **Height** and enter **30** for each of them.

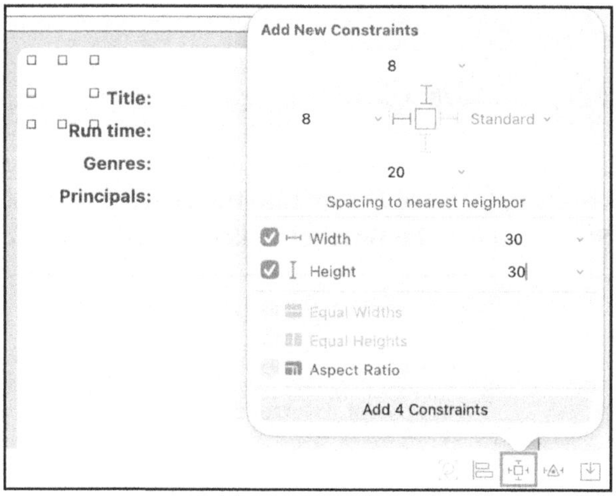

Setting button constraints.

Notice how you have red lines for the left and top spacings and not for the right and bottom. The lines show the spacings you're adding. Xcode turns them on automatically when you enter a value, but you can also click the red line to toggle them.

Click **Add 4 Constraints** to move and resize the button.

Next, **Shift-Option-click ViewController.swift** in the Project navigator to open it in a secondary editor.

You need to make two connections here: An **outlet** property that you can use to refer to the button in your code and an **action** method that the button can call when it's clicked. The nice thing is that Xcode knows which one of these you're adding, based on whether you drag to near the top of your code, or near the bottom.

Add some blank lines under `principalsLabel` and **Control-drag** from the button into this space. Xcode suggests adding an outlet. Set its name to **favButton** and click **Connect**:

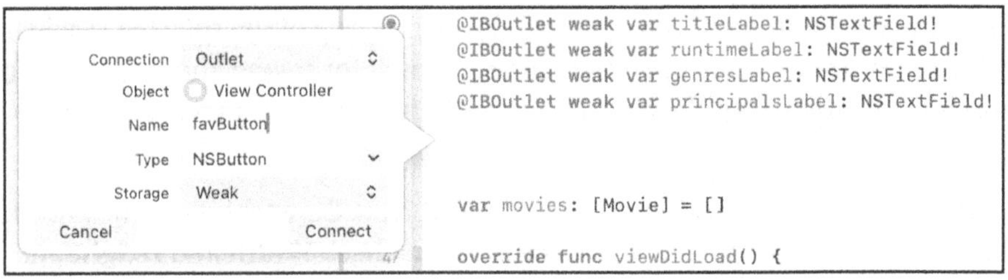

Connecting an outlet.

This fills in one line of code:

```
@IBOutlet weak var favButton: NSButton!
```

For the action, scroll down the page and add some blank lines before the final closing curly brace. **Control-drag** from the button into this space. This time, Xcode offers to create an action. Set its name to **favButtonClicked** and click **Connect**:

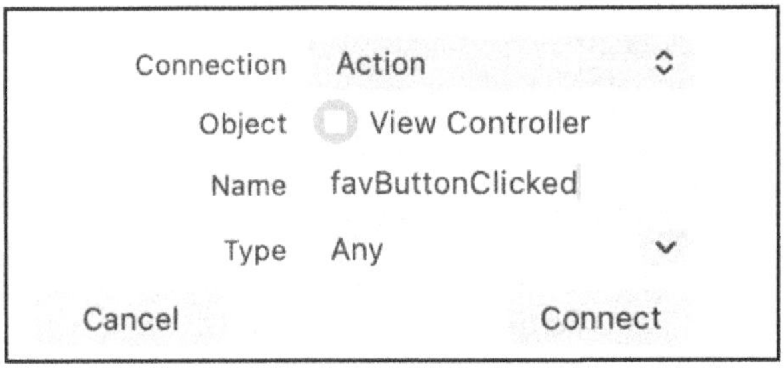

Connecting an action.

> **Note**: If Xcode gets it wrong, you can always swap between Outlet and Action using the menu at the top of the popup dialog.

That's it for the storyboard, so you can close its editor now. The next step is to show a suitable image in the button for favorite and non-favorite movies.

Open **TableData.swift** and find `clearSelectedMovie()`. When the user has no movie selected, you don't want any image appearing in the button, so add this line:

```
favButton.image = nil
```

By setting the button's image to `nil`, you blank the button.

The code in `showSelectedMovie(_:)` is a bit more complicated. You'll set an image depending on the value of `isFav`, and you want to use a colored image from SF Symbols, which is easy in SwiftUI but not quite so straightforward in AppKit.

Add this code to the end of `showSelectedMovie(_:)`:

```
// 1
let imageName = movie.isFav ? "heart.fill" : "heart"
// 2
let color = movie.isFav ? NSColor.red : NSColor.gray

// 3
let image = NSImage(
  systemSymbolName: imageName,
  accessibilityDescription: imageName)
// 4
let config = NSImage.SymbolConfiguration(paletteColors: [color])

// 5
favButton.image = image?.withSymbolConfiguration(config)
```

This is a lot of code for setting a button image!

1. Use the ternary operator to get an image name depending on the value of `isFav`. Both these names are from SF Symbols, or you can find them in Xcode's Symbols Library. A favorite movie gets a filled heart and a non-favorite gets an outline.

2. Get an `NSColor` for each state of `isFav` — red for a favorite and gray for others.

3. Create an `NSImage` from the symbol name using the name of the image as its accessibility label.

4. Create a `SymbolConfiguration` for the `NSImage`. This can take a palette of colors for multicolor symbols, but you only want one color, so set `paletteColors` to a single element array.

5. Finally, set the button's `image` using the image and its configuration. The image is an optional — you might have typed in an invalid name — so optional chaining only applies the configuration if the image exists.

That covers setting the image, but now you need to write the code to let the user toggle the setting. To make this easier, add a new property at the top of **ViewController.swift**:

```
var selectedMovie: Movie?
```

You'll use this to store the currently selected movie. It's an optional because the user may not have selected any movie.

To set this property, go back to **TableData.swift** and add this line to `clearSelectedMovie()`:

```
selectedMovie = nil
```

And add this to `showSelectedMovie(_:)`:

```
selectedMovie = movie
```

Now `selectedMovie` reflects the user's selection and is `nil` if the user hasn't selected anything.

With that property hooked up, zip back to **ViewController.swift** and insert this into `favButtonClicked(_:)`.

```
// 1
if let selectedMovie {
  // 2
  selectedMovie.isFav.toggle()
  // 3
  showSelectedMovie(selectedMovie)
}
```

How does this work?

1. Check to see if there's a value in `selectedMovie`. If there isn't, this method won't do anything.

2. Toggle `isFav` for the movie. This uses a Boolean method that swaps between `false` and `true`.

3. Call `showSelectedMovie(_:)` to update the display.

Time to try it out. Run the app and select a movie. Click the heart to turn it on. Select a different movie — the heart goes off. Go back to the first movie and your heart appears again.

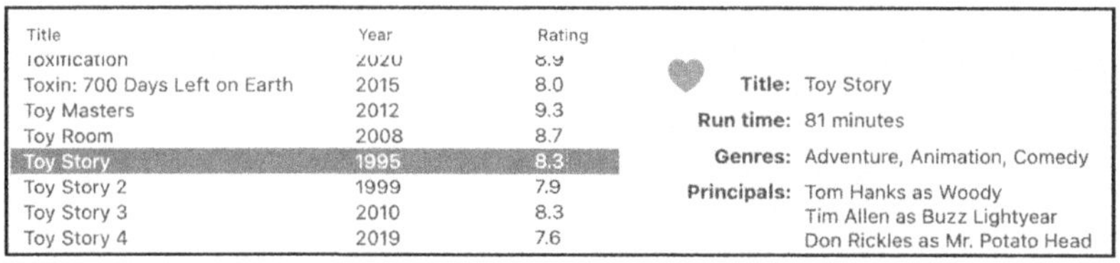

Favorite movie

For the moment, your favorite selections aren't stored anywhere, so when you quit the app, you lose all your hearts. :[In the next chapter, you'll learn how to save and restore the edited data.

Key Points

- `NSTableViewDelegate` can detect changes to the table selection.
- Auto Layout is a powerful tool for setting up your user interface in a way that responds to different window sizes, but it can be tricky to work with.
- JSON data can include nested data types.
- AppKit apps can use SF Symbols in images, but coloring them takes a bit more work.

Where to Go From Here?

You've created a table and filled it with data. Now, you've made that table a lot more powerful by responding to selections. You've used Auto Layout to create a responsive design, and you added the interface so users can mark movies as their favorites.

In the next chapter, you'll move on to powering the table itself, not only its selections. You'll add searching and sorting, and you'll implement data storage to save and restore user edits.

Chapter 13: Powering Up Your Table

By Sarah Reichelt

In the previous chapter, you designed and built the interface for users to select a movie and read its details.

Now, you'll move on to adding more features to the table itself. You'll create a toolbar with a search field and you'll make the table columns sortable.

You've already given users the ability to mark their favorite movies, but this data doesn't persist between app launches. In order to store the favorites settings, you'll learn how to save the data and reload it. This involves interacting with the Mac sandbox.

Adding a Search Field

With over 34,000 movies in the table, scrolling to find the one you want isn't easy. So it's time to add search. The appropriate place for a search field is in the window's toolbar, and that's where you'll add it.

Open Xcode with your project from the previous chapter or use the **starter** project from the downloads for this chapter.

Open **Main.storyboard** to set up the toolbar. You might expect to add it to `ViewController` since that's where you'll use it, but a toolbar is part of a window, so you add it to the window.

Scroll the display so you can see the window with the **Movies** title. Press **Shift-Command-L** to open the Library and search for **toolbar**, then drag a **Toolbar** into the window:

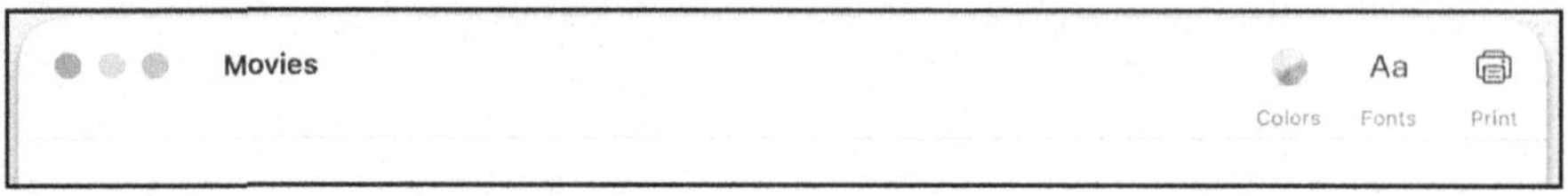

The default toolbar.

By default, the toolbar has three items (apart from spacers) and you don't want any of them. Double-click anywhere in the toolbar to open its editor:

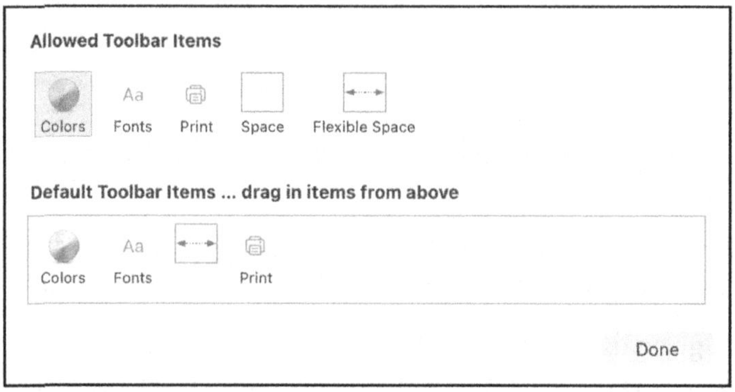

The toolbar editor

One at a time, select **Colors**, **Fonts** and **Print** from **Allowed Toolbar Items** and press **Delete**. Next, open the library again and search for **search**. :]

Drag a **Search Toolbar Item** into the toolbar in **Allowed Toolbar Items** and then drag it from the toolbar down into the **Default Toolbar Items** box:

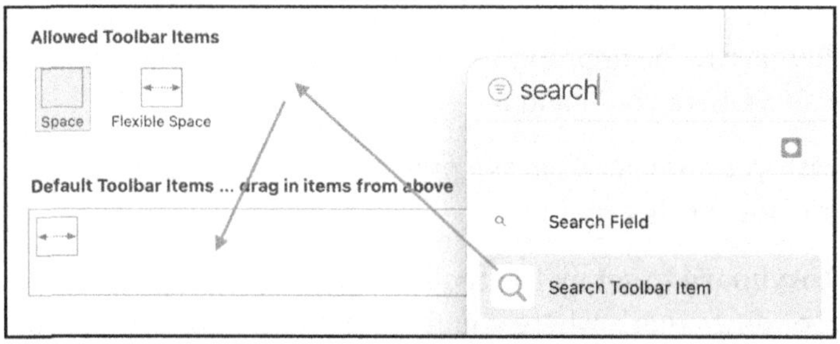

Adding the search item.

It ends up appearing twice, once in the allowed items box and once in the default items box.

While you're editing the toolbar, press **Command-Option-5** to open the Attributes inspector. Set **Display** to **Icon Only** so the search field doesn't have an unnecessary label:

Configuring the toolbar display mode.

Click **Done** to close the toolbar editor.

This adds the user interface, but it won't do anything until you write the code to detect any search input and filter the movies.

Processing Search Input

The search field is in the window, but you want its data in the view controller. You'll use the window controller to detect changes and pass them on.

You could create a custom subclass of `NSWindowController`, but you only need to add one method so you'll create an `extension` instead. You've used extensions on your own objects, but you can add them to any class or structure, even if you didn't write it.

Start by defining a property to hold the entered search text. Open **ViewController.swift** and add this property:

```
var searchText = ""
```

You'll add more code to process that soon, but this lets you continue without getting an error.

Right-click in the Project navigator and select **New Empty File**. Change its name to **WindowController.swift**.

Set the file contents to:

```
// 1
import AppKit
```

```
// 2
extension NSWindowController: @retroactive NSSearchFieldDelegate
{
}
```

These lines:

1. Import AppKit so you can use AppKit classes.
2. Create an extension of `NSWindowController` that conforms to `NSSearchFieldDelegate`. The `@retroactive` marker is a fix that Xcode suggests to remove a warning that this may not work if future versions of NSWindowController conform to `NSSearchFieldDelegate` automatically.

This delegate handles notifications coming from the search field.

Inside the extension, start typing `control` and select `controlTextDidChange(_ obj:)` from the autocomplete suggestions:

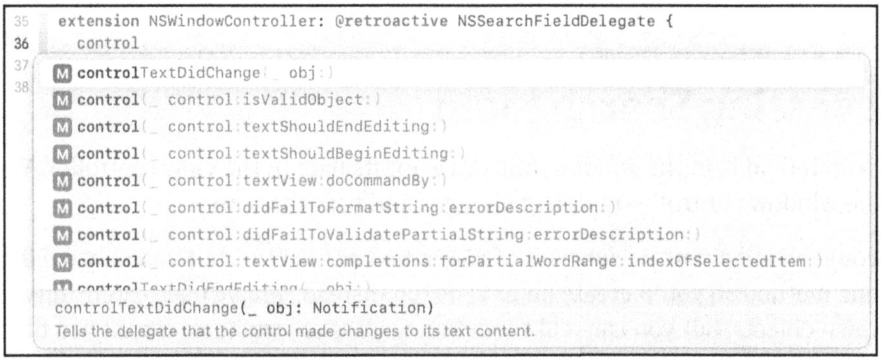

controlTextDidChange autocomplete

Xcode marks the method as `public` because that's what the protocol specifies. This access level allows you to access the method from any of your files.

Replace the `code` placeholder with:

```
// 1
guard
  // 2
  let searchField = obj.object as? NSSearchField,
  // 3
  let viewController = NSApp.keyWindow?.contentViewController
    as? ViewController
else {
  return
}
```

```
// 4
viewController.searchText = searchField.stringValue
```

Stepping through this, you:

1. Make two `guard` checks, returning if either fails.
2. First, check that the notification's `object` is a search field. All edit fields use this method, so you can't assume this is for the search.
3. Next, confirm that this window controller has access to a `ViewController`. You do this by asking the application for its active window and checking if that window's `contentViewController` is a `ViewController`.
4. If these checks pass, set the `ViewControllers` `searchText` property.

There's one last step to make this work. Open **Main.storyboard** and expand **Search** in the outline view so you can see **Search Field**. Select **Search Field** and open the Connections inspector using **Command-Option-7**.

Drag from the circle beside `delegate` to Window Controller in the outline view:

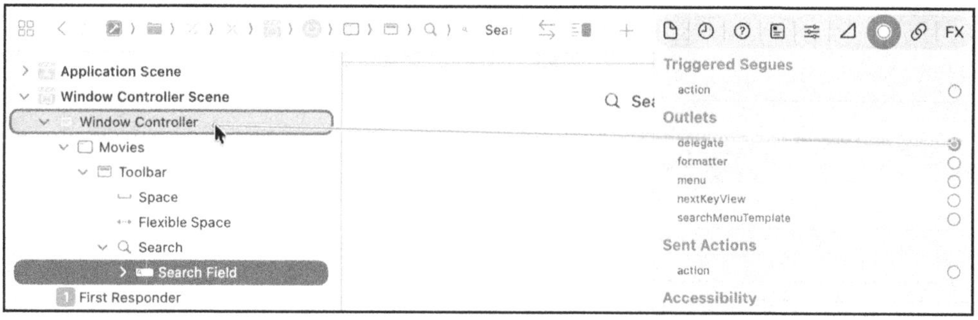

Setting the search field delegate.

This connects the search field to the delegate method you added to `NSWindowController`.

Responding to a Search

You've made the connections. Next, you need to respond to the user's search input.

Open **ViewController.swift** and find where you defined `searchText`. Replace that definition with:

```
var searchText = "" {
  didSet {
```

```
        print(searchText)
    }
}
```

This adds a property observer to detect changes.

Run the app and type in the search bar while watching the Xcode console:

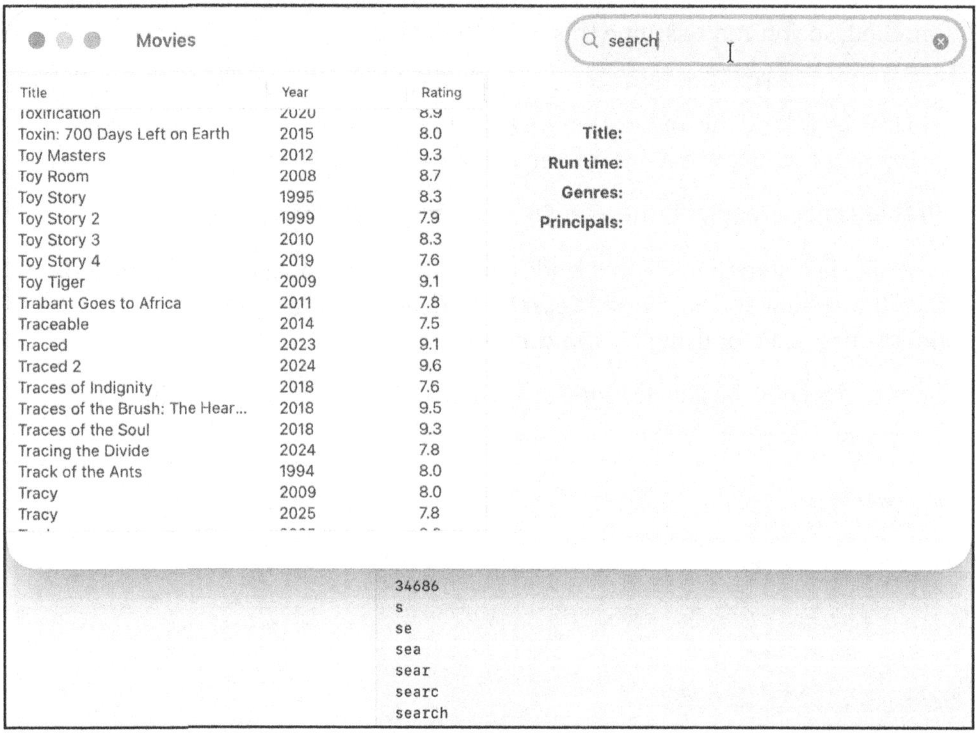

Search text

The delegate method sets `searchText`, so now you can use that to filter the table data. To do this, you'll make a copy of the `movies` array. The original stays complete and you adjust the copy to suit the search text. The table displays the copy. If you change the original array, you'll lose the movies that are filtered from the list.

Add this property to `ViewController`:

```
var visibleMovies: [Movie] = []
```

And in viewDidLoad, after the last line, add:

```
visibleMovies = movies
```

Next, add this method:

```
func searchMovies() {
  // 1
  if searchText.isEmpty {
    visibleMovies = movies
  } else {
    // 2
    visibleMovies = movies.filter { movie in
      // 3
      movie.title.localizedCaseInsensitiveContains(searchText)
    }
  }
  // 4
  moviesTableView.reloadData()
}
```

How does this search?

1. If there's no search text, set visibleMovies to the complete movies array.
2. If the user has typed in some search text, use filter to loop through each movie in movies.
3. Check if the title contains searchText using a String method that ignores case.
4. Reload the data displayed in the table to show the changes.

To use this method, go back to the searchText property observer and replace the print line with:

```
searchMovies()
```

This covers the data side of the search. To fix the display side, open **TableData.swift**.

Displaying Search Results

Here, you need to change every reference to `movies` to `visibleMovies`, but before you start typing, there's an easier way. :]

In `numberOfRows(in:)`, **right-click** on the word `movies` and select **Edit All in Scope** from the contextual menu:

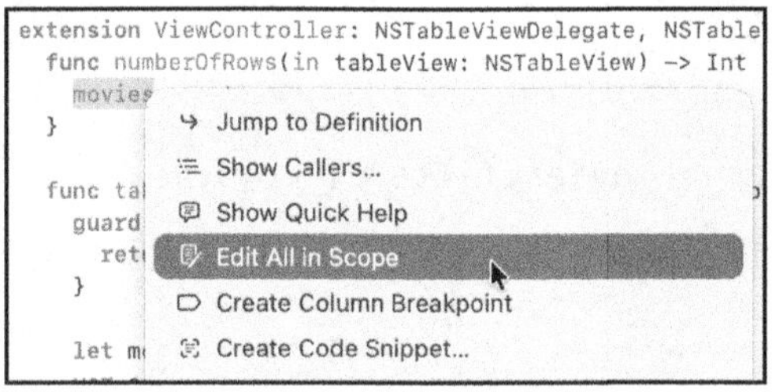

Edit All in Scope

This selects all the instances of `movies` in this file and makes the first one editable. Change it to **visibleMovies** and press **Return**.

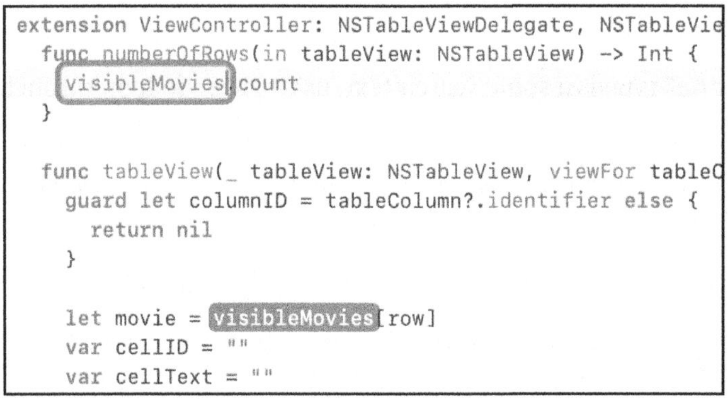

Renaming movies

As you type, you can see the change appear in the other instances. In this case, the **scope** is this extension, so nothing outside this file changes.

Run the app now and type something into the search field:

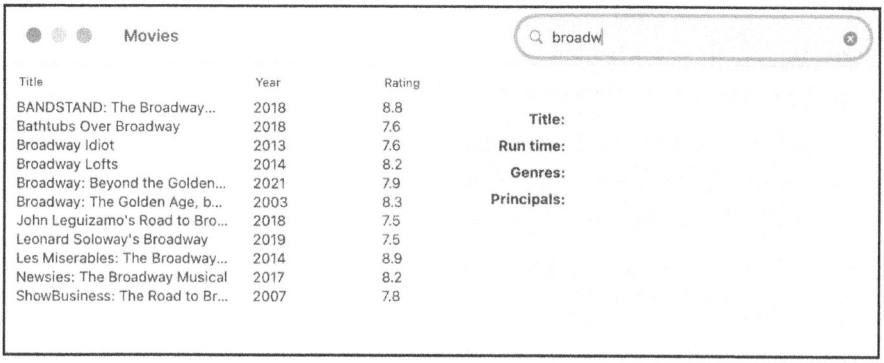

Searching the movies.

The app is a *lot* more usable now! But it can be even better.

Sorting the Table

The movies table shows three column headers, and Mac users expect to be able to sort the table by clicking these. You don't want to disappoint anyone, so that's what you'll add next.

You make a table column sortable by assigning a **sort descriptor** to it. A sort descriptor is a way of describing how to sort a collection. It includes the sort property, the sort direction and the sort method.

Open **TableData.swift** and add this method:

```
func addSortDescriptors() {
  // 1
  let titleSortDesc = NSSortDescriptor(
    key: "title",
    ascending: true,
    // 2
    selector:
#selector(NSString.localizedCaseInsensitiveCompare(_:)))
  // 3
  let yearSortDesc = NSSortDescriptor(key: "year", ascending:
true)
  let ratingSortDesc = NSSortDescriptor(key: "rating",
ascending: true)

  // set sort for each column
}
```

This creates a sort descriptor for each column:

1. The title sort is the most complex because it's case-insensitive. You initialize an `NSSortDescriptor` with a key — the property name. Set ascending to `true` so the initial sort is A to Z and not Z to A.
2. You supply the sort method as a **selector**. This is how you convert a method into an argument. You initialize a selector using `#selector` and, in this case, you supply an `NSString` method that compares two strings, ignoring case.
3. The `year` and `rating` descriptors are simpler. They use the default `compare` selector, so you don't have to include it in the initializer.

Now you've created these, you can assign them to each column.

Replace `// set sort for each column` with:

```
// 1
let titleColumnID = NSUserInterfaceItemIdentifier("TitleColumn")
// 2
let titleColumnIndex = moviesTableView.column(withIdentifier:
titleColumnID)
if titleColumnIndex > -1 {
  // 3
  moviesTableView.tableColumns[titleColumnIndex]
    // 4
    .sortDescriptorPrototype = titleSortDesc
}

// 5
let yearColumnID = NSUserInterfaceItemIdentifier("YearColumn")
let yearColumnIndex = moviesTableView.column(withIdentifier:
yearColumnID)
if yearColumnIndex > -1 {
  moviesTableView.tableColumns[yearColumnIndex]
    .sortDescriptorPrototype = yearSortDesc
}

let ratingColumnID =
NSUserInterfaceItemIdentifier("RatingColumn")
let ratingColumnIndex = moviesTableView.column(withIdentifier:
ratingColumnID)
if ratingColumnIndex > -1 {
  moviesTableView.tableColumns[ratingColumnIndex]
    .sortDescriptorPrototype = ratingSortDesc
}
```

This looks like a lot of code, but it's the same sequence repeated for each column:

1. Create an `NSUserInterfaceItemIdentifier` for the **Title** column, using the identifier you assigned in the storyboard.
2. Query `moviesTableView` for a column with this identifier. It returns an array index or `-1` if there's no matching column.
3. If the index is valid, use it to get the matching column from `moviesTableView.tableColumns`.
4. Set that column's `sortDescriptorPrototype` to the matching sort descriptor.
5. Repeat for the process for the **Year** column and the **Rating** column.

You have to do it this way because the user may have dragged columns around. You can't assume that the first column is the Title column. This is long-winded but it makes sure you assign the sort descriptors correctly, regardless of the user settings.

To call this method, open **ViewController.swift** and add this line at the end of `viewDidLoad`:

```
addSortDescriptors()
```

Run the app and click the table headers:

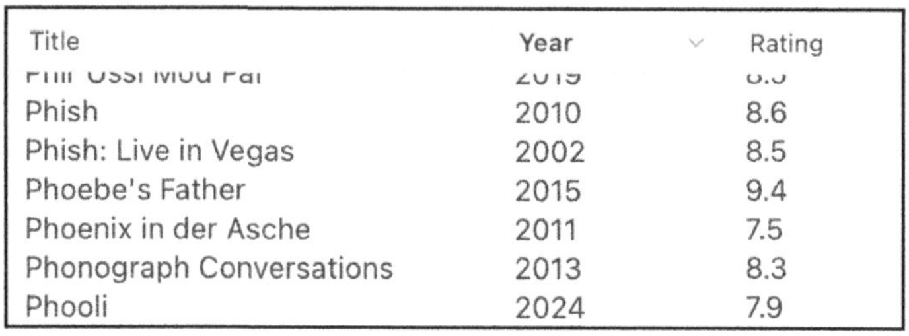

Title	Year	Rating
Phish	2010	8.6
Phish: Live in Vegas	2002	8.5
Phoebe's Father	2015	9.4
Phoenix in der Asche	2011	7.5
Phonograph Conversations	2013	8.3
Phooli	2024	7.9

Sort headers

The selected column header is slightly bolded and an arrow points up or down to indicate the direction of the sort. So far, no actually sorting takes place, but that's next on your to do list. :]

Applying the Sort

The `NSTableViewDataSource` receives a message when the user changes the sort. Open **TableData.swift** and make space at the end of the extension to add a new method.

Type `sort` and accept the only autocomplete suggestion:

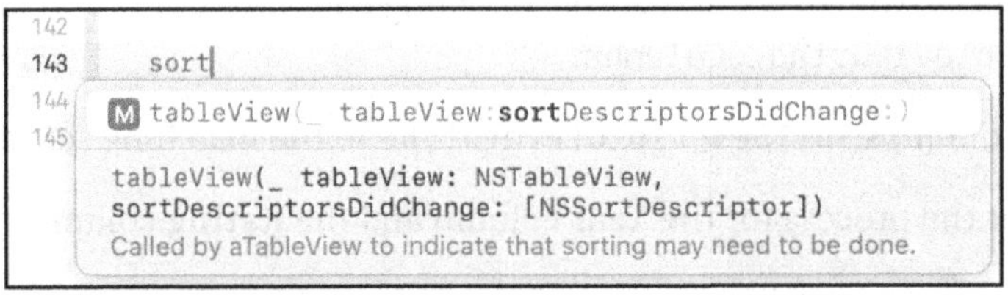

sort autocomplete

The `dataSource` calls this method whenever the user clicks a header to change the sort, but it's your responsibility to actually sort the data.

The nice thing is that with a bit of data type swapping, you can use the table's sort descriptors to do this for you.

Replace the `code` placeholder with:

```
// 1
if let sortedMovies = (visibleMovies as NSArray)
  // 2
  .sortedArray(using: moviesTableView.sortDescriptors) as?
[Movie] {
  // 3
  visibleMovies = sortedMovies
  // 4
  moviesTableView.reloadData()
}
```

How does this work?

1. In order to sort using the table's sort descriptors, convert the Swift Array into an Objective-C `NSArray`. Objective-C was Apple's language before Swift and a lot of the older frameworks still use it.

2. Use an `NSArray` method to sort using the sort descriptors you already assigned to each column. The table manages these and they change whenever the user clicks a header. Once that's finished, try to convert the `NSArray` back into a Swift array of `Movie` objects.

3. Converting to a Swift array can fail because an `NSArray` can contain any types of object where a Swift array only contains a single type. If the conversion succeeds, set `visibleMovies` to the sorted array.

4. Reload the table to show the sorted data.

Don't run the app yet or it'll crash. There's a twist to using an Objective-C method.

Adding Attributes

Whenever you want to be able to refer to a Swift class or property from an Objective-C method, you give it a special attribute. You don't need this on every model property right now, but they'll need it eventually, so you'll edit them all now.

Open **Data & Models** → **Movie.swift**. and replace the class definition line with:

```
@objc class Movie: NSObject, Codable {
```

The `@objc` attribute tells the Objective-C runtime that it can access this class. For this to work, the class has to be a subclass of `NSObject`, which is the ultimate parent of all Objective-C classes.

Next, you add this attribute to all the properties. There's a fast way to do this using multi-cursor editing.

Place the cursor before `let id`. Hold down **Option** and click and drag down to get a cursor at the start of each property line. Now, type `@objc` followed by a space, and watch it appear eight times as you type it once:

```
@objc class Movie: NSObject, Codable {
  @objc let id: String
  @objc var title: String
  @objc var runTime: Int
  @objc var rating: Double
  @objc var genres: String
  @objc var year: String
  @objc var isFav = false
  @objc var principals: [Principal]
```

Multi-cursor editing

Click anywhere else to revert to a single cursor. This style of editing can take a bit of getting used to, but it's a convenient tool to have at your disposal.

You have an error now because you applied the `@objc` attribute to `principals` before adding it to the `Principal` class, so open **Principal.swift**.

Change the class declaration to:

```
@objc class Principal: NSObject, Codable {
```

And insert `@objc` before each of the four properties like you did for `Movie`.

Now you can run the app and sort the columns:

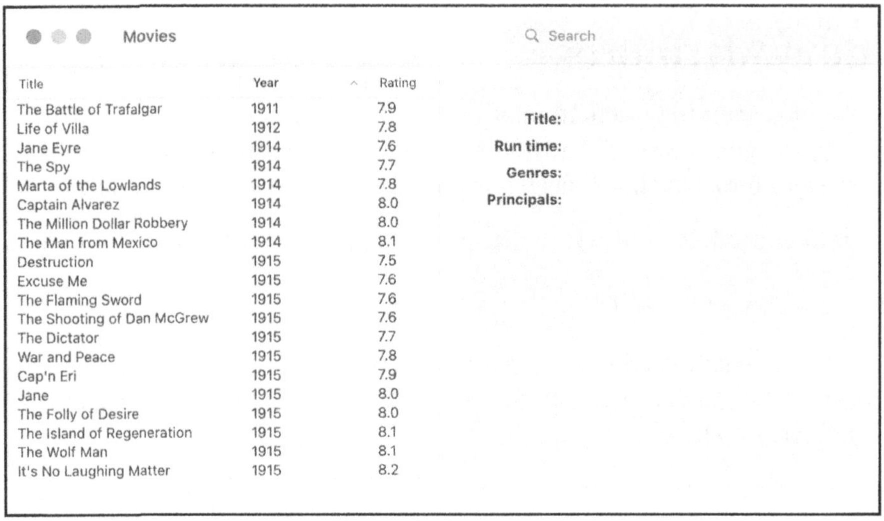

Sorting table columns.

But there's a bug. What happens if you sort by year and then do a search? The search results are still sorted by title!

Sorting the Search Results

Open **ViewController.swift** and find `searchMovies`. Before reloading the table, insert this:

```
if let sortedMovies = (visibleMovies as NSArray)
  .sortedArray(using: moviesTableView.sortDescriptors) as?
[Movie] {
  visibleMovies = sortedMovies
}
```

This is the same code as you used in the `dataSource` and does the same `NSArray` shuffle and Objective-C sorting for `visibleMovies`.

Run the app again, sort by year and enter some search text:

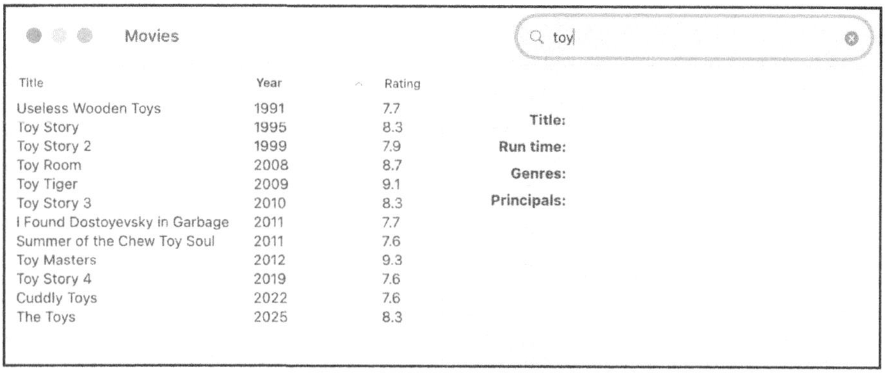

Sorted search results.

Hurray! It all works.

Saving the Table Setup

Run the app and change the way you display the table. Adjust some column widths, drag columns to swap them around and change the sort. Resize and move the window.

Next, quit and app and restart it. The window remembers where you left it, but your table has forgotten all its settings.

In an earlier chapter, you set an **Autosave** name for the window. This gave the app a key that it uses to save and restore your window size and location. You'll do the same thing for the table.

Open **Main.storyboard** and select the **Movies Table View** in the **View Controller Scene**. **Shift-right-click** the table to get the subview menu, so you can be sure you have the correct element selected.

Open the Attributes inspector using **Command-Option-5** and set Autosave to **MoviesTable**. Check **Column Information** to make sure this saves the column widths and positions too:

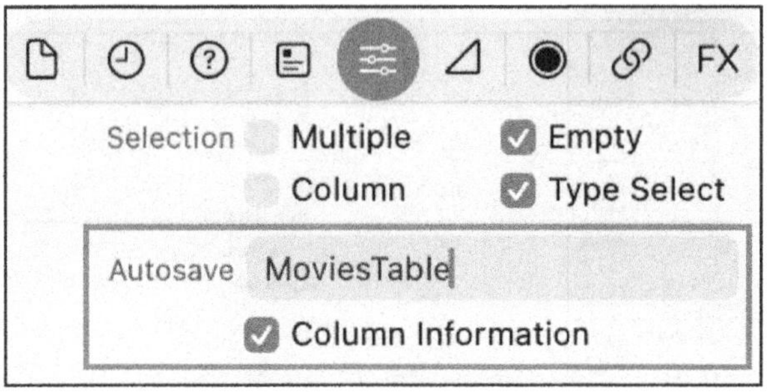

Setting table autosave.

Autosave names can be any string so long as each is unique in your project.

Run the app again, set up your columns, then quit and restart. This time, your columns are the way you left them:

Column setup restored.

You've reached the end of this long sorting section. You know how to set up a table for sorting, you know how to react to changes in the sort and you know how to save and restore the user's settings. Great work!

In the previous chapter, you allowed users to mark movies as their favorites. But each time the app restarted, these marks disappeared. You're saving your users' app settings, so now it's time to work out how to save their data changes too.

Saving Your Data

Every time the app starts, it reads in the list of movies from **movies.json**. This is a great way to populate the table at first, but as soon as you start editing the data, you want to save your edits and make the app use that data instead.

You'll create a new data structure to handle all data reading and writing.

Select **Data & Models** in the Project navigator and then use your preferred method to open the **New File from Template** dialog. Choose **Swift File** and name it **DataStore.swift**.

This object has three tasks: reading the original data, saving edited data and reading edited data, if it's available. Right now, you have an extension on `Movie` that reads the original, but you'll move that.

Start by adding this to your new file:

```
struct DataStore {
}
```

This sets up a structure called `DataStore`.

Next, open **Movie.swift** and find `readBundleData()`. Select the entire method and press **Command-X** to cut it from this file.

Swap back to **DataStore.swift** and press **Command-V** to paste the method in the structure. Delete the `static` keyword. This is now an instance method that you call on a `DataStore` object, not on the structure itself.

To tidy things up, go to **Movie.swift** and delete the now empty extension.

With these changes in place, the app won't display anything, so you'll fix that before you add any other methods.

Open **ViewController.swift** and add a new property:

```
var dataStore = DataStore()
```

This defines and initializes `dataStore` in a single line.

Scroll down to `viewDidLoad()` that now shows an error because `Movie` no longer has `readBundleData()`.

Change the error line to:

```
movies = dataStore.readBundleData()
```

This sets everything back to where it was before, but doesn't add anything new yet.

The Mac Sandbox

When you create an app project, it doesn't get access to everything on your Mac. It has its own **sandbox** where it's allowed to read and write files. Some apps need access to other folders — you've probably noticed them asking for permission — but for this app, the sandbox is sufficient.

But where is the sandbox?

Switch to **Finder** and open the **Go** menu. Hold down **Option** and when **Library** appears, choose it.

Find the folder called **Containers** and open it. It's full of folders, some of which have strange names and some of which even share names! They don't actually share names, but Finder shows you a friendly name for each one.

Scroll to find the folder called **MovieTables**. Select it and press **Command-I** to **Get Info** about it:

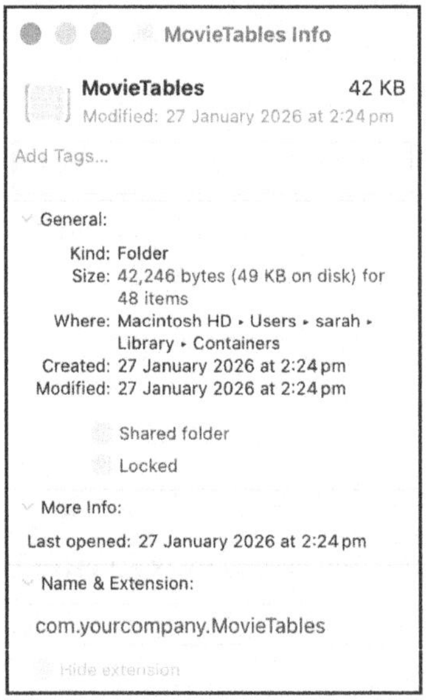

Container folder info

This shows data about the folder and tells you that its real name is **com.yourcompany.MovieTables**. (If you changed the bundle identifier from the starter project, you'll see that in the name.)

Inside this folder is a **Data** folder, and inside that is where things get interesting:

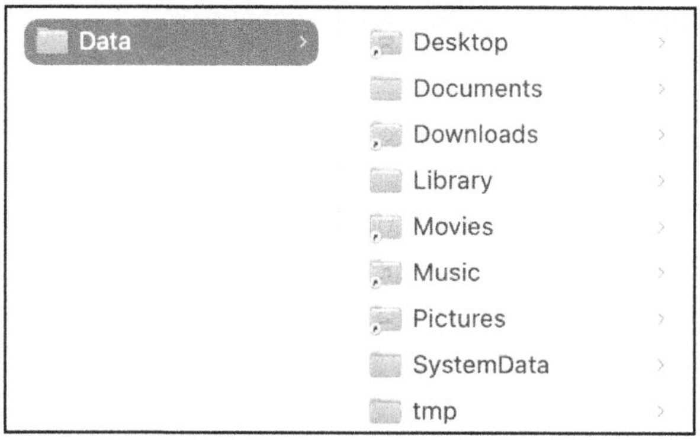

Container folder contents

Some of the folders have a small black arrow in the bottom left of the icon. These are aliases to standard folders on your Mac. If your app tried to access them, the user would see a permission prompt. The others are folders that belong to this app only. You can access them freely, but no other apps can. This allows you to save your data file to your app's own Documents folder, knowing that no other app can overwrite it.

The **Data → Library → Preferences** folder has a file called

com.yourcompany.MovieTables.plist that stores the window and table column settings.

> **Note**: You can do a complete reset of your app by quitting it and then deleting its container folder. It's always a good idea to do this before shipping an app, so you can test a fresh install.

But enough with the theory, it's time to save some data.

Saving Movie Data

Open **DataStore.swift** and add this computed property:

```
var savedDataURL: URL {
  URL.documentsDirectory.appending(component: "movies.json")
}
```

`URL` has a property to refer to the **Documents** directory or folder. This is the Documents folder inside the sandbox, not the main one in your user folder. Once you have a reference to the documents folder, you can append a file name.

Now, to convert the data and save it, add this method:

```
func saveData(movies: [Movie]) {
  // 1
  do {
    // 2
    let jsonData = try JSONEncoder().encode(movies)
    // 3
    try jsonData.write(to: savedDataURL)
  } catch {
    // 4
    print(error)
  }
}
```

Here's what's going on:

1. Since converting to JSON and writing to a file can both fail, use a `do` block to catch any errors.
2. Try to use a `JSONEncoder` to convert `movies` to `Data`. This is the reverse of the `JSONDecoder` method you used when reading the data.
3. Then, try to write this data to the file URL.
4. If any part of this fails, drop into the `catch` block and print an error report.

This is ready for use now, so open **ViewController.swift** and find `favButtonClicked(_:)`. After the `showSelectedMovie` line, add:

```
dataStore.saveData(movies: movies)
```

This means that every time you change an `isFav` property, `dataStore` saves your new data file. Because `Movie` is a class, it's passed around by reference. This means that changing a property of `selectedMovie` flows through to the `movies` array and the `visibleMovies` array.

Time to test this. Run the app, select the first movie in the list and set it as a favorite. Go back to Finder and your Container folder. Now, there's a **movies.json** file in Documents:

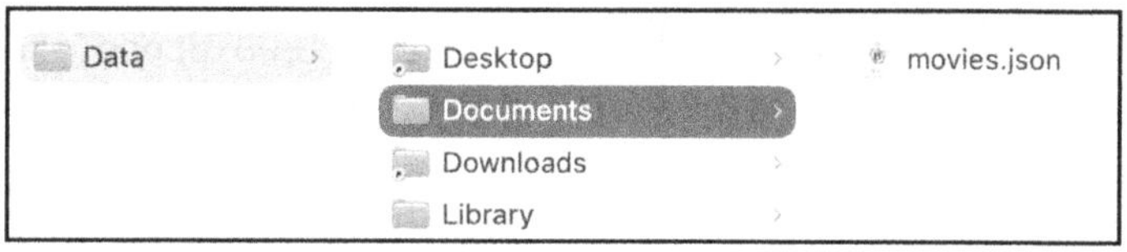

Saved data file in container

Don't try to open the file in Xcode — it'll choke and become unresponsive. To test whether the app saved your new data, you'll change the code to read data from this saved file.

Reading Saved Data

At the moment, you're calling `readBundleData()` in `DataStore` to read the default data file. You still want to use this method, but only if there's no stored data file.

Open **Data & Models → DataStore.swift** and add this new method:

```
// 1
func readStoredData() -> [Movie] {
  // 2
  do {
    let jsonData = try Data(contentsOf: savedDataURL)
    let movies = try JSONDecoder().decode([Movie].self, from:
jsonData)
    let sortedMovies = movies.sorted { movieA, movieB in
      movieA.title < movieB.title
    }
    return sortedMovies
  } catch {
    // 3
    return readBundleData()
  }
}
```

A lot of this is familiar:

1. The method returns an array of `Movie` objects.
2. Use do to try to read and process the saved data file. This is the same code as in `readBundleData()`.
3. Here's the big difference. If this fails, as it will if the file doesn't exist, use the `catch` block to fall back to reading the default data file.

With this in place, open **ViewController.swift** and in `viewDidLoad()`, replace `movies = dataStore.readBundleData()` with:

```
movies = dataStore.readStoredData()
```

Run the app and select the first movie to see your previously selected heart:

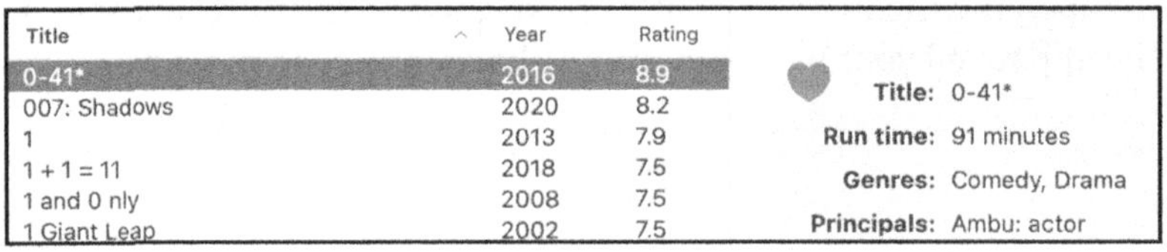

Displaying stored data.

To confirm the the fallback works, quit the app and delete **movies.json** from the app's container. When you run the app again, the movies data appears, but not your heart.

You're storing and reading the edited data and you have a working fallback solution.

Working with Threads

You may have noticed that when you click the heart to toggle a movie's favorite status, there's a slight delay. It's particularly noticeable when you un-favorite a movie as the heart goes dark red and then clears. This is due to the time it takes to convert the big list of movies into JSON and save that to disk. While your app is busy with that, it hasn't time to update the interface.

But aren't modern computers super-powerful? Why can't my Mac do more than one thing at a time? Well, it can, but by default, it doesn't.

When you run your app, it creates a series of **threads**. Each of these threads handles a different task, but everything that updates the display must happen on the **main thread**. Processing data and saving a file can happen on a **background thread** where it doesn't interfere with any interactions or display updates.

In **DataStore.swift**, replace the contents of `saveData(movies:)` with:

```
// 1
DispatchQueue.global().async { [savedDataURL] in
  do {
    let jsonData = try JSONEncoder().encode(movies)
    try jsonData.write(to: savedDataURL)
  } catch {
    print(error)
  }
// 2
}
```

There are only two new lines here, but the first one does a lot of work:

1. A `DispatchQueue` manages a series of tasks. When you add a task to this queue, it processes it when the queue has finished any previous tasks. The `global` dispatch queue is a system queue that you can always access. The `async` method asks the queue to perform this task asynchronously and not to pause the rest of the app by waiting until it's finished. Putting `savedDataURL` in square brackets **captures** it. This stores a value for `savedDataURL`, which the asynchronous block can use even if some other code changes it while the block is still working. Without this, you'll get an obscure warning about "Main actor-isolated property" if you're using Swift 6 or later.

2. The other new line closes the curly brace, so the entire `do` block happens asynchronously.

Run the app again and test clicking the heart. This time, the display updates immediately:

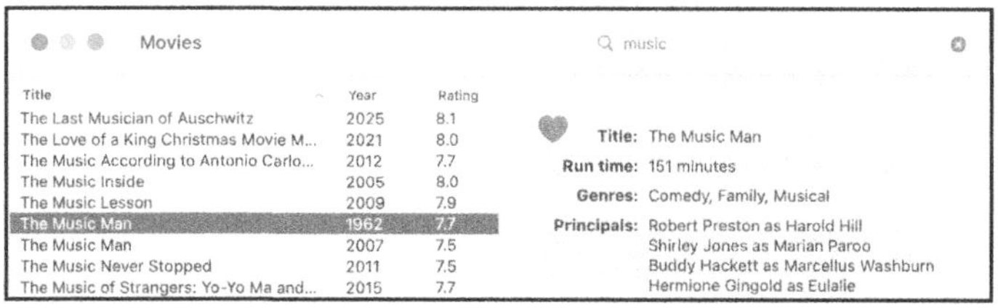

Saving asynchronously.

Now you're saving and loading data, while still providing a responsive experience for the user.

Key Points

- In an AppKit app, a toolbar is part of the window.
- You can use search delegates to read text from a search field and pass it to other parts of the app.
- Tables need sort descriptors to make columns sortable. Sorting based on sort descriptors uses NSArray methods.
- Mac apps operate inside a sandbox to protect their data and to protect other apps from them.
- Background threads can be used for tasks that don't change the display. This keeps your app's interface responsive.

Where to Go From Here?

You've done a lot of work in the main window, but so far, you haven't looked at the main menu bar. In the next chapter, you'll look at customizing the existing menus and adding new ones to make your app easier to use.

Chapter 14: Enhancing Your App

By Sarah Reichelt

In the previous chapters, you created a table-based app. Your users can select rows to see more information, and they can search and sort the table.

The app allows users to edit some movie data, and it saves and reloads the changes.

Every Mac app uses the system menu bar at the top of the screen. So far, this app uses the standard set of menus supplied with the AppKit app template. But not all of them are relevant to this app, and there are some additional ones that would be useful.

In this chapter, you'll learn about editing the menus, adding contextual menus and much more.

Examining the Menu Bar

Open the **MovieTables** project from the last chapter or use the **starter** from the downloads for this chapter. Run the app and look at the default menus in the menu bar:

Default menus

Working from left to right:

- The **Apple** menu is part of macOS and not under app control.
- The **MovieTables** menu is standard, so you won't change it.
- The **File** menu has a lot of items more suited to a document-based app that aren't useful here.
- The **Edit** menu has a lot of items dealing with formatted text. This app will add text editing later, but it doesn't need all this.
- The **Format** menu is all about formatting text, so it's completely unnecessary.
- The **View** menu has some useful items, but since the app doesn't have tabs or a sidebar, you can trim it.
- The **Window** menu is fine. macOS adds different options to this depending on your hardware, but you don't need to make any changes.
- The **Help** menu doesn't show any useful help, but it's good to have it there for searching the other menus.

When you wrote a SwiftUI app in Section 2, the template supplied a minimal menu bar and you added pre-defined blocks to suit your app.

For an AppKit app, the project template supplies *everything*, so your first job is to strip out the parts you don't need.

Open **Main.storyboard** and select **Application Scene** in the outline view. This shows the menu bar in the storyboard:

Application Scene

Expand **Application Scene** → **Application** → **Main Menu** → **File** → **Menu** in the outline:

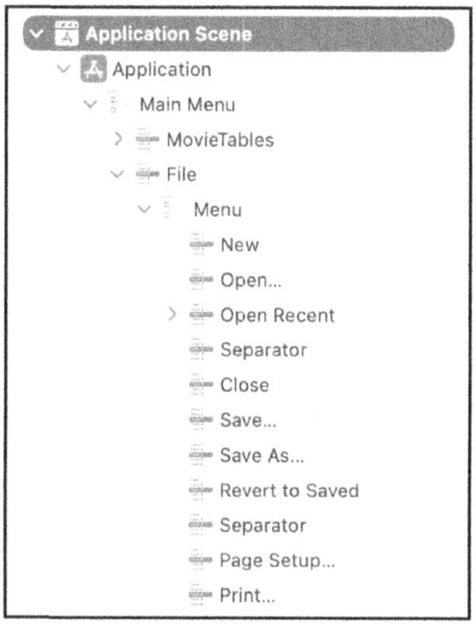

Menu structure

The structure takes some deciphering, so select **Main Menu** and press **Command-Option-4** to open the Identity inspector. The Class at the top shows that Main Menu is an `NSMenu`, which makes sense.

Now select and inspect **File**. Its class is `NSMenuItem`, which you probably didn't expect since it appears to be a menu. But it contains its own **Menu** and that *is* an `NSMenu`. All the objects inside that are `NSMenuItems`.

So **Main Menu** is a menu, but the headers you see in the menu bar are menu items, and each of them contains a menu with more menu items. That's not confusing at all. :]

Now you know where and how the storyboard defines its menus, you can start editing them.

Trimming the Menu Bar

You don't want the **Format** menu at all, so select it in the outline view and press **Delete**. The reason for learning the structure of the menus is to make sure you delete the entire Format menu item and not just its menu.

If you select Format in the storyboard and press **Delete**, you only trash its menu, and there will be a space between Edit and View in the display. If this happens to you, use the outline view to eradicate Format completely.

Click the **View** menu in the storyboard to open it, then delete **Show Sidebar**. The toolbar and full screen items can stay.

On to the **Edit** menu where you can get rid of a lot. Delete all the items after **Select All**, including the dividing line, which is a special type of menu item. Then delete **Paste and Match Style**.

And back at the **File** menu, delete everything except **Close**.

Run the app and have a look at the menus. They're a lot neater now. While it's great to supply menus for everything the user needs, it's also good design to remove anything that isn't necessary.

Take a look at the **View** menu. It still shows some tab bar options and so does the **Window** menu:

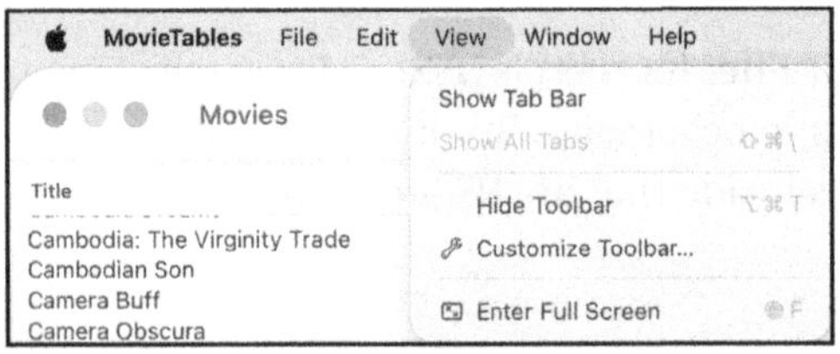

Edited View menu

These menu items don't appear in the Application Scene, so you can't get rid of them that way. The solution is to change a window setting so it doesn't support tabs.

Select the **Movies** window (in **Window Controller Scene → Window Controller**) in the storyboard and press **Command-Option-5** to open its Attributes inspector. Change **Tabbing Mode** to **Disallowed**:

Setting tabbing mode.

This gets rid of all tab bar options in the menus. Now you've removed all the unwanted items, and you're ready to add new ones.

Adding a New Menu Item

You'll add an item to the **Edit** menu to toggle the Favorite setting for a movie. It'll have a keyboard shortcut, so users can do this without clicking. It's often a good plan to replicate functions in the menus. It makes them more discoverable and adds visible keyboard shortcuts.

Open the **Edit** menu in the storyboard and press **Shift-Command-L** to open the **Library**. Search for **menu** and drag a **Menu Item** to the top of the menu. Open the **Library** again, and this time, drag a **Separator Menu Item** to below your new item:

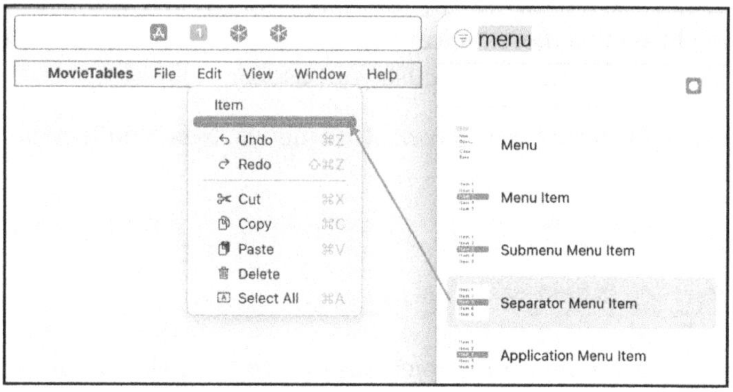

Adding a separator.

Select the new item and press **Command-Option-5** to get to the Attributes inspector. Set its **Title** to **Toggle Favorite**, then click in the **Key Equivalent box** and press **Command-T** to set the keyboard shortcut. If you mistype, click the **X** button in the box and try again. Next look further down the inspector to find **Image**.

Start typing “heart” in the box and select **heart.fill** from the menu that appears:

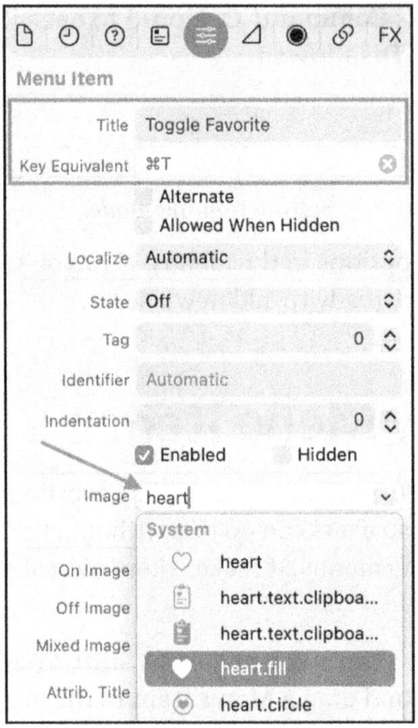

Setting menu item attributes.

Command-F might seem a more logical key equivalent, but that’s used for Find in most apps, and you don’t want to confuse your users.

You’ve removed and inserted items in existing menus. Now, you’ll create your own menu.

Inserting a New Menu

There are a lot of movies, and sometimes, it’s nice to see a shorter list. Listing only your favorite movies would also be useful. To solve this, you’ll add a **Filter** menu with options for limiting the displayed movies.

Remember, an entry in the menu bar is actually a menu item. Click the name to close any open menu in the storyboard. Open the **Library** and drag a **Menu Item** into the bar between **View** and **Window**. It appears in the bar as a blank space.

Use the Attributes inspector to change its title to **Filter**, but don’t worry that it still only appears as a blank.

Next, use the **Library** to drag a **Menu** into this blank space. Give the menu a title of **Filter**, and the name finally appears:

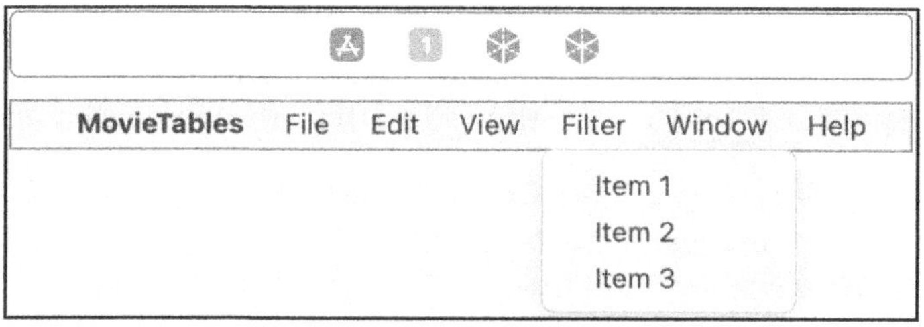

New Filter menu

The menu came prefilled with three items. Use the Attributes inspector to edit them as follows:

1. Title: **Show All Movies**, Key Equivalent: **Command-M**, Image: **movieclapper**
2. Title: **Favorites Only**, Key Equivalent: **Command-L** (L for Love), Image: **heart**
3. Title: **Highest Rated Movies**, Key Equivalent: **Command-R**, Image: **star**

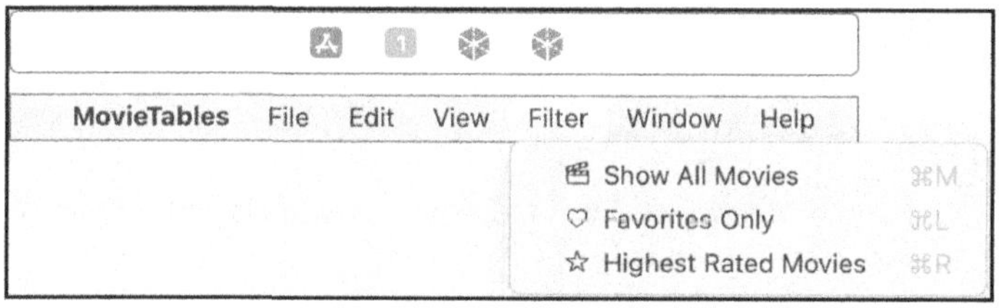

New Filter menu items

The UI is in place, so now it's time to connect these menu items to the code.

The First Responder

In AppKit, every app has a **First Responder**. This is whatever is active and can receive events at the time. It could be a text field, a button, a view or a window. For an app like this one, the chain flows from view → superviews → window → window controller → application.

Checking the storyboard, each scene includes a First Responder object to accept input and events. The preset menu items all send messages to the First Responder.

To see this, select **File → Close** in the **Application Scene** and press **Command-Option-7** to open the Connections inspector. The action for this menu item sends `performClose` to the First Responder. When you choose this menu item, the message travels up the responder chain until it gets to an object that can handle this method. Since `performClose` is an `NSWindow` method, the window handles this action.

For your own menu items, you'll create action methods in `ViewController`, which is part of the responder chain.

Adding Menu Actions

Previously, to create an action, you **Control-dragged** from the storyboard into `ViewController`. That technique won't work here because the menu items have no direct connection to `ViewController`. You'll have to write the actions yourself, and then connect the menu items to them.

Open **ViewController.swift** and scroll to the bottom. Make some space before the closing curly brace and add this:

```
// 1
// MARK: - Menu Actions

// 2
@IBAction func showAllMovies(_ sender: Any) {
  // 3
  print("Show all movies")
}

// 4
@IBAction func showFavs(_ sender: Any) {
  print("Show favorites")
}

@IBAction func showHighRated(_ sender: Any) {
  print("Show highest rated")
}
```

Stepping through this:

1. A `MARK` is a special comment that adds a label to the jump bar navigator at the top of the code pane. If it has a dash before the text, it adds a divider line too. This makes navigating around your code easier as your program gets longer.

2. This is the same format as the action Xcode inserted for `favButtonClicked(_:)`. `@IBAction` marks this as a method that the storyboard can access. The `sender` is the object that initiated this call, and it can be any type.
3. This action will eventually show all movies, but for now, print something to show it works.
4. Create similar actions for showing favorite movies and highest rated movies.

Back in **Main.storyboard**, open the **Filter** menu and **Control-drag** from **Show All Movies** to the orange **1** icon in the bar above. This represents the First Responder:

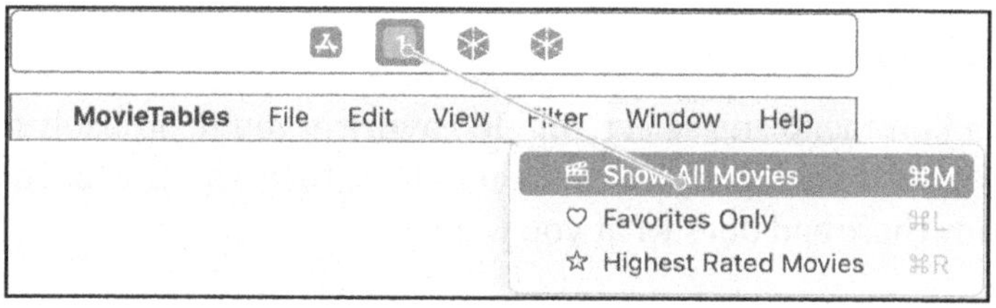

Control-drag to First Responder

You'll see a huge scrolling list of possible actions.

Type **show** to scroll to the actions starting with `show` and select **showAllMovies:**:

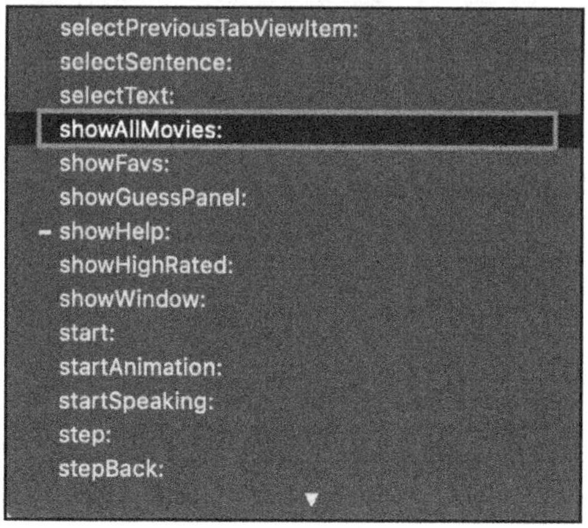

Connecting to First Responder.

Repeat this for the other two Filter menu items, selecting **showFavs:** and **showHighRated:**.

When you've done that, select the **First Responder** icon and open its Connections inspector. There are a *lot* of connections, but they're in alphabetical order, so scroll down until you find the `show...` actions. Mouse over them, and the storyboard highlights the connected menu items so you can confirm that you linked the right menu item to the right method:

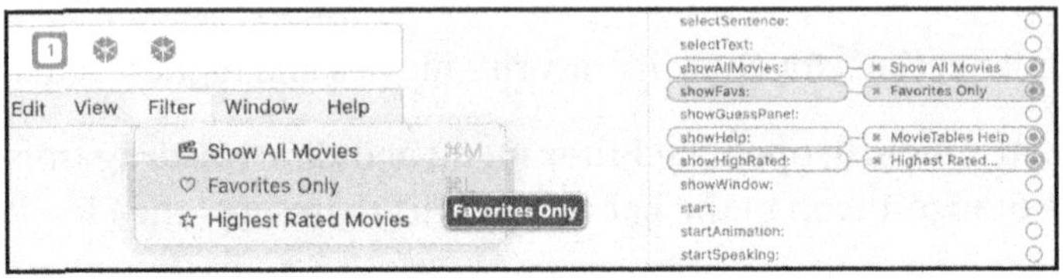

First Responder connections

Next, open the **Edit** menu and select **Toggle Favorite**. You're probably starting to type another `@IBAction` already, but you don't have to. :] The `favButtonClicked` action is already there and does what you want.

Control-drag from **Toggle Favorite** to **First Responder** and choose `favButtonClicked:`. You're duplicating functionality in the menu, but you don't have to duplicate the code.

Run the app now and test your new menu items:

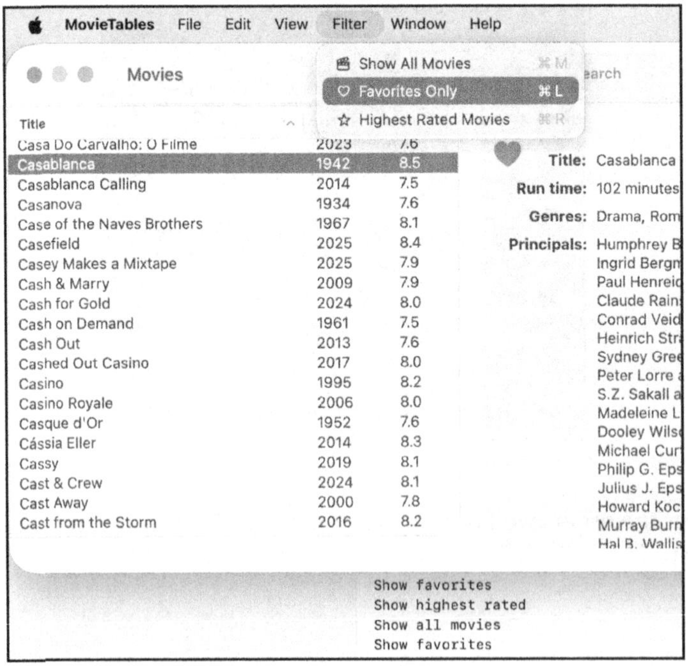

Testing the menus

Toggle Favorite works already, and the others print the expected reports, whether you select the item from the menu or use the keyboard shortcut.

You've made all the links between the storyboard and `ViewController`. Next, you'll fill in the code.

Coding the Menus

You've set up menus to switch between three different view modes. An enumeration is always a good choice to manage a set of states like this.

Select the **Data & Models** folder in the Project navigator and make a new empty file called **ViewMode.swift**.

Add this enumeration:

```
enum ViewMode {
  case allMovies
  case favsOnly
  case highRating
}
```

This sets up a `case` for each of the three possible modes.

Next, open **ViewController.swift** and add these properties:

```
var viewMode = ViewMode.allMovies {
  didSet {
    searchMovies()
  }
}
var highRatingLimit = 9.0
```

This creates a `ViewMode` property and sets it to `allMovies` by default. Any time you set a new value, call `searchMovies()` to update the list of displayed movies. It also sets up a property to hold the limit for a high rated movie.

You already have a method to search and sort the movies. This is the logical place to add the filter, so scroll to `searchMovies()`. Add some blank lines at the start of the method and insert this code:

```
// 1
var moviesToShow = movies
// 2
if viewMode == .favsOnly {
```

```
    // 3
    moviesToShow = movies.filter { movie in
      movie.isFav
    }
  } else if viewMode == .highRating {
    // 4
    moviesToShow = movies.filter { movie in
      movie.rating >= highRatingLimit
    }
  }
```

What does this do?

1. Make a copy of the complete `movies` array. This is the default list for display.
2. If `viewMode` is `favsOnly`, loop through `movies`, using `filter` to find the favorites only.
3. Or if `viewMode` is `highRating`, use `filter` to find the ones with a rating higher than or equal to `highRatingLimit`.

Now `moviesToShow` contains the movies matching the view mode, but you aren't using it yet.

Applying the View mode

Lower in the method, replace `visibleMovies = movies` with:

```
visibleMovies = moviesToShow
```

And replace `visibleMovies = movies.filter { movie in` with:

```
visibleMovies = moviesToShow.filter { movie in
```

This starts any search with the filtered `moviesToShow`.

You're nearly at the end of the menu processing now. Use the navigation jump bar to move to `showAllMovies`:

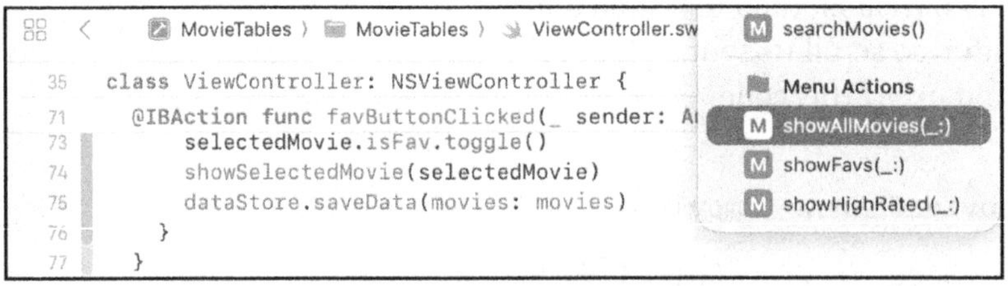

Navigation jump bar

Replace the `print` line with:

```
viewMode = .allMovies
```

This sets the correct `viewMode` and the property observer you created earlier calls the search method to process it.

Similarly, replace the `print` in `showFavs(_:)` with:

```
viewMode = .favsOnly
```

And in `showHighRated(_:)`, use:

```
viewMode = .highRating
```

Time to check it out. Run the app, make sure you have a few favorite movies marked and test the menu:

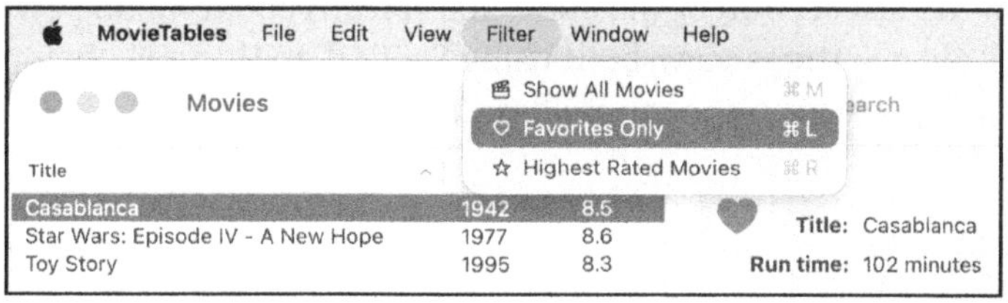

Showing favorites

Test the **Highest Rating** mode too. Sort by **Rating** to make sure you can't see anything with a rating lower than 9.0.

You're nearly done with the system menu bar, but there's just one more thing... :]

The MovieTables Menu

Your app has some standard menu items in the **MovieTables** menu. One of these is **About MovieTables**. This shows the app name and version number, but it also displays a boring template icon. Adding a custom icon would improve this dialog and the Dock display.

In the **assets** folder in the downloads for this chapter, you'll find an **AppIcon.icon** folder that contains a pre-built icon. To install this, drag **AppIcon.icon** from the **assets** folder into the Project navigator. Press **Shift-Command-K** to clean the build folder, then run the app.

Select **MovieTables** → **About MovieTables** to see your new icon in the **About** box:

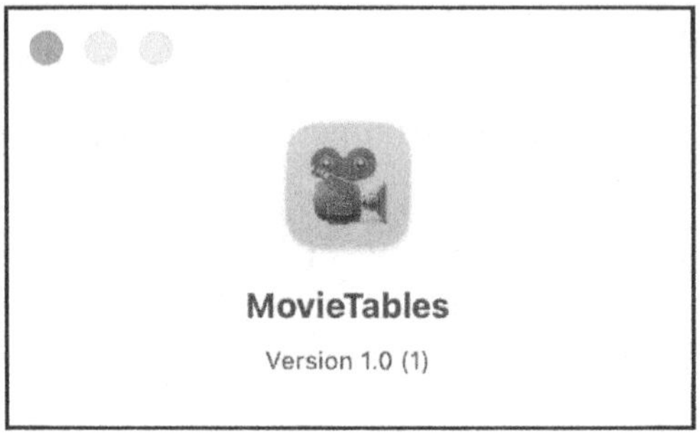

About dialog with icon

The **MovieTables menu** also contains a disabled item for **Settings...**. One of the constant themes of this book has been to supply the features the Mac users expect, and they definitely expect a Settings window. So why isn't there one for this app?

It's coming. In the last section of the book, you'll learn about mixing SwiftUI and AppKit. You'll add a Settings view, built using SwiftUI, to this app. So for now, leave the menu item in place even though it doesn't do anything.

App Delegate

You've learned about using delegates for the table and the search bar, but you haven't looked at `AppDelegate` yet. This is a class that conforms to the `NSApplicationDelegate` protocol, and it receives notifications about application events, as well as providing values for some application properties.

Open **AppDelegate.swift** to see the three methods supplied in the standard template.

- `applicationDidFinishLaunching(_:)` gives you a place to perform any app-wide initialization.
- `applicationWillTerminate(_:)` is the opposite and allows you to take actions before the app closes.
- `applicationSupportsSecureRestorableState(_:)` specifies whether this app should restore its previous state on launch.

This app doesn't do any of these things, and since unnecessary code is bad code, delete everything inside the `AppDelegate` class definition.

But, there's one thing you need to add. Right now, if you run the app and close the window, you're stuck. This is a single window app, and there's no way to get the window back if you close it.

The solution is to add this method to `AppDelegate`:

```
func applicationShouldTerminateAfterLastWindowClosed(
    _ sender: NSApplication
) -> Bool {
    true
}
```

This is a message that the app sends to `AppDelegate` when the last window closes, and as it returns `true`, the app then quits. This is good behavior for a single window app.

Contextual Menus

So far, you've looked at menus in the system menu bar, but you can attach menus to other objects in your interface. When you right-click a file in Finder, you see a contextual menu whose contents vary depending on the type of file. You'll add a similar menu to the table.

Start with the visuals. Open **Main.storyboard** and scroll to see the view with the table. Click the bar above the **ViewController** to make it active. Press **Shift-Command-L** to open the **Library** and search for `menu`. Drag a **menu** into the bar:

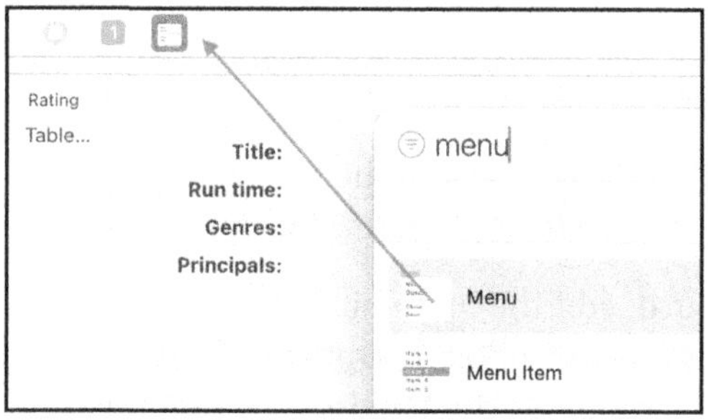

Adding a menu to View Controller Scene

This adds the menu to the scene, but it's not connected to the table. Select **Movies Table View** using the **Shift-right-click** menu. Press **Command-Option-7** to open the Connections inspector.

In the **Outlets** section, drag from the circle beside **menu** to the menu you just added to the bar:

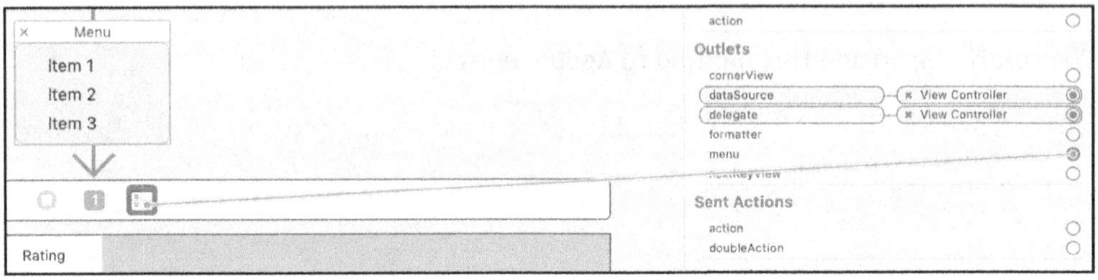

Connecting the menu to the table.

Run the app and right-click anywhere in the table to make the menu appear, showing the default three items:

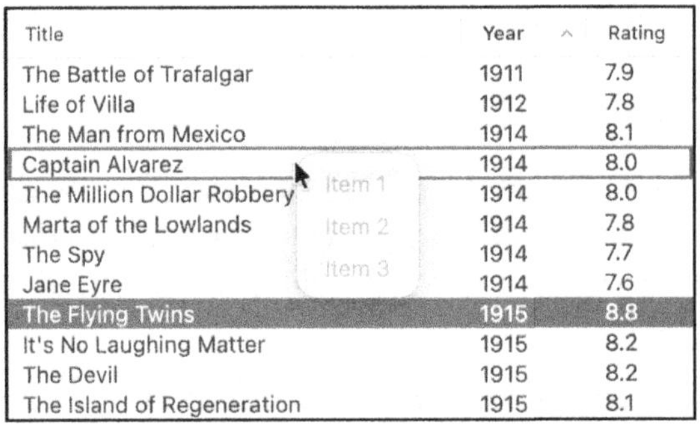

Default contextual menu

There are a few things to note here. The menu only appears when you right-click in the table, not anywhere else. The items are inactive because you haven't connected them to any actions yet.

Most interestingly, the selected line and the line that activated the menu aren't necessarily the same. Your code has to allow for this.

Back in **Main.storyboard**, edit the three menu items: Use the Attributes inspector or double-click the text in the menu. Using **Option-;** to type the three dots as a single character, set the menu items to **Edit Movie…**, **Delete Movie…** and **Show in Browser**.

The first two menu items end in an ellipsis because they'll lead the user to another window or dialog.

Open the **Library** again and drag a **Separator Menu Item** between the second and third items, so your menu looks like:

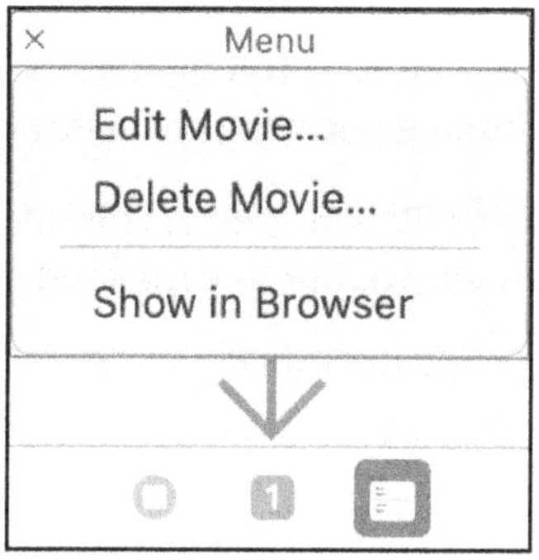

Contextual menu items

With the items in place, your next task is to set up their actions.

Setting a Contextual Action

Open **ViewController.swift** and scroll to the bottom. Add some blank lines and then insert this:

```
// 1
// MARK: - Contextual Menu Actions

// 2
var clickedMovie: Movie? {
  // 3
  let row = moviesTableView.clickedRow
  // 4
  if row > -1 {
    return visibleMovies[row]
  }
  // 5
  return nil
}

// 6
@IBAction func editMovie(_ sender: Any) {
  // 7
  guard let movie = clickedMovie else {
    return
  }
  // 8
  print("Editing \(movie.title)")
}
```

Taking this bit by bit:

1. Add another `MARK` to divide up the code.
2. Create a computed property to return the right-clicked movie, if possible. All three menu items need this, so it's worth separating out for easy access.
3. Query the table for its `clickedRow` property. This gives the index of the row the user right-clicked in, which may not be the selected row.
4. If the user right-clicked outside the table rows, `row` is `-1`. Otherwise, use `row` to find the movie in `visibleMovies`.
5. If `row` is `-1`, return `nil` to tell the actions to do nothing.
6. Add another `@IBAction` that you can connect to the menu item.
7. It starts by looking for a valid `clickedMovie` and returns if there isn't one.
8. Editing movies comes later, so for now, print the movie title to show the menu works.

Now to connect the menu item to this action. Open **Main.storyboard** and select the **Edit Movie** menu item.

Control-drag from the menu item to the circular icon in the bar that represents the **View Controller** and choose `editMovie:` from the menu:

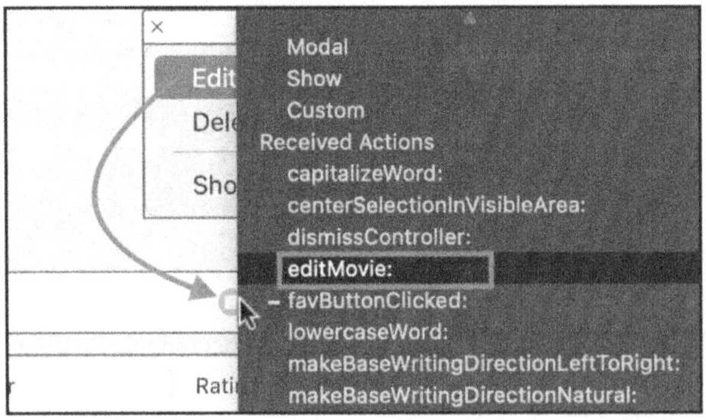

Connecting the Edit Movie menu item.

> **Note**: This demonstrates a different way to make a connection. Before you used the Connections inspector, or you Control-dragged into the outline view. Try them all and use whichever you find most intuitive.

You've only linked one menu item, but that's enough to test the menu. Run the app, right-click a movie and select **Edit Movie** to see the expected text appear in the Xcode console:

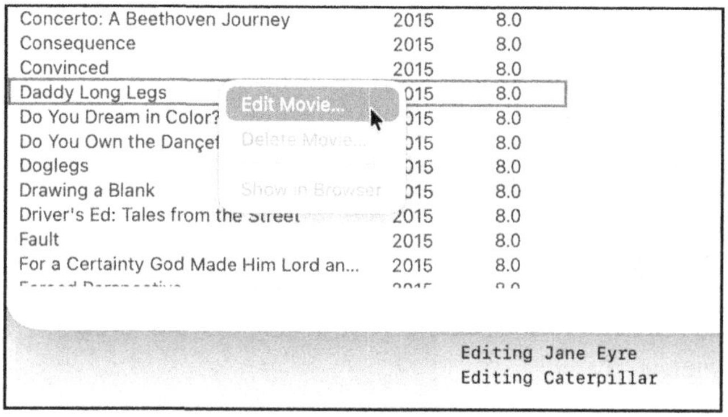

Selecting Edit Movie.

You've coded one menu item and connected the action to the item. Now, it's time to complete the other two.

Showing a Movie in the Browser

Start by adding the **Show in Browser** action. Open **ViewController.swift**, scroll to the end and add this:

```
// 1
@IBAction func showInBrowser(_ sender: Any) {
  // 2
  guard let movie = clickedMovie else {
    return
  }

  // 3
  let address = "https://www.imdb.com/title/\(movie.id)/"
  // 4
  guard let url = URL(string: address) else {
    return
  }
  // 5
  NSWorkspace.shared.open(url)
}
```

What's happening here?

1. Set up an `@IBAction` as before.
2. Again, check the user has right-clicked a movie.
3. Each movie has an `id` property that identifies it in the IMDb database. Assemble a web address for the selected movie by interpolating its `id`.
4. Check that this creates a valid `URL`.
5. `NSWorkspace` is a class that can interact with other apps. `NSWorkspace.shared` gives you the workspace that's available to the app and `open` uses the default application for the URL. Since this URL is a web address, it opens it in the user's default browser.

With the action in place, head back to **Main.storyboard** to connect it up. **Control-drag** from **Show in Browser** to **View Controller** and select `showInBrowser:`.

Time to test this one. Run the app, right-click any movie and select **Show in Browser**:

Showing movie in browser.

It works! Time to implement the last action.

Deleting a Movie

Deleting a movie is complicated because you shouldn't do something destructive without confirmation. So, this action needs to show a dialog.

In **ViewController.swift,** add this method:

```
// 1
@IBAction func deleteMovie(_ sender: Any) {
  guard let movie = clickedMovie else {
```

```
      return
    }

    // 2
    let alert = NSAlert()
    alert.alertStyle = .warning
    alert.messageText = "Really delete '\(movie.title)'?"

    // 3
    alert.addButton(withTitle: "Delete")
    alert.addButton(withTitle: "Cancel")

    // 4
    let response = alert.runModal()

    // 5
    if response == .alertFirstButtonReturn {
      // 6
      movies.removeAll {
        $0.id == movie.id
      }

      // 7
      clearSelectedMovie()
      searchMovies()
      dataStore.saveData(movies: movies)
    }
  }
```

This is quite a chunk of code:

1. The first section is familiar to you — create an `@IBAction` and check if the user right-clicked a movie.

2. Create an `NSAlert`, which is the class that displays a dialog box. Set its style — the options are `critical`, `warning` or `informational` — and set the message using the movie's title.

3. Add two buttons to the alert. The first one added is always the default selection if the user presses **Return**.

4. Run the alert to show it and wait for the user to respond. This returns an `NSApplication.ModalResponse`.

5. Since the second button does nothing, you only need to check if the user clicked the first button, which returns `alertFirstButtonReturn`.

6. Use an `Array` method to delete any movies that match the criteria. In this case, `id` is a unique identifier, so you'll only remove one.

7. Clear the detail display, use `searchMovies()` to update the table, then save the edited data.

Phew, that's quite a method! Now, you to connect it to its menu item.

I'm sure you've guessed what's coming. Open **Main.storyboard** and **Control-drag** from **Delete Movie** to **View Controller**. Select `deleteMovie:` to complete the link.

Ready to test? Run the app and try deleting a movie:

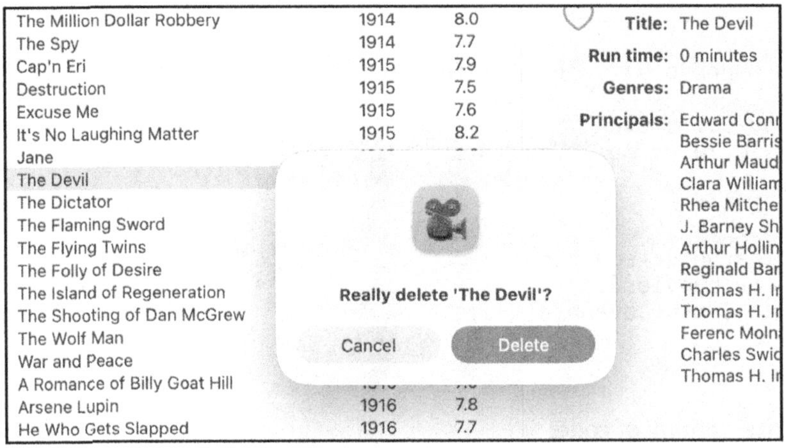

Delete movie confirmation

Click either button to test. Or, press **Escape** to *click* Cancel or **Return** to *click* the default Delete.

> **Note**: If you ever want to return to the default list of movies, quit the app and switch to **Finder**. Open **Library → Containers → MovieTables → Data → Documents** and delete **movies.json**. Next time you run the app, it'll read the default data file.

Great work! Your table now has a contextual menu, and two of the three items are fully functional.

Showing the Movie Count

When the app reads the movies data file, it prints the number of movies. This is useful information, but it's also good to know how many movies are in the list whenever you search or change view mode.

To add this, open **Main.storyboard** and scroll to see the blank space underneath the table in **View Controller**. You left that space there for this exact purpose. :]

Open the **Library** and drag a **Label** into this space.

Click **Add New Constraints** and set top spacing and left spacing to **Standard**. Click **Add 2 Constraints**:

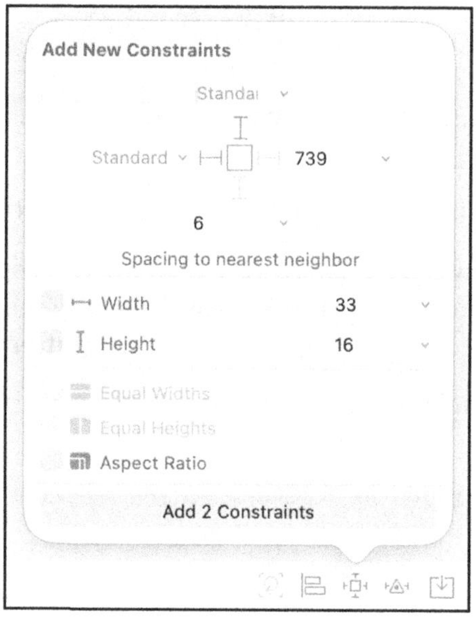

Setting label constraints.

Control-drag from the new label into the table area and choose **Trailing** from the popup menu. This locks the right edge of the label to the right, or trailing, edge of the table box:

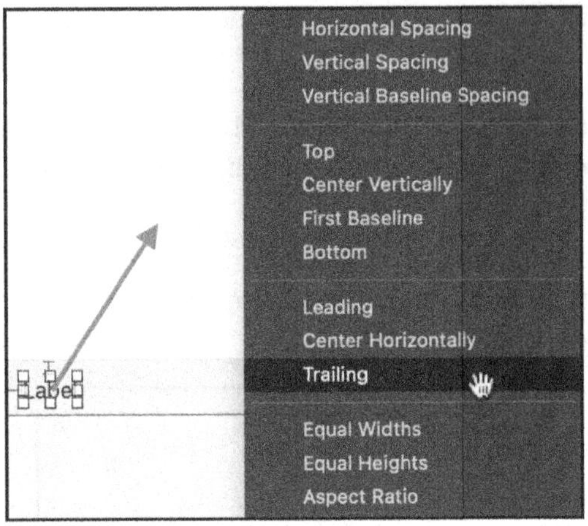

Adding a trailing constraint.

You've positioned the label, but now it needs a name, so the code can access it.

Shift-Option-click ViewController.swift in the Project navigator to open it in a secondary editor. Scroll to the top and **Control-drag** from the new label to where you defined the other `@IBOutlet` properties. Insert an **Outlet** called **statusLabel**.

After `searchMovies()`, add this new method:

```
func showMovieCount() {
  statusLabel.stringValue = "\(visibleMovies.count) movies."
}
```

This sets the text of the status label to the number of movies displayed in the table, accounting for searches and filters.

In `viewDidLoad()`, add this line at the end to call your new method:

```
showMovieCount()
```

And, since this now displays the count in the app, delete the `print` line.

Finally, scroll to the end of `searchMovies()` and add the same line.

Run the app and check the count:

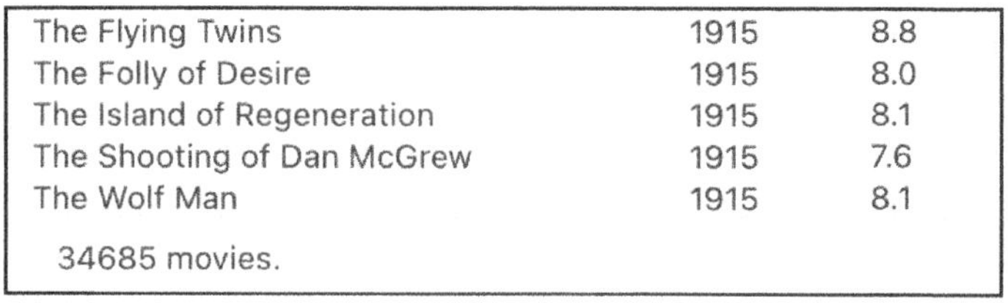

Counting the movies.

Do a search and change the view mode to confirm that the status label shows the number of visible movies.

This is good, but large numbers are easier to read if they're formatted.

Formatting the Count

Adding the thousands separator will make the movie count much more readable. But this isn't easy to do. Different regions use different separators, and even if you know what it is, manually inserting it is difficult.

Fortunately, Apple has provided a number formatting class for this.

Replace the contents of `showMovieCount()` with:

```
// 1
let formatter = NumberFormatter()
// 2
formatter.numberStyle = .decimal
// 3
formatter.locale = Locale.current

// 4
let numberString = formatter.string(for: visibleMovies.count)
  // 5
  ?? "\(visibleMovies.count)"

// 6
statusLabel.stringValue = "\(numberString) movies."
```

Going through these lines:

1. Create a number formatter.
2. Set its style to the one that shows thousands separators. The number of movies is an `Int`, so even though you've chosen the `decimal` style, it won't show any numbers after the decimal point.

3. Set the region for the formatter to the user's locale. This uses a comma for the thousands separators in the US, a space in France and whatever is appropriate all around the world.
4. Use the formatter to convert `visibleMovies.count` into a formatted string.
5. The conversion can fail, so fall back to converting `visibleMovies.count` into a string, if necessary.
6. Display the string in the status label.

Run the app now, and check the display with all the movies visible:

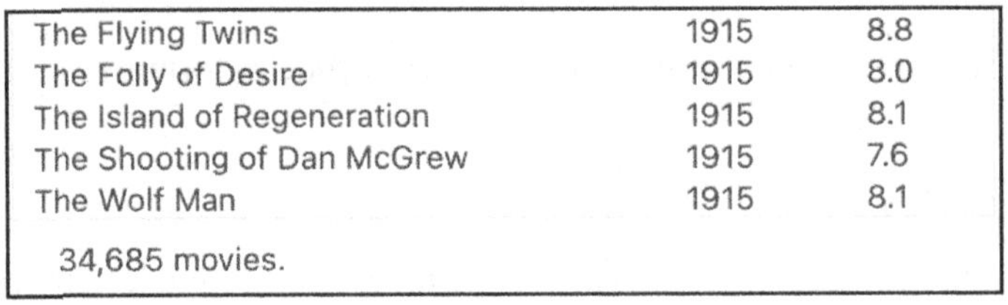

Formatting the movie count.

That's a much clearer display.

Key Points

- The menu bar is an important part of any Mac app. Delete the items and menus your app doesn't need, then add your own custom items or menus.
- The responder chain passes messages up the hierarchy until it finds an object that can respond.
- You can add a menu and connect it to any view to create a contextual menu.
- A number formatter makes numeric data more readable.

Where to Go From Here?

You've covered a lot in this chapter. You know how to delete and add menus and menu items to the system menu bar. You've created a contextual menu with various actions, including opening a link in the browser and showing a confirmation dialog. And finally, you added a status label with a number formatter. That was a lot of work!

Over the next two chapters, you'll make a new window for editing movies. You'll learn a different way to set up a table, and you'll handle editable text fields.

Chapter 15: Creating the Edit Interface

By Sarah Reichelt

In the previous chapter, you created a contextual menu for the movies table. One of the menu items is for editing a movie, but at the moment, it doesn't do anything.

Over the next two chapters, you'll add and configure a new window for doing these edits, with edit fields for the data like the movie title and year, plus a table for listing and editing the movie principals.

When you finish, the edit window will look like this:

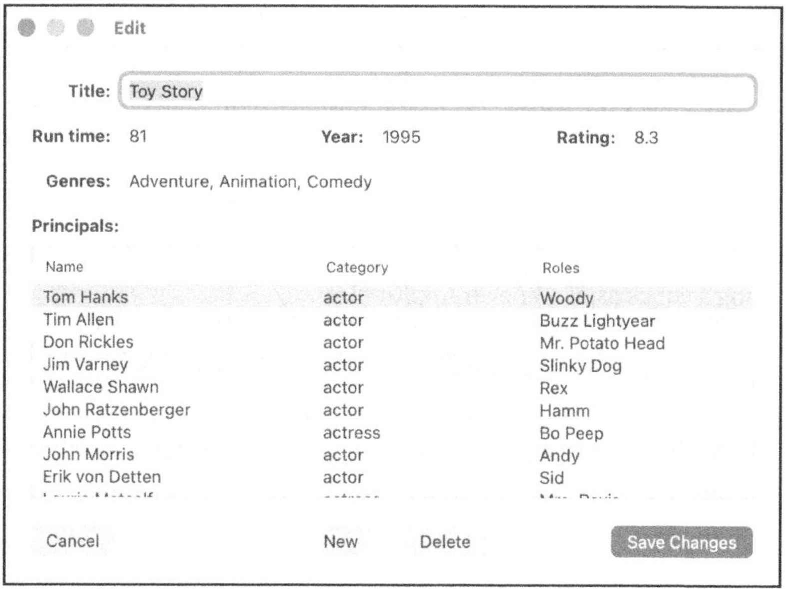

Final edit window.

Adding a New Window

Launch **Xcode** and open your **MovieTables** project or get the **starter** project from the downloads for this chapter.

The first task is to add a new window controller and view controller in the storyboard. Open **Main.storyboard** and then open the Library using the + button in the bottom toolbar or by pressing **Shift-Command-L.**

Search for **win** and drag a **Window Controller** into any blank area in the storyboard. This adds a Window Controller with a window and a connected View Controller with a view.

Select the window and press **Command-Option-5** to open the Attributes inspector. Set its **Title** to **Edit**. The window and view are too small, so switch to the next inspector along — the Size inspector — and set the Width to **600** and Height to **400**. Press **Tab** or **Return** to process your new size, then check **Minimum Content Size** and make sure the same numbers appear there.

How do you decide what sizes to set? Looking at the design, the table is the widest component. It needs three columns, each of which will be between 150 and 200 pixels wide. Rounding that to a neat number gives a width of 600. For the height, you want to use a fraction of the width. Two-thirds of the width gives 400, which looks good. You may need to change this later as the design develops, but this provides a decent starting point.

Next, select the **View Controller → View** and set its width and height to 600 and 400 to match.

This View Controller needs its own class. Press **Command-N** to open the new file template chooser. This time, choose **macOS → Source → Cocoa Class**. This gives a file containing a subclass of a known AppKit class.

Click **Next** and set the Class to **EditViewController**. Choose **NSViewController** from the **Subclass of:** popup. Uncheck **Also create XIB file for user interface**. You'll use Main.storyboard for the design, so you don't need a separate design file.

Make sure Language is set to **Swift** and press **Next**, then **Create**:

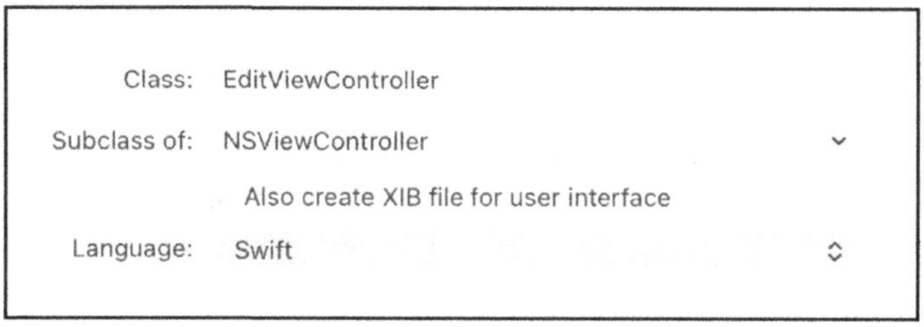

Adding a view controller.

This gives your project a new `NSViewController` class and now you can set it as the class for the newly added View Controller.

In **Main.storyboard**, select the new View Controller. Use the outline view to be sure you select the controller and not its view. Press **Command-Option-4** to open the Identity inspector and use the Class popup to change it to **EditViewController**:

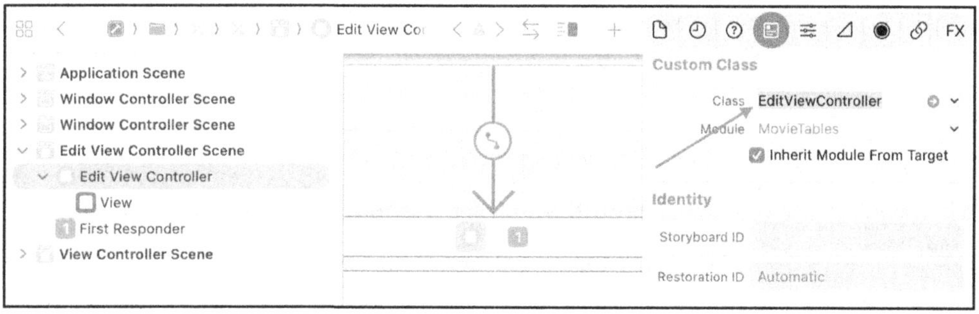

Assigning the view controller class.

When you do this, the names in the outline view change too, making it easier to identify this view controller from now on.

Segueing to the New Window

The navigation link between two view controllers is a **segue** (pronounced SEG-way). To create a segue, position the objects in the storyboard so you can see the original View Controller and the new Edit window's Window Controller. Click in the bar at the top of the View Controller so you can see its buttons. **Control-drag** from the View Controller icon into the new Edit **Window** Controller, not the Edit **View** Controller:

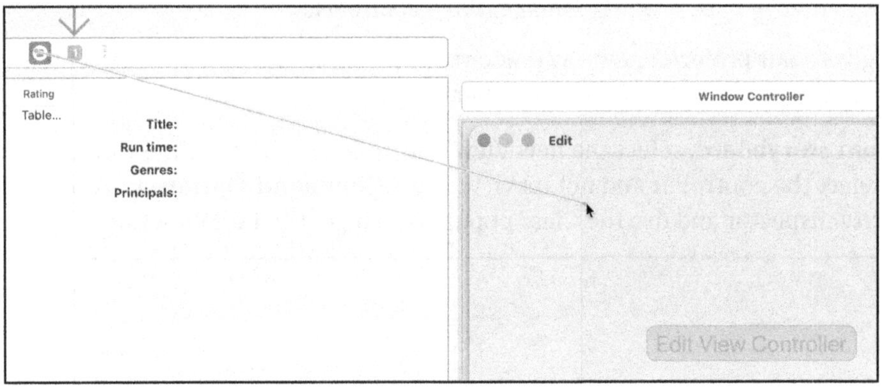

Creating a segue.

When you release the mouse button, you'll see a menu. Choose **Show** as the segue style.

This draws a line between the two objects, with an icon in the middle — this represents the segue, or in full, the `NSStoryboardSegue`.

Click the icon and press **Command-Option-5** to open the Attributes inspector for the segue. Set the Identifier to **showEditWindow**:

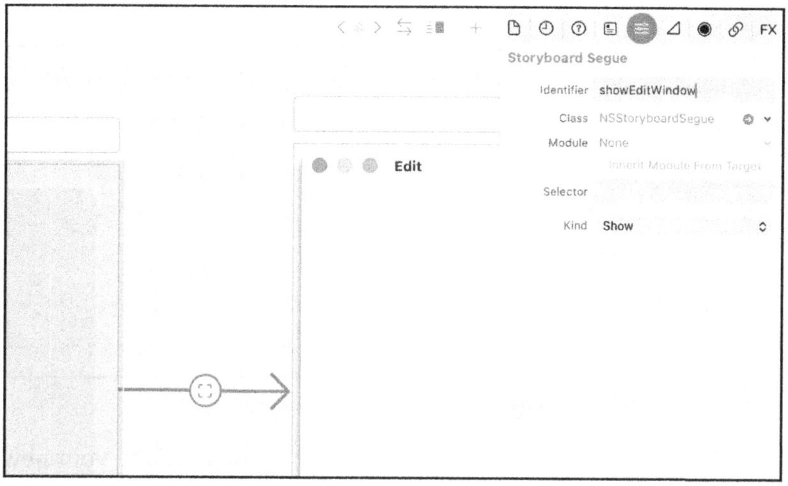

Identifying the segue.

Now you have a name you can use to run this segue and show the new window.

Open **ViewController.swift** and scroll or jump to `editMovie(_:)`. Replace the `print` line with:

```
performSegue(withIdentifier: "showEditWindow", sender: movie)
```

This activates the segue, sending in the clicked movie. The movie doesn't do anything yet, but you've done enough to test the transition.

Run the app, **right-click** any row in the table and select **Edit Movie...**:

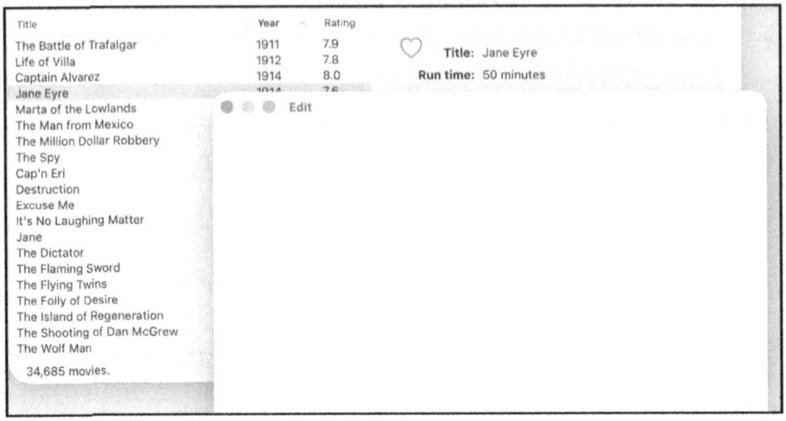

Segueing to the Edit window.

The new window appears! Now, you need to send the movie data to your new window.

Preparing Data for the Edit Window

When you initiate a segue, it triggers a method called `prepare(for:sender:)`. You can override this method to customize what happens during the transition. At this point, the segue knows where it's heading, so this is a great place to set some properties on the destination.

Start by opening **EditViewController.swift**. It needs the `Movie` object for editing, but there's a problem. `Movie` is a class and as such, it's a reference type. If you passed a movie to `EditViewController`, you'd actually be passing a reference to that movie — its address in your computer's memory — not the values in the movie properties. When your edit window changed any properties, these changes would apply directly to the original, but you want to send a copy, so users can cancel their edits and leave the original unchanged.

One way round this is to use JSON encoding to pass the movie to `EditViewController` as `Data` and decode it there to get a completely new copy.

Add these properties to `EditViewController`:

```
// 1
var movie: Movie?
```

```
// 2
var originalMovieData: Data? {
  // 3
  didSet {
    // 4
    if let originalMovieData {
      // 5
      movie = try? JSONDecoder().decode(Movie.self, from:
originalMovieData)
      // 6
      print("In EditViewController")
      print(movie)
    }
  }
}
```

Stepping through these:

1. The `movie` property stores an optional `Movie`.
2. `originalMovieData` is optional `Data`.
3. Add a property observer to `originalMovieData` to detect whenever it's set.
4. Check if there's any data in the optional.
5. If there is, try to decode the JSON data into a `Movie` and use it to set the `movie` property.
6. Print some debug information. This shows a warning but you can ignore it since this line is only temporary.

This is rather long-winded but it solves the problem.

Passing the Data

Next, open **ViewController.swift** and add this new method underneath `editMovie(_:)`:

```
// 1
override func prepare(for segue: NSStoryboardSegue, sender:
Any?) {
  // 2
  guard segue.identifier == "showEditWindow" else {
    return
  }

  // 3
  guard
```

```
    let movie = sender as? Movie,
    let movieData = try? JSONEncoder().encode(movie)
  else {
    return
  }

  // 4
  print("Leaving ViewController")
  print(movie)

  // 5
  if
    let windowController = segue.destinationController as?
NSWindowController,
    let editViewController = windowController
      .contentViewController as? EditViewController {
    // 6
    editViewController.originalMovieData = movieData
  }
}
```

What does this do?

1. Provide an override method for your segues.
2. Confirm this is the `showEditWindow` segue.
3. Check the segue's `sender` is a `Movie` and try to encode it into JSON data. You set the sender value when you called `performSegue(withIdentifier:sender:)`.
4. Print some debug information.
5. Now you have to work your way through the view hierarchy. The segue's destination is a window controller and that window controller has a `contentViewController`. You need to make sure this is an `EditViewController` so you can set its properties.
6. If the segue ends up at the correct type of view controller, set its `originalMovieData`, which then sets its `movie` property.

The edit window has no UI yet, but there's enough in place to test the data flow. Run the app, **right-click** any movie and select **Edit Movie...**:

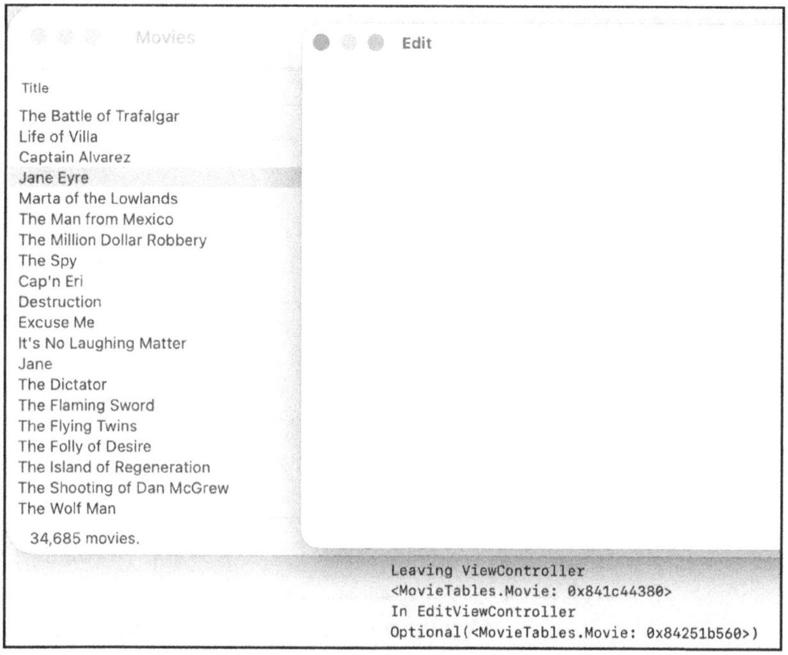

Movie for editing

Check the Xcode console. The key thing is the hexadecimal numbers shown for each movie (yours will be different to the ones in the screenshot). These are the memory addresses for the two movies and they're not identical, which confirms you've got two distinct `Movie` objects. This is why you went through all this encoding and decoding. If you'd sent `movie` directly to `EditViewController`, the addresses would have been the same and any edits would have changed the main data array.

Now you've proved that the data transfer works, delete the two `print` lines in **ViewController.swift** and the two in **EditViewController.swift**.

With the data transfer in place, you can start work on the interface.

The Editing Interface

The edit window has three main sections. The top section is for the single chunks of data: title, year etc. The middle is a table for the list of principals. And finally the bottom has the **Cancel** and **Save Changes** buttons.

Open **Main.storyboard** and scroll to see the Edit View Controller. Starting at the bottom, open the Library and search for **button**.

Drag a **Push Button** into the bottom left corner until you see the two blue alignment guides. Place the button with its bottom left corner at the intersection of these lines:

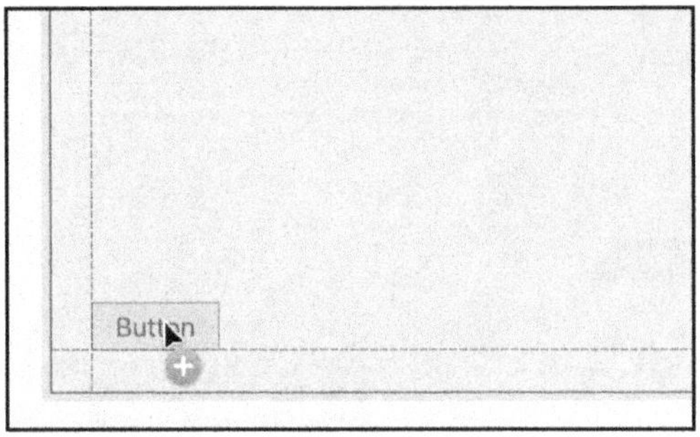

Aligning a button.

Repeat the process, dragging another **Push Button** to the bottom right corner.

Select the left button and open the Attributes inspector. Set the Title to **Cancel**. Press **Tab** or **Return** to finish editing and Xcode sets the Key Equivalent to **Escape**:

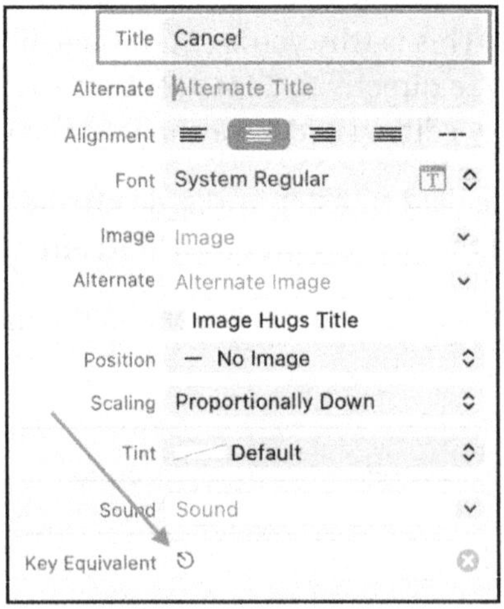

Cancel button attributes

Select the other button and set its Title to **Save Changes**. This time you'll have to set the Key Equivalent yourself, so click in the Key Equivalent box and press **Return**. This applies the default button appearance.

The new title makes the button wider, so drag it back to the alignment guides.

Select both buttons, click **Resolve Auto Layout Issues** and choose **Reset to Suggested Constraints**:

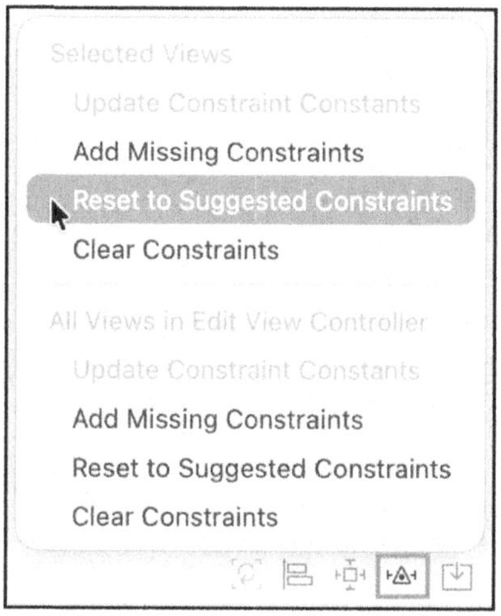

Reset to suggested constraints

This pins them both to the bottom and sides, but doesn't fill in a constraint for the gap in the middle.

Select the Cancel button, **Control-drag** to the Save Changes button and choose **Horizontal Spacing**:

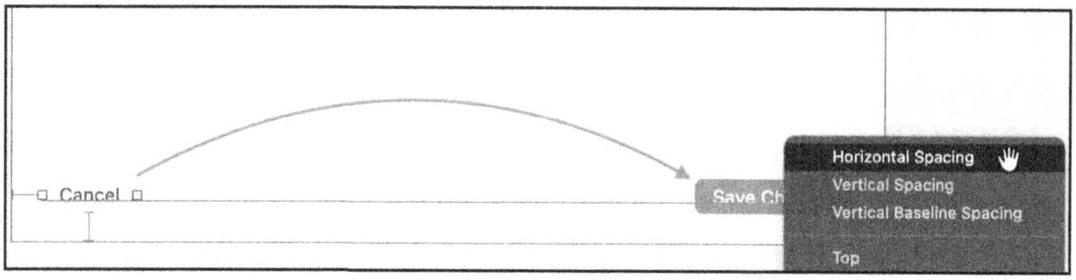

Adding horizontal spacing

This sets a fixed spacing between them, but you want a more flexible setup.

With the Cancel button still selected, swap to the Size inspector. Click the **Edit** button in the **Trailing Space to: Save Changes** constraint and change the **Constant** popup to greater than or equal to:

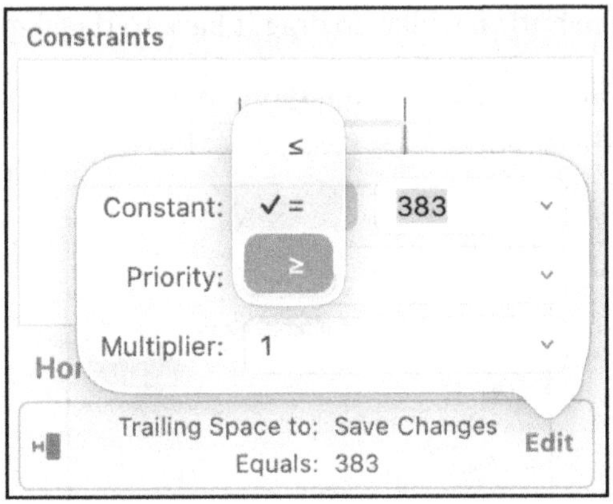

Changing the constraint constant.

That's all for the buttons. Now, it's time to set up the table.

Placing the Table View

Find **Table View** in the Library and drag it so it aligns with the left alignment guide and clicks into the standard spacing above the Cancel button:

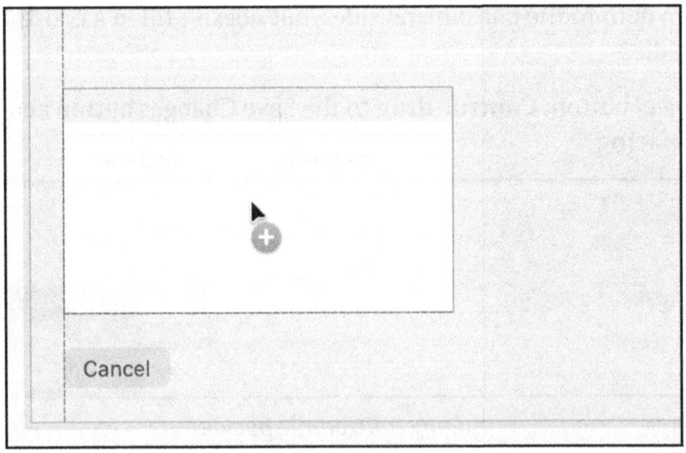

Adding a table view.

Drag the right side of the table until it reaches the alignment guide on the right. To fix the table in place, click **Add New Constraints**. Set the top spacing to **150** and click the lines going left, right and down to turn them red and set them to **Standard**.

Check **Width** and leave it at **560**. Check **Height** and change it to **190**. Then click **Add 6 Constraints**:

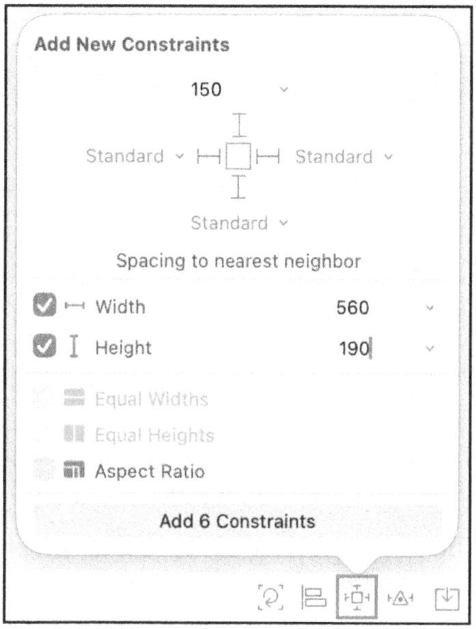

Setting table constraints.

This sets a fixed height for the table, but you want this to be its minimum height, so in the Size inspector, find the Height constraint and use the **Edit** button to change it to greater than or equal to 190:

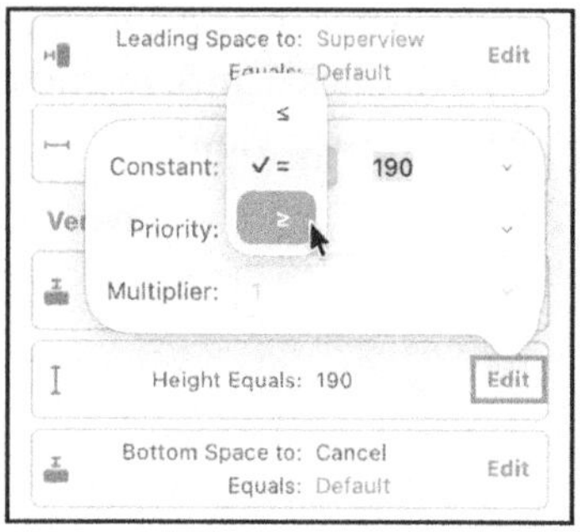

Editing table height.

Do the same for the Width constraint, setting it to greater than or equal to 560.

This fixes the table but leaves it independent of any elements you add later. Setting the minimum height and width fixes the entire view so it can never be smaller than the minimum size. This gets round Xcode's nasty tendency to adjust view sizes when you close and re-open a project.

To finish the table, give it a label. Drag a Label from the Library into the view. Use the Attributes inspector to set its Title to **Principals:** and its Font to **Text style - Headline**:

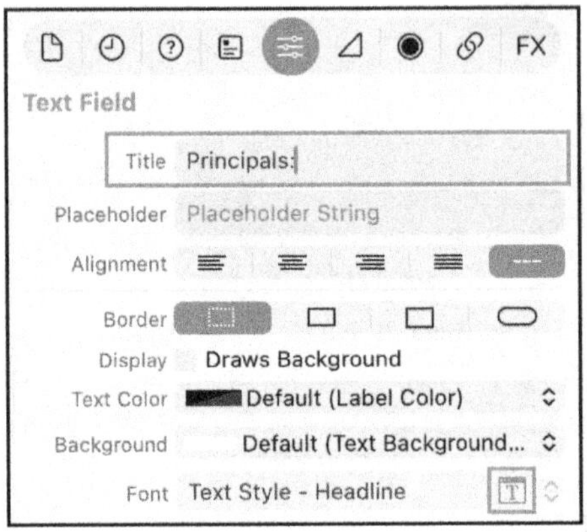

Principals label

Drag the label to above the top left corner of the table, using the alignment guides to position it. Click **Resolve Auto Layout Issues** and **Reset to Suggested Constraints** to lock it into place.

This gives two layout warnings. Click the yellow arrow button beside Edit View Controller Scene to see them. One of the warnings mentions width — click the yellow triangle beside it and choose **Set Constraint to >= Current Width**. This allows the label to expand if a different language requires more space. Next, click the remaining yellow triangle and select **Use Fixed Leading and Resizing Trailing Constraints** because this is to the left of the view. Click **Confirm** and the last warning disappears. Click **< Structure** to get back to the outline view.

All that remains is to build the top section.

Setting up the Text Edit Fields

Checking the screenshot at the start of this chapter, the top section is the most complicated.

Start by adding the edit fields. Open the Library and search for **text**. Drag a **Text Field** into the view.

Move it to align the top right corner with the guides near the top right of the view, then drag the left side out until the width is **490**:

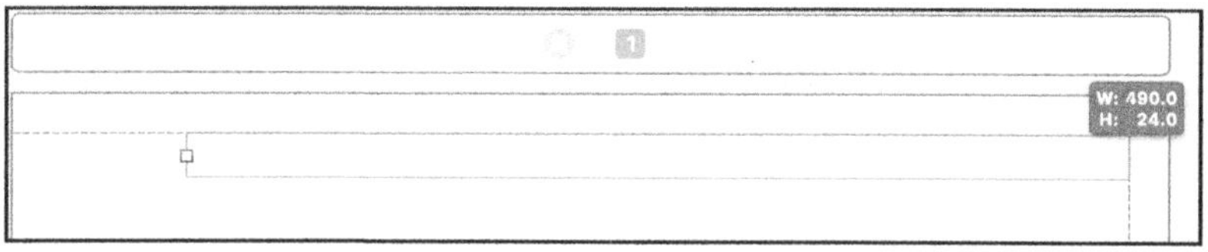

Positioning the top edit field.

Option-drag the field down to create a copy. Make sure it aligns left and right and is the standard distance below the original. Repeat this so you have three edit fields down the display.

Click the middle text field, grab the handle at the right side and drag it left until the width is **100**. Duplicate (**Option-drag**) this shorter field and move it towards the middle until it gets a central alignment guide from the longer text fields, not from the table or window. Then, duplicate again and align this one to the guide at the right:

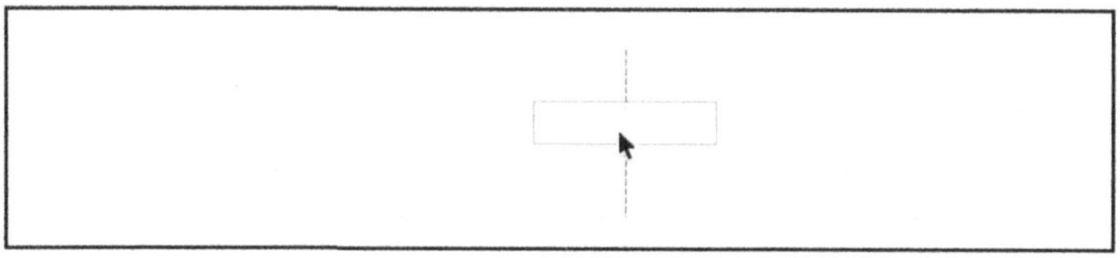

Aligning the text fields.

Drag to select all five of these fields before clicking **Resolve Auto Layout Issues** and **Reset to Suggested Constraints** for the selected views.

Time to see if this has worked. Run the app, **right-click** any row in the table and select **Edit Movie...**. Resize the Edit window to see what works:

Testing the Auto Layout.

Nearly everything is good. Hurray for **Reset to Suggested Constraints**. The only thing not right is the central edit field. It correctly stays centered, but its width grows. The middle row of fields is for run time, year and rating, so they don't need to expand.

Back in **Main.storyboard**, things are about to get a bit messy.

Select the middle text field and open the Size inspector using **Command-Option-6**. The vertical constraints are fine, but the horizontal ones aren't giving the desired result. The one that aligns the center X is great. The problem is the fixed spacing to one or both of the text fields on either side — the text field has to expand to maintain these. Delete the **Trailing Space to: Text Field** and **Leading Space to: Text Field** constraints by selecting each one and pressing the **Delete** key.

Without these constraints, the text field no longer has enough information to position and resize itself. Fix this by setting a specific width. Click **Add New Constraints**.

Check **Width**, make sure its value is **100** and click **Add 1 Constraint**:

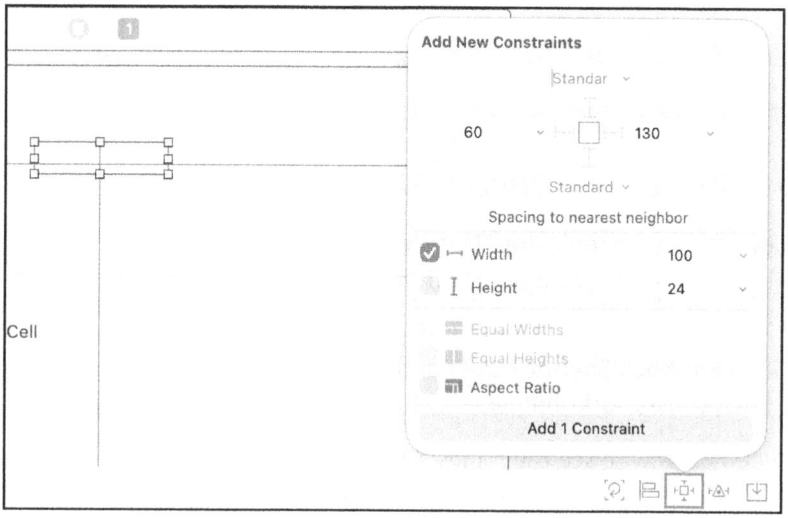

Constraining the width.

That fixes the middle field, but now the one on the right needs some help. Select it and use **Add New Constraints** to set its **Width** to **100**.

That gets rid of all the errors and warnings, so now you can label these fields.

Labeling the Edit Fields

The Principals label is set up the way you want, so select it and use **Command-D** or **Option-Drag**, whichever you prefer, to duplicate it. Drag the copy up to beside the top edit field. These field labels align to the left of their matching edit fields, so use the Attributes inspector to set the alignment to **Right**.

Duplicate this field four more times, positioning each copy beside an edit field, aligning the text baselines and spacing the standard distance apart. The baseline shows two alignment guides in the bottom half of the fields:

> **Note:** If you're having trouble positioning the labels beside the text fields, you can add a trailing constraint with standard spacing for each label so you don't need to adjust the spacing between the labels and the text fields manually.

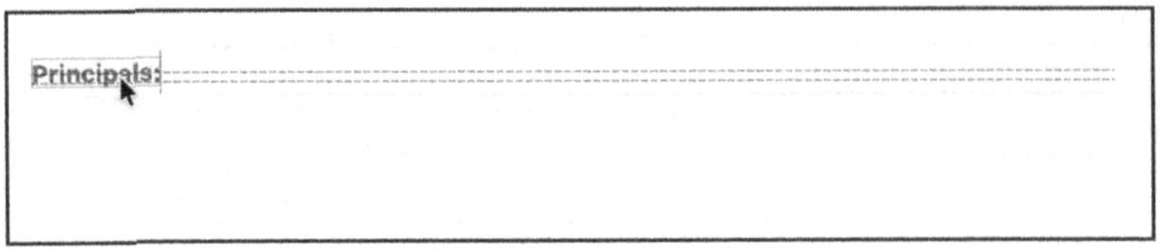

Aligning baselines.

Set the titles of these labels to **Title:**, **Run time:**, **Year:**, **Rating:**, and **Genres:**.

Now, you need to set up their Auto Layout constraints. Select all the labels. You can't drag to select without including the edit fields, so select one and **Command-click** the other four.

Time for **Resolve Auto Layout Issues** and **Reset to Suggested Constraints** for the selected views, which works but leaves you with the yellow warning again.

Click the yellow arrow to see the issues. Click the yellow triangle for each of them, and this time choose **Use Resizing Leading and Fixed Trailing Constraints** for each one. Even though some are on the left, you want them to stick to their edit fields.

That gets rid of all the warnings, so click **< Structure** to get back to the outline view, and then run the app. Edit a movie and test resizing the window:

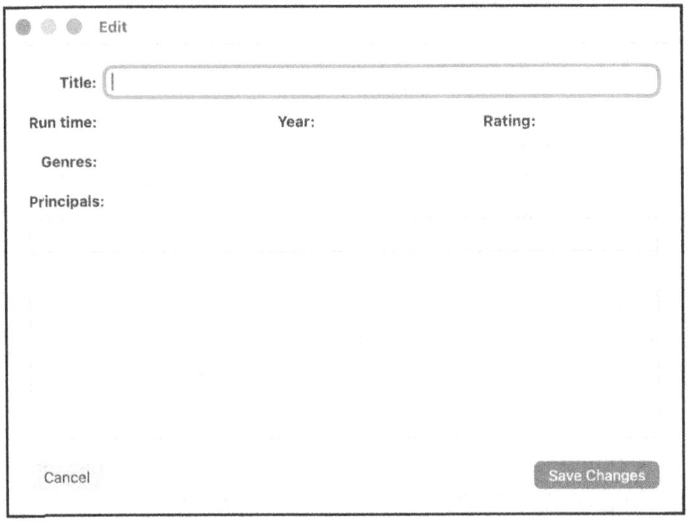

Complete layout

You did it! You worked through all those Auto Layout settings and ended with a great looking Edit window that resizes as expected. That's never easy. Auto Layout is something you have to work at, but it gives a responsive and flexible result in the end.

> **Note**: It's easy to get confused in Auto Layout. If things aren't working, or you get more warnings than expected, click **Resolve Auto Layout Issues** and **Clear Constraints** for the entire view controller, then work through them again. You can also check the final project for this chapter and read the constraints set there.

Now, it's time to start bringing the edit window alive.

Coding the Buttons

With **Main.storyboard** still open, **Shift-Option-click EditViewController.swift** in the Project navigator to open it in a secondary editor.

Add some blank lines before the last closing curly brace, then **Control-drag** from the **Cancel** button into this space. Connect an action called **cancelEdits**.

Do the same for the **Save Changes** button, creating an action called **saveEdits**.

Add this code to `cancelEdits(_:)`:

```
view.window?.close()
```

The view controller has a view, and that view can try to access its containing window. If that works, call the window's `close()` method. And that's all the **Cancel** button needs.

The **Save Changes** button has more work to do, so add this code to `saveEdits(_:)`:

```
// 1
view.window?.makeFirstResponder(nil)

// 2
// tell parent view controller to save

// 3
view.window?.close()
```

Going through these lines:

1. When you type in a text edit field, the changes aren't processed until you click out of the field or press Tab or Return. You've seen this when editing in the inspectors. This line sets the first responder to `nil`, which causes any active control to resign its focus. If this is a text field, it triggers the edit processing so the data in the active edit field becomes part of the saved data.
2. The save process is going to happen in `ViewController`, which already has methods to save the data and update the display.
3. Then, use the same technique for closing the window.

Run the app now and edit a movie. There's nothing new to see, but either of the buttons closes the Edit window. The Escape and Return keys do the same.

Now, it's time to finish the **Save Changes** code.

Saving the Edits

In order for `EditViewController` to call a method in `ViewController`, it needs access to that view controller.

Close the secondary editor pane, open **EditViewController.swift** and add this property:

```
weak var parentVC: ViewController?
```

This gives `EditViewController` an optional reference to the main `ViewController`. It's a `weak` reference to avoid the connection hanging around in memory.

You supply this property to `EditViewController` in `ViewController`'s `prepare(for:sender:)` method.

Open **ViewController.swift** and find that method. Below where you set `editViewController.originalMovieData` add:

```
editViewController.parentVC = self
```

In this case, `self` is `ViewController`.

Next, add the `ViewController` method to do the actual save:

```
// 1
func saveEdits(for movie: Movie) {
  // 2
  let index = movies.firstIndex {
    $0.id == movie.id
  }

  if let index {
    // 3
    movies[index] = movie
  } else {
    // 4
    movies.append(movie)
  }

  // 5
  searchMovies()
  if selectedMovie?.id == movie.id {
    showSelectedMovie(movie)
  }

  // 6
  dataStore.saveData(movies: movies)
}
```

This method has a bit going on:

1. Call the method with a `Movie` to save. The argument has an external label of `for` and an internal label of `movie` to make calling and using both read logically.
2. Search the `movies` array for the index of a movie with the matching `id`.
3. If the search found an existing movie, replace it in the database.
4. If this is an unknown movie, append it to the array. The app doesn't have the ability to add movies, but maybe you'll decide to add that later. This line future-proofs this method.
5. Update the display using `searchMovies()` and update the selected movie display, if appropriate.
6. Save the edited `movies` array.

Now `EditViewController` has a way to access `ViewController` and `ViewController` has a method for saving an edited movie.

Open **EditViewController.swift** and in `saveEdits(_:)`, replace `// tell parent view controller to save` with:

```
if
  let parentVC,
  let movie {
  parentVC.saveEdits(for: movie)
}
```

Both `parentVC` and `movie` are optionals, so only call `saveEdits(for:)` if they both have values.

You have both the buttons completely set up and coded. In the next chapter, you'll show the data and allow users to edit it.

Making Editing Easier

Before getting into the actual editing, there's a feature you can add to the main table to make editing faster and easier. How about letting the user double-click a line to open the Edit window?

Open **Main.storyboard**, scroll to the main window, and use the **Shift-right-click** menu to select **Movies Table View**.

Open the Connections inspector (**Command-Option-7**) and drag from **Sent Actions → doubleAction** to the View Controller box in the bar above the window:

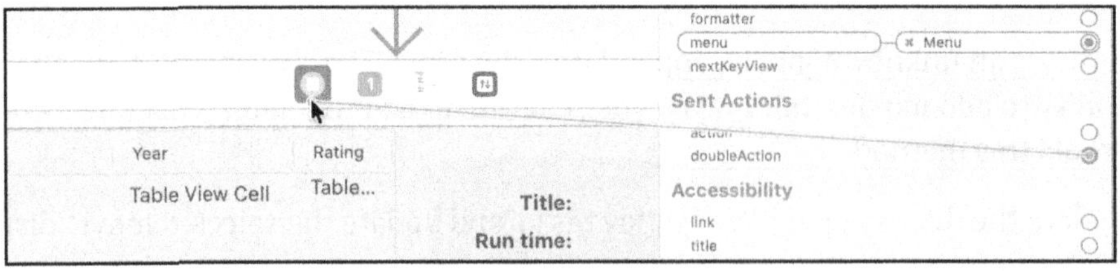

Connecting the doubleAction.

Release the mouse and choose **editMovie:** from the list. This is the `@IBAction` you created for the contextual menu, but there's no reason why the `doubleAction` can't use it too.

Now, run the app and double-click any movie:

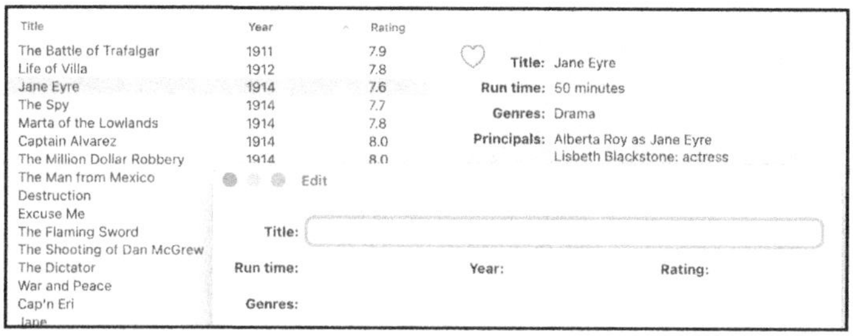

Double-click editing.

The neat thing about this is that it selects and edits, all with a single user action.

Now you have a great UI set up, ready to display editable data.

Key Points

- To show a secondary window, add a Window Controller and a View Controller to the storyboard.
- Use a segue to transition to the new window.
- Attach data to the segue to send it to the secondary window.

Where to Go From Here?

The next step is to show the data in the fields and table. You'll also want to configure the fields for editing and set up the table for sorting and editing. That's all in the next chapter.

Chapter 16: Using Cocoa Bindings

By Sarah Reichelt

In the last chapter, you designed the movie edit window. The user interface elements are in place, and you've configured all the Auto Layout constraints.

Now, you have to display the data and allow the users to edit it. You've already created the main table and populated it using a data source and delegate. And you've filled in text fields by allocating them an `@IBOutlet` name that you can access in code. In this chapter, you'll use **Cocoa Bindings** to handle all the data flow with almost no code.

Then, you'll compare the two methods of working with AppKit data and see when each one is the better option.

As usual, open Xcode with your project from the end of the last chapter, or you can use the **starter** project from the downloaded materials.

Binding the Title Field

When showing the movie details in `ViewController`, you set up an `@IBOutlet` for each field and manually inserted the matching properties into each one.

This time, you'll do it a different way; you'll use **Cocoa Bindings**. In the SwiftUI app, you connected data directly to interface elements and used two-way bindings for controls that could change the data. Cocoa Bindings is an older technology, but it has a similar effect. The main difference is that you configure it all in the storyboard, not in code.

Start with the title. Open **Main.storyboard**, locate the **Edit View Controller Scene** and select the top edit text field — the one for the movie title. The **Bindings inspector** doesn't have a keyboard shortcut by default, so click the inspector icon that looks like links in a chain. Expand the **Value** section at the top.

Check **Bind to** and select **Edit View Controller** from the popup.

Enter **self.movie.title** in the **Model Key Path** field:

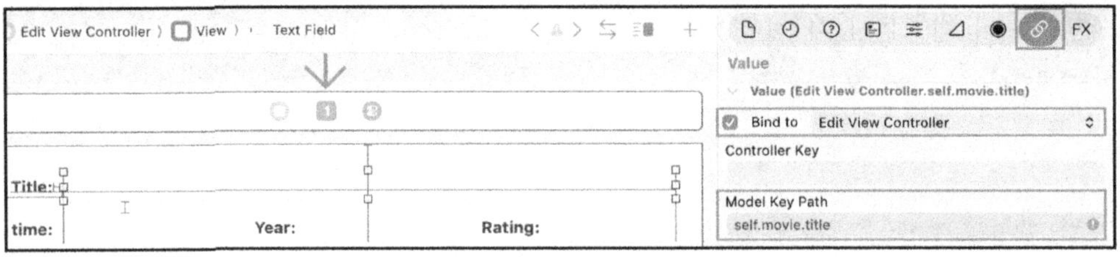

Binding the title field.

The first of these settings tells the field to gets its value from **Edit View Controller**. The second tells it what property to use. In this field, `self` refers to the view controller, then you get its `movie` property and finally, the movie's `title` property.

> **Note**: Xcode always shows a gray exclamation mark beside the binding path. You only need to worry if it shows a red error marker.

You've bound one field, so that's enough for a test. But you need to make one change to the data first.

Open **EditViewController.swift** and replace `var movie: Movie?` with

```
@objc dynamic var movie: Movie?
```

Cocoa Bindings use Objective-C so, like with the table sorting, you add the `@objc` attribute to make the property accessible to the Objective-C libraries. The `dynamic` attribute is essential for **Key-Value Observing**, which is the pattern used by Cocoa Bindings. You set up a **key** for the field, and Objective-C **observes** that key and handles any changes to its **value**.

Now run the app, select a movie, **right-click** and select **Edit Movie...**. The movie title appears in the edit field:

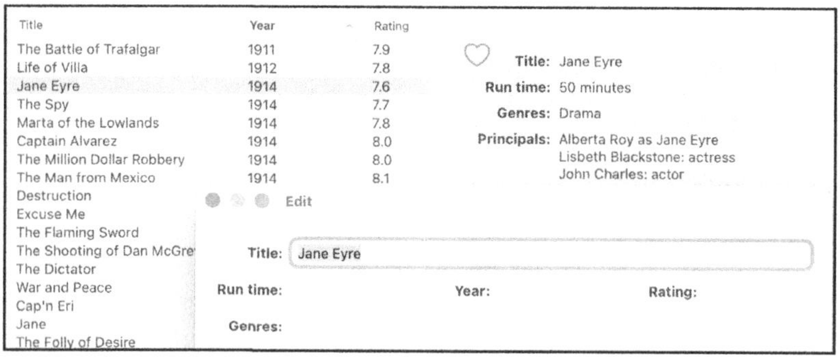

Editing the title.

Now for the cool part. Change the title and click **Save Changes**. The Edit window closes and your new title appears in the table and in the movie details:

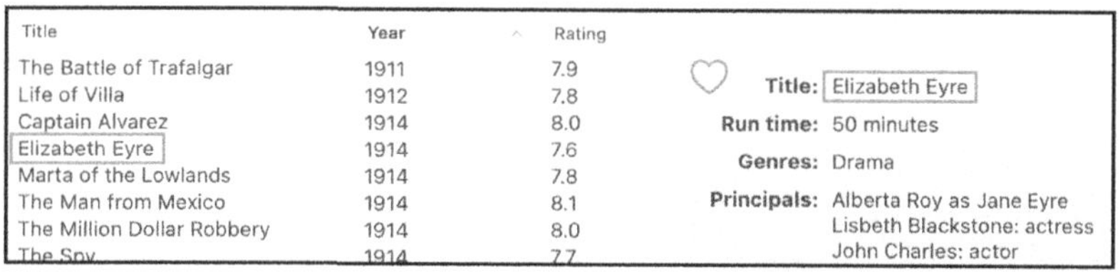

Edited title.

How's that for a no-code solution? And when you quit and restart the app, your edit is still there.

Adding More Bindings

Next, you'll set up bindings for the other text entry fields, so open **Main.storyboard** again.

Select the field beside the **Run time** label and open the Bindings inspector. Expand the **Value** section at the top if it isn't already expanded.

Check **Bind to** and select **Edit View Controller** from the popup.Enter **self.movie.runTime** in the **Model Key Path** field.

Repeat this for the Year, Ratings and Genres fields. For each one, check **Bind to** and select **Edit View Controller**. Make sure you set the properties on the text entry fields, not their matching title labels.

Enter the respective **Model Key Path**:

- Year: **self.movie.year**
- Rating: **self.movie.rating**
- Genres: **self.movie.genres**

These match the properties in the `Movie` class. Cocoa Bindings does the work of converting the properties into strings and back again if needed. Make sure you press **Return** or **Tab** to finish editing the last one, or Xcode won't process it and the app will crash.

Run the app, **double-click** a movie to open the edit window and test all these fields:

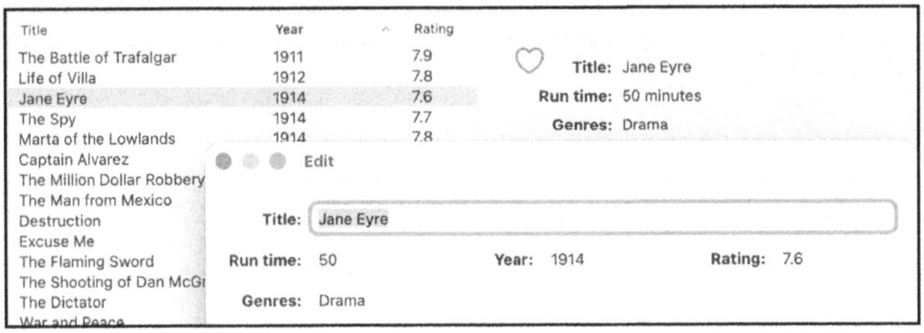

All the edit fields.

Right now, these text fields accept any text input. But in the `Movie` class, `runTime` is an `Int` and `rating` is a `Double`. What happens if you type in the wrong sort of data?

Validating the Entries

Cocoa Bindings does its best to transform the data you enter into the correct type for the model class, but if you set a `runTime` of **3 hours**, it converts it to 3, which displays as 3 minutes. Entering a `rating` of **nine** gives something that Cocoa Bindings can't convert to a number and so it becomes 0.

Neither of these options is ideal, so you'll add a `NumberFormatter` to both the numeric fields to validate the entries.

Open **Main.storyboard** and arrange the views so you can see the **Run time** and **Rating** entry fields. Open the **Library** and search for `number`. Drag a **Number Formatter** into each of these fields.

The two formatters appear in the outline view, attached to each field. Select the first one, and the **Run time** field highlights in the storyboard. Open the Attributes inspector and change **Style** to **Decimal**:

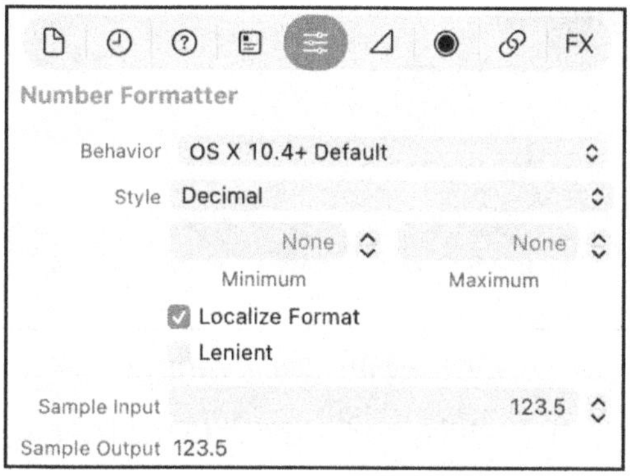

Decimal number formatter

Now, select the **Rating** formatter in the outline view. Make sure it highlights the correct entry field:

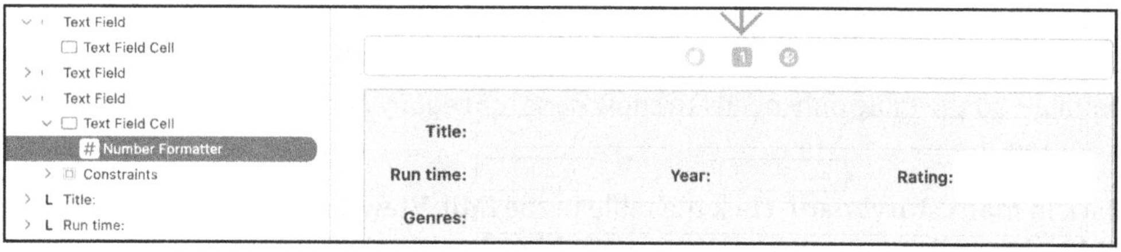

Selecting the Ratings formatter.

Over in the Attributes inspector, set **Style** to **Decimal** again. But this time, you'll set limits. The rating must be between 1 and 10, so set the **Minimum** to **1** and the **Maximum** to **10**.

Time to test this. Run the app, edit a movie and try typing invalid data into the **Run time** and **Rating** fields, pressing **Tab** to trigger the formatter:

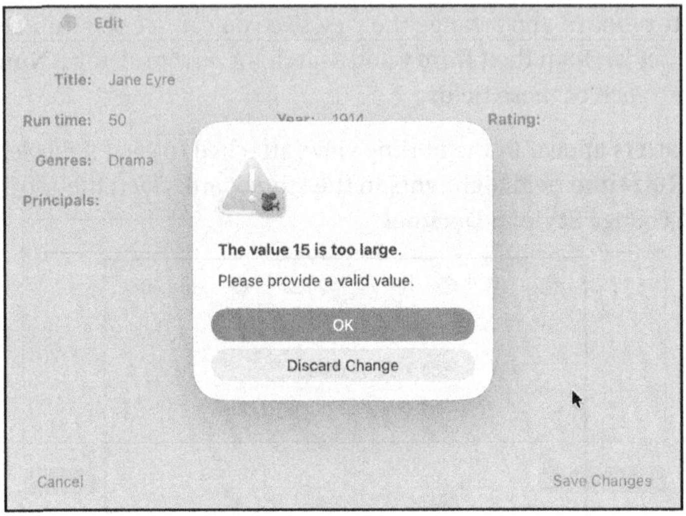

Entering an invalid rating.

That finishes the editing and validation for the data fields. Now, it's time to populate the principals table.

Configuring the Table Columns

Open **Data & Models** → **Principal.swift** to check the properties. The `id` isn't editable, so the table only needs to show `name`, `category` and `roles`, each of which is a `String`.

Back in **Main.storyboard**, click the table in the **Edit View Controller**, and use the **Shift-right-click** menu to drill down to **Table View**.

Use **Command-Option-5** to open the Attributes inspector and change the number of columns to **3**. The outline view shows the three columns, two with automatic identifiers and the new one:

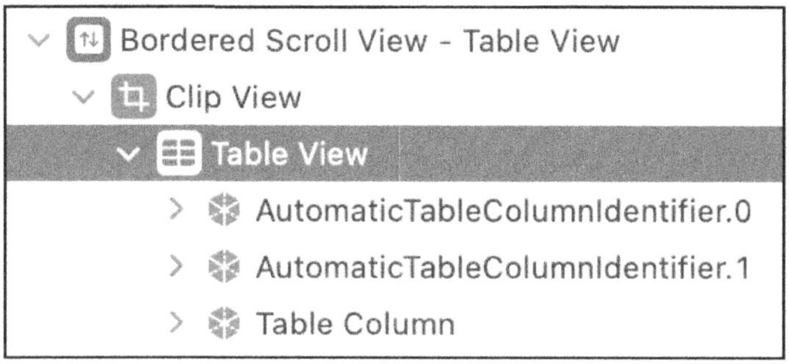

Table columns in outline

Select the first column in the outline view and use the Attributes inspector to set its **Title** to **Name**. Switch to the Size inspector and set its **Width** to **200**.

Use the same technique to set the second column's **Title** to **Category** and its **Width** to **150**.

Finally set the third column to **Roles**. This needs a width that completely fills the table at the table's current default width. Use the stepper arrows beside the width number to step up and down until you see it lined up exactly with the edge of the table. It'll end up at **162**.

Finally, go back to **Table View** and, in the Attributes inspector, check **Alternating Rows** to improve the look of the entire table.

Assigning Sort Descriptors

In the main table, you created sort descriptors manually and assigned them to each column. In the Edit window, you're setting everything up in the storyboard.

Select the **Name** column in the outline and return to the Attributes inspector. Set the **Sort Key** to **name** and press **Return**. This fills in the default sort selector or method — `compare:` — but you want a case-insensitive sort. Replace `compare:` with **localizedCaseInsensitiveCompare:**, which is the sort method you applied to the movie titles in the main table.

Now, this column sorts on the `name` property using a case-insensitive sort method:

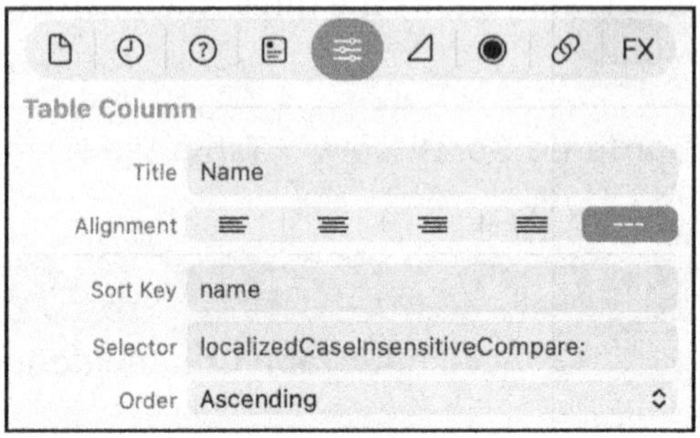

Name column sort

Repeat this for the other two columns, setting the **Sort Key** to **category** and **roles** respectively. They can both use the default `compare:` selector.

Linking the Data

In the text input fields, you bound them to properties of the view controller's `movie`. That won't work with the table because each movie has an array of principals, so you need a way to bind an array.

The tool for this is an `NSArrayController`, which gives you a controller that manages the binding for a collection of objects.

Still in **Main.storyboard**, open the **Library** and find **Array Controller**. Drag it into the bar above the **Edit View Controller**:

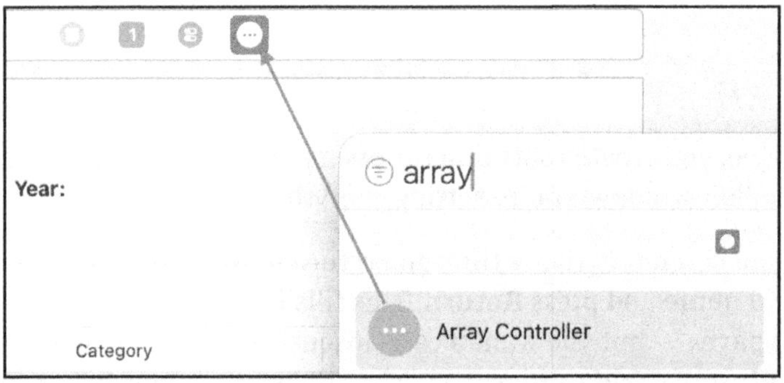

Adding an array controller.

Now you can bind this array controller to the principals data.

Make sure you have the array controller selected in the top bar, then open the Bindings inspector. Expand **Controller Content → Content Array**, check **Bind to** and select **Edit View Controller**.

Set **Model Key Path** to **self.movie.principals**. This is the same pattern you used for the text input fields, but you're binding the property to an array controller instead of a field.

With the array controller set up, you can link it to the table. Select the **Table View** and make sure you're still in the Bindings inspector.

Expand **Table Content → Content**. Check **Bind to** and select **Array Controller** if Xcode doesn't have it as the default. The **Controller Key** is preset to `arrangedObjects`, which refers to the sorted objects in the array controller's binding, and this is correct.

You haven't finished yet, but run the app and **double-click** to edit a movie:

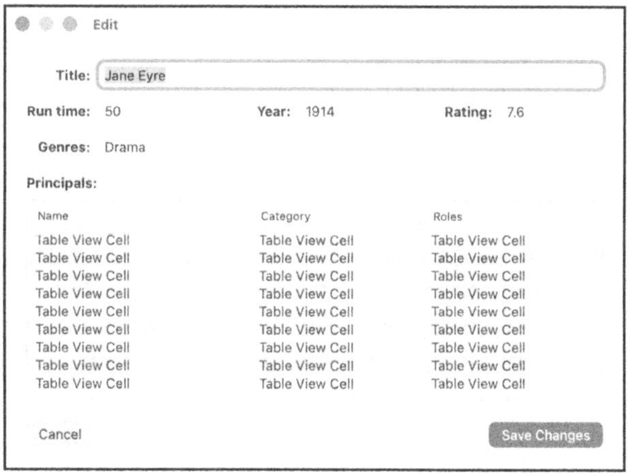

Table showing placeholder data.

The table fills in the correct number of rows for the principals. Next, you'll tell the table cells what to show for each row.

Listing the Names

Setting up the cells involves diving deeper into the structure of each table column.

Option-click the disclosure arrow beside the **Name** column in the outline view to expand it fully. (If it was already partially expanded, collapse it and then Option-click.) Ignoring the Constraints for now, you have this structure:

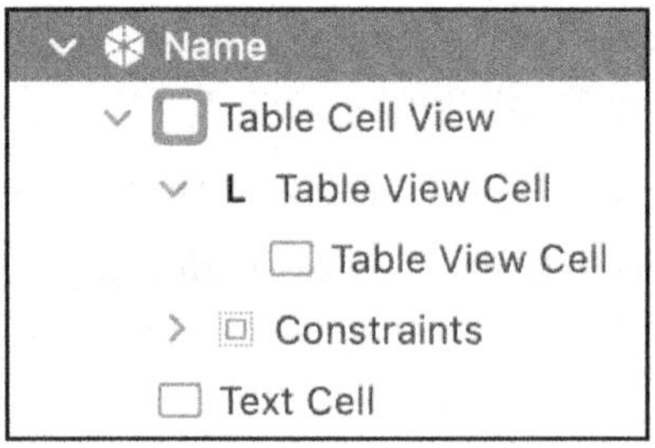

Name column structure

Press **Command-Option-4** to open the Identity inspector so you can see the class of each element as you step through them.

Name is an `NSTableColumn`.

It contains **Table Cell View** — an `NSTableCellView` — and **Text Cell** — an `NSTextFieldCell`.

Table Cell View contains a **Table View Cell** — notice how the words have swapped around — but this one has an **L** icon and is an `NSTextField`. It holds another **Table View Cell** and this one is another `NSTextFieldCell`. So many parts with very confusing names.

The important one is the outermost **Table View Cell** with the **L** icon. Select it and use the Identity inspector to confirm you've selected an `NSTextField`.

Switch to the Binding inspector and expand the **Value** section if necessary.

Check **Bind to**. The default selection is **Table Cell View** and that's correct. In **Model Key Path**, enter **objectValue.name**:

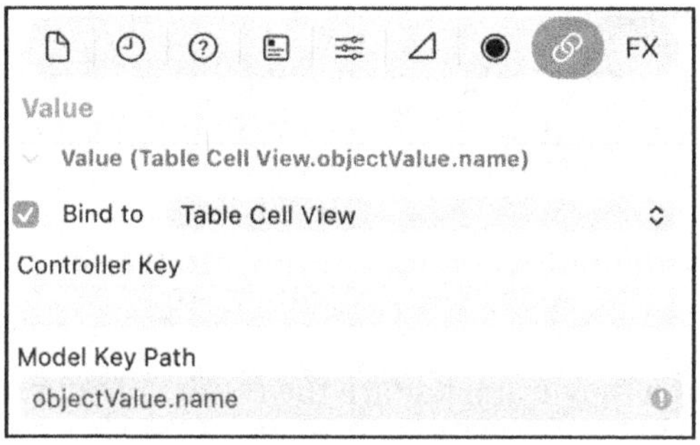

Binding the name cell value.

You've already bound the entire table to the Array Controller and this provides an `objectValue` property for each row and cell. You're telling this cell to take its value from the `name` of this object.

Run the app and edit a movie:

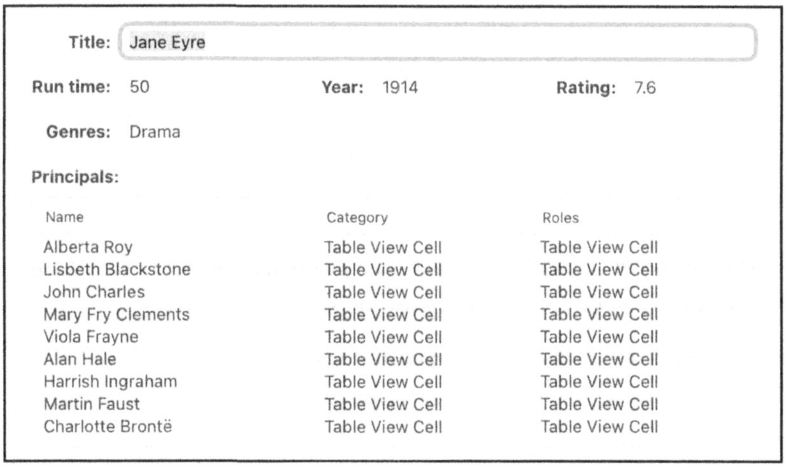

Name column data

And there are the names for the principals in the Name column.

Next, apply the same logic to the remaining columns. Back in **Main.storyboard**, click the disclosure arrow beside **Name** to collapse it and **Option-click** the disclosure arrow for **Category**.

Find the first **Table View Cell** — the one with the **L** icon — and select it. In the Bindings inspector, check **Bind to** and choose **Table Cell View**. Set **Model Key Path** to **objectValue.category**.

Repeat this process for the **Roles** column, setting **Model Key Path** to **objectValue.roles**.

Run the app again, edit a movie and admire the results of your work:

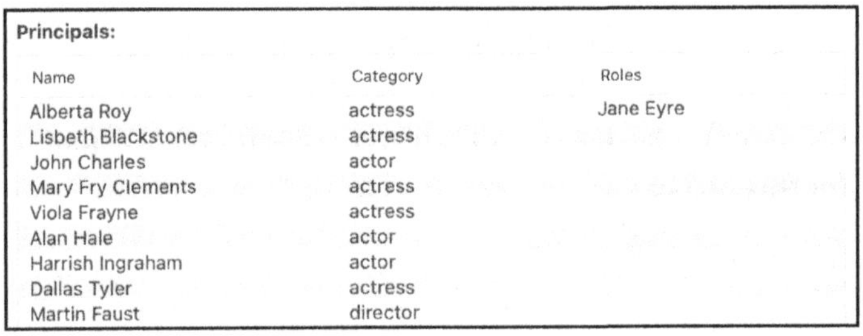

Principals:

Name	Category	Roles
Alberta Roy	actress	Jane Eyre
Lisbeth Blackstone	actress	
John Charles	actor	
Mary Fry Clements	actress	
Viola Frayne	actress	
Alan Hale	actor	
Harrish Ingraham	actor	
Dallas Tyler	actress	
Martin Faust	director	

Principals table

Auto Layout Again

Before going any further, it's time to fix the yellow layout warning in the outline view. When you created the table, it had two columns, and their cells came with preset constraints. The cell in the third column has no constraints.

In **Main.storyboard**, expand the **Name** column in the outline and select the **Table View Cell** — the one with the **L** icon. Open the Size inspector and check the constraints:

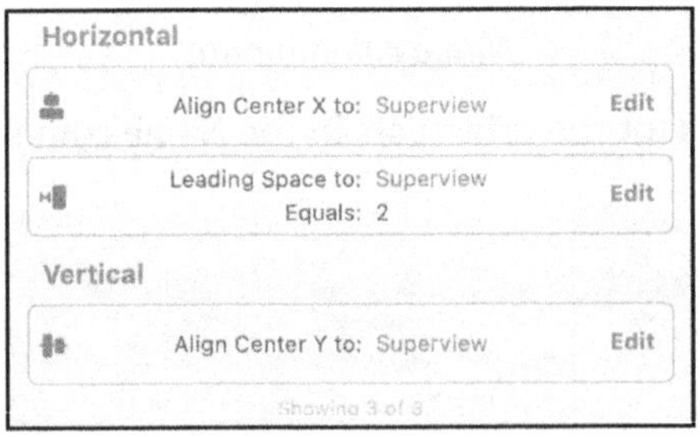

Name cell constraints

These align Center X And Center Y to the superview and give a leading spacing of 2.

Select the matching **Table View Cell** in the **Roles** column and click **Align** in the bottom toolbar. It's to the left of Add New Constraints.

Check **Horizontally in Container** and **Vertically in Container** and then click **Add 2 Constraints**:

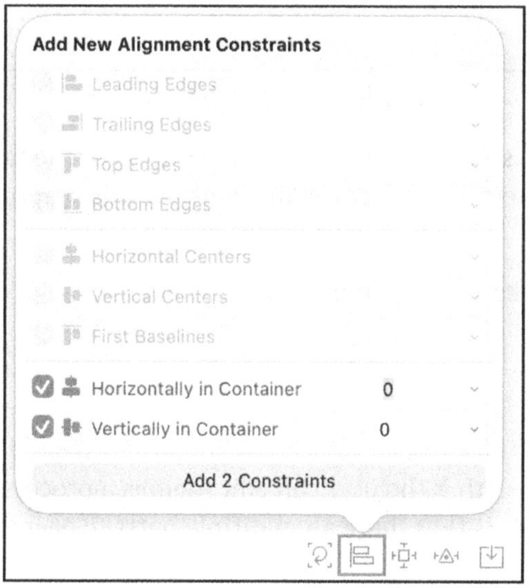

Adding alignment constraints.

This sets two of the three constraints but moves the cell into the center of the column. Click **Add New Constraints** and set the left spacing to **2**. Click **Add 1 Constraint** to apply this and set the cell to be the same as the other two. And this gets rid of the yellow warning. Hurray!

Sorting the Table

You added sort keys and selectors to each column, but they aren't working. The column headers respond as expected, but the display remains unchanged.

It's time for another binding!

Select **Table View** and swap to the Binding inspector. Expand **Table Content →**

Sort Descriptors. Check **Bind to** and make sure it's set to **Array Controller**. This time, set **Controller Key** to **sortDescriptors**. If you start typing it, autocomplete suggests it.

Run the app and edit a movie. Sort the principals table by different columns and sort again to change from ascending sort to descending:

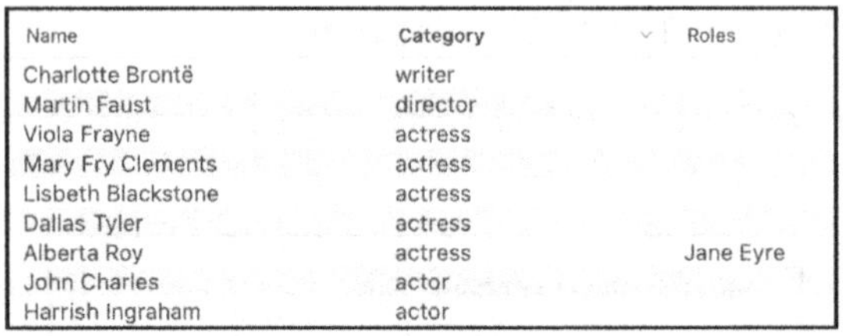

Sorting the principals table.

You already set up the sort descriptors for each column of the table. This configuration binds them to the array controller's sort descriptors, so now it all just works!

The next step is to make the table editable.

Editing the Table

Setting the table cells so that the user can edit them is a process that can be quite confusing. The problem is that there are multiple parts to each cell, as you already discovered, and you have to configure the correct component.

In **Main.storyboard**, **Shift-right-click** in the first cell of the first column of the principals table and select the first **Table View Cell**. That's the one with the **Label** icon because right now, it's a **Label**:

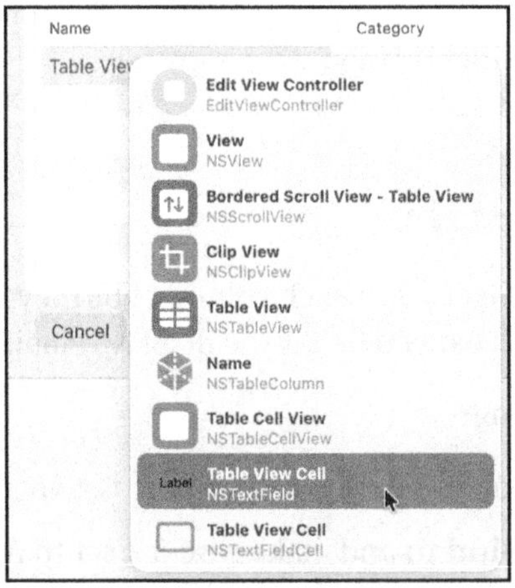

Select Table View Cell

Open the Attributes inspector and change **Behavior** to **Editable**:

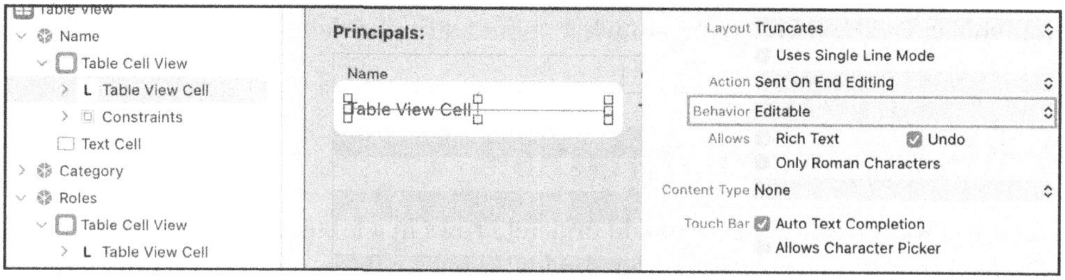

Changing Behavior to Editable.

Next, select the first **Table View Cell** in the **Category** column and set its **Behavior** to **Editable**.

Repeat this process for the **Roles** column.

It won't happen immediately, but eventually Xcode works out that these are now edit fields, instead of labels, and changes their icons in the outline view:

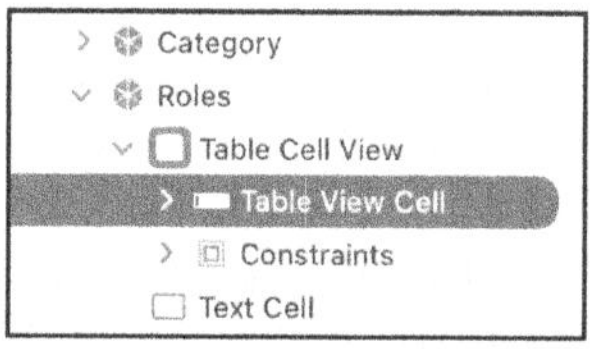

Editable cell icon

Time to test this. Run the app and **double-click** to edit a movie. Select a row in the table and then click the text, or click anywhere in an empty cell. This lets you change the data in that cell:

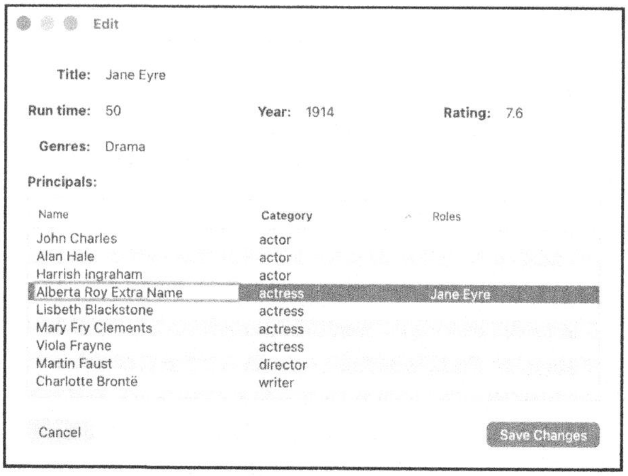

Editing a principal's name.

Click **Save Changes**, and the new data appears in the main window.

Now you can edit existing data, but what about adding or deleting rows?

Adding More Controls

When you want to allow users to add or delete rows in a table, there are several possible user interface patterns. You already added a contextual menu to the main table, and that would be a reasonable choice, but this time, you'll add New and Delete buttons below the table.

Use the **Library** to drag two **Push Buttons** into the view, between the Cancel and Save Changes buttons. Use the Attributes inspector to set their Titles to **New** and **Delete**.

These new buttons need Auto Layout constraints. Since they're functionally linked, you'll keep them together on either side of the center.

Select the **New** button and click **Align**. You used Align earlier to center the cell in the third column, but this time, you'll add an alignment with an offset value.

Check **Horizontally in Container** and set the value to **-40** instead of the default 0. A negative value pushes the constrained object to the left:

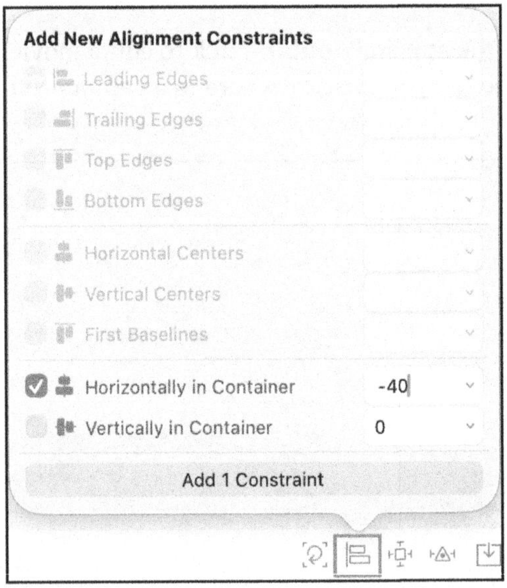

Offset alignment

You're familiar now with the standard **Add New Constraints** popup. Use it to set the bottom spacing below the button to **Standard**.

Repeat this for the **Delete** button, but this time, use an alignment offset of **40**. A positive offset pushes to the right.

Now that the new buttons are properly positioned, it's time to make them work.

Implementing the Delete Button

Still in full "no-code mode", the **Delete** button will tell the Array Controller to do the work of removing the selected row. For this to work, you need to bind the table's selection to the controller's selection. That way the Array Controller knows which row to delete.

Click in the table area and use **Shift-right-click** to select the **Table View**. Open the Bindings inspector and expand **Table Content → Selection Indexes**.

Check **Bind to** and confirm it's set to **Array Controller**. In the **Controller Key** field, start typing **select** and choose **selectionIndexes**:

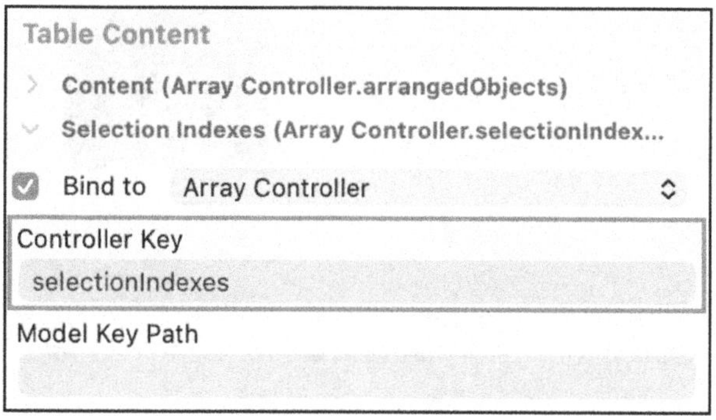

Binding the table selection.

Since the table only allows a single selection at a time, you might think to choose `selectionIndex`, but don't do it. Your app will crash unless you set this to `selectionIndexes`.

You only want to enable the Delete button if there's a selected row to delete. This requires another binding to another array controller property.

Select the **Delete** button and, in the Bindings inspector, expand **Availability → Enabled**.

Check **Bind to** — it's set to **Array Controller** by default. Enter **canRemove** in the **Controller Key** field. This is a Boolean property on Array Controller that's `true` whenever it's possible to remove a row. Connecting this to the enabled state of the button is perfect.

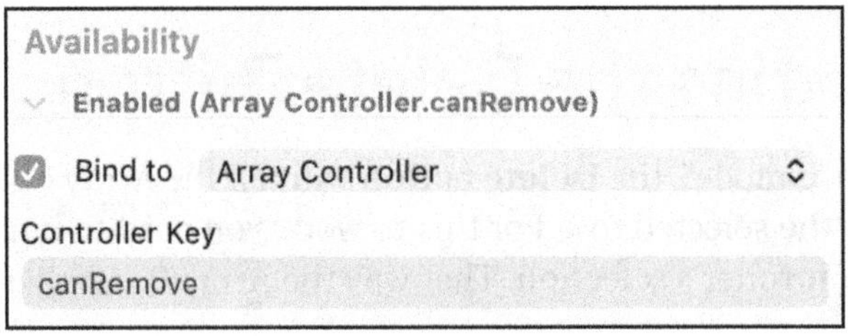

Enabling the Delete button.

There's one more step to complete the implementation. **Control-drag** from the **Delete** button up to **Array Controller** in the top bar. Select `remove:` from the menu that appears when you release the mouse button:

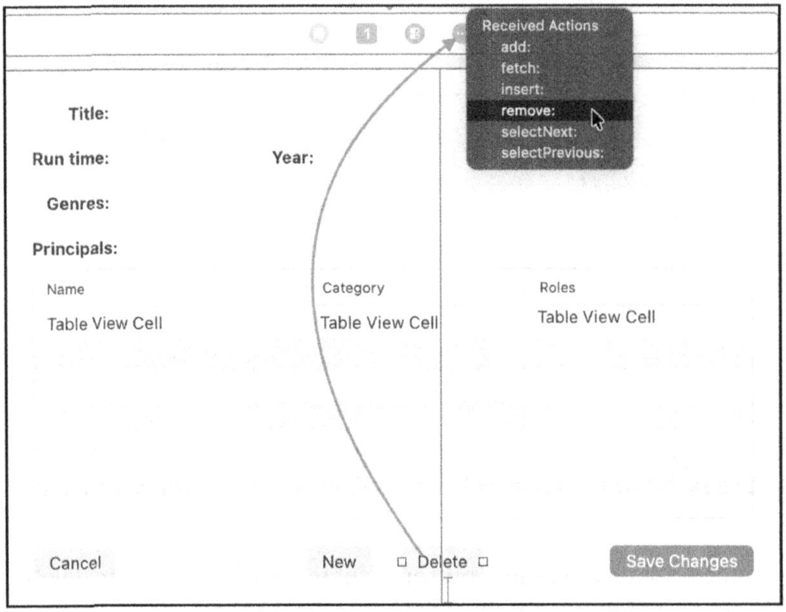

Connecting the remove action.

And that's it. Time for a trial run. Run the app, edit a movie, select a principal and click the **Delete** button:

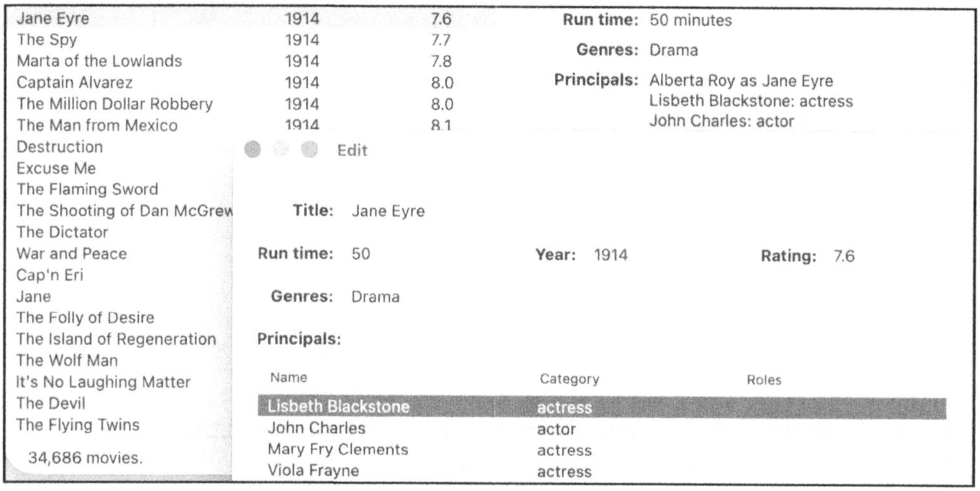

Deleting a principal

> **Note**: For this screenshot, I edited Jane Eyre (1914) and deleted Alberta Roy, so her name still appears in the main window, but not in the principals table. Once I click **Save Changes**, she disappears from the main window too.

Command-click the selected row to deselect everything and disable the Delete button.

You may be wondering why there's no dialog here to confirm a destructive operation. It isn't necessary because the user can always click Cancel to exit without saving any changes. But if you considered a confirmation dialog, that's a good instinct.

Now, it's time to complete your app by implementing the New button.

Inserting a New Principal

Again, Array Controller does the work here, but it needs some help. Before it can add a new object, it has to know what type of object to add.

Still in **Main.storyboard**, select **Edit View Controller Scene → Array Controller** in the outline view and open the Attributes inspector.

In the **Object Controller** section, **Mode** is already set to **Class**, which is correct. In the **Class** menu, choose **Principal**:

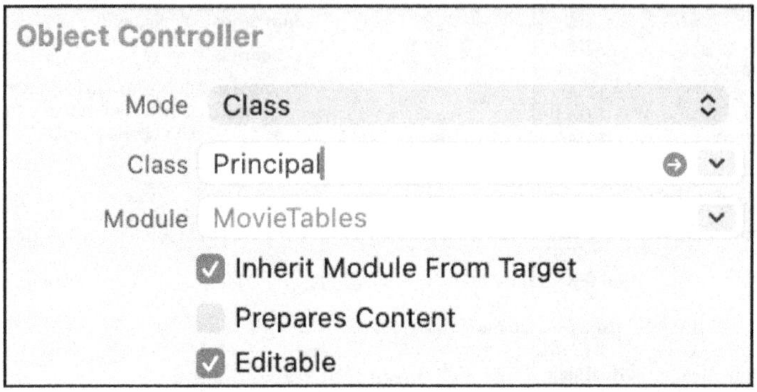

Setting the array controller's class.

Xcode sorts the list alphabetically, which puts Principal way down the list, but with the menu open, start typing **prin** to scroll directly to it.

This makes sure that Array Controller adds a new `Principal` when adding a new record.

When Array Controller creates a new object, it calls that object's class `init`. Right now, `Principal` doesn't have such a method.

Open **Data & Models → Principal.swift** and add this:

```
//
override init() {
  // 2
  id = UUID().uuidString
  // 3
  name = "New Person"
  category = ""
  roles = ""
}
```

With this method you:

1. Override the standard `init` to provide some default property values.
2. Create a unique `id`. UUID is its own object type, but its `uuidString` property is a `String`, which suits this class.
3. Provide default values for the other properties. You need to have text in at least one of these properties or the new row appears empty.

And finally, you're ready to connect the button.

Jump back to **Main.storyboard**, **Control-drag** from the **New** button to the **Array Controller** and select `insert:`. There are two possible methods you could use: `add` appends the new record to the end of the table but since it doesn't scroll the table to the new record, it can seem like it hasn't worked. `insert` puts the new record before the current selection and then selects it, which provides a better user experience.

Run the app, edit a movie and click **New**:

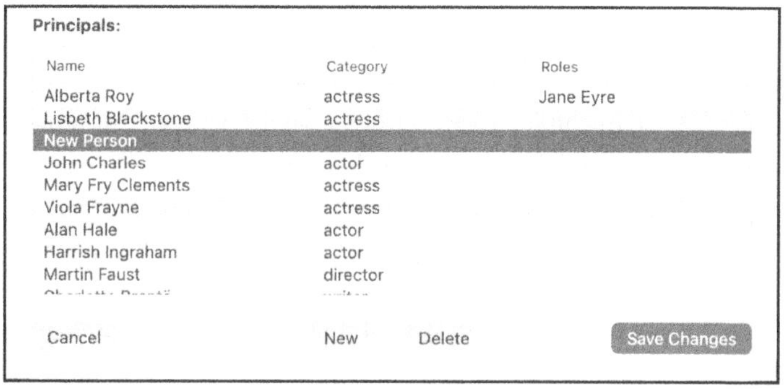

Adding a new principal

There's your new row, showing the default data you provided. You can edit its details and save the changes.

You've done it! The app is complete. You can view the list of movies, mark your favorites, sort and search. You can set different view modes, navigate to the movies web page and delete movies. And now, you can edit every detail about any movie. There's a *lot* packed into this app, and you should feel very proud of yourself for having got through it all.

What Method to Use?

You've now used two different techniques for managing data. But which is the best?

The main window uses a data source and delegate to manage its table data, sorting and selections. When the user selects a table row, you have a series of labels set up as `@IBOutlets` that you populate with the movie data.

In the editing window, you use Cocoa Bindings exclusively. The `EditViewController` has very little code, where `ViewController` and its extension in **TableData.swift** have a lot of methods.

By now, you've probably decided which one you prefer, but which *should* you use?

The answer is **it depends**. :]

Let's consider some arguments in favor of using the **data source - delegate - IBOutlet** method:

Maintainability: When you open a project that's new to you, or maybe one you haven't touched in a year, the data source - delegate - IBOutlet method is more obvious. It's easier to work out what parts of the code provide and manipulate the data.

By contrast, when you open a project that uses Cocoa Bindings, the data seems to appear by magic, and it can take a lot of detective work to track down exactly what's happening.

Source control: Swift files are plain text and, when you use a source control system like `git`, you can track all the edits and revert any changes if you break things.

In a Cocoa Bindings app, all the action is in the storyboard file. Under the hood, this is XML text, but it uses a custom format and while you can track changes in the XML, using that as a way of reverting changes is tricky.

Also Xcode changes the storyboard file periodically, editing time stamps and internal identifiers. This adds confusion and noise to your attempts to track edits.

Now for some advantages to using **Cocoa Bindings**.

Table Editing: When you set up a data source and delegate table for editing, you use a delegate method to detect text field changes. Once you have a change, there's a lot of code involved in working out exactly what cell in what row the user edited. And then you apply that manually to the model object. With Cocoa Bindings, it all just works.

Less Code: You write a lot less code when using bindings and this leads to fewer bugs. If you set up the bindings incorrectly, your app either displays no data or it crashes. This means you detect errors quickly. When you write a lot of lines of code, there's always the possibility of some subtle logic error that may look right, but isn't correct.

My general recommendation is to use the data source - delegate - IBOutlet method, unless you need in-table editing. If you come to a project that's already set up, it may not be your decision, but now you have the tools to work with either technology.

As a side note, you may be wondering how SwiftUI fits into this. It uses bindings but sets them up in code. This is the best of both worlds as it gives you maintainable code but still offers the *magic* of data binding.

Key Points

- Cocoa Bindings are a way to connect interface elements and data, using a storyboard.
- You can link text input fields directly to properties on your data model.
- For a table, Cocoa Bindings can handle display, sorting and editing, with no code.

Where to Go From Here?

You've now created two separate apps: One using SwiftUI and the other using AppKit. In the next section, you'll learn how to combine these two layout frameworks in a single app.

Section IV: Combining SwiftUI & AppKit

Apple has made it simple to include pieces of both user interface frameworks in a single app. In this section, you'll do just that in order to add some finishing touches to both of the apps from the previous sections.

Chapter 17: Using AppKit in SwiftUI

By Sarah Reichelt

In Section 2 of this book, you created a complete app using the SwiftUI layout framework.

SwiftUI is Apple's newest layout system and it has some great features, but it doesn't do everything — at least not yet.

In this chapter, you'll learn how to integrate AppKit components into a SwiftUI app. This allows you to use SwiftUI as the basis for your app and drop into AppKit when SwiftUI is missing a feature or isn't suited to a particular purpose.

Showing a Warning Bar

Open your **Snowman** project from the end of Chapter 10, "Adding Toolbars & Menus", or use the **starter** project from the downloads for this chapter.

Run the app and play a few games to remind yourself what you built:

Starting app with some games played.

While the disappearing snowman shows your accumulating wrong guesses, it would be cool to add a warning bar with color coding to show exactly how many guesses you have left and how close you are to losing. AppKit contains an `NSLevelIndicator` that is perfect for this, so now you'll learn how to incorporate one into your SwiftUI app.

> **Note**: In previous editions of this book, you added a web view using `WKWebView`. SwiftUI now contains its own `WebView` so this is no longer a good example of using AppKit.

Creating a Level Indicator

To show any AppKit view in a SwiftUI app, you first convert it into a SwiftUI view. The `NSViewRepresentable` protocol provides the means for doing this.

Start by making a new file. Select **Views** in the Project navigator to position the new file. Right-click and choose **New Empty File**, then set its name to **WarningBar.swift**.

Set the file contents to:

```
// 1
import SwiftUI
import AppKit

// 2
struct WarningBar: NSViewRepresentable {
  // 3
  let guessesLeft: Int
}
```

Stepping through this:

1. Import the two libraries you need: one for the SwiftUI protocol and one for the AppKit view.
2. Create a structure called `WarningBar` and mark it as conforming to `NSViewRepresentable`. `WarningBar` is your name for the SwiftUI view you'll create from AppKit's `NSLevelIndicator`.
3. Provide the number of guesses left. You'll pass this in when you display this view.

You've got an error now because `WarningBar` doesn't conform to the protocol. Click the red dot on the error indicator and then click **Apply**:

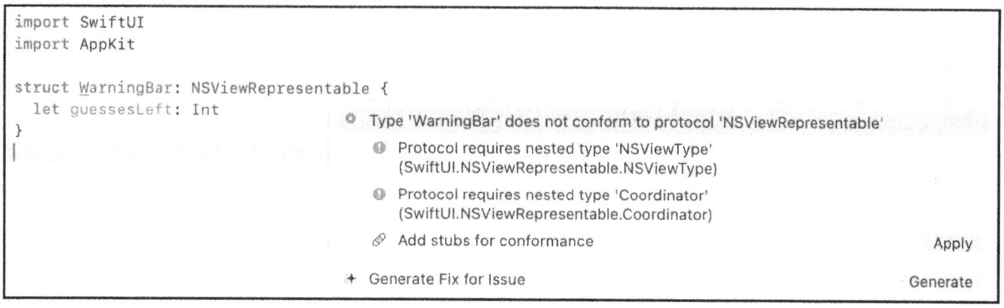

Fixing the protocol error.

This isn't as helpful as you probably hoped, as it adds a second error. But it has inserted this line:

```
typealias NSViewType = type
```

The `NSViewRepresentable` protocol can work with any AppKit view, so this line asks you to state what type of view you want to use. Replace the `typealias` line with:

```
typealias NSViewType = NSLevelIndicator
```

Now you're back to a single error, but this time, the **Apply** button actually fixes it by providing stubs for the two required methods. It was able to do this because your `typealias` specified the AppKit view type:

```
struct WarningBar: NSViewRepresentable {
  func makeNSView(context: Context) -> NSLevelIndicator {
    code
  }

  func updateNSView(_ nsView: NSLevelIndicator, context: Context) {
    code
  }

  typealias NSViewType = NSLevelIndicator

  let guessesLeft: Int
}
```

Really fixing the protocol error.

Filling in the Methods

The first of these methods makes the AppKit view, so in `makeNSView(context:)`, replace the placeholder with:

```
NSLevelIndicator()
```

This creates an instance of `NSLevelIndicator` and returns it.

The second required method is the one that SwiftUI calls to refresh the display whenever the data changes: in this case `guessesLeft`. This method updates the level indicator to reflect that number.

Fill in `updateNSView(_:context:)` with:

```
nsView.intValue = Int32(guessesLeft)
```

Set the `intValue` of the `NSLevelIndicator` to the number of guesses left. The level indicator expects an `Int32`, so you need to convert the `Int` value of `guessesLeft` to the correct type.

When you initialize the view, you provide a value for `guessesLeft`, which triggers this method. That means that you don't need to set `intValue` in `makeNSView(context:)`.

That's everything you need to display the level indicator, but so far, you don't have a way of showing it in your app.

Setting Up the Data Flow

Your new `WarningBar` structure expects an `Int` containing the number of guesses left, but right now, there's no property that supplies that information directly. It sounds like something `Game` should do, so open **Game.swift** and add this computed property:

```
// 1
var guessesLeft: Int {
  // 2
  7 - incorrectGuessCount
}
```

This adds a computed property:

1. The property is called `guessesLeft` and it returns an `Int`.
2. It calculates the number of guesses left by subtracting the number of incorrect guesses made so far from the maximum of 7.

`Game` uses the value **7** three times now, so it would be good practice to create a constant to hold this value. That way if you ever change the game to allow a different number of guesses, you only have to change it in one place.

Add this constant to the top of the `Game` structure:

```
let maxGuesses = 7
```

Next, search **Game.swift** for the number **7** and replace all three occurrences with `maxGuesses`. These replacements are in `processGuess(letter:)`, `checkForGameOver()` and `guessesLeft`, which now looks like this:

```
var guessesLeft: Int {
  maxGuesses - incorrectGuessCount
}
```

This is a much more maintainable way to write this code and avoids having a magic number appearing in several places.

Now, you have all the pieces you need to display the warning bar.

Adding the View

The logical place for this bar is underneath the snowman image inside `GameView`. Open **GameView.swift** and find the `Image` that displays the snowman. Select the Image line and its three modifier lines, then press **{**. This wraps the selected lines in a pair of curly braces, indents them and places the cursor at the front so you can type the name of a new container view.

Type `VStack` and a space to embed the `Image` in a vertical stack. Now you can add the `WarningBar` underneath the snowman.

Add this line before the closing curly brace for the new `VStack`:

```
WarningBar(guessesLeft: game.guessesLeft)
```

The bar now appears below the snowman. Run the app and play a game to see how it updates as you make wrong guesses:

Warning bar with default settings.

The good news is that it appears and it does change as you make wrong guesses. The bad news is that its too wide, it doesn't have the correct number of blocks and it doesn't show any different colors. Time to go back to `WarningBar` and add some more settings.

Configuring the Level Indicator

`NSLevelIndicator` has several properties that you can change to make it look the way you want. To see the effect of your changes as you make them, open **GameView.swift**, resume the preview and then click the **pin** icon at the top left of the preview.

Switch to **WarningBar.swift**, where you can still see the `GameView` preview, and replace the contents of `makeNSView(context:)` with:

```
let levelIndicator = NSLevelIndicator()
// set properties here
return levelIndicator
```

Before, you returned the new `NSLevelIndicator` immediately, using an implicit `return`. Now, you're creating the level indicator and assigning it to a constant, so you can set some properties before returning it.

One property that changes how to level indicator looks is `levelIndicatorStyle`. Replace the `// set properties here` comment with this line:

```
levelIndicator.levelIndicatorStyle = .
```

When you type the period, Xcode will suggest the different styles. Experiment with the four styles: `continuousCapacity`, `discreteCapacity`, `rating` and `relevancy`. For this app, `discreteCapacity` is the best choice, so select that once you've checked out the others.

The next task is to set the number of blocks to show in the level indicator. You could set this to **7**, but you just created a `maxGuesses` constant in `Game`, so it would be better to pass that to the `WarningBar` and use it.

Start by adding this property to `WarningBar`, underneath `guessesLeft`:

```
let maxGuesses: Int
```

Jump back to **GameView.swift** to see the error that this has caused. Change the line showing the error to:

```
WarningBar(guessesLeft: game.guessesLeft, maxGuesses:
game.maxGuesses)
```

Back in **WarningBar.swift**, add this line to `makeNSView(context:)`, under where you set the style:

```
levelIndicator.maxValue = Double(maxGuesses)
```

This sets the maximum value for the level indicator to the number of guesses allowed in the game. You have to convert it to a `Double` because that's the type that `maxValue` expects. Resume the `ContentView` preview to see the change:

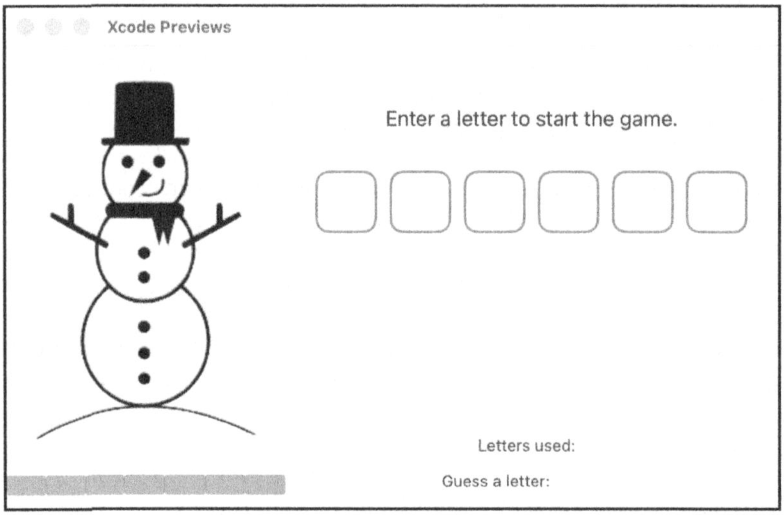

Preview after setting max value.

The warning bar is now showing 7 discrete blocks, but they'll all show the same color, even when the value changes. You want them to change color as the number of guesses left decreases, so add these two property settings:

```
levelIndicator.warningValue = 3
levelIndicator.criticalValue = 1
```

Run the app and enter lots of wrong guesses to see the colors change as you approach losing:

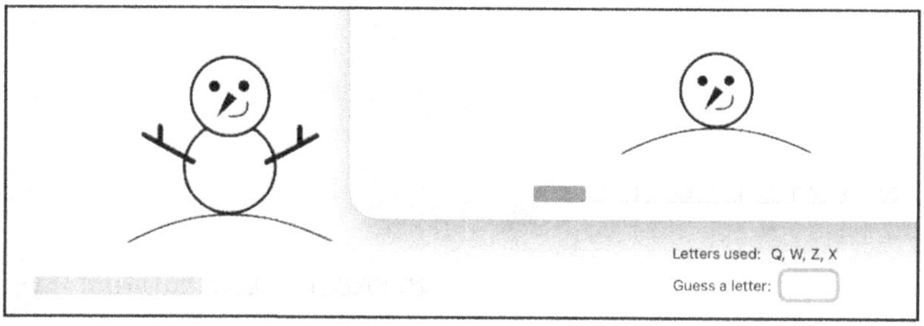

Warning bar with colors.

And when you finally lose the game, there are no blocks showing.

The remaining problem is that the warning bar is too wide, so open **GameView.swift** where the snowman image has a fixed with of 230. To apply this to the entire `VStack`, select the `frame(width: 230)` line and press **Option-Command-]** to move the line down. Keep pressing those keys until this modifier is outside the `VStack`. Finally, add this modifier to the `WarningBar` itself:

```
.padding(.horizontal)
```

This spaces it out from the sides but not from the top or bottom and now the preview shows the warning bar with a suitable width:

The resized warning bar.

Run the app and play a few games to test it out. It's a bit scary when you get near the end!

Now you know how to convert any AppKit view into a SwiftUI view and how to display it.

Using a Coordinator

You're sending data from the SwiftUI view to the AppKit view, but what if you want to communicate back the other way?

The answer is to set up a custom **coordinator**. The `NSViewRepresentable` methods have a `context` argument that contains information about your view. One of its properties is a coordinator for communication between the two frameworks. You can provide a custom coordinator to do what your app needs.

First, open **WarningBar.swift** and add a new property after `maxGuesses`:

```
@Binding var showHint: Bool
```

This is an `@Binding` property so when `WarningBar` changes it, the new value flows back to the SwiftUI view that supplied the property.

Next, insert a `Coordinator` class **inside** `WarningBar`:

```
class Coordinator {
}
```

This does nothing at the moment, but it sets up the new view to have a coordinator that it can use to handle interactions.

It causes an error because `WarningBar` knows there's a `Coordinator` class, but isn't using it. The **Apply** button comes to the rescue again, adding:

```
func makeCoordinator() -> Coordinator {
  code
}
```

To pass data from `Coordinator` back to `WarningBar`, `Coordinator` needs access to it. Add this property and initializer to `Coordinator`:

```
// 1
var parent: WarningBar
```

```
// 2
init(_ parent: WarningBar) {
  // 3
  self.parent = parent
}
```

You configure `Coordinator` by:

1. Giving it a `WarningBar` property called `parent`.
2. Creating an initializer. The underscore for the external argument label means the caller can omit it.
3. Setting `Coordinator`'s parent to the supplied `WarningBar`.

Now you can fill in `makeCoordinator()`, replacing the code placeholder with:

```
Coordinator(self)
```

This returns a `Coordinator` object, initialized with the containing `WarningBar` as its `parent`. This gives you a place to handle interactions.

Setting Up the Action and Target

The purpose of this coordinator is to detect and respond to clicks inside the level indicator. AppKit views do this with a target and action system. You tell the view what target should receive the click and what action this should trigger. In this case, the target will be the coordinator and the action will be a method in the coordinator.

First, add the action method to the `Coordinator` class:

```
// 1
@objc func handleClick(sender: NSLevelIndicator) {
  // 2
  parent.showHint.toggle()
}
```

What's happening here?

1. Add a method to respond to clicks in the `NSLevelIndicator`. This must have the `@objc` marker so `NSLevelIndicator` can recognize and call it.
2. When the user clicks, toggle the value of `showHint` in the parent `WarningBar`. This is a binding, so it will flow back to the SwiftUI view that supplied it.

Next, configure the target and action. In `makeNSView(context:)`, add these lines after setting the properties, but before the `return`:

```
// 1
levelIndicator.target = context.coordinator
// 2
levelIndicator.action = #selector(Coordinator.handleClick)
```

This is how you set up the target and action for an AppKit view programmatically:

1. Tell the level indicator that its target is the coordinator, which you can access through the `context` argument.
2. Set its action, using `#selector` to specify the method in the coordinator. This is the same technique that you used to specify sort descriptor methods in Chapter 13: "Powering Up Your Table".

There's one more wrinkle in this, which is due to the way SwiftUI views are redrawn as required. Every time the `WarningBar` view updates, you need to reset the coordinator's parent. If you don't do this, hints will only work for the first game.

Add this line to `updateNSView(_:context:)`:

```
context.coordinator.parent = self
```

Now, the level indicator will detect clicks and call `handleClick(sender:)` in the coordinator. This method toggles a binding in the parent view, allowing SwiftUI to react to the change. So, how can you use this information?

Showing Hints

Right now, the app doesn't build. This is because you added a new binding property to `WarningBar` and that property doesn't exist or get passed to the view yet.

Start by opening **Game.swift** and adding this property to `Game`:

```
var showHint = false
```

Next, open **GameView.swift** and replace the line that creates the `WarningBar`, which is showing an error:

```
// 1
WarningBar(
  // 2
```

```
    guessesLeft: game.guessesLeft,
    maxGuesses: game.maxGuesses,
    // 3
    showHint: $appState.games[appState.gameIndex].showHint
  )
```

What does this do?

1. Split the call over multiple lines, to make it easier to read now that it's getting longer.
2. Provide two game properties as before.
3. Use the longer form of accessing the current game to be able to pass it as a binding. The $ prefix means that when `WarningBar` changes this, the new value flows back to the game. This is the same way you passed a binding to `GuessesView`.

Now `showHint` is being passed to `WarningBar` and clicks in `WarningBar` will toggle this value, so you can use it to show helpful hints.

Open **Game.swift** and add this computed property to `Game`:

```
// 1
var hint: String? {
  // 2
  if gameStatus != .inProgress || !showHint {
    return nil
  }

  // 3
  if guesses.count == 0 {
    return "Starting with a vowel is always a good idea."
  }

  // 4
  let numberOfVowelsGuessed = guesses.count {
    "AEIOU".contains($0)
  }
  if numberOfVowelsGuessed == 0 {
    return "Try guessing a vowel."
  } else if numberOfVowelsGuessed < 3 {
    return "Try guessing another vowel."
  }

  // 5
  let commonConsonants = ["T","N","S","H","R"]
  let unusedCommons = commonConsonants.filter {
    !guesses.contains($0)
  }
```

```
    if !unusedCommons.isEmpty {
      return "These are commonly used consonants that you haven't
tried yet: "
        + unusedCommons
        .joined(separator: ", ")
    }

    // 6
    return "It's generally best to avoid uncommon letters like Z,
Q and X."
  }
```

This generates a hint based on the current game state:

1. `hint` is a computed property that returns an optional `String`.
2. If the game is over or `showHint` is false, return `nil`.
3. If the player hasn't made any guesses, advise them to start with a vowel.
4. If the player has made some guesses but no or few vowels, recommend a vowel.
5. If the player has guessed some vowels already, but hasn't tried some of the most common consonants, suggest trying those.
6. If none of these conditions are met, show them uncommon letters that are unlikely to be useful.

Feel free to change the hints to be more helpful or more fun, but this is a good starting point.

Finally, open **GameView.swift** and add this computed property:

```
// 1
var statusOrHint: String {
  // 2
  if let hint = game.hint {
    return hint
  }
  return game.statusText
}
```

What's this for?

1. `statusOrHint` is a computed property that returns a `String`.
2. Check to see if `game.hint` is not `nil`. If so, return the hint.
3. Otherwise, return the normal status text.

To display this, replace `Text(game.statusText)` with:

```
Text(statusOrHint)
```

Now the text above the letters boxes will show a hint when the user clicks the level indicator to request a hint, and it will show the normal status text at all other times.

There's one final tweak to add. The hint shouldn't stay visible once it's been used, so jump back to **Game.swift** and find `processGuess(letter:)`. Before the `checkForGameOver()` call, add this line:

```
showHint = false
```

Now the player can ask for a hint and it disappears as soon as they make their next guess.

Run the app and test it out:

Asking for a hint.

This is quite a complex chain of data passing, so here's a review of the complete sequence:

1. `Game` has the properties `maxGuesses` and `showHint`, as well computed properties for `guessesLeft` and `hint`.
2. `GameView` displays `WarningBar`, passing it `guessesLeft` and `maxGuesses` as integers.
3. `GameView` also sends `showHint` as a binding, so when `WarningBar` changes it, the new value flows back to `Game`.

4. `WarningBar` uses `maxGuesses` to configure the `NSLevelIndicator` and `guessesLeft` to set its value.
5. `WarningBar` sets up a `Coordinator` as the target for the `NSLevelIndicator` click event, providing itself as the parent view.
6. `Coordinator` detects clicks in the `NSLevelIndicator` and toggles the `showHint` property in its parent `WarningBar`.
7. Because this is a binding, it flows back to the enclosing `GameView` which then changes its display accordingly using the `hint` property in `Game` to generate a relevant hint.

As soon as you need an AppKit view to be able to change data in a SwiftUI view, things get complicated, so take your time and follow this chain through the different files.

The project now has four views that are involved in displaying the game, so to make the project more organized, move **GameView.swift**, **GuessesView.swift**, **LettersView.swift** and **WarningBar.swift** into a new folder called **Game**:

Game views folder.

Next, you'll learn another way of including AppKit features in a SwiftUI app.

Observing Events

You've seen how to convert an AppKit view into a SwiftUI view for presentation in your SwiftUI app, but AppKit has more than views. One thing it's extremely good at is event handling.

SwiftUI has modifiers to trap certain events. You've used `onAppear` to take action when a view first appears and you've used `onChange` to detect data changes.

Press **Shift-Command-L** to open the Xcode Library. Select the **Modifiers** tab — the one with the sliders icon — and scroll down to find the Events section. There are lots of events, but nothing to detect key presses. That's why you used a text entry field for the player's guesses.

Using an AppKit method, you'll add key press detection and make entering guesses look and feel a lot more natural.

Trapping Key Strokes

Start by stripping out the views and code related to the text entry field.

Open **Views → Game → GuessesView.swift** and double-click the closing curly brace at the end of the `LabeledContent` line. This selects the contents of this view and all its modifiers. Press **Delete** to get rid of it and then delete the `LabeledContent` line itself.

In the properties for this view, delete `entryFieldHasFocus` but leave the others in place. You'll still use `nextGuess`, but you'll populate it differently.

You've eliminated the current method for guessing letters so now, it's time to replace it.

Still in **GuessesView.swift**, add this method to the structure, outside `body`:

```
func startMonitoringKeystrokes() {
  // 1
  NSEvent.addLocalMonitorForEvents(matching: .keyDown) { event
in
    // 2
    print(event.characters)
    // 3
    return event
  }
}
```

This method uses an AppKit class:

1. `NSEvent` is a class that provides information about user actions. In this case, use a class method to monitor this app only and watch for the user pressing a key.

2. The method passes an `NSEvent` into the attached closure where you'll process it. For now, print its `characters` to see what's happening. Ignore the warning since you'll delete this line in a minute.
3. Return the `event` for any other part of the app to handle as usual.

To activate this method, attach a modifier to the `VStack`:

```
.onAppear(perform: startMonitoringKeystrokes)
```

This is a different way to use `onAppear`, passing the name of a method as its `perform` argument. Notice how there's no need to add the parentheses after the method name. If a called method doesn't have any arguments, this is a neat way of writing `onAppear`.

Run the app now and start pressing buttons on your keyboard:

```
Optional("p")
Optional("R")
Optional("1")
Optional("]")
Optional("\u{10}")
Optional("ª")
Optional("\\")
Optional("\'")
```

Detecting key presses.

The Xcode console shows the optional characters for keys you pressed, with a mix of uppercase, lowercase, numbers, symbols and strange control sequences.

Now, you can decide which keys you want the game to process.

Processing Key Strokes

The first step is to work out if the player pressed a valid key.

Replace `print(event.characters)` with:

```
// 1
guard let key = event.characters(byApplyingModifiers: .shift)
else {
  return event
}

// 2
if key >= "A" && key <= "Z" {
```

```
    // 3
    nextGuess = key
    return nil
  }
```

This does two checks:

1. See if the event had any characters after you apply the Shift key. This means if the user presses either **a** or **Shift-a**, `key` is **A**. If the event has no characters, `key` is `nil` and this returns the event immediately.
2. The second test confirms the typed character is between **A** and **Z**. The `byApplyingModifiers: .shift` has changed everything to upper case, so there's no need to check for **a** to **z**.
3. If both checks pass, set `nextGuess` to the typed character and return `nil` to indicate that you've handled the event and it doesn't need to be passed on to the rest of the app.

Finally, everything is in place to handle the entered letters, so add this modifier after `onAppear`:

```
// 1
.onChange(of: nextGuess) {
  // 2
  if game.gameStatus == .inProgress {
    // 3
    game.processGuess(letter: nextGuess)
  }
  // 4
  nextGuess = ""
}
```

Working through these lines:

1. Watch for changes to `nextGuess`.
2. When there's a change, check if the game is still in progress. Previously, you used a modifier to disable the input field for completed games, but events can arrive at any time, so now you have to check manually.
3. Process the guess as before.
4. Clear the value in `nextGuess`. This is necessary when you have more than one active game. If you press **E** for game 1 and then switch to game 2 and press **E** again, there's no change in the value of `nextGuess` to trigger `onChange`. Clearing `nextGuess` means that any key press triggers `onChange`.

Run the app now and play a game:

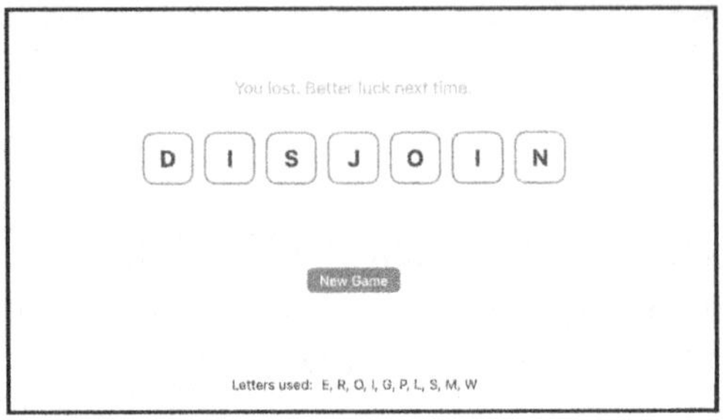

Playing with key press detection.

It doesn't make the game any easier to win :] but the interface is cleaner and you've eliminated a lot of bother with the text entry field and its focus.

> Note: You might think that it'd be easier to process the guess directly from the `NSEvent` handler. The problem is that if you access `game` inside the event handler's closure, it **captures** the value for `game` as it's created. This means that inside the closure, `game` never updates, but always refers to the first game. Setting `nextGuess` gets around this by doing the processing outside the closure using the current value for `game`.

There's one final wrinkle before this new feature is complete.

Watching for the Command Key

Run the app and press **Command-N** to try to start a second game. Try quitting the app using **Command-Q**. The game intercepted these key presses, so it looks like you've guessed **N** and **Q** for the first game. You didn't get a new game, and the app didn't quit.

However, `NSEvent` can tell if the **Command** key was down at the time of the event, so you can allow for it.

Add this to `startMonitoringKeystrokes()` in `GuessesView`, before checking if `key` is between **A** and **Z**:

```
// 1
if event.modifierFlags.contains(.command) {
  // 2
```

```
    return event
  }
```

How does this help?

1. An `NSEvent` has a `modifierFlags` option set, which lists its modifier keys. You can query this to see if it contains any particular modifier. The possibilities are all properties of `NSEvent.ModifierFlags`. This includes `shift`, `control`, `option` and others, but the only one that matters for this app is `command`.
2. If the event includes the **Command** key, return it immediately. This allows the menus to work as expected and stops the game from processing the associated character.

You've implemented a new feature using AppKit, and you've added code to handle some edge cases. Great work!

When Should You Start With SwiftUI?

You've made a SwiftUI app and you've made an AppKit app. Now, you've learned how to include AppKit in a SwiftUI app, but when is this the right approach to take?

For a brand new project, there are only two cases where I would **not** start with SwiftUI: Apps that include long-form text editing and apps that display more than a few thousand records in a list.

For every other project type, start with SwiftUI and see what happens.

As you progress, you may find a sticking point where SwiftUI doesn't do what you want. At that stage, ask yourself these three questions:

1. Can I restructure the app, the data or the data flow, so that SwiftUI does what I need?
2. Is there an AppKit feature that I can include in the app to solve this problem?
3. Would swapping to AppKit make everything work, realizing that I can include SwiftUI views in an AppKit app?

Your answers dictate what you do next: Take action based on the first question that gets a **Yes** answer.

For this app, when looking to add a level indicator, the answers were **No**, **Yes** and **Yes**, so you included AppKit.

Over time, you'll develop your own sense of what works best for your individual programming style, but this is a good guide to start with.

SwiftUI has a limited number of view types and although Apple adds new views every year, it can't compete yet with the huge scope of AppKit. A hybrid app, combining the speed and convenience of SwiftUI development with the power and depth of AppKit, is a terrific option. Apple continues to expand SwiftUI, reducing the need to use AppKit, but the mix-and-match approach will be necessary for many years.

Challenges

1. Add a tooltip to `WarningBar` that shows how it can be used to display a hint.
2. Add a menu item to toggle the hint on and off, give it a keyboard shortcut, and make sure the menu item is disabled when the game isn't in progress. Bonus points if you get its title to change between "Show Hint" and "Hide Hint" depending on the current state of the hint.

Have a go at these yourself, but check out **SnowmanApp.swift** in the **challenge** folder if you get stuck.

Key Points

- `NSViewRepresentable` lets you create a SwiftUI version of an AppKit view.
- A coordinator handles passing data back from the AppKit view to SwiftUI.
- You can include non-view AppKit features, like `NSEvent`, in a SwiftUI app.
- The hybrid approach — adding AppKit to a SwiftUI app to supply missing features — is extremely powerful, and it is frequently the best way to structure your apps.

Where to Go From Here?

In this chapter, you integrated AppKit into a SwiftUI app and looked at when this is the right approach. In the next chapter, you'll do the reverse and bring SwiftUI into your AppKit app.

Chapter 18: Using SwiftUI in AppKit

By Sarah Reichelt

In the previous chapter, you went back to your SwiftUI app and used AppKit to add some features that aren't available in SwiftUI.

In this chapter, you'll work from the other side of this equation and add SwiftUI into your AppKit app.

When coding a SwiftUI app, there are things you can't do without AppKit. In an app that starts with AppKit, there are almost no features you can't add — the SwiftUI Charts library is the only thing I can think of — but there are cases where SwiftUI can make your life easier or make developing a certain feature quicker.

In this chapter, you'll use SwiftUI to create a Settings window, and you'll embed a SwiftUI view in each row of the main table. Then, you'll examine when this is the best way to build an app.

Adding a Hosting Controller

In the previous chapter, you used `NSViewRepresentable` to create a SwiftUI view from an AppKit view. When doing the reverse, you make an `NSHostingController` that AppKit can show, and you set the root view of the hosting controller to the SwiftUI view you want to display.

Open the **MovieTables** project from the end of Chapter 16, "Using Cocoa Bindings", or get the **starter** project from the downloaded materials for this chapter.

Run the app and take a look at the **MovieTables** menu:

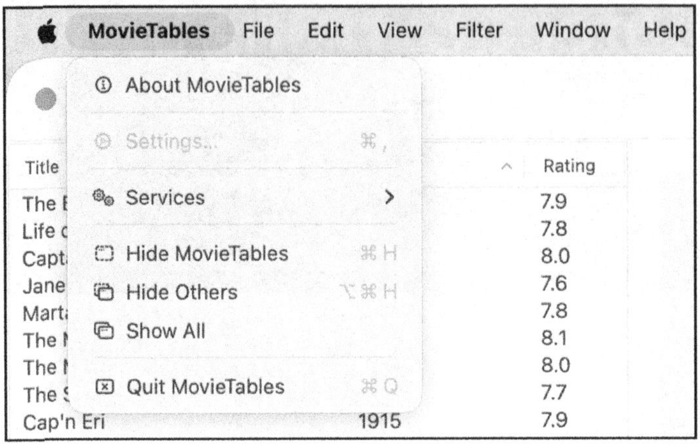

MovieTables menu

There's a **Settings...** menu item, but you haven't linked it to a window, so your app disables the item.

Open **Main.storyboard** and, in **Application Scene**, open the **MovieTables** menu. You're probably surprised to see a **Preferences...** menu item there. Until macOS Ventura, Settings were called Preferences. Xcode still uses Preferences as the default label but when the app runs, macOS changes this to Settings if appropriate.

Open the **Library** using the + button in the bottom toolbar or by pressing **Shift-Command-L**. Make sure you're in the **Objects** tab and search for **host**. Drag a **Hosting View Controller** into the storyboard, near the menu bar:

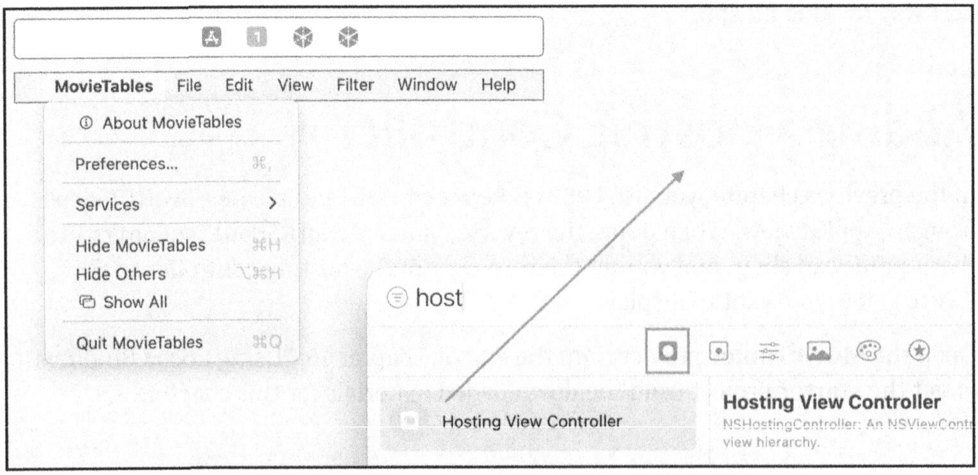

Adding a Hosting View Controller.

With that in place, **Control-drag** from the **Preferences...** menu item to the new **Hosting Controller** and select **Show** from the popup options:

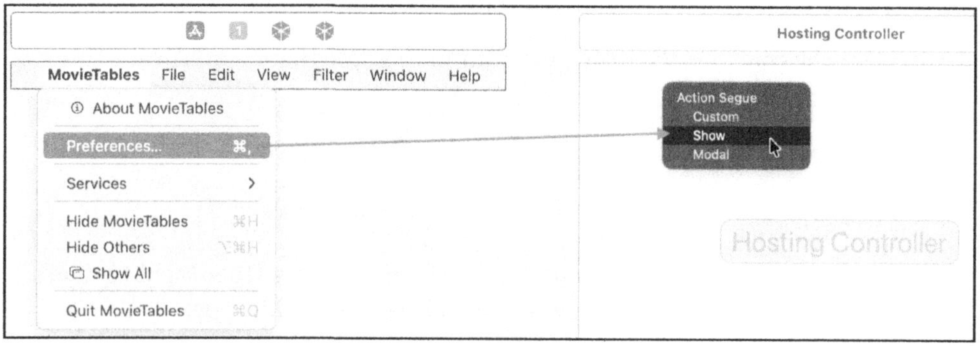

Creating a segue.

This creates a segue so that choosing **Settings...** opens the hosting controller. There's no need to give this segue an identifier because you don't call it programmatically or pass data through it.

Next, you'll make a SwiftUI view for the hosting controller to host.

Creating the Settings View

The Settings view will be pure SwiftUI. Select **EditViewController.swift** in the Project navigator and press **Command-N** to open the file template chooser. Select **SwiftUI View** and set the name to **SettingsView.swift**.

What settings will this control?

Open **ViewController.swift** and jump to `searchMovies()`. There are two options that could usefully appear in Settings. The first is the default `viewMode`. Right now, the app starts up showing all the movies, but some users may prefer a different starting mode.

The second option is the limit for showing highest rated movies. It's set to 9.0, but your users may be more or less picky about movies.

Back in **SettingsView.swift**, add these two `@AppStorage` properties to `SettingsView`:

```
@AppStorage("defaultViewMode") var defaultViewMode =
ViewMode.allMovies
@AppStorage("highRatingLimit") var highRatingLimit = 9.0
```

These lines create properties that the app stores and reloads, using SwiftUI's `@AppStorage` wrapper. The first one gives an error because this storage mechanism can only store basic data types, and it doesn't know how to store `ViewMode` cases.

You'll fix this by changing `ViewMode` to conform to a type that `@AppStorage` can handle.

Open **ViewMode.swift** and change the `enum` declaration line to:

```
enum ViewMode: Int {
```

This gives every case in the enumeration its own integer `rawValue`. `@AppStorage` has no trouble handling an `Int` and can now store properties of this type.

Back in **SettingsView.swift**, it's time to add the interface to go with the properties.

Coding the Interface

Replace the default contents of `body` with:

```
// 1
VStack(alignment: .leading, spacing: 30) {
  // 2
  Picker("Default View Mode:", selection: $defaultViewMode) {
    // 3
    Text("All Movies").tag(ViewMode.allMovies)
    Text("Favorites Only").tag(ViewMode.favsOnly)
    Text("Highest Rated").tag(ViewMode.highRating)
  }
  // 4
  .pickerStyle(.radioGroup)

  // 5
  Slider(value: $highRatingLimit, in: 7.5 ... 10.0) {
    // 6
    HStack {
      Text("High Rating Limit:")
      // 7
      Text(highRatingLimit,
format: .number.precision(.fractionLength(1)))
    }
  }
}
// 8
.frame(width: 300, height: 120)
.padding()
```

You've had quite a bit of experience with SwiftUI views by now but there are some new features here:

1. By default, a `VStack` aligns all its views centrally and close together. These arguments pin the views to the leading side and add more spacing between them.
2. A `Picker` is a good interface choice when deciding between a fixed set of options. This initializer gives it a title and binds its selection to `defaultViewMode`.
3. Inside the `Picker`, each option has its own `Text` display with a `tag` linking it to its associated `ViewMode` case.
4. SwiftUI offers several `pickerStyle` options. A segmented control often works well for enumerations, but in this case the labels are long, so a `radioGroup` looks best.
5. Set up a `Slider` to control the numeric `highRating` property. Bind its value to `highRatingLimit` and set its limits using a closed range. The data file only includes movies with a rating of at least 7.5, so there's no need to let the slider go any lower.
6. The contents of the `Slider` shows its associated label: a title and the currently selected value, wrapped in an `HStack`.
7. When showing a number in a `Text` view, you can supply a `format`. This is a `FormatStyle` that specifies how the number looks. The `number` style, when applied to a floating point number, has a `precision` method for setting various other options. This configuration shows the number with one digit after the decimal point.
8. Finally, set the view `frame` and add some `padding` to inset the subviews from the edges.

Press **Command-Option-P** to resume the preview and you'll see your Settings view:

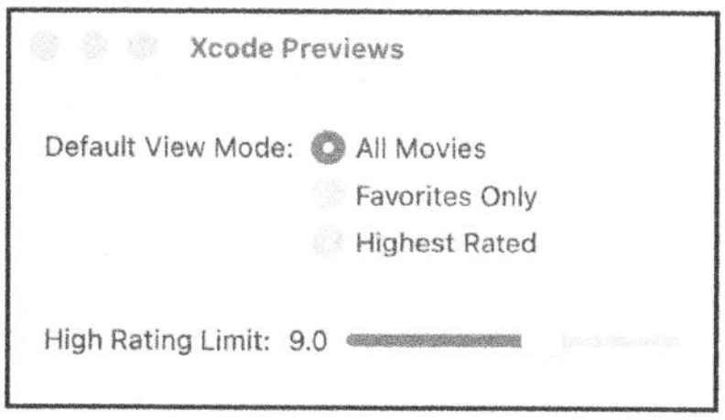

Previewing the Settings view.

Now that you have a view to show, you can tell the hosting controller to show it.

Customizing the Hosting Controller

An `NSHostingController` has a `rootView` property to tell it what SwiftUI view to host. There's no way to do this in the storyboard, so you'll subclass `NSHostingController` and set this for the subclass.

Use your preferred method to add a new empty file called **SettingsHostingController.swift**.

Set the contents of the new file to:

```
// 1
import SwiftUI

// 2
class SettingsHostingController: NSHostingController {
  // 3
  required init?(coder: NSCoder) {
    // 4
    super.init(coder: coder, rootView: SettingsView())
  }
}
```

Working through these lines:

1. `NSHostingController` looks like an AppKit class with that `NS` prefix, but it's defined in the SwiftUI library, so import that. The SwiftUI import also brings in AppKit and Foundation, so there's no need to import them separately.

2. Define a class called `SettingsHostingController` that's a subclass of `NSHostingController`. This line shows an error, but it's a useful error, so leave it in place for now.

3. Whenever you initialize a controller from a storyboard, it calls `init(coder:)`, so this is `required`. The coder *decodes* the storyboard data to create the user interface.

4. Since this is a subclass, call the inherited class's `init`. For an `NSHostingController`, this requires the `coder` and the `rootView`. Create a `SettingsView` and pass it to the hosting controller.

That's quite a chunk of code, but now you can go back to the storyboard and finish the job.

Open **Main.storyboard** and select the **Hosting Controller**. Press **Command-Option-4** to show the Identity inspector. Change **Class** to **SettingsHostingController** and press **Return**:

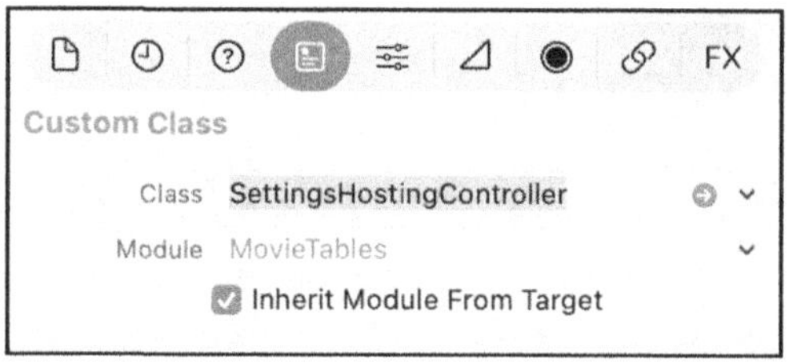

Setting host controller class.

This is the reason for the error in **SettingsHostingController.swift**. If you'd written that correctly, Xcode wouldn't have shown anything in the Class popup menu. You could have typed it in manually, or copied and pasted, but this is a more reliable way of getting it exactly right and avoiding a crash.

While you're in the storyboard, open the Attributes inspector and set the hosting controller's **Title** to **Settings** and set **Presentation** to **Single** so only one copy of this window is ever open at a time:

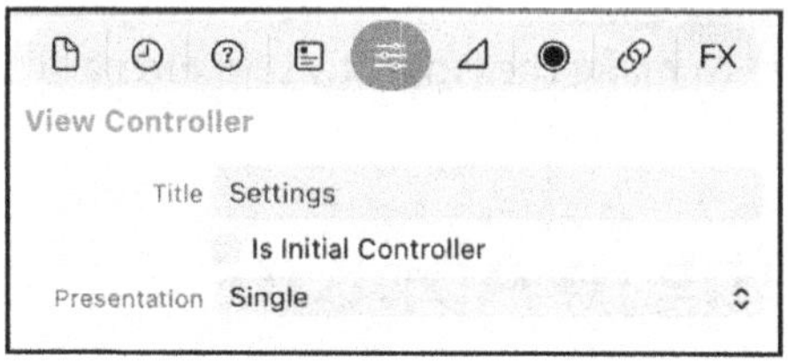

Setting hosting controller attributes.

Now that you've set the class, you can go back to **SettingsHostingController.swift** to fix the error. Change the class declaration line to:

```
class SettingsHostingController:
NSHostingController<SettingsView> {
```

The name inside the angle brackets tells `SettingsHostingController` the type of the SwiftUI view it's to host.

You're ready for a test run now. Press **Command-R** to run the app and use **MovieTables → Settings...** to open the Settings window.

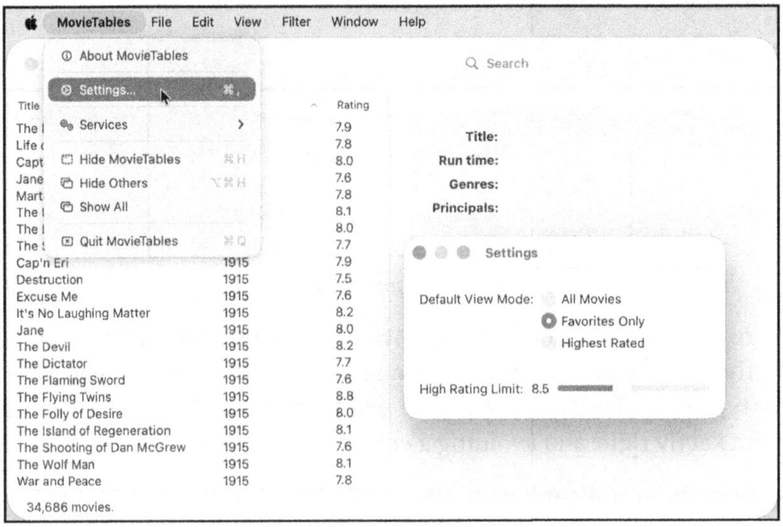

Opening the Settings view.

Change the options, quit the app and reopen the Settings window. Your changes are all there. The next step is to make the AppKit `ViewController` use them.

Using a Setting in AppKit

The Settings window stores two different settings using the `@AppStorage` property wrapper. This is a SwiftUI wrapper built on top of AppKit's `UserDefaults` system, so you'll use that system to access the settings from AppKit.

The first setting only matters when the app starts. It allows the user to set the default view mode — the one that appears initially.

Open **ViewController.swift**, find `viewDidLoad()` and replace all its code with:

```
// 1
super.viewDidLoad()
movies = dataStore.readStoredData()

// 2
addSortDescriptors()
```

```
// 3
let defaultViewModeSetting = UserDefaults.standard
  .integer(forKey: "defaultViewMode")
// 4
if let defaultViewMode = ViewMode(rawValue:
defaultViewModeSetting) {
  // 5
  viewMode = defaultViewMode
}

// 6
searchMovies()
```

Stepping through this:

1. Call `viewDidLoad()` for the super class and read the `movies` array, as before.
2. Add the sort descriptors to the table before doing anything that will change what the table shows.
3. Query `UserDefaults.standard` for an integer with the key `defaultViewMode`. `UserDefaults` is the settings storage mechanism and its `standard` property gives you access to the settings for this app. When setting up `@AppStorage`, you made `ViewMode` conform to `Int`, so that's what it stored for this setting, and the key is the label you set for the `@AppStorage` property. `integer(forKey:)` always returns an `Int`, using `0` if the key doesn't exist yet.
4. Try to convert this integer into a `ViewMode`. You didn't assign a `rawValue` directly to each `ViewMode` case, but by conforming it to `Int`, you set the first case to 0 by default, and this increments for each subsequent case. This means that a stored value of 0 *or* a missing value both give `allMovies`, which is perfect.
5. If the integer is a valid `rawValue` for `ViewMode`, use the result to set `viewMode`. This `ViewController` property dictates the list of movies to show or search.
6. Instead of setting `visibleMovies` to the full `movies` array, call `searchMovies()` to apply the default view mode setting.

Time to test this. Run the app and make sure you have some favorites marked. Use **Settings** to change the default view mode to **Favorites Only**.

Quit the app and run it again to confirm that it defaults to the correct mode:

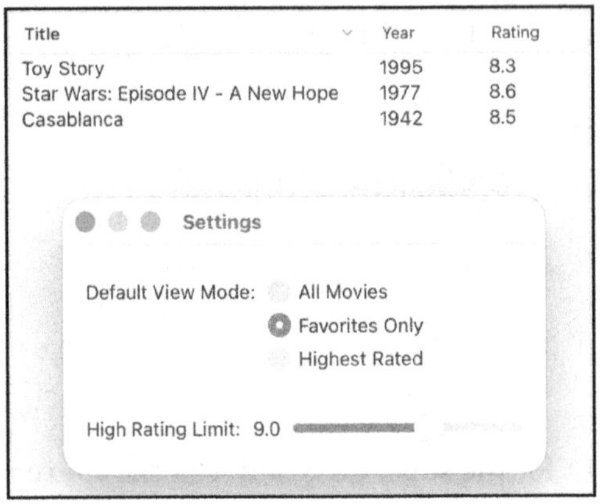

Default view mode.

The default view mode setting only matters when the app starts. After that, the user can change the default setting without needing to trigger a display change. This isn't the case for the other setting.

Watching for a Change

Whenever a user changes the high rating limit, they expect the new setting to take effect immediately. You can't ask them to quit the app and restart to implement their change.

In SwiftUI, this isn't a problem. The `@AppStorage` property wrapper handles this sort of thing for you and changes to any `@AppStorage` property triggers updates to the display. With `UserDefaults`, you have to do more of the work.

To detect when the user edits this setting, you'll watch for a notification.

Still in **ViewController.swift**, add this to the end of `viewDidLoad()`, after all the other code:

```
// 1
NotificationCenter.default.addObserver(
  // 2
  forName: UserDefaults.didChangeNotification,
  // 3
  object: nil,
  // 4
  queue: .main) { _ in
    // 5
```

```
    // process notification
}
```

What does this do?

1. `NotificationCenter` is a mechanism for sending and receiving broadcast notifications. `NotificationCenter.default` is the notification center for the app and you add an **observer** to detect a specific type of notification.
2. The `forName` argument takes an `NSNotification.Name` to tell it what to observe. You can create your own notifications and names, but this observer watches for `UserDefaults` to post a notification called `UserDefaults.didChangeNotification`. It does this whenever any `UserDefault` setting changes. This includes when `@AppStorage` has handled the change.
3. Some notifications come with an attached `object`, usually the notification sender. You're only interested in knowing that there was a change, so you can ignore this by setting it to `nil`.
4. The third argument sets the `queue` that'll run the attached code block. Since this change triggers an interface refresh, it must run on the main queue.
5. The code to run when any notification arrives goes in this closure.

That's a complex sequence of events, but to summarize:

`UserDefaults` broadcasts a predefined notification whenever anything changes. Any object registered as an **observer** to that event receives the **notification**.

Now that you're detecting changes, you can take appropriate action.

Processing the New Setting

Add a new `ViewController` method:

```
func userDefaultsChanged() {
  // 1
  let newLimit = UserDefaults.standard.double(forKey:
"highRatingLimit")
  // 2
  let roundedLimit = round(newLimit * 10) / 10
  // 3
  if roundedLimit == highRatingLimit {
    return
```

```
    }

    // 4
    highRatingLimit = roundedLimit

    // 5
    if viewMode == .highRating {
      searchMovies()
    }
  }
```

You'll call this from the observer, but what does it do?

1. This time, you query `UserDefaults.standard` for a `Double`. The key is the one you set for the `@AppStorage` property. If this isn't set — for example, when the user has just installed your app — you'll get `0` as the value for `newLimit`. You'll fix this in a minute.
2. A `Double` can have a lot of digits after the decimal point and this can cause problems. If you thought you set a limit of 8.0 but it was actually 8.00000001, then you wouldn't see movies with a rating of 8.0. To solve this, round the number to one decimal place. You can do this for any number by multiplying it by 10, rounding it to get rid of any digits after the decimal point, and then dividing by 10.
3. Check if this new limit is the same as the current `highRatingLimit`. If it is, there's no need to do anything, so return. Remember that any setting change triggers this notification, so `highRatingLimit` may still be the same as it was.
4. Use the new value to change `highRatingLimit`.
5. Since this setting only affects the display when the user is in `highRating` mode, check for this before calling `searchMovies()`. The changed `highRatingLimit` applies next time the user selects this view mode, even if it isn't used now.

This gives you the method for processing changes, so now make the observer call it.

Inside the `addObserver` block, replace `// process notification` with:

```
self.userDefaultsChanged()
```

This calls `userDefaultsChanged()` but why does it have a `.self` prefix? The method is in `ViewController`, but any object can receive notifications. Using `self` lets the block **capture** the current value of `self`, which is `ViewController`. That way, the block always knows where to find the method.

You don't need to remember when to add `self` — if you leave it out when it's needed, Xcode shows an error and suggests fixes.

To handle the case where the user hasn't yet set a value for the high limit, add the following line to `viewDidLoad()`, before the call to `NotificationCenter`:

```
UserDefaults.standard.register(defaults: ["highRatingLimit":
9.0])
```

`UserDefaults` provides a mechanism where you provide a dictionary of default values. Any time you read a value that isn't already set, it will look in this dictionary and return whatever it finds there.

Time to test this feature. Run the app and press **Command-R** to get to the **Highest Rated Movies** view. Sort by **Rating** and sort again if needed to show the lowest rated movies at the top.

Press **Command-,** to open **Settings** and start sliding the slider. The list updates as you drag:

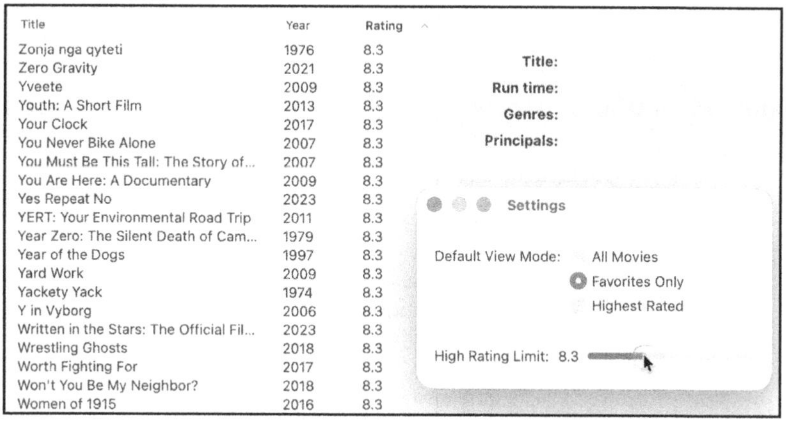

Changing the high rating limit setting.

That's the end of the first SwiftUI addition to your AppKit app. Creating a window in SwiftUI is quicker and easier than doing it in AppKit, mostly because you don't have to struggle with Auto Layout. And handling user settings takes a lot less code in SwiftUI.

Now on to something a bit different.

Jazzing Up the Table

Run the app if it isn't still running and take a look at the main movies table:

Title	Year	Rating
The Battle of Trafalgar	1911	7.9
Life of Villa	1912	7.8
Jane Eyre	1914	7.6
The Spy	1914	7.7
Marta of the Lowlands	1914	7.8
The Million Dollar Robbery	1914	8.0
Captain Alvarez	1914	8.0
The Man from Mexico	1914	8.1

The movies table

The information is all there, but the display is a bit boring. The first thing you can do is apply alternate row colors. This makes a table more visually stimulating and easier to read.

Open **Main.storyboard** and select the table in **View Controller Scene**. Remember, you can **Shift-right-click** in the table area and select **Movies Table View** from the popup menu.

Press **Command-Option-5** to show the Attributes inspector and check **Alternating Rows**:

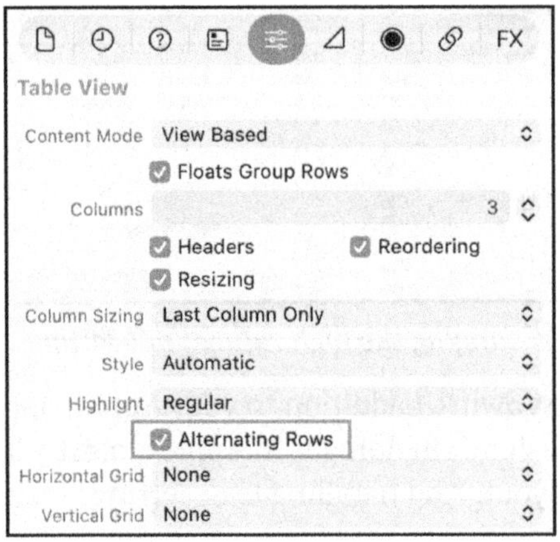

Turning on alternating rows.

With the default size settings, this makes the rows look too squashed together, so **Command-Option-6** over to the Size inspector and set **Row Size Style** to **Medium**:

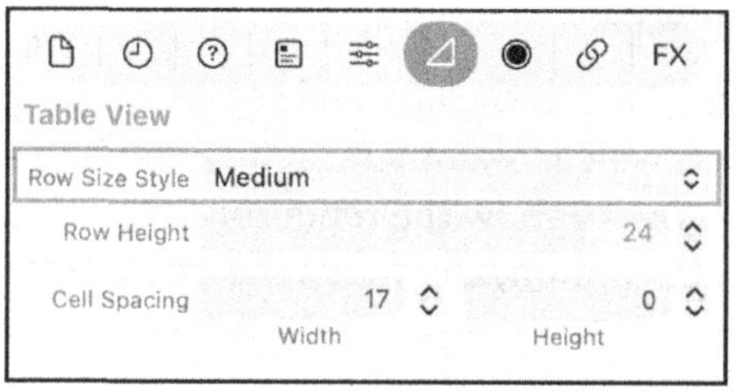

Setting the row size

Leave **Row Height** empty and showing its placeholder of 24. The table works out the row height from the style.

Run the app and check out the improved look:

Title	Year	Rating
The Battle of Trafalgar	1911	7.9
Life of Villa	1912	7.8
Jane Eyre	1914	7.6
The Spy	1914	7.7
Marta of the Lowlands	1914	7.8
The Million Dollar Robbery	1914	8.0

Table with alternating and taller rows.

You can't see as many movies in the same height window, but readability is more important.

That improves the table as a whole, now to add some sparkle to the rating column.

Designing a Rating Cell

Frequently, an app or web page shows a rating as a line of stars with some colored or filled in to indicate the rating. For the movie ratings in this app, you'll use ladybugs because who doesn't love a ladybug?

Actually, the real reason to use a ladybug is that SF Symbols has a multicolored ladybug icon with a filled version that shows colors and a plain version that's only gray. A strip of these will look great as the rating display.

If you don't already have the **SF Symbols app**, download it from Apple Developer (https://developer.apple.com/sf-symbols/). The Xcode Library lists all the symbols, but the app shows a lot more information.

Once you have it installed, launch the app and search for **ladybug**. You'll see the plain and filled variants as well as six others. Select **ladybug.fill** and click the paint brush tab in the right sidebar to show the rendering inspector. The fourth version of the image is the **Multicolor** option, and that's the one you'll use:

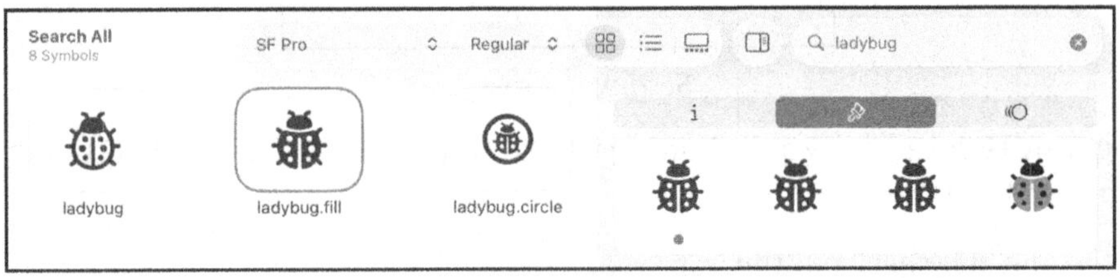

Searching SF Symbols.

The movies in the list have ratings between 7.5 and 10, so there's no point in having the display account for ratings from 1 to 7.5. The display will show five multicolored ladybugs for a rating of 10 and five gray images for a rating of 7.5 with more colors appearing as the rating increases. Still in **SF Symbols**, with **ladybug.fill** selected, choose **Secondary** in the **Color** popup to see the gray version.

Now that you've worked out what to display, you can set up the SwiftUI view for it.

Creating the Rating View

Back in Xcode, press **Command-N** and create a new **SwiftUI View** file called **RatingView.swift**. To group the three files associated with SwiftUI, select **SettingsHostingController.swift**, **SettingsView.swift** and **RatingView.swift** in the Project navigator. **Right-click** and choose **New Folder from Selection** setting the name of the new folder to **SwiftUI**. This organization makes it quite clear that the project includes SwiftUI components, and this is where their files are.

Open **RatingView.swift** and add these two properties:

```
// 1
let rating: Double
// 2
let ladybugImage = Image(systemName: "ladybug")
  .symbolRenderingMode(.multicolor)
```

These provide:

1. The rating for the movie, as supplied to the view.
2. An `Image` view for the ladybug icons, using the SF Symbol name and pre-configured to use multicolor rendering.

This gives an error in the preview, but ignore it for now as you'll set up multiple previews soon.

Replace the `Text` view in `body` with:

```
// 1
HStack(spacing: 2) {
  // 2
  ladybugImage.symbolVariant(rating >= 8 ? .fill : .none)
  ladybugImage.symbolVariant(rating >= 8.5 ? .fill : .none)
  ladybugImage.symbolVariant(rating >= 9 ? .fill : .none)
  ladybugImage.symbolVariant(rating >= 9.5 ? .fill : .none)
  ladybugImage.symbolVariant(rating >= 10 ? .fill : .none)
}
// 3
.font(.title3)
// 4
.foregroundStyle(.secondary)
```

How does this show the rating?

1. Use an `HStack` to draw the five images side-by-side and close together.
2. For each image, check if `rating` meets a certain threshold. Set the symbol variant to `fill` if the the rating is high enough or `none` if not. The `none` variant gives the original image, which isn't multicolored.
3. Set the size of the symbol using a `font` modifier. You can treat SF Symbols like text when it comes to sizing.
4. Set the foreground style to the secondary system color. This only affects the plain variant.

To confirm this works for different ratings, you'll add a range of previews.

Replace the contents of `#Preview` with:

```
VStack {
  RatingView(rating: 7.5)
  RatingView(rating: 8)
  RatingView(rating: 8.5)
  RatingView(rating: 9)
```

```
    RatingView(rating: 9.5)
    RatingView(rating: 10)
}
```

Resume the preview to admire your work:

Previewing the RatingView.

This does exactly as planned with multicolored ladybugs appearing as the rating increases. But how can you make this appear in the table?

Inserting SwiftUI into the Table

You used `NSHostingViewController` to display a SwiftUI view in its own window, as if it was a view controller. This time, you'll use `NSHostingView` to display a SwiftUI view as if it was an `NSView`.

Open **TableData.swift** and, since you'll need SwiftUI features, replace the import line at the top with:

```
import SwiftUI
```

In `tableView(_:viewFor:row:)`, find the `case "RatingColumn":` section. Delete the two lines setting `cellID` and `cellText` for the rating column and replace them with:

```
// 1
let view = RatingView(rating: movie.rating)
// 2
let host = NSHostingView(rootView: view)
```

```
// 3
return host
```

What's happening here?

1. Create a SwiftUI `RatingView` using the rating for the current movie.
2. Initialize an `NSHostingView`, setting its `rootView` to the newly created `RatingView`.
3. Return the `NSHostingView`. The method requires you to return an `NSView`. Until now, you used `cellID` to get an `NSTableCellView` from the storyboard, and populated its `textField` with a String. Now you're returning an `NSHostingView` for the table to show in the rating column for this row.

Run the app and see how this looks:

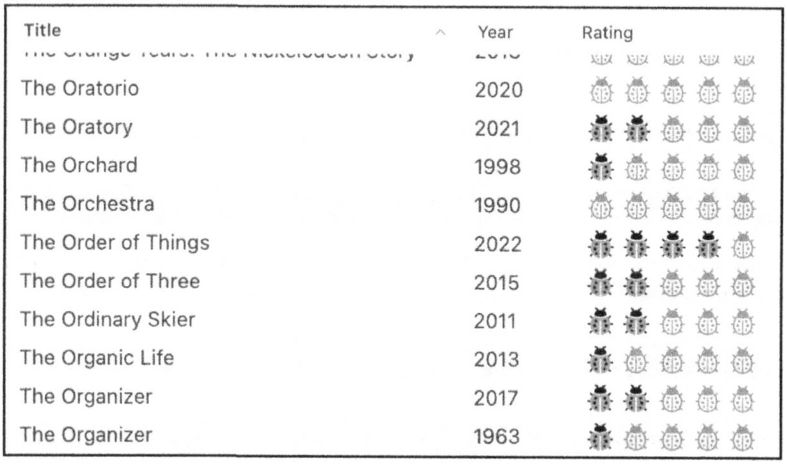

SwiftUI rating view

When you look back at the screenshot of the original table, I think you'll agree that this is a big improvement. There's nothing here that you couldn't have done in pure AppKit, but it would have taken a *lot* more code and effort.

> **Note**: When integrating SwiftUI into an iOS app that uses UIKit, there's a class called `UIHostingConfiguration` specifically designed for use in table cells or collection view cells. Unusually for SwiftUI, there's no AppKit equivalent. If Apple ever creates `NSHostingConfiguration`, it'll replace the use of `NSHostingView` here, but for now, this is a perfectly functional system.

When Should You Start With AppKit?

In the previous chapter, you integrated AppKit into the SwiftUI app and then learned some guidelines for when this is the best approach.

This chapter covers the reverse process, so when is AppKit the best way to build an app?

There are a lot of AppKit apps out there, and you may come across one that you have to maintain. It's always tempting to throw the whole thing out and start again using the newest technology, but that's probably not a great idea. An established app has been well tested and debugged, with all the edge cases handled. You don't want to lose all that.

In that circumstance, the best thing is to add SwiftUI incrementally. If you're making a new window, consider using SwiftUI for it. Or maybe use SwiftUI for a single view. As you saw with the table, you can use `NSHostingView` anywhere you can use `NSView`, but you have to add it programmatically and not through the storyboard.

This lets you keep the proven parts of the AppKit app in place while you gradually move towards the convenience of SwiftUI.

If you're creating a new app, then the guidance from the previous chapter applies: Apps that include long-form text editing or that display thousands of records in a list are best suited to AppKit.

Minimum System Versions

There's one other consideration when picking what sort of app to build, and that's to decide the oldest version of macOS you want your app to support. Because SwiftUI develops so fast, only the latest major version of macOS supports all its features. You can build SwiftUI apps for macOS 10.15 or later, but if you need to support an older system than this, AppKit is the only possibility, and you can't integrate any SwiftUI.

Even if you only support macOS 10.15 and later, a lot of SwiftUI features won't work. AppKit is more mature and stable — it still gets new features, but at a much slower rate, meaning that if you want to support old systems, you can do so without losing a lot of functionality.

To demonstrate this, select the project at the top of the Project navigator, choose the target and then the **General** tab. Set the **Minimum Deployments** popup to **macOS 11 Big Sur** which fills in a minimum system version of **11.5**:

Go to Xcode's **Settings** → **General** and turn off **Stop build on first error**. This stops Xcode from giving up in despair midway through a flood of issues. :]

Press **Shift-Command-K** to clean the build folder and then **Command-B** to build. Use **Command-5** to open the **Issue navigator** to view the list of problems:

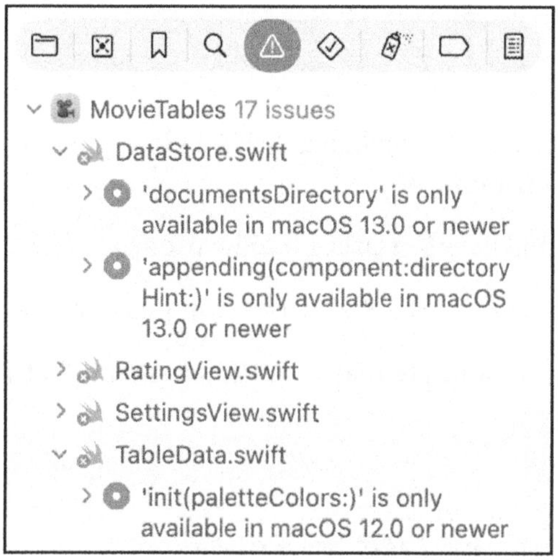

Build errors for macOS 11

Ignoring the two SwiftUI files, there are three issues, most of which are easily worked around without changing the end result. The SwiftUI files use features that are only available in macOS 12.0 or later, so with minor tweaks, you could make this app available for macOS 12. After that, it would need more changes, particularly in `RatingView`, to make it work on macOS 11, but it is feasible.

> **Note**: You may see more errors related to files that you didn't write like MovieTables.abi.json. You can ignore them as they refer to previous builds.

In contrast to this, open the **Snowman** project from the last chapter. Building for macOS 11.0 or for macOS 12.0 gives more than 80 issues, and fixing them would require you to remove significant portions of the app.

Switch both apps back to macOS 26 Tahoe and build again to get them to a working state.

In Summary

- To support old versions of macOS, use AppKit.
- For long-form text editing or for thousands of records, use AppKit.
- For existing AppKit apps, add SwiftUI gradually.
- For everything else, start with SwiftUI and include AppKit as needed.

Key Points

- Use `NSHostingController` to embed a SwiftUI view in its own view controller for display in an AppKit window.
- Both `@AppStorage` and `UserDefaults` handle user settings.
- `NSHostingView` lets you insert a SwiftUI view in place of an `NSView`.
- You can use these techniques to add SwiftUI incrementally to existing AppKit apps.

Where to Go From Here?

At WWDC 2022, there was a video that's relevant to this chapter and the previous one: Use SwiftUI with AppKit (https://developer.apple.com/videos/play/wwdc2022/10075/). Despite the title, it also covers using AppKit with SwiftUI.

19 Conclusion

We hope you're excited by this glimpse into the world of macOS development that lies before you!

By completing this book, you've gained the knowledge and tools you need to build beautiful and functional macOS apps. Set your imagination free and couple your creativity with your newfound knowledge to create some impressive apps of your own.

There is so much more to the macOS ecosystem and Kodeco has the resources to help your continued growth as a macOS developer:

- The many video courses and free tutorials on Kodeco explore diverse topics from MapKit to Core Data to animation and much more. While many seem geared to iOS, these frameworks exist on macOS as well and including them can really amp up your macOS apps!

- *macOS Apps Step by Step* (formerly published by Kodeco as *macOS by Tutorials* and now self-published by Sarah) will expand your knowledge of macOS and explores more advanced developer topics.

If you have any questions or comments as you work through this book, please stop by our forums at https://forums.kodeco.com and look for the particular forum category for this book.

Thank you again for purchasing this book. Your continued support is what makes the books, tutorials, videos and other things we do at Kodeco possible. We truly appreciate it!

– Sarah, Audrey, Ehab and Richard

The *macOS Apprentice* team

Made in United States
North Haven, CT
20 September 2026

18832780R00267